Contents

CÆDMON'S HYMN

(FL. 658–680)

CÆDMON is the earliest English poet whose name is known. His only surviving work is called "Cædmon's Hymn." Cædmon was an Anglo-Saxon herdsman at the monastery in Whitby Abbey, the ruins of which can still be seen in Yorkshire, England. By accounts, he learned to write songs during a dream he had one night. He later became a monk and a pious poet. Cædmon's story is told in the *Historia ecclesiastica gentis Anglorum* or *Ecclesiastical History of the English People* written by St. Bede. Cædmon is one of twelve different Anglo-Saxon poets identified in medieval texts and one of only three for whom somewhat contemporary biographical information and literary examples have survived.

"Cædmon's Hymn" is nine lines long and is written in the alliterative style with a caesura (break or deep pause) in every line, which characterizes old English. English was very influenced by the medieval French language at this time. This poem is one of the earliest examples of Old English literature and may be the earliest example of Old English poetry (there are two other contenders). The hymn is also noted for being one of the first examples of sustained poetry in a Germanic language. A *hymn* is a Christian song of praise or worship for a deity and Cædmon's work is noted for its sweetness and humility. The poem reminds humans to aspire to heaven and not put too much importance in the earthly world.

Cædmon's Hymn

Now we must praise   the kingdom of heaven's
    guardian
The might of the Creator   and his purpose,
The work of the Father of Glory   as he of each
    miracle,
Eternal Lord,   established the beginning.
He first created   for the sons of the earth
Heaven as a roof,   holy Creator.
Then the middle earth,   mankind's guardian,
Eternal Lord,   afterwards adorned
The earth with people,   the Lord Almighty.

Cædmon's Hymn
original Old English

Nu we sculon herigean   heofonrices Weard,
Meotodes meahte   ond his modgeþanc,
weorc Wuldorfæder,   swa he wundra gehwæs,
ece Drihten,   or onstealde.
He ærest sceop   eorthan bearnum
heofon to hrofe,   halig Scyppend.
Tha middangeard   monncynnes Weard,
ece Drihten,   æfter teode
firum foldan,   Frea ælmihtig.

from BEOWULF

(C. 521–C. 1026)

B*eowulf* IS A FAMOUS old English heroic epic poem that has sometimes been referred to as "England's national epic." It was sung by Anglo-Saxon bards or *scops* for several centuries before being recorded on paper around 750 A.D. The narrative of Beowulf follows the Swedish hero as he goes to slay the monster Grendel—and then Grendel's mother when she comes to avenge her son's death—at the request of the Danish king Hrothgar whose people are ravaged by Grendel. Beowulf returns home rich and famous and becomes king of the Geats. Later, when he is older and weaker but still brave, he is called upon to slay a dragon. He kills the dragon but is mortally wounded in the fight. Before dying, Beowulf appoints a young warrior, Wiglaf, as his successor.

Notable for its lengthiness, Beowulf is 3,183 lines. It is written in the alliterative style with a caesura (gap or deep pause) in every line and strong stresses, which characterizes Old English. The Old English line is based on stressed syllables only—unstressed syllables are not counted in the rhythm. There are many translations of Beowulf, including the Noble Laureate poet, Seamus Heaney's *Beowulf: A New Translation*, published in 2000.

PRELUDE OF THE
FOUNDER OF THE DANISH HOUSE[1]

Lo, praise of the prowess of people-kings
of spear-armed Danes, in days long sped,
we have heard, and what honor the athelings won!
Oft Scyld the Scefing[2] from squadroned foes,
from many a tribe, the mead-bench[3] tore,
awing the earls. Since erst he lay
friendless, a foundling, fate repaid him:
for he waxed under welkin, in wealth he throve,
till before him the folk, both far and near,
who house by the whale-path, heard his mandate,
gave him gifts: a good king he!
To him an heir was afterward born,
a son in his halls, whom heaven sent
to favor the folk, feeling their woe
that erst they had lacked an earl for leader
so long a while; the Lord endowed him,
the Wielder of Wonder, with world's renown.
Famed was this Beowulf:[4] far flew the boast of him,
son of Scyld, in the Scandian lands.
So becomes it a youth to quit him well
with his father's friends, by fee and gift,
that to aid him, aged, in after days,
come warriors willing, should war draw nigh,

---

[1] This excerpt was translated by Francis Barton Gummere (1855–1919).

[2] "Scyld the Scefing" refers to King Skjöld who was the son of Sceaf and the husband of Gefyon in Norse mythology.

[3] A "mead-bench" is the place to drink mead, a fermented alcoholic beverage made of honey, water, and yeast.

[4] This refers to another Beowulf, not the hero of this epic.

liegemen loyal: by lauded deeds
shall an earl have honor in every clan.

Forth he fared at the fated moment,
sturdy Scyld to the shelter of God.
Then they bore him over to ocean's billow,
loving clansmen, as late he charged them,
while wielded words the winsome Scyld,
the leader beloved who long had ruled. . . .
In the roadstead rocked a ring-dight vessel,
ice-flecked, outbound, atheling's barge:
there laid they down their darling lord
on the breast of the boat, the breaker-of-rings,[5]
by the mast the mighty one. Many a treasure
fetched from far was freighted with him.
No ship have I known so nobly dight
with weapons of war and weeds of battle,
with breastplate and blade: on his bosom lay
a heaped hoard that hence should go
far o'er the flood with him floating away.
No less these loaded the lordly gifts,
thanes' huge treasure, than those had done
who in former time forth had sent him
sole on the seas, a suckling child.
High o'er his head they hoist the standard,
a gold-wove banner; let billows take him,
gave him to ocean. Grave were their spirits,
mournful their mood. No man is able
to say in sooth, no son of the halls,
no hero 'neath heaven,—who harbored that freight!

---

[5] A king or chieftain would break off gold from his spiral rings
   (often worn on the arms) to reward his followers.

PRELUDE OF THE
FOUNDER OF THE DANISH HOUSE
original Old English

Hwæt! We Gardena   in geardagum,
theodcyninga,   thrym gefrunon,
hu tha æthelingas   ellen fremedon.
Oft Scyld Scefing   sceathena threatum,

monegum mægthum,   meodosetla ofteah,
egsode eorlas.   Syththan ærest wearth
feasceaft funden,   he thæs frofre gebad,
weox under wolcnum,   weorthmyndum thah,
oththæt him æghwylc   thara ymbsittendra
ofer hronrade   hyran scolde,
gomban gyldan.   thæt wæs god cyning!
Thæm eafera wæs   æfter cenned,
geong in geardum,   thone god sende
folce to frofre;   fyrenthearfe ongeat

the hie ær drugon   aldorlease
lange hwile.   Him thæs liffrea,
wuldres wealdend,   woroldare forgeaf;
Beowulf wæs breme   (blæd wide sprang),
Scyldes eafera   Scedelandum in.

Swa sceal geong guma   gode gewyrcean,
fromum feohgiftum   on fæder bearme,
thæt hine on ylde   eft gewunigen
wilgesithas,   thonne wig cume,
leode gelæsten;   lofdædum sceal

in mægtha gehwære   man getheon.
Him tha Scyld gewat   to gescæphwile
felahror feran   on frean wære.
Hi hyne tha ætbæron   to brimes farothe,
swæse gesithas,   swa he selfa bæd,

thenden wordum weold   wine Scyldinga;
leof landfruma   lange ahte.
Thær æt hythe stod   hringedstefna,
isig ond utfus,   æthelinges fær.
Aledon tha   leofne theoden,

beaga bryttan,   on bearm scipes,
mærne be mæste.   Thær wæs madma fela
of feorwegum,   frætwa, gelæded;
ne hyrde ic cymlicor   ceol gegyrwan
hildewæpnum   ond heathowædum,

billum ond byrnum;   him on bearme læg
madma mænigo,   tha him mid scoldon
on flodes æht   feor gewitan.
Nalæs hi hine læssan   lacum teodan,
theodgestreonum,   thon tha dydon

the hine æt frumsceafte   forth onsendon
ænne ofer ythe   umborwesende.
Tha gyt hie him asetton   segen geldenne
heah ofer heafod,   leton holm beran,
geafon on garsecg;   him wæs geomor sefa,

murnende mod.   Men ne cunnon
secgan to sothe,   selerædende,
hæleth under heofenum,   hwa thæm hlæste
    onfeng.

I Tha wæs on burgum   Beowulf Scyldinga,
leof leodcyning,   longe thrage

folcum gefræge   (fæder ellor hwearf,
aldor of earde),   oththæt him eft onwoc
heah Healfdene;   heold thenden lifde,
gamol ond guthreouw,   glæde Scyldingas.
Thæm feower bearn   forth gerimed

in worold wocun,   weoroda ræswan,
Heorogar ond Hrothgar   ond Halga til;
hyrde ic thæt   wæs Onelan cwen,
Heathoscilfingas   healsgebedda.
Tha wæs Hrothgare   heresped gyfen,

wiges weorthmynd,   thæt him his winemagas
georne hyrdon,   oththæt seo geogoth geweox,
magodriht micel.   Him on mod bearn
thæt healreced   hatan wolde,
medoærn micel,   men gewyrcean

GEOFFREY CHAUCER

(c. 1343–1400)

G EOFFREY CHAUCER was the foremost Middle English poet and is especially celebrated for his master-piece *The Canterbury Tales*. Chaucer was also a philosopher, courtier, and diplomat. He has been called the father of English literature, because he is considered by some to be the first writer to prove the artistic merit of writing in English rather than French or Latin. Born in London, the exact date and location of his birth are unknown. His father and grandfather were both vintners (winemakers). Chaucer became a noblewoman's page as well as working as a courtier, diplomat, and civil servant. At the start of the Hundred Years' War, King Edward III invaded France and Chaucer traveled as part of the English army. He was captured and became a prisoner of war until King Edward paid his ransom.

Chaucer married Philippa de Roet, a lady in waiting to the queen, around 1366. In 1367 he became an official member of the royal court of Edward III. He traveled abroad many times as part of his duties. On a trip to Italy he probably became familiar with medieval Italian poetry which would influence his work. King Edward honored Chaucer with "a gallon of wine daily for the rest of his life" and this honor is considered to be a precursor to the later poet laureates of England. When King Richard II came to power, the wine was converted into a monetary grant. In 1374 Chaucer became Comptroller of the Customs for the port in London, a job that he held for twelve years. He moved to Kent and became a member of Parliament in 1386. He continued to serve the court in various positions until the overthrow of King Richard II in 1399. He is thought to have died on October 25, 1400, but the only evidence for this date is the engraving on his tomb, which was built more than one hundred years after Chaucer's death.

from THE GENERAL PROLOGUE

Whan that Aprill with his shoures soote[1]
The droghte of March hath perced to the roote,
And bathed every veyne[2] in swich licour
Of which vertu[3] engendred is the flour;
Whan Zephirus[4] eek[5] with his sweete breeth
Inspired hath in every holt and heeth[6]
The tendre croppes,[7] and the yonge sonne
Hath in the Ram[8] his half cours yronne,
And smale foweles maken melodye,
That slepen al the nyght with open ye
(So priketh[9] hem Nature in hir corages),[10]
Thanne longen folk to goon on pilgrimages,

---

[1] Sweet-smelling showers.
[2] Vein (of the plants).
[3] Power.
[4] West Wind.
[5] Also.
[6] Wood and field.
[7] Tender new leaves.
[8] Aries.
[9] Incites.
[10] Hearts.

And palmeres[11] for to seken straunge strondes,[12]
To ferne halwes,[13] kowthe in sondry londes;[14]
And specially from every shires ende
Of Engelond to Caunterbury they wende,[15]
The hooly blisful martir[16] for to seke,
That hem hath holpen[17] whan that they were seeke.[18]

from THE WIFE OF BATH'S PROLOGUE

Experience, though noon auctoritee[19]
Were in this world, is right ynough[20] for me
To speke of wo that is in mariage:
For lordinges,[21] sith I twelf yeer was of age—
Thanked be God that is eterne on live[22]—
Housbondes at chirche dore I have had five
(If I so ofte mighte han wedded be),
And alle were worthy men in hir degree.[23]
But me was told, certain, nat longe agoon is,
That sith that Crist ne wente nevere but ones[24]
To wedding in the Cane of Galilee,

---

[11] Pilgrims.
[12] Foreign shores.
[13] Distant shrines.
[14] Known in different lands.
[15] Travel.
[16] Holy, blessed martyr.
[17] Helped.
[18] Sick.
[19] No written authority.
[20] Good enough.
[21] Gentlemen.
[22] Eternally alive.
[23] Their way.
[24] Once.

That by the same ensample[25] taughte he me
That I ne sholde wedded be but ones.
Herke eek,[26] lo, which a sharp word for the nones,[27]
Biside a well, Jesus, God and man,
Spak in repreve of the Samaritan:
"Thou hast yhad five housbondes," quod he,
"And that ilke[28] man that now hath thee
Is nat thyn housbonde." Thus saide he certain.
What that he mente therby I can nat seyn,[29]
But that I axe why the fifthe man
Was noon housbonde to the Samaritan?
How manye mighte she han in mariage?
Yit herde I nevere tellen in myn age[30]
Upon this nombre diffinicioun.[31]
Men may devyne and glosen[32] up and down,
But wel I woot, expres,[33] withouten lie,
God bad[34] us for to wexe[35] and multiplye:
That gentil text can I wel understonde.

---

[25] Example.
[26] Listen also.
[27] Purpose.
[28] Same.
[29] Say.
[30] Lifetime.
[31] A definition of this anwer.
[32] Conjecture and interpret.
[33] Know expressly.
[34] Commanded.
[35] Grow fruitful.

from SIR GAWAIN AND THE GREEN KNIGHT

(c. 1375–1400)

S*ir Gawain and the Green Knight* is an alliterative romance that was recorded in a single manuscript, although the authorship remains unknown. The unidentified poet is also believed to be the author of the poems *Pearl, Patience, and Cleanness* and is sometimes referred to as "the *Pearl* poet."

Drawing on Arthurian legend and the court of Camelot, the plot follows a green knight who intrudes on a New Year's Even banquet. The Green Knight challenges the knights at the banquet to cut off his head and if he survives, the knight who failed must be beheaded exactly one year later. Gawain accepts the green knight's offer and lops off his head. Unfortunately the Green Knight is able to pick up his head and put it back on, so a year later Gawain sets out on a journey to keep his bargain. Gawain is given hospitality at a Lord's castle for three days and then goes to the Green chapel to meet his fate. There the Green Knight reveals that he was the lord of the castle in another guise and that he will spare Gawain's life because he honored his promise and conducted himself virtuously at the castle.

This epic poem is written in distinctive verse stanzas composed of long alliterative lines. Each stanza ends in a form called the "bob and wheel." The "bob" is a single line of one foot (two syllables) and the "wheel" that follows consists of a quatrain (four lines) of trimeter lines (six syllables) rhyming with the "bob."

from PART I

List! wen Arthur he was King,
He had all att his leadinge[1]
    The broad Ile of Brittaine.
England and Scottland one was,[2]
And Wales stood in the same case,
    The truth itt is not to layne.[3]

He drive allyance[4] out of this Ile.
Soe Arthur lived in peace a while,
    As men of mickle maine,[5]
Knights strove of their degree,[6]
Which of them hyest shold bee;
    Therof Arthur was not faine.[7]

Hee made the Round Table for their behove,[8]
That none of them shold sitt above,
    But all shold sitt as one,
The King himselfe in state royall,
Dame Guenever our Queene withall,
    Seemlye[9] of body and bone.

---

[1] Command.
[2] England and Scotland were united.
[3] Conceal or hide.
[4] Drove foreigners.
[5] Great might.
[6] Argued about rank.
[7] Arthur was not glad about that.
[8] On their behalf.
[9] Handsome; becoming.

14

Itt fell againe[10] the Christmase
Many came to that Lords place,
  To that worthye one,
With helme[11] on head and brand[12] bright,
All that tooke order of knight;
  None wold linger att home.

There was noe castle nor manour free
That might harbour that companye,
  Their puissance[13] was soe great.
Their tents up they pight[14]
For to lodge there all that night;
  Therto were sett to meate.

Messengers there came and went
With much victualls verament,
  Both by way and streete.
Wine and wild fowle thither was brought—
Within[15] they spared nought
  For gold, and they might itt gett.

---

[10] Happened upon. King Arthur created the Round Table so that
   his knights wouldn't argue about who had the highest rank.
[11] Helmet.
[12] Sword.
[13] A crowd or force of people.
[14] Pitched.
[15] In all.

Now of King Arthur noe more I mell,[16]
But of a venterous knight I will you tell
    That dwelled in the west countrye.[17]
Sir Bredbeddle, for sooth he hett:[18]
He was a man of mickele might[19]
    And Lord of great bewtye.[20]

---

[16] Tell; speak.
[17] The poem is set in the northwest midlands of England, near the
  Welsh border.
[18] Was called.
[19] Great strength.
[20] Beauty.

Charles d'Orleans

(1391–1465)

CHARLES D'ORLEANS was a French duke and poet. The nephew of King Charles VI, he became a duke at the age of fifteen after his father was assassinated. In 1415, d'Orleans was wounded and captured in the battle of Agincourt during the English invasion of France (he makes an appearance in Shakespeare's *Henry V* as the "Duke of Orleans"). He remained a prisoner in England until 1440 when he was ransomed. During his imprisonment he wrote much of his poetry. After he returned to France he spent the rest of his life writing poetry and socializing in literary circles. There are over 500 of his poems still in existence today.

D'Orleans is noted for his expert *rondels*. He wrote mainly in this form and his subject matter was love and spring. The *rondel* was invented in France in the 14th century and is very similar to the *rondeau*. It contains fourteen lines and the initial couplet is repeated in the middle and at the close of the poem. The rhyme scheme is abba abab abbaab.

SPRING

The year has changed his mantle cold
Of wind, of rain, of bitter air;
And he goes clad in cloth of gold,
Of laughing suns and season fair;
No bird or beast of wood or wold[1]
But doth with cry or song declare
The year lays down his mantle cold.
All founts, all rivers, seaward rolled,
The pleasant summer livery wear,
With silver studs on broidered vair;[2]
The world puts off its raiment old,
The year lays down his mantle cold.

---

[1] Open, rolling plain or moor.
[2] Fur, most often squirrel, used in medieval times to trim robes.

Anonymous
Middle English Lyrics

Western Wind[1]

Western wind, when wilt thou blow,
    That the small rain down can rain?
Christ, that my love were in my arms,
    And I in my bed again!

The Cuckoo Song

Sumer is ycomen in,
Loude sing cuckou!
Groweth seed and bloweth meed[2],
And springth the wode now.
Sing cuckou!

Ewe bleteth after lamb,
Loweth after calve cow,
Bulloc sterteth, bucke verteth,
Merye sing cuckou!
Cuckou, cuckou,
Wel singest thou cuckou:
Ne swik[3] thou never now!

---

[1] This intensely emotional lyric probably dates from the 15th or
    16th century.
[2] A fitting reward or gift.
[3] Cease.

William Dunbar

(c. 1460–c. 1520)

WILLIAM DUNBAR was a Scottish poet who wrote in Old Scots. He is not considered an intellectual poet although he was well-educated, earning a master's degree at the University of St. Andrews. Dunbar went to France as a wandering friar. He was given an annual salary by King James IV as a member of the royal household. By 1504 he had become a priest, but it is not clear that he ever had a parish. It is probable that Dunbar was a clerk or envoy for the court. His poems show a knowledge of the law. William Dunbar was highly thought of by his successors and Sir Walter Scott wrote that he was "unrivalled by any which Scotland has produced." Over one hundred poems are attributed to him, mostly short pieces, but also some longer work. His verse includes the dream allegory, "The Goldyn Targe;" the wedding song celebrating the marriage of James IV and Margaret Tudor, "The Thrissill and the Rois;" a satiric rebuttal to a poetic rival, "The Flying of Dunbar and Kennedie;" a devotional piece, "Of the Nativity of Christ;" and the ribald "The Two Married Women and the Widow." One of his most famous poems is the pessimistic "Lament for the Makers" with its noted refrain "Timor mortis conturbat me"—"the fear of death confuses me." Dunbar was the principle *makar* or courtly poet, during a flourishing time of Scottish poetry.

from LAMENT FOR THE MAKERS[1]

I that in heill[2] was and gladness
Am trublit now with great sickness
And feblit[3] with infirmitie:—
Timor Mortis conturbat me[4]

Our plesance here is all vain glory,
This fals world is but transitory,
The flesh is bruckle,[5] the Feynd is slee:—[6]
Timor Mortis conturbat me.

The state of man does change and vary,
Now sound, now sick, now blyth, now sary,[7]
Now dansand mirry[8], now like to die:—
Timor Mortis conturbat me.

No state in Erd[9] here standis sicker;[10]
As with the wynd wavis the wicker[11]
So wannis this world's vanitie:—
Timor Mortis conturbat me.

---

[1] "Makers" is the Scots word for poets.
[2] Health.
[3] Enfeebled.
[4] The fear of death confuses me.
[5] Brittle.
[6] "Fyend is slee" means fiend is sly.
[7] Sorry.
[8] "Dansand mirry" means dancing merrily.
[9] Earth.
[0] Secure.
[11] Twig.

Unto the Death gois all Estatis,
Princis, Prelatis, and Potestatis,[12]
Baith rich and poor of all degree:—
Timor Mortis conturbat me.

He takis the knichtis in to the field
Enarmit under helm and scheild;
Victor he is at all mellie:—[13]
Timor Mortis conturbat me.

That strong unmerciful tyrand
Takis, on the motheris breast sowkand,[14]
The babe full of benignitie:—
Timor Mortis conturbat me.

He takis the campion[15] in the stour,[16]
The captain closit in the tour,
The lady in bour full of bewtie:—
Timor Mortis conturbat me.

He spairis no lord for his piscence,[17]
Na[18] clerk for his intelligence;
His awful straik[19] may no man flee:—
Timor Mortis conturbat me.

---

[12] Potentates or rulers.
[13] Fight.
[14] Sucking.
[15] Champion.
[16] Battle.
[17] Puissance.
[18] No.
[19] Stroke.

John Skelton

(1460–1529)

JOHN SKELTON was a poet, scholar, and satirist who received a classical education, studying at Cambridge. He found a patron in the pious and learned countess of Richmond, King Henry VII's mother. In the 1490s he tutored the young Prince Henry. He also was ordained a priest at this time. Skelton was the unofficial Poet Laureate of England under King Henry VII, who was a great admirer of his poetry. Prince Henry took the throne of England as King Henry VIII in 1509. Skelton wrote most of his best work later in life. He is known for his humorous poetry written in very short rhymed lines with a pronounced rhythm. The term "Skeltonics" is sometimes used to describe poetry similar in style to John Skelton's—a form of humorous poetry that consists of very short rhymed lines and a pronounced rhythm.

To Mistress Margaret Hussey

Merry Margaret,
As midsummer flower,
Gentil as falcon
Or hawk of the tower;[1]
    With solace and gladness,
Much mirth and no madness,
All good and no badness,
So joyously,

---

[1] A hawk that has been trained to fly very high.

So maidenly,
So womanly
Her demeaning
In every thing,—
Far, far passing
That I can endite[2]
Or suffice to write
Of merry Margaret,
As midsummer flower,
Gentil as falcon
Or hawk of the tower.
    As patient and as still
And as full of good will
As fair Isiphill,[3]
Coliander,[4]
Sweet pomander,[5]
Good Cassander;[6]
Steadfast of thought,
Well made, well wrought;
Far may be sought
Erst that ye can find
So curteise, so kind
As merry Margaret,
This midsummer flower,
Gentil as falcon
Or hawk of the tower

---

[2] Surpassing anything that the poem's speaker can compose.

[3] In Greek mythology Hypsipyle, Queen of Lemnos, is renowned for her devotion to her father and children.

[4] A sweet-smelling herb that is supposed to soothe pain (coriander).

[5] A mixture of perfumed substances made into a ball.

[6] Cassandra is a figure in Greek myth. She was the daughter of Priam of Troy and her beauty was so great that Apollo gave her the gift of prophecy.

Sir Thomas Wyatt

(1503–1542)

Thomas Wyatt was a courtier, diplomat, and the leading English poet during the reign of King Henry VIII. He lived a tumultuous life full of political intrigue. Thomas Wyatt and his friend, Henry Howard, Earl of Surrey, were the first poets to introduce the Petrarchan or Italian sonnet (sonnet is from the French, meaning "little song") to the English language. Wyatt and Surrey share the title of "Father of the English sonnet."

Wyatt's first known appearance in court was in 1516 as "Sewer Extraordinaire." Marrying around age seventeen, he had one child, Thomas Wyatt, Jr. Wyatt later separated from his wife, accusing her of adultery. In the early to mid 1520s he fell in love with the young Anne Boleyn. He wrote love poems for her and became one of her admirers. When Boleyn came to King Henry's attention, Wyatt and Henry quarreled over her. As an ambassador for the court, Wyatt was sent to Rome to petition the Pope to allow Henry to divorce his wife, Catherine of Aragon. Wyatt was knighted in 1535, but a year later was imprisoned in the Tower of England because he was suspected of being one of Anne Boleyn's lovers. While in the Tower, Wyatt witnessed Boleyn's beheading and wrote a poem about it. He was released later the same year and went back to his diplomatic duties. Then in 1541 he was again charged with treason and pardoned under the condition that he reconcile with his wife. He died shortly thereafter.

Wyatt wrote satirical verse about court life, translations of Petrarch's sonnets, and accomplished poems in other new forms, such as the *terza rima* and the *rondeau*. None of Wyatt's poems were published during his lifetime— aristocratic poets rarely published their poems themselves at that time. It took fifteen years before they were first printed by Richard Tottel, alongside Henry Howard's poems, in what is now called *Tottle's Miscellany*. Ninety-seven of Wyatt's sonnets and lyrics were gathered in Tottle's collection. The rest of Wyatt's poems were "rediscovered" in the 19th and 20th centuries. Sir Thomas Wyatt was a pioneer in bringing the poetic forms of the Italian Renaissance to England.

They Flee from Me

They flee from me that sometime did me seek,
With naked foot stalking[1] in my chamber.
I have seen them gentle, tame, and meek
That now are wild and do not rèmember
That sometime they put themselves in dangèr[2]
To take bread at my hand; and now they range
Busily seeking with a continual change.[3]

---

[1] Gliding or walking stealthily.
[2] Under obligation or in debt to the speaker.
[3] "Continual change" refers to persistent fickleness.

Thanked be Fortune it hath been otherwise,
Twenty times better; but once in special,[4]
In thin array,[5] after a pleasant guise,[6]
When her loose gown from her shoulders did fall,
And she me caught in her arms long and small,[7]
And therewith all sweetly did me kiss,
And softly said, "Dear heart,[8] how like you this?"

It was no dream: I lay broad waking.[9]
But all is turned, thorough[10] my gentleness,
Into a strange fashion of forsaking;[11]
And I have leave to go, of her goodness,[12]
And she also to use newfangleness.[13]
But since that I so kindely[14] am served,[15]
I would fain know what she hath deserved.

---

[4] Especially.

[5] "In thin array" means in diaphanous dress.

[6] "After a pleasant guise" means in a pleasing style or manner.

[7] Slender.

[8] Possibly a play on "hart" (a female deer).

[9] "Broad waking" means wide awake.

[10] Through.

[11] Rejecting.

[12] "Of her goodness" means ironically "through her consent" or "with her gracious permission."

[13] To be inconsistent, following the fashion.

[14] "Kindely" is to be pronounced as having three syllables and is meant ironically. It can also mean according to nature, as a wild animal would behave.

[15] The speaker has been given his "walking papers," i.e., told to leave.

Whoso List to Hunt[16]

Whoso list[17] to hunt, I know where is an hind,
But as for me, hélas, I may no more.
The vain travail hath wearied me so sore,
I am of them that farthest cometh behind.
Yet may I by no means my wearied mind
Draw from the deer, but as she fleeth afore
Fainting I follow. I leave off therefore,
Sithens in a net I seek to hold the wind.
Who list her hunt, I put him out of doubt,
As well as I may spend his time in vain.
And graven with diamonds in letters plain
There is written, her fair neck round about:
Noli me tangere,[18] for Caesar's I am,[19]
And wild for to hold, though I seem tame.

---

[16] This poem is believed to have been written about Anne Boleyn who is depicted as a deer with a jeweled collar. The poem flirts with concealment and revelation. As a court poet, it would be traditional for Wyatt to keep his love interests secret since marriages were of great political interest and often arranged by the monarch.

[17] "List" means would wish.

[18] "Noli me tangere" means "touch me not."

[19] This line has been interpreted as a reference to Wyatt's involvement with Anne Boleyn. The hind (Boleyn) belongs to the ruler (Henry VIII).

Henry Howard,
Earl of Surrey

(c. 1517–1547)

Henry Howard (also known as Surrey) was an English aristocrat who was descended from kings on both sides of his family. He was also a major poet of his day and helped usher in the English poetry renaissance. Along with his friend Sir Thomas Wyatt he popularized the Petrarchan or Italian sonnet in England. Although Wyatt and Surrey probably both inspired each other, it is likely that Wyatt lead the way in introducing new poetic forms. As well as being known for his sonnets, Henry Howard translated two books of Virgil's *Aeneid*, in which he introduced blank verse to English. At court, some of his poetry circulated in manuscript form and he self-published his "Epitaph of Sir Thomas Wyatt." But most of his poetry was published, along with Wyatt's, in *Tottel's Miscellany* in 1557, ten years after his death. He is the only poet mentioned on the title page of that compilation.

Henry Howard fought with his father in a military campaign against rebels to defend Henry VIII's policy of dissolving monasteries. But political intrigue and false accusations of treason resulted in his imprisonment on several occasions, although the Howard family had always been loyal to the king. In his paranoia, Henry VIII believed falsely that Henry Howard wanted to usurp the throne from his son Edward—goaded by Surrey's brashness in boasting about his royal heritage and for his statement that the king's son would be under Surrey's father's protection. In 1547 he was charged again with treason and executed.

Together, Henry Howard and Sir Thomas Wyatt are known as "Fathers of the English Sonnet." They established the sonnet form (three quatrains and a couplet, with a rhyme scheme of abab cdcd efef gg) that was later perfected by Shakespeare and others.

The Soote Season[1]

The soote[2] season, that bud and bloom forth brings,
With green hath clad the hill and eke[3] the vale.
The nightingale with feathers new she sings;
The turtle[4] to her make[5] hath told her tale.
Summer is come, for every spray now springs,
The hart hath hung his old head on the pale;
The buck in brake his winter coat he slings;
The fishes flete with new repaired scale;
The adder all her slough away she slings;
The swift swallow pursueth the flies smale[6]
The busy bee her honey now she mings;[7]
Winter is worn that was the flowers' bale.[8]
And thus I see among these pleasant things
Each care decays, and yet my sorrow springs!

---

[1] This poem is one of the earliest examples of the Petrarchan sonnet in the English language.

[2] Sweet.

[3] Also.

[4] Turtledove.

[5] Mate.

[6] Small.

[7] Mingles or remembers.

[8] Destruction.

ANNE ASKEW

(1521–1546)

ANNE ASKEW was an English Protestant who was persecuted for being a heretic. Forced to marry at age fifteen by her prominent family, she refused to take her husband's name. Her husband was a Catholic but Anne was a supporter of Martin Luther. Anne left her husband and went to London where she gave sermons and handed out banned Protestant books. She also tried to get a divorce from her husband. She was arrested and her husband was ordered to take her back home to Lincolnshire but she escaped and returned to London to continue preaching. Anne was again arrested. This time she was tortured on the rack in the Tower of London in an attempt to get her to name other Protestants. Askew refused to recant her religion or name names although she was badly crippled. At her trial she was sentenced to death and burnt at the stake.

While in the Tower she wrote accounts of being interrogated, which were smuggled out of England and later published. She wrote, "They did put me on the rack, because I confessed no ladies or gentlemen . . . I said that I would rather die than break my faith." Askew is also thought to have written a ballad while awaiting execution, "I Am a Woman Poor and Blind." It was a popular ballad for over a century after Askew's death and various versions exist.

I Am a Woman Poor and Blind

The Ballad which Anne Askew made and sang
when she was in Newgate

I am a woman poor and blind
and little knowledge remains in me,
Long have I sought, but fain[1] would I find,
what herb in my garden were best to be.

A garden I have which is unknown,
which God of his goodness gave to me,
I mean my body, wherein I should have sown
the seed of Christ's true verity.

My spirit within me is vexed sore,
my flesh striveth against the same:
My sorrows do increase more and more,
my conscience suffereth most bitter pain:

I, with myself being thus at strife,
would fain[2] have been at rest,
Musing and studying in mortal life,
what things I might do to please God best.

With whole intent and one accord,
unto a Gardener[3] that I did know,
I desired him for the love of the Lord,
true seeds in my garden for to sow.

---

[1] Gladly.
[2] Ibid.
[3] Alludes to Stephen Gardiner, Bishop of Winchester.

Then this proud Gardener seeing me so blind,
he thought on me to work his will,
And flattered me with words so kind,
to have me continue in my blindness still.

He fed me then with lies and mocks,
for venial[4] sins he bid me go
To give my money to stones and stocks,[5]
which was stark lies and nothing so.

With stinking meat then was I fed,
for to keep me from my salvation,
I had trentals[6] of mass, and bulls[7] of lead,
not one word spoken of Christ's passion.

In me was sown all kind of feigned seeds,
with Popish ceremonies many a one,
Masses of requiem[8] with other juggling[9] deeds,
till God's spirit out of my garden was gone.

Then was I commanded most strictly,
If of my salvation I would be sure,
To build some chapel or chantry,[10]
to be prayed for while the world doth endure.

---

[4] Minor.
[5] Images of saints made from stone and wood.
[6] A series of thirty requiem masses.
[7] Papal edicts.
[8] Mass for the souls of the dead.
[9] Misleading.
[10] A chapel that is endowed in order to say prayers for its founder.

"Beware of a new learning," quoth he, "it lies,
which is the thing I most abhor,
Meddle not with it in any manner of wise,
but do as your fathers have done before."

My trust I did put in the Devil's works,
thinking sufficient my soul to save,
Being worse then either Jews or Turks,
thus Christ of his merits I did deprave.

I might liken my self with a woeful heart,
unto the dumb man in Luke the Eleven,
From whence Christ caused the Devil to depart,
but shortly after he took the other seven.

My time thus, good Lord, so wickedly spent,
alas, I shall die the sooner therefore.
Oh Lord, I find it written in thy Testament,
that thou hast mercy enough in store

For such sinners, as the scripture sayeth,
that would gladly repent and follow thy word,
Which I'll not deny whilst I have breath,
for prison, fire, fagot,[11] or fierce sword.

Strengthen me good Lord in thy truth to stand,
for the bloody butchers have me at their will,
With their slaughter knives ready drawn in their hand
my simple carcass to devour and kill.

---

[11] A fagot is a bundle of sticks used to start a fire.

O Lord forgive me mine offense,
for I have offended thee very sore,
Take therefore my sinful body from hence,
Then shall I, vile creature, offend thee no more.

I would with all creatures and faithful friends
for to keep them from this Gardener's hands,
For he will bring them soon unto their ends,
with cruel torments of fierce firebrands.

I dare not presume for him to pray,
because the truth of him it was well known,
But since that time he hath gone astray,
and much pestilent seed abroad he hath sown.

Because that now I have no space,
the cause of my death truly to show,
I trust hereafter that by God's holy grace,
that all faithful men shall plainly know.

To thee O Lord I bequeath my spirit,
that art the work-master of the same,
It is thine, Lord, therefore take it of right,
my carcass on earth I leave, from whence it came.

Although to ashes it be now burned,
I know thou canst raise it again,
In the same likeness as thou it formed,
in heaven with thee evermore to remain.

Queen Elizabeth I

(1533–1603)

Queen Elizabeth I was ruler of England during a time of religious and political instability (conflict between Catholics and Protestants tore at the foundations of British society) and enormous cultural flourishing. The daughter of Henry VIII and Anne Boleyn, she came to the throne in 1558. A highly educated woman (she knew Greek, Latin, French, Italian, Spanish, and German), Elizabeth was proud of her linguistic skills and celebrated by others for her intellectual prowess. Not only was Elizabeth a great patron of the arts (drama, poetry, music, etc.), but she was a well-read woman who wrote poetry of her own and translated books such as Boethius's *Consolation of Philosophy* and Horace's *Art of Poetry*.

Edmund Spenser wrote his epic "Faerie Queen" for Elizabeth, associating her with the romance tradition and making her a figure of Arthurian legend. She inspired many poets, including Sir Walter Ralegh and Sir Philip Sidney. When William Shakespeare killed off Sir John Falstaff in *Henry IV*, Elizabeth asked that the character be brought back and Shakespeare honored her request by writing *The Merry Wives of Windsor*. She was a muse for many writers of the era who considered her to be the model of female power. Her reign was considered to usher in the Golden Age of England and she is quoted as having said, "Be ye ensured that I will be as good unto you as ever a Queen was unto her people." Only a handful of poems by Queen Elizabeth exist today.

ON MONSIEUR'S DEPARTURE[1]

I grieve and dare not show my discontent,[2]
I love and yet am forced to seem to hate,
I do, yet dare not say I ever meant,
I seem stark mute but inwardly to prate.[3]
I am and not, I freeze and yet am burned.[4]
Since from myself another self I turned.

My care is like my shadow in the sun,
Follows me flying, flies when I pursue it,
Stands and lies by me, doth what I have done.
His too familiar care doth make me rue it.
No means I find to rid him from my breast,
Till by the end of things it be supprest.[5]

---

[1] "On Monsieur's Departure" is probably Queen Elizabeth's most
   famous poem. Queen Elizabeth had numerous suitors but never
   married. Although there is no proof that connects the poem to
   her suitor Sir Francis de Valois, Duke of Alençon, it has often
   been assumed that the poem is about his departure from England. He left after growing tired of the politics of making a royal
   match. The Duke of Alençon was her last suitor and she is said
   to have been very fond of him, calling him her "little frog." It
   has also been conjectured that the poem is about the English
   Earl of Leicester, Robert Dudley, one of her favorite courtiers.
   Elizabeth is said to have been in love with him, but didn't marry
   him because it was not politically advantageous.
[2] This opening line is an example of the poetic convention of
   antithesis.
[3] The first four lines of the poem show how the speaker must not
   reveal her true feelings of love.
[4] An antithesis or oxymoron typical of Elizabethan poetry.
[5] This stanza illustrates that it is impossible for the speaker to stop
   loving her "Monsieur".

Some gentler passion slide into my mind,
For I am soft and made of melting snow;
Or be more cruel, love, and so be kind.
Let me or float or sink, be high or low.
Or let me live with some more sweet content,
Or die and so forget what love ere meant.[6]

---

[6] The speaker wants to either die or forget her love completely. She
longs to live freely without the burden of love.

The Doubt of Future Foes[7]

The doubt of future foes exiles my present joy,
And wit me warns to shun such snares as threaten mine
annoy;
For falsehood now doth flow, and subjects' faith doth
ebb,
Which should not be if reason ruled or wisdom weaved
the web.
But clouds of joy untried do cloak aspiring minds,
Which turn to rain of late repent by changed course of
winds.
The top of hope supposed the root upreared shall be,
And fruitless all their grafted guile, as shortly ye shall
see.
The dazzled eyes with pride, which great ambition
blinds,
Shall be unsealed by worthy wights whose foresight
falsehood finds.
The daughter of debate that discord aye doth sow
Shall reap no gain where former rule still peace hath
taught to know.

---

[7] This poem focuses on the danger presented to Queen Elizabeth
by her many enemies, especially Mary Stuart, Elizabeth's cousin,
better known as Mary, Queen of Scots (mother to the first Stuart
monarch, James I). Mary was a Roman Catholic who had been
expelled from Scotland by rebellious Protestant subjects. She
was involved with failed Catholic plots to overthrow Elizabeth.
Under pressure from her supporters, Elizabeth reluctantly
agreed to have her executed.

No foreign banished wight shall anchor in this port;
Our realm brooks not seditious sects, let them
    elsewhere resort.[8]
My rusty sword through rest shall first his edge employ
To poll their tops[9] that seek such change or gape for
    future joy.

---

[8] England will not let foreign powers take over the throne. After
    Elizabeth rejected a marriage proposal from Philip II of Spain,
    the Spanish King, infuriated by English piracy and forays in
    New World exploration, sent his feared Armada to raid England.
    England won the naval battle easily.
[9] A botanical image: the speaker threatens seditionists with
    beheading.

ARTHUR GOLDING

(c. 1536–c. 1605)

ARTHUR GOLDING was an English translator and essayist famous for having published the first English translation of Ovid's *Metamorphoses*. His father was an auditor of the Exchequer and he is thought to have been educated at Queens' College, Cambridge. He lived for some time in the house of Lord Burghley, along with his nephew, the poet Edward de Vere, Earl of Oxford. Golding had strong Puritan sympathies and translated much of John Calvin's work.

Golding's major work was his translation of Ovid's *Metamorphoses* from Latin into English. It was from Golding that many Elizabethans drew their knowledge of classical mythology. Most notably, William Shakespeare used Golding's book as a source for his plays, including *A Midsummer's Night's Dream*. Golding probably intended to portray Ovid's bawdy tales as moral examples for readers. His only original work is *Discourse*, a prose piece about the earthquake of 1580, in which he saw God's judgment on man's wickedness.

from METAMORPHOSES
excerpt from BOOK III

All such as doo in flattring freaks, and hawks, and
  hownds delyght,
And dyce, and cards, and for to spend the tyme both
  day and nyght
In foule excesse of chamberworke, or too much meate
  and drink:
Uppon the piteous storie of Acteon[1] ought to think.
For theis and theyr adherents usde excessive are in
  deede
The dogs that dayly doo devour theyr followers on
  with speede.
Tyresias[2] willes inferior folk in any wyse to shun
Too judge betweene their betters least in perill they
  doo run.
Narcissus[3] is of scornfulnesse and pryde a myrror
  cleere,

---

[1] In Greek mythology Acteon (or Actaeon) was the son of the king
of Thebes and while he was deer hunting he wandered away
from his friends and caught a glimpse of Artemis bathing. In
punishment Artemis transformed Acteon into a stag and his own
hounds chased him down and killed him.

[2] Tyresias was a famous Theban seer who saw two snakes mating
and struck them apart with a staff. For this interference in nature
the Greek gods turned him into a woman for seven years.

[3] Narcissus was a beautiful young man who spurned the advances of
women.

Where beawties fading vanitie most playnly may
  appeere.
And Echo[4] in the selfsame tale dooth kyndly represent
The lewd behaviour of a bawd, and his due
  punishment.

---

[4] Echo was a nympth who fell in love with Narcissus but because he
  ignored her she faded until she became only a whisper. The goddess Nemesis punished Narcissus by making him fall in love
  with his own reflection. He could do nothing but watch his
  reflection until he wasted away. It is possible that the relationship between Echo and Narcissus was Ovid's own creation.

ISABELLA WHITNEY

(C. 1540–AFTER 1580)

ISABELLA WHITNEY is considered to be the first professional secular female poet in England. She published
two volumes of nonreligious verse. Unlike most of the
other women poets of the Renaissance, Whitney was
middle class rather than an aristocrat, and probably not
formally educated (though from her poetry it is evident
that she was familiar with the literary conventions of her
day). Very little is known about Isabella Whitney's life.
She may have been a lady-in-waiting for a noble family—being a servant to the upper class was considered an
honorable profession for members of the middle class.

Whitney first published *Copy of a Letter . . . in Meter
by a Young Gentlewoman to her Unconstant Lover* when
she was about eighteen. The poem warns women to
protect their honor from the wiles of untrustworthy
men. It has been speculated that the poem was inspired
by a broken engagement. Much of Isabella Whitney's
poetry is written in the form of a verse epistle or a letter, and is addressed to members of her family. Whitney was a pioneer in writing saleable poetry that
appealed to the public at a time when women were
supposed to write only devotional literature and translations of male writers' works.

from THE ADMONITION BY THE AUTHOR
TO ALL YOUNG GENTLEWOMEN:
AND TO ALL OTHER MAIDS BEING IN LOVE

Ye Virgins, ye from Cupid's[1] tents[2]
  do bear away the foil,[3]
Whose hearts as yet with raging love
  most painfully do boil.

To you I speak: for you be they
  that good advice do lack:
Oh, if I could good counsell get,[4]
  my tongue should not be slack.

But such as I can give, I will
  here in few words express,
Which, if you do observe, it will
  some of your care redress.

Beware of fair and painted[5] talk,
  beware of flattering tongues:
The Mermaids do pretend no good
  for all their pleasant songs.

---

[1] The Roman god of love whose arrows cause pain.
[2] Probes that keep wounds open.
[3] Fencing weapon; small sword.
[4] "Get" means make.
[5] Pleasing.

Some use the tears of crocodiles,
   contrary to their heart:
And if they cannot always weep,
   they wet their cheeks by art.

Ovid,[6] within his Art of Love,
   doth teach them this same knack
To wet their hand and touch their eyes,
   so oft as tears they lack.

Why have ye such deceit in store?
   have you such crafty wile?
Less craft than this, God knows, would soon
   us simple souls beguile.

And will ye not leave off? but still
   delude us in this wise?
Sith it is so, we trust we shall
   take heed to fained lies.

Trust not a man at the first sight
   but try him well before:
I wish all maids within their breasts
   to keep this thing in store.

For trial shall declare his truth
   and show what he doth think,
Whether he be a lover true,
   or do intend to shrink.[7]

---

[6] A Roman poet who wrote *Metamorphosis* (43 B.C.-A.D. 18).
[7] Depart.

Sir Walter Ralegh

(c. 1552–1618)

Sir Walter Ralegh (or Raleigh) was a celebrated poet, courtier, soldier, and explorer during the English Renaissance, known for his wit and womanizing, as well as falling in and out of Queen Elizabeth I's favor. Ralegh's family was Protestant and narrowly escaped persecution during the rule of Queen Mary, also known as Bloody Mary for her treatment of Catholics. Ralegh developed a hatred of Catholicism in his childhood. After fighting in military engagements in France, Ireland, and elsewhere, he established himself as a beloved courtier in Queen Elizabeth's court. Ralegh established the first English colony in the New World. It was located at Roanoke Island, Virginia. The unsuccessful settlers were forced to abandon the island.

In 1591 Ralegh was clandestinely married to one of Elizabeth's ladies-in-waiting, Elizabeth ("Bess") Throckmorton, who was pregnant. When the Queen found out about the unsanctioned marriage she dismissed Bess and imprisoned Ralegh. Ralegh returned to Elizabeth's favor in a few years and the marriage was a successful one. But after Elizabeth's death, Ralegh was tried for treason and imprisoned in the Tower of London for over twelve years. He was set free in order to lead an expedition in search of El Dorado, a kingdom in South America that was supposed to contain a legendary golden king. During their journey, Ralegh's men attacked the town of San Thome, a Spanish outpost. When Ralegh returned to England, the Spanish ambassador insisted that King James I restore Ralegh's death sentence. In 1618, Ralegh was beheaded. On viewing the axe that would behead him, his last words were, "This is a sharp Medicine, but it is a Physician for all Diseases." It was reported that Bess had his head "embalmed and kept it by her side, frequently inquiring of visitors if they would like to see Sir Walter" (according to the biography by J. H. Adamson and H. F. Holland, *Shepherd of the Ocean*, Gambit, 1969).

Ralegh's poetry is characteristically straightforward and unadorned. He drew more on the literature of the Middle Ages than the optimistic humanism of the Italian Renaissance. While a prisoner he wrote A *Historie of the World* about ancient Greece and Rome. He and Edmund Spenser traveled to London together where Spenser presented some of his allegorical poem, *The Faerie Queen* to Elizabeth. Ralegh is considered one of the most distinguished poets of the Elizabethan era.

The Nymph's Reply to the Shepherd[1]

If all the world and love were young,
And truth in every shepherd's tongue,
These pretty pleasures might me move
To live with thee and be thy love.

---

[1] This poem was written as a response to Christopher Marlowe's poem "The Passionate Shepherd to His Love." It was published in John Bodenham's *England's Helicon* in 1600. Other poets such as John Donne and Robert Herrick also replied famously to Marlowe's poem. Marlowe's poem can be seen as representing youthful exhuberance and optimism, while Ralegh's poem is more world-weary.

Time drives the flocks from field to fold
When rivers rage and rocks grow cold,
And Philomel becometh dumb;[2]
The rest complains of cares to come.

The flowers do fade, and wanton fields
To wayward winter reckoning yields;
A honey tongue, a heart of gall,
Is fancy's spring, but sorrow's fall.

The gowns, thy shoes, thy beds of roses,
Thy cap, thy kirtle,[3] and thy posies
Soon break, soon wither, soon forgotten,—
In folly ripe, in reason rotten.

Thy belt of straw and ivy buds,
Thy coral clasps and amber studs,
All these in me no means can move
To come to thee and be thy love.

But could youth last and love still breed,
Had joys no date[4] nor age no need,
Then these delights my mind might move
To live with thee and be thy love.

---

[2] The Greek myth of Philomel (or Philomela) recounts how she
was raped by King Tereus of Thrace who was married to
Philomel's sister, Procne. Tereus cut out Philomel's tongue and
imprisoned her so she couldn't reveal his terrible crime. Tereus
later turned Procne into a swallow and Philomel into a nightingale. Thus the nightingale is often called Philomel in poems.
[3] A long dress, often worn under an outer garment.
[4] "Date" here means ending date.

What is Our Life?[5]

What is our life? a play of passion,
~~Our mirth the musicke of division,~~
Our mothers wombes the tyring houses[6] be,
When we are drest for this short Comedy,
Heaven the Judicious sharpe spector[7] is,
That sits and markes still who doth act amisse,
Our graves that hide us from the searching Sun,
Are like drawne curtaynes when the play is done,
Thus march we playing to our latest[8] rest,
Onely we dye in earnest, that's no Jest.

---

[5] This poem reveals a *contemptus mundi* or contempt of the world attitude that harkens to the writing of the Middle Ages.
[6] "Tyring houses" comes from the term "attiring house," which was the room where actors dressed before a performance.
[7] "Spector" means spectator, as well as being a play on specter or ghost.
[8] "Latest" here means last.

EDMUND SPENSER

(1552–1599)

EDMUND SPENSER is one of the most famous courtier poets during the Elizabethan era and is most renowned for his allegorical romantic epic *The Faerie Queen*, an homage to Queen Elizabeth I. He is also remembered for his pastoral *Shepeardes Calendar* published in 1579 and for his lyric ode about marriage, *Epithalamion*, published in 1595.

Spenser is celebrated for pioneering the "Spenserian stanza" or a nine-line stanza consisting of eight lines of iambic pentameter and a last line of iambic hexameter, using the rhyme scheme ababbcbcc. He uses this stanza in *The Fairie Queen*, which was first published in 1609, and is a creative defense of Protestantism as well as a glorification of England and Elizabeth's reign.

from THE FAERIE[1] QUEEN

BOOK I, CANTO I

1

Lo I the man, whose Muse whilome did maske,
As time her taught in lowly Shepheards[2] weeds,[3]
Am now enforst a far unfitter taske,
For trumpets sterne to chaunge mine Oaten reeds,[4]
And sing of Knights and Ladies gentle deeds;
Whose prayses having slept in silence long,
Me, all too meane, the sacred Muse areeds
To blazon broad emongst her learned throng:
Fierce warres and faithful loves shall moralize my song.

2

Helpe then, O holy Virgin chiefe of nine,[5]
Thy weaker Novice to performe thy will,
Lay forth out of thine everlasting scryne
The antique rolles, which there lye hidden still,
Of Faerie knights and fairest Tanaquill,[6]
Whom that most noble Briton Prince[7] so long

---

[1] An archaic variant of "fairy," used by Spenser to signify the imaginary land, corresponding to England, where his poem is set.
[2] Spenser's *The Shepheardes Calender*, a work of pastoral poetry, was published in 1579.
[3] Clothing.
[4] Shepherds' pipes were supposed to made of oaten reeds.
[5] Refers to the chief of the Nine Muses of Greek mythology, probably Clio, the Muse of History.
[6] Tanaquil was the wife of Tarquinius Priscus, the 5th King of Rome.
[7] King Arthur.

Sought through the world, and suffered so much ill,
That I must rue his undeserved wrong:
O helpe thou my weake wit, and sharpen my dull tong.

3

And thou most dreaded impe of highest Jove,[8]
Faire Venus sonne,[9] that with thy cruell dart
At that good knight so cunningly didst rove,
That glorious fire it kindled in his hart,
Lay now thy deadly Heben[10] bow apart,
And with thy mother milde come to mine ayde:
Come both, and with you bring triumphant Mart,[11]
In loves and gentle jollities arrayd,
After his murdrous spoiles and bloudy rage allayd.

4

And with them eke, O Goddesse heavenly bright,
Mirrour of grace and Majestie divine,
Great Lady of the greatest Isle, whose light
Like Phoebus[12] lampe throughout the world doth
    shine,
Shed thy faire beames into my feeble eyne,
And raise my thoughts too humble and too vile,
To thinke of that true glorious type of thine,
The argument of mine afflicted stile:
The which to heare, vouchsafe, O dearest dred a-while.

---

8 In Roman myth, Jupitor is the chief god.
[9] In Roman myth, Venus is the goddess of love and beauty and her
    son is Cupid.
[10] Ebony.
[11] Mars, in Roman myth he is the god of war and the lover of Venus.
[12] In Greek myth, Phoebus is the god of the sun.

from EPITHALAMION[13]

Ye learned sisters,[14] which have oftentimes
Beene to me ayding, others to adorne,
Whom ye thought worthy of your gracefull rymes,
That even the greatest[15] did not greatly scorne
To heare theyr names sung in your simple layes,
But joyed in theyr praise;
And when ye list your owne mishaps to mourne,
Which death, or love, or fortunes wreck did rayse,
Your string could soone to sadder tenor turne,
And teach the woods and waters to lament
Your dolefull dreriment:
Now lay those sorrowfull complaints aside;
And, having all your heads with girlands crownd,
Helpe me mine owne loves prayses to resound;
Ne let the same of any be envide:
So Orpheus[16] did for his owne bride!
So I unto my selfe alone will sing;
The woods shall to me answer, and my Eccho ring.

---

[13] "Epithalamion" was first published in 1595 along with the sonnet
sequence *Amoretti*. The poem commemorates Spenser's marriage. Spenser was married twice, but it is thought that this verse
refers to his first marriage to Elizabeth Boyle as she is also
referred to in *Amoretti*.
[14] Refers to the nine Muses, daughters of Memory.
[15] Queen Elizabeth I.
[16] In Greek myth, Orpheus played the lyre and held wild beasts
spellbound as he rescued his wife Eurydice from Hades.

My Love is Like to Ice

My love is like to ice, and I to fire:
How comes it then that this her cold so great
Is not dissolved through my so hot desire,
But harder grows the more I her entreat?
Or how comes it that my exceeding heat
Is not allayed by her heart-frozen cold,
But that I burn much more in boiling sweat,
And feel my flames augmented manifold?
What more miraculous thing may be told,
That fire, which all things melts, should harden ice,
And ice, which is congeal's with senseless cold,
Should kindle fire by wonderful device?
Such is the power of love in gentle mind,
That it can alter all the course of kind.

Sir Philip Sidney

(1554–1586)

Sir Philip Sidney was one of the most famous Elizabethan courtier poets and considered the ideal
Renaissance gentleman. He was also a soldier and
statesman and is noted in particular for his 1591 *Astrophel and Stella*, as well as The *Defence of Poesy* or *An
Apology for Poetry*, published in 1595 and *The Countess of
Pembroke's Arcadia*, published in 1590 (none of his writing was published during his lifetime). Born in Pen-
shurst, Kent, his father was Sir Henry Sidney, Lord
Deputy of Ireland, and after being tutored, Philip studied at Shrewsbury School, beginning on the same day
as the poet Fulke Greville, Lord Brooke. Fulke Greville and Sidney became close friends and later Greville
wrote Sidney's biography. Sidney attended Oxford, but
left without graduating so that he could travel Europe.
He went to Paris, Frankfurt, Venice, Vienna, and other
cities. Sidney became one of the most important members of Queen Elizabeth I's court. He served on several
diplomatic missions. In 1583 he married Frances Wals-
ingham. As a soldier in the Netherlands he was
wounded and died from an infection.

Arcadia, a series of verse idylls connected by prose
narrative, was written for his sister Mary, countess of
Pembroke and is the earliest celebrated pastoral in English literature. *Astrophel and Stella* (probably written
around 1581) was inspired by Sidney's love for his aunt's
married ward, Penelope Devereux, later Lady Rich. It is
considered the greatest Elizabethan sonnet sequence

after William Shakespeare's sonnets. Containing one hundred and eight sonnets and eleven songs, Sidney got the name Astrophel from the Greek words "aster" or star and "phil" or lover while Stella came from the Latin word for star, thus Astrophel is the star lover and Stella is his star. In *Astrophel and Stella* Sidney utilized principles he put forth in his *Defense of Poetry*—poetry's liveliness or energia and its power to move readers—to revive the two-hundred-and-fifty-year-old Petrarchan sonnet sequence. The sonnet cycle shows how sympathy becomes love, then love becomes desire, and desire ultimately subverts and destroys the real love. John Donne was very influenced by *Astrophel and Stella*, as were George Herbert, Henry Vaughan, Richard Crashaw, Thomas Traherne, Thomas Carew, Andrew Marvell, and many others.

from ASTROPHIL AND STELLA

SONNET XXXI[1]

With how sad steps, O Moon, thou climb'st the skies !
How silently, and with how wan a face !
What, may it be that even in heavenly place
That busy archer his sharp arrows tries?
Sure, if that long with love-acquainted eyes
Can judge of love, thou feel'st a lover's case;
I read it in thy looks;   thy languisht grace
To me that feel the like, thy state descries.
Then, even of fellowship, O Moon, tell me,
Is constant love deemed there but want of wit?
Are beauties there as proud as here they be?
Do they above love to be loved, and yet
        Those lovers scorn whom that love doth possess?
        Do they call virtue there, ungratefulness?

SONNET LXXXIV[2]

Highway, since you my chief Parnassus[3] be,
And that my Muse, to some ears not unsweet,
Tempers her words to trampling horses' feet
More oft than to a chamber melody;
Now, blessed you, bear onward blessed me

---

[1] This sonnet from *Astrophel and Stella* is sometimes known as "His Lady's Cruelty."

[2] This sonnet from *Astrophel and Stella* is sometimes known as "The Highway."

[3] Parnassus is a mountain in central Greece. In Greek myth it was home to the Muses as well as being sacred to the sun god Apollo.

To her, where I my heart safe left shall meet;
My Muse and I must you of duty greet
With thanks and wishes, wishing thankfully.
Be you still fair, honoured by public heed,
By no encroachment wronged, nor time forgot,
Nor blamed for blood, nor shamed for sinful deed;
And that you know I envy you no lot
    Of highest wish, I wish you so much bliss:
    Hundreds of years you Stella's feet may kiss.

THE BARGAIN

My true love hath my heart, and I have his,
By just exchange one for another given:
I hold his dear, and mine he cannot miss,
There never was a better bargain driven:
My true love hath my heart, and I have his.

His heart in me keeps him and me in one,
My heart in him his thoughts and senses guides:
He loves my heart, for once it was his own,
I cherish his because in me it bides:
My true love hath my heart, and I have his.

ROBERT SOUTHWELL

(1561–1595)

ROBERT SOUTHWELL was a poet and a Jesuit priest, venerated by Roman Catholics as a martyr. He came from an aristocratic Catholic family and was ordained in Rome in 1584. That same year it was outlawed for any English-born subject to stay more than forty days in England if they had become a Roman Catholic priest. The punishment was death. However, Southwell requested to go back to England as a missionary where he ministered to oppressed Catholics. In 1592, after six years in England, he was arrested and imprisoned. He was so badly tortured that his father petitioned Queen Elizabeth I to have his son removed from Westminster or brought to trial and put to death. Southwell was moved to the Tower of London where he stayed for three years and was tortured further. Finally he was tried for treason in 1595. He pleaded not guilty, refuting that he had "entertained any designs or plots against the queen or kingdom," but the jury convicted him. He was sentenced to be hung, drawn, and quartered. In 1970 Southwell was canonized by Pope Paul VI.

Southwell wrote religious tracts and his poetry is deeply devotional, praising the exquisiteness of the spiritual world as opposed to the material one. He wasn't published until after his death and most of his poetry was written in prison. He employed the poetic conventions of antithesis and paradox frequently in his poetry. Most of his poems are euphuistic—a mannered and ornate style of writing that got its name from John Lyly's work.

"The Burning Babe" is probably Southwell's most renowned poem. Ben Jonson stated that he would gladly have destroyed much of his own work to be able to take credit for this poem, a powerful example of Southwell's handling of devotional subjects.

THE BURNING BABE

As I in hoary winter's night stood shivering in the snow,
Surprised I was with sudden heat which made my heart
    to glow;
And lifting up a fearful eye to view what fire was near,
A pretty babe all burning bright did in the air appear;
Who, scorchèd with excessive heat, such floods of tears
    did shed
As though his floods should quench his flames which
    with his tears were fed.
Alas, quoth he, but newly born in fiery heats I fry,
Yet none approach to warm their hearts or feel my fire
    but I!
My faultless breast the furnace is, the fuel wounding
    thorns,[1]
Love is the fire, and sighs the smoke, the ashes shame
    and scorns;
The fuel justice layeth on, and mercy blows the coals,
The metal in this furnace wrought are men's defilèd
    souls,

---

[1] Southwell utilizes a great deal of alliteration in his poetry. This line demonstrates his use of alliteration with the words "faultless," "furnace," and "fuel." Throughout "The Burning Babe" Southwell repeats "f" and "s" sounds to intensify the poem.

For which, as now on fire I am to work them to their
    good,
So will I melt into a bath to wash them in my blood.
With this he vanished out of sight and swiftly shrunk
    away,
And straight I callëd unto mind that it was Christmas
    day.

GEORGE CHAPMAN

(c. 1559–1634)

GEORGE CHAPMAN was an English poet, dramatist, and translator famous for his poetic translations of Homer's *Iliad* and *Odyssey*. Chapman was a classical scholar, who studied either at Oxford or Cambridge. His work was influenced by the Roman Stoic philosophers, Epicetus and Seneca. Working with Ben Jonson and John Marston, he contributed to the comedy *Eastward Ho!*, a play that landed the three authors in jail because of satirical references to the Scottish court. Chapman's greatest tragedies were based on recent French history. He wrote several metaphysical poems, translated Petrarch and Hesiod, and completed Christopher Marlowe's *Hero and Leander*. Chapman is considered by some to be the "rival poet" referred to in Shakespeare's sonnets.

Chapman published his translation of the *Iliad* in installments. The complete *Iliad* and *Odyssey* appeared in 1616 in *The Whole Works of Homer*, which was the first complete English translation. Chapman's *Homer* was much admired by poets such as Samuel Taylor Coleridge and John Keats, the latter who wrote a poem called, "On First Looking into Chapman's Homer." They found the work grand, spirited, and faithful. However, criticism of Chapman's *Homer* being overly romantic and laborious has caused his version to be much less widely read today. Chapman was devoted to the craft of poetry and felt a great duty to take his vocation seriously. His version of Homer is still considered a masterpiece of his age.

BRIDAL SONG

O come, soft rest of cares! come, Night!
    Come, naked Virtue's only tire,[1]
The reapàed harvest of the light
    Bound up in sheaves of sacred fire.
      Love calls to war:
        Sighs his alarms,
      Lips his swords are,
        The field his arms.
Come, Night, and lay thy velvet hand
    On glorious Day's outfacing face;
And all thy crownàed flames command
    For torches to our nuptial grace.
      Love calls to war:
        Sighs his alarms,
      Lips his swords are,
        The field his arms.

---

[1] "Tire" means attire or apparel.

Mary Sidney Herbert,
Countess of Pembroke

(1562–1621)

Mary Sidney Herbert was one of the first women in England to attain renown for her poetry, literary translations, and patronage of the arts. Mary was sister to the famous courtier poet, Sir Philip Sidney. Like a small number of aristocratic women, she was educated at home in music and classical languages. Queen Elizabeth I favored Mary and invited her to court in 1575. Mary wed Henry Herbert, 2nd Earl of Pembroke in 1577. She made their house into a center of literary activity—a gathering place for poets, musicians and artists. Edmund Spenser, Michael Drayton, Samuel Daniel, and Sir John Davies all commended her literary benefaction.

Mary's literary work includes various translations and a few original poems, among them an elegy for her brother, "The Dolefull Lay of Clorinda." She also wrote a pastoral for Queen Elizabeth. Philip was working on a new English version of the *Book of Psalms* when he died and Mary finished the book, supplying 107 of the 150 psalms. The psalms were made from previous English translations, not the original Hebrew text. A copy of the book was given to Queen Elizabeth I in 1599. The book is usually referred to as "The Sidney Psalms" or "The Sidneian Psalms." It had a significant influence on the development of English poetry, and inspired George Herbert and John Donne, among others. Both Philip and Mary's versions of the psalms demonstrate great imagination and dynamic language, as well as showcasing a wide array of different verse forms.

PSALM 58[1]

And call ye this to utter what is just,
    You that of justice hold the sovereign throne?
And call ye this to yield, O sons of dust,
    To wronged brethren every man his own?
O no: it is your long malicious will
    Now to the world to make by practice known,
With whose oppression you the balance fill,
    Just to yourselves, indifferent else to none.
But what could they, who even in birth declined,
    From truth and right to lies and injuries?
To show the venom of their cancered mind
    The adder's[2] image scarcely can suffice;
Nay scarce the aspic[3] may with them contend,
    On whom the charmer all in vain applies
His skilful'st spells: ay missing of his end,
While she self-deaf and unaffected lies.

---

[1] Mary Sidney Herbert's psalms utilize more urgent, dramatic language than previous English versions of the psalms. Mary takes the passionate language used for love poetry and applys it to religious verse. The Sidney Psalms are a great example of devotional poetry during the Renaissance.

[2] "Adder" in this poem refers to a snake believed to be poisonous, though adders are actually any of several kinds of nonvenomous snakes, such as the milk snake of North America.

[3] An "aspic" is an asp or viper. It is also synonymous with adder. It is a venomous or supposedly venomous snake. Biblical references to serpents connote treachery and malice.

Lord, crack their teeth; Lord, crush these lions' jaws,
    So let them sink as water in the sand.
When deadly bow their aiming fury draws,
    Shiver the shaft ere past the shooter's hand.
So make them melt as the dis-housed snail
    Or as the embryo, whose vital band
Breaks ere it holds, and formless eyes do fail
    To see the sun, though brought to lightful land.
O let their brood, a brood of springing thorns,
    Be by untimely rooting overthrown,
Ere bushes waxed they push with pricking horns,
    As fruits yet green are oft by tempest blown.
The good with gladness this revenge shall see,
    And bathe his feet in blood of wicked one;
While all shall say: the just rewarded be;
    There is a God that carves to each his own.

Samuel Daniel

(1562–1619)

Samuel Daniel was a prominent English poet, playwright, and historian of the Renaissance who was offered the position of Poet Laureate upon Edmund Spenser's death. It appears that he resigned from the post shortly after in favor of Ben Jonson. He first published in 1592 and this volume of poetry contains a cycle of sonnets to Delia. Twenty-seven of these sonnets had already been printed without Daniel's consent at the end of Sir Philip Sidney's *Astrophel and Stella*. Like Michael Drayton, Daniel wrote a historical poem about the Wars of the Roses in *ottava rima*. He wrote a prose essay "A Defence of Rime" to answer the poet Thomas Campion's essay "Observations on the Art of English Poesie," which argued that rhyme was inappropriate for the English language. In 1603 Daniel became master of Queen Elizabeth's revels and wrote masques and pastoral tragic comedies.

Although he is not well-known now, during his time Samuel Daniel was acknowledged as a leading writer. William Shakespeare and George Chapman visited him at his secluded home. During the 18th century, when little Elizabethan literature was read, Daniel remained renowned. He was praised by Samuel Taylor Coleridge, Charles Lamb, and others in the 19th century. He is important for being one of the pioneering sonneteers of the English Renaissance, along with Henry Constable and others.

Delia XXXI[1]

Look, *Delia*,[2] how we 'steem the half-blown[3] Rose,[4]
The image of thy blush and Summer's honor,
Whilst in her tender green she doth enclose
That pure sweet Beauty Time bestows upon her.

No sooner spreads her glory in the air,
But straight her full-blown pride is in declining;
She then is scorn'd that late adorn'd the Fair;
So clouds thy beauty after fairest shining.[5]

No April can revive thy wither'd flowers,
Whose blooming grace adorns thy glory now;
Swift speedy Time, feather'd with flying hours,
Dissolves the beauty of the fairest brow.[6]

O let not then such riches waste in vain,
But love whilst that thou mayst be lov'd again.[7]

---

[1] There are two slightly different versions of this sonnet. This is the 1592 version. The other version is from 1623, after Daniel's death.

[2] Daniel's sonnet sequence about Delia, who lived on the banks of Shakespeare's river, the Avon, were inspired by her memory when the poet was in Italy.

[3] "Half-blown" means half in bloom.

[4] This sonnet uses the extended metaphor of a rose to celebrate the speaker's beloved Delia. In the first stanza, the metaphor focuses on the purity and sweetness of a rose that is starting to blossom.

[5] As soon as a rose is in full-bloom, its beauty begins to pale.

[6] When the rose has faded, its beauty can never come back.

[7] Since time is of the essence, one must love in the prime of youth, before it is too late. This theme is a very important one in poetry. Christopher Marlowe's "Shepherd to a Young Nymph" is a more famous example of this subject.

MICHAEL DRAYTON

(1563–1631)

MICHAEL DRAYTON was a very prominent and prolific English poet during the Renaissance, although he is not read much today. His work is influenced by Sir Edmund Spencer and is most often compared to that of his contemporary, Samuel Daniel. He was a favorite in the court of Queen Elizabeth I, but on James I's accession his services were ridiculed and rejected. He was also friends with some of the most famous literary men of the era, including Ben Johnson, George Wither, William Browne, and William Drummond. It is possible that he was a friend of Shakespeare, as the vicar of Stratford-on-Avon states that "Shakespear, Drayton and Ben Johnson had a merry meeting, and it seems, drank too hard, for Shakespear died of a feavour there contracted."

Drayton had a long career and he continually revised and republished his poems. He published his first collection, containing spiritual poems, in 1581, but all except forty copies of the book were confiscated by the Archbishop of Canterbury and destroyed. Drayton published a final version of his sixty-four sonnet sequence in 1619, called *Idea's Mirror*. He also wrote historical poems, of which one of the most significant is the lengthy "Mortimerades," later renamed "The Barons' Wars," about the Wars of the Roses, written in *ottava rima*. Other important poems by Drayton are his ballad "The Battle of Agincourt" and "Nimphidia, the Court of Faery," which is an epic about fairyland influenced by Shakespeare's *A Midsummer Night's Dream*. The latter poem inspired the metaphysical poet Robert Herrick. Drayton died in London and was buried in Westminster Abbey where an epitaph written by Ben Johnson is engraved on his tomb.

Sonnet LXI: Since There's No Help[1]

Since there's no help, come, let us kiss and part,
Nay, I have done, you get no more of me,
And I am glad, yea, glad with all my heart,
That thus so cleanly I myself can free.
Shake hands for ever, cancel all our vows,
And when we meet at any time again
Be it not seen in either of our brows
That we one jot of former love retain.
Now at the last gasp of Love's latest breath,
When, his pulse failing, Passion speechless lies,
When Faith is kneeling by his bed of death,
And Innocence is closing up his eyes.
    Now, if thou wouldst, when all have given him over,
    From death to life thou might'st him yet recover.

----

[1] This is sonnet thirty-nine out of sixty-four sonnets from *Idea's Mirror*. It is thought Sir Henry Goodere's daughter, Anne, whom Drayton was in love with, inspired these sonnets. Sonnet LXI is considered Drayton's most accomplished sonnet. It was published in its final version in 1619, a quarter century after he first sought to be considered a sonneteer by the Elizabethan public. The poem uses the passionate directness characteristic of Elizabethan love poetry. There is also a hint of metaphysical poetry in the poem with its depiction of the death of Love, Passion, Faith, and Innocence. Drayton associated himself with the sonneteering movement.

CHRISTOPHER MARLOWE

(1564–1593)

CHRISTOPHER MARLOWE was a famous English poet and playwright who was often considered Shakespeare's greatest rival. The son of a shoemaker, Marlowe was born two months earlier than Shakespeare in Canterbury. He studied at Cambridge where he earned an undergraduate and masters degree. In London in 1587 Marlowe joined the acting troupe The Admiral's Men, and his play *Tamburlaine the Great* (c. 1587) became a great success. His other great plays include *Dr. Faustus* (c. 1588), *The Jew of Malta* (c. 1589) and *Edward II* (c. 1592). Marlowe's heroic dramas usually focus on a person of overreaching drive who is ultimately ruined by his own ambition. The plays are full of violence, passion, and beautifully crafted language written in blank verse (verse with regular meter—usually iambic pentameter—but no rhyme). It is probable that his work influenced Shakespeare, especially in *Titus Andronicus* and *King Henry VI*.

"The Passionate Shepherd to his Love" is Marlowe's most famous and enduring poem. The opening lines "Come live with me, and be my love;/And we will all the pleasures prove" have been quoted or alluded to by many poets, including Sir Walter Ralegh, John Donne, and Robert Herrick. Ralegh's "The Nymph's Reply to the Shepherd," is the best known response to Marlowe's poem. Marlowe is also noted for his long poem *Hero and Leander* (1598), which he never completed and which was finished by the poet and translator George Chapman.

Marlowe also translated Ovid's *Amores*, which was published posthumously (as were all his works except for the two parts of *Tamburlaine*, printed in 1590) and subsequently banned as being offensive. Marlowe died dramatically, stabbed in a bar fight by a drinking companion. It is possible that the murder was part of a plot as it is thought Marlowe worked as a government agent or spy.

The Passionate Shepherd to His Love[1]

Come live with me, and be my love;
And we will all the pleasures prove
That hills and valleys, dales and fields,
Woods or steepy mountain yields.

And we will sit upon the rocks,
Seeing the shepherds feed their flocks
By shallow rivers, to whose falls
Melodious birds sing madrigals.

And I will make thee beds of roses,
And a thousand fragrant posies;
A cap of flowers, and a kirtle[2]
Embroider'd all with leaves of myrtle;

---

[1] This poem is one of the best-known love poems in the English language and is famous for its insistence on *carpe diem*, seizing the day. It is a poem of seduction. Sir Walter Ralegh, Robert Herrick, John Donne, and other poets wrote replies to Marlowe's poem. Written in pastoral style, the structure of the poem is six stanzas composed of two rhyming couplets in iambic tetrameter (four feet of unstressed/stressed syllables).

[2] Scots word for slip.

A gown made of the finest wool
Which from our pretty lambs we pull;
Fair-lined slippers for the cold,
With buckles of the purest gold;

A belt of straw and ivy-buds,
With coral clasps and amber studs:
An if these pleasures may thee move,
Come live with me, and be my love.

The shepherd-swains shall dance and sing
For they delight each May morning:
If these delights thy mind may move,
Then live with me, and be my love.

from TAMBURLAINE THE GREAT
"Accurs'd be he that first invented war!"

Accursed be he that first invented war!
They knew not, ah, they knew not, simple men,
How those were hit by pelting cannon-shot
Stand staggering like a quivering aspen-leaf
Fearing the force of Boreas'[3] boisterous blasts!
In what a lamentable case where I,
If nature had not given me wisdom's lore!
For kings are clouts that every man shoots at,
Our crown the pin that thousands seek to cleave:
Therefore in policy I think it good
To hide it close; a goodly stratagem,
And far from any man that is a fool:
So shall not I be known; or if I be,
They cannot take away my crown from me.
Here will I hide it in this simple hole.

---

[3] In Greek myth Boreas is the god of the North Wind.

WILLIAM SHAKESPEARE

(1564–1616)

WILLIAM SHAKESPEARE is arguably the best known writer in the English language. He was famous as a playwright and poet, and acted as well. However, for all his great renown, little is known about his private life, as is true of many writers of his day, including his contemporary Christopher Marlowe. Shakespeare was born in Stratford-Upon-Avon and attended the local school where he would have been educated in the classics, particularly Latin. His father, John, was a successful businessman when William was a young child, but later had financial troubles. In 1582 Shakespeare married Anne Hathaway, who was eight years older and pregnant at the time of their marriage. They had three children, Susanna, born in 1583, and twins, Hamnet and Judith, born in 1585. Shakespeare emerged as a London playwright around 1592. He joined the Lord Chamberlain's Men as an actor and playwright in 1594. Under King James I, the company became the King's Men and Shakespeare stayed with it until the end of his career. In 1596 he acquired a coat of arms and in 1597 he bought a house in Stratford (he lived there after his retirement). In 1599 he became a part owner of the Globe Theater and in 1608 he became part owner of the Blackfriars Theatre.

Shakespeare's first published works were the long narrative poems *Venus and Adonis* in 1593 and *The Rape of Lucrece* in 1594. In 1601 his love elegy, *The Phoenix and the Turtle*, was published. Shakespeare's sonnets were first published in 1609 and were probably written in the

1590s. The first 126 sonnets (there are 154 sonnets in all) are addressed to a young man whose identity is unknown, while sonnets 127 to 152 are addressed to a dark lady who is also unknown. Many conjectures have been made about the identity of both and some scholars think the young man was Henry Wriothesley, Earl of Southampton (Shakespeare dedicated his two narrative poems to Wriothesley) while others believe the man might be William Herbert, Earl of Pembroke. Some scholars believe the "Dark Lady" was the poet Ameilia Lanyer. Shakespeare's sonnets are often about youthful beauty being destroyed by time or the capability of love and art to transcend time.

Sonnet I: From Fairest Creatures We Desire Increase[1]

From fairest creatures we desire increase,[2]
That thereby beauty's rose might never die,
But as the riper should by time decease,
His tender heir might bear his memory:
But thou contracted to thine own bright eyes,

---

[1] The speaker of this sonnet is trying persuade a young man to marry and have children. This poem sets the tone for sonnets 1–17 (sometimes called the "procreation" sonnets). Many of the ideas of the later sonnets are introduced here: the young man's beauty, his defenselessness in the face of time's cruelty, his potential for harm (to the world, to himself, and to his lovers), nature's beauty, which pales in comparison to his, the menace of disease, and the need to see the world in a larger sense than through one's own self-interested vision.

[2] Offspring.

Feed'st thy light's flame with self-substantial fuel,
Making a famine where abundance lies,
Thy self thy foe, to thy sweet self too cruel:
Thou that art now the world's fresh ornament,
And only herald to the gaudy spring,
Within thine own bud buriest thy content,
And, tender churl,[3] mak'st waste in niggarding:[4]
Pity the world, or else this glutton be,
To eat the world's due, by the grave and thee.

SONNET XVIII: SHALL I COMPARE THEE TO A SUMMER'S DAY?[5]

Shall I compare thee to a summer's day?
Thou art more lovely and more temperate.[6]
Rough winds do shake the darling buds of May,
And summer's lease[7] hath all too short a date.
Sometime too hot the eye of heaven shines,
And often is his gold complexion dimmed;
And every fair[8] from fair sometime declines,
By chance, or nature's changing course, untrimmed;[9]
But thy eternal summer shall not fade,
Nor lose possession of that fair thou ow'st,[10]

---

[3] Country fellow; rustic.

[4] Miserly.

[5] This sonnet is about the ability of art to make love immortal although human beauty decays: "thy eternal summer shall not fade."

[6] Gentler.

[7] Duration.

[8] Beauty.

[9] Stripped of its decoration.

[10] Possessed.

Nor shall death brag thou wand'rest in his shade,
When in eternal lines to Time thou grow'st.
So long as men can breathe, or eyes can see,
So long lives this, and this gives life to thee.

SONNET LXXI: NO LONGER MOURN FOR ME WHEN I AM DEAD[11]

No longer mourn for me when I am dead
Than you shall hear the surly sullen bell
Give warning to the world that I am fled
From this vile world with vilest worms to dwell.
Nay if you read this line, remember not
The hand that writ it, for I love you so
That I in your sweet thoughts would be forgot
If thinking on me then should make you woe.
O, if, I say, you look upon this verse,
When I perhaps compounded am with clay,
Do not so much as my poor name rehearse,
But let your love even with my life decay,
Lest the wise world should look into your moan
And mock you with me after I am gone.

[11] This sonnet is the embodiment of contradiction: it declares that it is best for the beloved one to be buried without any commemoration and on the other hand it is itself a memorial to love.

SONNET CXXX: MY MISTRESS' EYES ARE NOTHING LIKE THE SUN[12]

My mistress' eyes are nothing like the sun;
Coral is far more red than her lips' red;
If snow be white, why then her breasts are dun;[13]
If hairs be wires,[14] black wires grow on her head.
I have seen roses damasked,[15] red and white,
But no such roses see I in her cheeks;
And in some perfumes is there more delight
Than in the breath that from my mistress reeks.
I love to hear her speak, yet well I know
That music hath a far more pleasing sound;
I grant I never saw a goddess go;
My mistress when she walks treads on the ground.
And yet, by heaven, I think my love as rare[16]
As any she belied with false compare.

---

[12] In this sonnet Shakespeare writes that true love is loving some-one's imperfections. This is also a satire of sonneteers who over-praise their love by comparing the lover to everything beautiful under the sun.

[13] Dull gray-brown color. In Elizabethan poetry breasts were often compared to ivory and pearl.

[14] In Elizabethan poetry women's hair was often likened to golden wire or thread.

[15] The damask rose is a pinkish color.

[16] Precious.

80

Full Fathom Five[17]

Full fathom five thy father lies;
    Of his bones are coral made;
Those are pearls that were his eyes:
    Nothing of him that doth fade
But doth suffer a sea-change
Into something rich and strange.
Sea-nymphs hourly ring his knell:
    Ding-dong.
Hark! now I hear them,—ding-dong, bell.

---

[17] Ariel sings this song to punish Ferdinand for his past sins in *The Tempest*, Act I, scene 2. He falsely tells Ferdinand that his father has drowned, when in actuality he is still alive.

Aemilia Lanyer

(1569–1645)

AEMILIA LANYER is known as the first professional female poet in England and is also speculated to be the "Dark Lady" made famous in Shakespeare's sonnets. She published one book of poems in 1611. Her father was a royal musician and thus considered part of the lesser gentry. She was educated in the household of dowager Countess of Kent. She had an affair with Queen Elizabeth I's first cousin, Henry Carey, for several years and in 1592, upon becoming pregnant, was married to Alfonso Lanyer, a court musician. They did not have a happy marriage.

Her book focuses on the title poem, "Salve Deus Rex Judaeorum", a lengthy narrative of over 200 stanzas, which tells the story of Christ's passion almost exclusively from the point of view of the women around him. In a prose preface, Lanyer defends "virtuous women" against disbelievers. Lanyer dedicates her shorter poems to aristocratic women, including Queen Elizabeth. Lanyer's poem dedicated to the Countess of Cumberland, "Description of Cookham," is the first published English country house poem. Country house poems became popular in 17th century England as a genre in which the poet compliments a wealthy patron or friend through a description of his or her country house.

Lanyer's lover, Henry Carey or Lord Hunsdon, became a patron of Shakespeare's theater company and it has been conjectured that Lanyer is Shakespeare's "Dark Lady." She is supposed to have been strikingly beautiful and her musical skills fit the picture of the Lady in the sonnets.

Eve's Apology in Defense of Women[1]

Till now your indiscretion sets us free
And makes our former fault much less appeare;
Our Mother Eve, who tasted of the Tree,
Giving to Adam what shee held most deare,
Was simply good, and had no powre to see,
That after-comming harm did not appeare:
The subtill Serpent that our Sex betraide,
Before our fall so sure a plot had laide.

That undiscerning Ignorance perceav'd
No guile, or craft that was by him intended;
For had she knowne, of what we were bereav'd,
To his request she had not condiscended.
But she (poor soule) by cunning was deceav'd,
No hurt therein her harmelesse Heart intended:
For she alleadg'd God's word, which he denies
That they should die, but even as Gods, be wise.

But surely Adam can not be excusde,
Her fault though great, yet hee was most to blame:
What weaknesse offered, Strength might have refusde,
Being Lord of all, the greater was his shame:

---

[1] In part a response to John Milton's Par*adise Lost*, in which Eve's
   sin is the reason for humankind's fall. Lanyer is trying to rehabil-
   itate Eve in this poem and in doing so is attacking conventional
   gender roles of the day. Lanyer is defending the equal worth of
   women to men by writing about Adam's complicit role (in fact,
   in her poem Adam is "most to blame") in the expulsion from
   the garden of Eden.

Although the Serpent's craft had her abusde,
God's holy word ought all his actions frame,
For he was Lord and King of all the earth,
Before poore Eve had either life or breath.

Who being fram'd by God's eternall hand,
The perfect'st man that ever breath'd on earth;
And from God's mouth receiv'd that strait command,
The breach whereof he knew was present death:
Yea having powre to rule both Sea and Land,
Yet with one Apple wonne to loose that breath
Which God had breathed in his beauteous face,
Bringing us all in danger and disgrace.

And then to lay the fault on Patience backe,
That we (poore women) must endure it all;
We know right well he did discretion lack,
Being not perswaded thereunto at all;
If Eve did erre, it was for knowledge sake,
The fruit being faire perswaded him to fall:
Not subtill Sperent's falsehood did betray him,
If he would eate it, who had powre to stay him?

Not Eve, whose fault was onely too much love,
Which made her give this present to her Deare,
That what shee tasted, he likewise might prove,
Whereby his knowledge might become more cleare;
He never sought her weakenesse to reprove
With those sharpe words, which he of God did heare:
Yet Men will boast of Knowledge, which he tooke
From Eve's fair hand, as from a learned Booke.

If any Evill did in her remaine,
Beeing made of him, he was the ground of all;
If one of many Worlds could lay a staine
Upon our Sexe, and worke so great a fall
To wretched Man, by Satan's subtill traine;
What will so fowle a fault amongst you all?
Her weakenesse did the Serpent's words obay,
But you in malice God's deare Sonne betray.

Whom, if unjustly you condemne to die,
Her sinne was small, to what you doe commit:
All mortal sinnes that doe for vengeance crie,
Are not to be compared unto it:
If many worlds would altogether trie,
By all their sinnes the wrath of God to get;
This sinne of yours, surmounts them all as farre
As does the Sunne, another littlle starre.

Then let us have our Libertie againe,
And challendge to your selves no Sov'raigntie;
You came not in the world without our paine,
Make that a barre against your crueltie;
Your fault being greater, why should you disdaine
Our beeing your equals, free from tyranny?
If one weake woman simply did offend,
This sin of ours, hath no excuse, nor end.

JOHN DONNE

(1572–1631)

JOHN DONNE is considered the greatest of the metaphysical poets and his love of poetry, as well as his religious and philosophical verse, is highly celebrated. Raised a Roman Catholic, Donne studied at Oxford, Cambridge, and law at Lincoln's Inn. He traveled abroad and when he returned to England he became a secretary to Sir Thomas Egerton. He also became a celebrated poet and public figure. During this time he wrote some of his *Songs and Sonnets*, as well as *Problems and Paradoxes*, books that included love lyrics and satirical verse. However, Donne's court career came to an end after it was discovered that he was secretly married to Anne More in 1601 and he was briefly imprisoned. After this, Donne's poetry became more solemn and after a long time of financial hardship, during which he was a member of Parliament twice, Donne took holy orders at the behest of King James I in 1615. In 1617 his wife died and his poetry further deepened. After Donne was ordained, he wrote more religious works. He was considered one of the most expressive preachers of his time. In 1621 Donne became dean of St. Paul's Cathedral, a job which he held until his death.

Donne's poetry is noted for its originality and its mixture of passion and logic, as well as its use of paradox and hyperbole. He writes about the interconnectedness of spiritual and physical love. His devotional poems show Donne's preoccupation with death, decay, damnation, and the possibility of union with God. Some of his most renowned poems include "The Sun Rising," "A Valedic-tion: Forbidding Mourning" and his Holy Sonnet, "Death, Be Not Proud." Donne's poetry was neglected for almost two hundred years until 20th century critics rediscovered his work, which influenced poets such as W.B. Yeats, T.S. Eliot, and W.H. Auden.

The Sun Rising[1]

Busy old fool, unruly sun,
Why dost thou thus,
Through windows, and through curtains call on us?
Must to thy motions lovers' seasons run?
Saucy pedantic wretch, go chide
Late school-boys and sour prentices,
     Go tell court-huntsmen, that the king will ride,
     Call country ants to harvest offices;
Love, all alike,[2] no season knows, nor clime,
Nor hours, days, months, which are the rags of time.

Thy beams, so reverend, and strong
Why shouldst thou think?
I could eclipse and cloud them with a wink,
But that I would not lose her sight so long;
     If her eyes have not blinded thine,
     Look, and tomorrow late, tell me,
     Whether both th' Indias of spice and mine[3]

---

[1] This is one of Donne's most famous love poems, noted for its vivid use of hyperbole.

[2] Unchanging.

[3] The East Indies was known for its perfumes and spices and the West Indies for its gold and mines.

Be where thou leftst them, or lie here with me.
Ask for those kings whom thou saw'st yesterday,
And thou shalt hear, All here in one bed lay.
She's all states, and all princes, I,
Nothing else is.
Princes do but play us; compared to this,
All honour's mimic; all wealth alchemy.[4]
 Thou sun art half as happy as we,
  In that the world's contracted thus;
  Thine age asks ease, and since thy duties be
  To warm the world, that's done in warming us.
Shine here to us, and thou art everywhere;
This bed thy centre is, these walls, thy sphere.

Holy Sonnet XIV: Batter my heart, three-person'd God[5]

Batter my heart, three-person'd God; for you
As yet but knock ; breathe, shine, and seek to mend;
That I may rise, and stand, o'erthrow me, and bend
Your force, to break, blow, burn, and make me new.
I, like an usurp'd town, to another due,
Labour to admit you, but O, to no end.
Reason, your viceroy in me, me should defend,
But is captived, and proves weak or untrue.
Yet dearly I love you, and would be loved fain,
But am betroth'd unto your enemy;
Divorce me, untie, or break that knot again,

---

[4] Counterfeit gold.
[5] The dates of Donne's nineteen "Holy Sonnets" are not known.
 Most were probably written around 1609.

Take me to you, imprison me, for I,
Except you enthrall me, never shall be free,
Nor ever chaste, except you ravish me.

HOLY SONNET X: DEATH, BE NOT PROUD

Death, be not proud, though some have called thee
Mighty and dreadful, for thou art not so;
For those, whom thou think'st thou dost overthrow,
Die not, poor Death, nor yet canst thou kill me.
From rest and sleep, which but thy pictures be,
Much pleasure, then from thee much more must flow,
And soonest our best men with thee do go,
Rest of their bones, and soul's delivery.
Thou'rt slave to Fate, chance, kings, and desperate
    men,
And dost with poison, war, and sickness dwell,
And poppy, or charms can make us sleep as well,
And better than thy stroke; why swell'st thou then?
One short sleep past, we wake eternally,
And Death shall be no more; Death, thou shalt die.

THE BAIT[6]

Come live with me, and be my love,
And we will some new pleasures prove
Of golden sands, and crystal brooks,
With silken lines, and silver hooks.

---

[6] This poem is a satiric response to Christopher Marlowe's pastoral
love poem "The Passionate Shepherd to His Love."

There will the river whispering run
Warm'd by thy eyes, more than the sun;
And there the 'enamour'd fish will stay,
Begging themselves they may betray.

When thou wilt swim in that live bath,
Each fish, which every channel hath,
Will amorously to thee swim,
Gladder to catch thee, than thou him.

If thou, to be so seen, be'st loth,
By sun or moon, thou dark'nest both,
And if myself have leave to see,
I need not their light having thee.

Let others freeze with angling reeds,
And cut their legs with shells and weeds,
Or treacherously poor fish beset,
With strangling snare, or windowy net.

Let coarse bold hands from slimy nest
The bedded fish in banks out-wrest;
Or curious traitors, sleeve-silk flies,
Bewitch poor fishes' wand'ring eyes.

For thee, thou need'st no such deceit,
For thou thyself art thine own bait:
That fish, that is not catch'd thereby,
Alas, is wiser far than I.

The Canonization[7]

For God's sake hold your tongue, and let me love;
 Or chide my palsy, or my gout;
 My five gray hairs, or ruin'd fortune flout;
With wealth your state, your mind with arts improve;
  Take you a course, get you a place,
  Observe his Honour, or his Grace;
Or the king's real, or his stamp'd face[8]
 Contemplate ; what you will, approve,
 So you will let me love.

Alas! alas! who's injured by my love?
 What merchant's ships have my sighs drown'd?
 Who says my tears have overflow'd his ground?
When did my colds a forward spring remove?
  When did the heats which my veins fill
  Add one more to the plaguy bill?
Soldiers find wars, and lawyers find out still
 Litigious men, which quarrels move,
 Though she and I do love.

Call's what you will, we are made such by love;
 Call her one, me another fly,

---

[7] In this love poem Donne writes in the voice of a worldly-wise and
 jaded courtier who is nevertheless utterly caught up by his passion. The poem parodies old concepts of love while creating
 elaborate new ones, eventually concluding that even if the love
 affair is impossible in the real world, it can become legendary
 through art, and the speaker and his lover will become saints to
 subsequent generations of lovers. The title refers to the process
 by which people are inducted into the canon of saints.
[8] Refers to coins.

We're tapers too, and at our own cost die,
And we in us find th' eagle and the dove.[9]
  The phoenix riddle hath more wit
  By us; we two being one, are it;
So, to one neutral thing both sexes fit.
  We die and rise the same, and prove
  Mysterious by this love.

We can die by it, if not live by love,
  And if unfit for tomb or hearse
  Our legend be, it will be fit for verse;
And if no piece of chronicle we prove,
  We'll build in sonnets pretty rooms;
  As well a well-wrought urn becomes[10]
The greatest ashes, as half-acre tombs,
  And by these hymns, all shall approve
  Us canonized for love;

And thus invoke us, "You, whom reverend love
  Made one another's hermitage;
  You, to whom love was peace, that now is rage;
Who did the whole world's soul contract, and drove
  Into the glasses of your eyes;
  So made such mirrors, and such spies,
That they did all to you epitomize—
  Countries, towns, courts beg from above
  A pattern of your love."

---

[9] The eagle is a symbol of fierceness and the dove is a symbol of
 tenderness.
[10] Suits.

BEN JONSON

(1573–1637)

BEN JONSON was a master poet, playwright, and actor who rose to become the most celebrated literary figure of his age. From humble origins he became the subject of fame and admiration rivaling, and perhaps even outshining, his close friend William Shakespeare. He is renowned for his satirical plays *Volpone* (1606) and *The Alchemist* (1610). Jonson was a learned man of vast reading. He lived a tumultuous life, including killing a man in a duel (he escaped execution by claiming right of clergy, i.e., that he could read and write). He also had an unparalleled literary influence on writers of the Renaissance and his followers were called "the sons of Ben." Born in London, he started out as a bricklayer, his stepfather's trade, and serving in the military he began working as an actor and playwright for Philip Henslowe. In 1598 his first significant play was produced, *Every Man in His Humour.* Shakespeare was one of the actors in the play. He went on to write *Every Man out of His Humor, The Poetaster,* and collaborated with George Chapman and Marston on *Eastward Ho!,* which offended King James I, and the three writers were briefly jailed. Later, Jonson became a favorite of King James and wrote many court masques for him. In 1616 Jonson's fortunes declined—his final plays were unsuccessful and King Charles I (who came to the throne in 1625) did not appreciate him as James did.

Ben Jonson's poem "To the Memory of my Beloved, The Author Mr. William Shakespeare" prefaces the first folio of his collected plays. The well-known poem praises Shakespeare, and the line "He was not of an age, but for all time" is especially famous. Jonson also wrote the poetry volumes *Epigrams* and *The Forest* in 1616. From the latter book come two of his celebrated songs, "Drink to me only with thine eyes" and "Come, my Celia, let us prove." Like his drama, Jonson's poetry is influenced by his classical learning.

To the Memory of My Beloved, The Author Mr. William Shakespeare

To draw no envy, Shakespeare, on thy name,
Am I thus ample to thy book and fame;
While I confess thy writings to be such,
As neither Man nor Muse can praise too much.
'Tis true, and all men's suffrage.[1] But these ways
Were not the paths I meant unto thy praise;
For seeliest[2] ignorance on these may light,
Which, when it sounds at best, but echoes right;
Or blind affection,[3] which doth ne'er advance
The truth, but gropes, and urgeth all by chance;
Or crafty malice might pretend this praise,
And think to ruin where it seemed to raise.
These are, as some infamous bawd or whore
Should praise a matron; what could hurt her more?
But thou art proof against them, and, indeed,
Above the ill fortune of them, or the need.

---

[1] Consent.
[2] Simple.
[3] Feeling.

I therefore will begin: Soul of the age!
The applause! delight! the wonder of our stage!
My Shakespeare rise! I will not lodge thee by
Chaucer, or Spenser, or bid Beaumont lie
A little further, to make thee a room:[4]
Thou art a monument without a tomb,
And art alive still while thy book doth live
And we have wits to read, and praise to give.
That I not mix thee so my brain excuses,
I mean with great, but disproportioned[5] Muses:[6]
For if I thought my judgment were of years,
I should commit thee surely with thy peers,
And tell how far thou didst our Lyly outshine,
Or sporting Kyd, or Marlowe's mighty line.[7]
And though thou hadst small Latin and less Greek,
From thence to honour thee, I would not seek
For names : but call forth thund'ring Aeschylus,
Euripides, and Sophocles to us,
Pacuvius, Accius, him of Cordova dead,[8]
To life again, to hear thy buskin[9] tread
And shake a stage : or when thy socks[10] were on,
Leave thee alone for the comparison

---

[4] Geoffrey Chaucer, Edmund Spenser, and John Beaumont are buried in Westminster Abbey.

[5] Not comparable.

[6] Poets.

[7] John Lyly, Thomas Kyd, and Christopher Marlowe are Elizabethan poets and playwrights.

[8] Marcus Pacuvius and Lucius Accius were Roman tragic playwrights. "Him of Cordova" refers to the Roman tragedian Seneca.

[9] "Buskin" refers to the high-heeled boot worn by actors in Greek tragedies.

[10] Actors in Greek comedies wore low shoes.

Of all that insolent Greece or haughty Rome
Sent forth, or since did from their ashes come.
Triumph, my Britain, thou hast one to show
To whom all scenes[11] of Europe homage owe.
He was not of an age, but for all time!
And all the Muses still were in their prime,
When, like Apollo, he came forth to warm
Our ears, or like a Mercury to charm!
Nature herself was proud of his designs,
And joyed to wear the dressing of his lines!
Which were so richly spun, and woven so fit,
As, since, she will vouchsafe no other wit.
The merry Greek, tart Aristophanes,
Neat Terence, witty Plautus,[12] now not please;
But antiquated and deserted lie,
As they were not of Nature's family.
Yet must I not give Nature all; thy art,
My gentle Shakspeare, must enjoy a part.
For though the poet's matter nature be,
His art doth give the fashion: and, that he
Who casts to write a living line, must sweat,
(Such as thine are) and strike the second heat
Upon the Muses' anvil; turn the same,
And himself with it, that he thinks to frame;
Or for the laurel he may gain a scorn;
For a good poet's made, as well as born.
And such wert thou! Look how the father's face
Lives in his issue, even so the race
Of Shakspeare's mind and manners brightly shines

---

[11] Stages or theaters.
[12] Aristophanes was a Greek comic playwright. Terence and Plautus were Roman comic playwrights.

In his well torned and true filed lines;
In each of which he seems to shake a lance,[13]
As brandisht at the eyes of ignorance.
Sweet Swan of Avon! what a sight it were
To see thee in our waters yet appear,
And make those flights upon the banks of Thames,[14]
That so did take[15] Eliza, and our James![16]
But stay, I see thee in the hemisphere
Advanced, and made a constellation there!
Shine forth, thou Star of Poets, and with rage
Or influence,[17] chide or cheer the drooping stage,
Which, since thy flight from hence, hath mourned like
    night,
And despairs day, but for thy volume's light.

COME MY CELIA, LET US PROVE[18]

Come my Celia, let us prove,
While we may, the sports of love.
Time will not be ours for ever:
He at length our good will sever.
Spend not then his gifts in vain;
Suns that set may rise again,

---

[13] A pun on Shakespeare's name.
[14] The Globe Theater was located on the Thames.
[15] Pleased or charmed.
[16] Queen Elizabeth I and King James I.
[17] The power the stars supposedly possessed over human destiny.
[18] This poem appears in Jonson's poetry collection *The Forest* and in his play *Volpone* (Act III, scene 7) where Volpone is courting Celia in vain. It was inspired by the Roman poet Catullus and it in turn inspired Herrick's famed poem "To the Virgins, to Make Much of Time."

But if once we lose this light
'Tis, with us, perpetual night.
Why should we defer our joys?
Fame and rumour are but toys.
Cannot we delude the eyes
Of a few poor household spies?
Or his easier ears beguile,
So removed by our wile?
'Tis no sin love's fruit to steal,
But the sweet theft to reveal;
To be taken, to be seen,
These have crimes accounted been.

ON MY FIRST SON[19]

Farewell, thou child of my right hand, and joy;
    My sin was too much hope of thee, lov'd boy.
Seven years thou wert lent to me, and I thee pay,
    Exacted by thy fate, on the just day.
Oh, could I lose all father now! For why
    Will man lament the state he should envy?
To have so soon 'scaped world's and flesh's rage,
    And if no other misery, yet age!
Rest in soft peace, and, asked, say, Here doth lie
    Ben Jonson his best piece of poetry.
For whose sake henceforth all his vows be such
    As what he loves may never like too much.

---

[19] "On My First Son" was written in 1603, the year that Jonson's
    son died from the plague that ravaged London. The poem is
    written in heroic couplets (two rhymed lines consisting of iambic
    pentameter).

CYRIL TOURNEUR

(c. 1575–1626)

CYRIL TOURNEUR was a Jacobean playwright and poet who enjoyed success during King James I's reign. The most famous play attributed to Tourneur is *The Revenger's Tragedy*, printed in 1607. The play was published anonymously and wasn't accredited to Tourneur until the 1650s. There is some evidence that Thomas Middleton wrote the play, but its true authorship remains unknown. Tourneur wrote *The Atheist's Tragedie*, published in 1611 and considered by critics to be crude and uneven. He also wrote a poetical satire *The Transformed Metamorphosis*, an elegy on King James's son's death, and an epicede, or funeral song, on Sir Francis de Vere, which illustrates the poet's conception of the perfect knight. *The Revenger's Tragedy* is notable for its violent and macabre imagery. Like John Webster's work, it is a masterpiece of brutality, articulate villains, and dark word play about the gruesome state of human nature.

Adultery Is My Nature[1]

Adultery is my nature.
~~Faith, if the truth were known, I was begot~~
After some gluttonous dinner; some stirring dish
Was my first father, when deep healths went round,
And ladies' cheeks were painted red with wine,
Their tongues, as short and nimble as their heels,
Uttering words sweet and thick; and when the rose,
Were merrily disposed to fall again.
In such a whispering and withdrawing hour,
When base male-bawds kept sentinel at stair-head,
Was I stol'n softly. Oh damnation meet!
The sin of feasts, drunken adultery!
I feel it swell me; my revenge is just!
I was begot in impudent wine and lust.

---

[1] This poem is from *The Revenger's Tragedy*, published in 1607. It is of questionable authorship.

JOHN WEBSTER

(c. 1580–c. 1632)

JOHN WEBSTER was a Jacobean playwright (the term "Jacobean" is associated with the reign of King James I of England from 1603–1625) who is most famous for his tragedies *The White Devil* and *The Duchess of Malfi*, which are considered masterpieces of the early 17th century theater. Not much is known about Webster's life, including the dates of his birth and death. His father was a carriage maker and his mother was a blacksmith's daughter. It is probable that Webster was a lawyer, though he never practiced, and an interest in legal affairs is apparent in his plays. By 1602 Webster was writing history plays with Michael Drayton, Thomas Dekker, Thomas Middleton, and Anthony Munday. His first solo effort was the tragi-comedy *The Devil's Law Case*, written around 1610. *The White Devil*, based on Italian sources, was not a success when performed in 1612, probably because it was too unusual and complex for its audience. *The Duchess of Malfi*, also based on Italian sources, was more successful. It was performed by the King's Men in 1614 and published in 1623.

Webster's major plays are gruesome, unsettling works that can be seen as precursors to 18th-century Gothic literature. His writing combines intense violence with sophisticated word play. Webster's work shows a bleak and unflinchingly dark conception of mankind. His tragedies present a horrifying, desperate vision of human nature. In his poem "Whispers of Immortality," T. S. Eliot famously refers to Webster's ability to see "the skull beneath the skin." During the 18th and 19th centuries, many critics dismissed Webster's writing, but his reputation flourished again in the 20th century.

CALL FOR THE ROBIN-REDBREAST AND THE WREN[1]

Call for the robin-redbreast and the wren,
　　Since o'er shady groves they hover,
　　And with leaves and flowers do cover
The friendless bodies of unburied men.
　　Call unto his funeral dole[2]
　　The ant, the field-mouse and the mole,
To raise him hillocks that shall keep him warm,
And (when gay tombs are robb'd) sustain no harm;
But keep the wolf far thence, that's foe to men,
For with his nails he'll dig them up again.[3]

---

[1] This poem is sometimes known as "A Dirge." It comes from the play *The White Devil*, published in 1612. The language and imagery is typical of Webster's work in its macabre and disturbing quality and its unsparing view of death.

[2] Sorrow.

[3] Even in death there is no comfort or rest or safety.

LADY MARY WROTH

(c. 1587–c. 1651)

Lady Mary Wroth was one of the first female
British writers to achieve a lasting reputation. She
was from a well-connected English family. Her mother,
a wealthy heiress, was a cousin of Sir Walter Ralegh,
while her father was brother to Philip Sidney, one of the
most famous Elizabethan poet courtiers. Wroth grew up
in the home of Mary Sidney, Countess of Pembroke.
King James I had her marry Robert Wroth. The marriage was an unfortunate one and Wroth's husband
seems to have been a gambler, womanizer, and drunkard
who left her in debt when he died. After his death, she
had a relationship with her cousin William Herbert, 3rd
Earl of Pembroke, which was considered scandalous.

After becoming a widow, Wroth wrote a prose
romance, *Urania* that caused a scandal when it was published in 1621. It was considered a *roman à clef* and she
was accused of slander. Her most famous work of prose
is the romance *The Countess of Mountgomeries Urania*.
This is considered to be the earliest piece of long fiction
by an Englishwoman. In this romance a sonnet sequence
focuses on a woman who is in love, in contrast to the
male point of view typically seen in Petrarchan sonnets.
Cupid becomes a creature worthy of worship rather than
a blind boy who hits people with his arrows.

SONNET II

Love like a Jugler comes to play his prize

Love like a Jugler comes to play his prize,
    And all mindes draw his wonders to admire,
    To see how cunningly he (wanting eyes)
    Can yet deceive the best sight of desire.

The wanton Childe,[1] how he can faine his fire
    So prettily, as none sees his disguise,
    How finely doe his trickes; while we fooles hire
    The badge, and office of his tyrannies.

For in the ende such Jugling he doth make,
    As he our hearts instead of eyes doth take;
    For men can onely by their slights abuse.

The sight with nimble, and delightful skill,
    But if he play, his gaine is our lost will.
    Yet Childe-like we cannot his sports refuse.

---

[1] The "wanton Childe" is Cupid, the Roman god of love.

ROBERT HERRICK

(1591–1674)

ROBERT HERRICK was a leading English Cavalier poet who was deeply influenced by Ben Jonson and became an Episcopal minister. His father was a wealthy goldsmith who killed himself by jumping from the fourth-floor window of his house when Herrick was one year old. Because of the suicide, the Herrick family had to pay the British monarchy a substantial fee so that the estate wouldn't be taken possession of by the crown. Herrick became an apprentice goldsmith to his uncle and then studied at Cambridge, graduating in 1617. Herrick became a disciple of Ben Jonson during his twenties—he was the oldest of a group of poets called the "Sons of Ben"—and wrote five poems about him. He took holy orders and became a vicar in Devonshire in 1629. In 1647, Herrick was removed from the position because of his royalist sympathies during the Great Rebellion. He regained his post after the restoration of King Charles II and remained there until his death.

Herrick lived a secluded live in Devonshire and wrote some of his best work there, but he never completely stopped longing for the pleasures of London. Herrick never married and it is believed that most of the women referred to in his poems were fictional. His major work was *Hesperides; or, the Works Both Human and Divine of Robert Herrick, Esq.* published in 1648 and consisting of 1200 poems. Herrick's poetry was inspired by classical Roman poetry. He mostly wrote pastoral poems that deal with English country life. The poet Algernon Swinburne called Herrick "The greatest songwriter ever born of English race." His well-known poem "To the Virgins, to Make Much of Time" is written in response to Christopher Marlowe's "The Passionate Shepherd to His Love" and is similar in theme to Andrew Marvell's poem "To His Coy Mistress." Herrick also wrote a number of Julia poems, which are love poems written to an invented mistress. They include "Upon Julia's Clothes," "Upon Julia's Breasts," and "The Night Piece, to Julia," as well as many others.

To the Virgins, to Make Much of Time[1]

Gather ye rosebuds while ye may,
    Old time is still a-flying:
And this same flower that smiles to-day
    To-morrow will be dying.

The glorious lamp of heaven, the sun,
    The higher he's a-getting,

---

[1] This well-known poem is a light and witty verse about seizing the day (*carpe diem*) and uses the same themes as Christopher Marlowe's "The Passionate Shepherd to His Love," calling on women to marry and have sex before they are no longer young. The poem was also inspired by Ben Jonson's "Come, My Celia, Let Us Prove." The form of the poem is a variation of the hymnal stanza or common measure. The hymnal stanza is a ballad form typical of church hymns. It usually consists of four-line stanzas in iambic meter arranged in rhymed pairs (here the rhyme scheme is abab) with a line of four stressed syllables followed by three stressed syllables. Herrick adds an unstressed foot at the end of the second line of each quatrain.

The sooner will his race be run,
    And nearer he's to setting.

That age is best which is the first,
    When youth and blood are warmer;
But being spent, the worse, and worst
    Times still succeed the former.

Then be not coy, but use your time,
    And while ye may go marry:
For having lost but once your prime
    You may for ever tarry.

DELIGHT IN DISORDER

A sweet disorder in the dress
Kindles in clothes a wantonness:[2]
A lawn[3] about the shoulders thrown
Into a fine distraction:
An erring lace which here and there
Enthrals the crimson stomacher:[4]
A cuff neglectful, and thereby
Ribbons to flow confusedly:
A winning wave (deserving note)
In the tempestuous petticoat:
A careless shoe-string, in whose tie
I see a wild civility:

---

[2] Here "wantonness" means both unchaste and playful.
[3] Fine linen.
[4] A heavily embroidered or jeweled garment consisting of a
    V-shaped panel worn over the chest and stomach.

Do more bewitch me than when art
Is too precise in every part.

Upon Julia's Clothes[5]

Whenas in silks my Julia goes,
Then, then, methinks, how sweetly flows
That liquefaction of her clothes.

Next, when I cast mine eyes and see
That brave vibration each way free;
O how that glittering taketh me!

---

[5] This poem is one of many about an invented love that Herrick
named Julia. Many poems that mention Julia are alluding to
Herrick's Julia poems.

Henry King

(1592–1669)

Henry King was an English Metaphysical poet and Anglican bishop who became a friend and follower of both John Donne and Ben Jonson. His father, John King, was the Bishop of London. King was educated at Oxford and then entered the church, rising to become the Bishop of Chichester in 1642. During the English War he was expelled from his position and imprisoned by the Parliamentary army. After being released he found asylum and was reinstated after King Charles II was restored to the throne. King wrote many elegies about his friends and royalty, including a moving poem about his first wife's early death, "The Exequy." "The Exequy" is considered by some critics to be one of the best elegies in the English language. His works include *Poems, Elegies, Paradoxes and Sonets* (1657), *The Psalmes of David from the New Translation of the Bible, turned into Meter* (1651), and several sermons. He served as one of the executors of Donne's estate and wrote an elegy as a preface for a 1663 edition of Donne's poetry.

A Contemplation upon Flowers

Brave flowers—that I could gallant it like you,
And be as little vain!
You come abroad, and make a harmless show,
And to your beds of earth again.
You are not proud: you know your birth:
For your embroider'd garments are from earth.

You do obey your months and times, but I
Would have it ever Spring:
My fate would know no Winter, never die,
Nor think of such a thing.
O that I could my bed of earth but view
And smile, and look as cheerfully as you!

O teach me to see Death and not to fear,
But rather to take truce!
How often have I seen you at a bier,
And there look fresh and spruce!
You fragrant flowers! then teach me, that my breath
Like yours may sweeten and perfume my death.

GEORGE HERBERT

(1593–1633)

GEORGE HERBERT was one of the most celebrated English Metaphysical poets, as well as an orator and priest. He was born to a distinguished, artistic family and his mother was a patron to illustrious poets such as John Donne, who dedicated his *Holy Sonnets* to her. Herbert studied at Cambridge and became a public orator for the university in 1620. In 1627 he married and took holy orders in the Church of England in 1630, becoming a rector. For the rest of his life he preached and wrote poetry, while also helping to rebuild the church with his own money. Herbert's *A Priest to the Temple* was published after his death and has been enormously successful. Herbert's poems are full of deep religious devotion, precise language, metrical dexterity, and inventive use of conceit. Herbert is ranked with Donne as one of the greatest Metaphysical poets.

THE FLOWER

How fresh, O Lord, how sweet and clean
Are thy returns! ev'n as the flowers in spring;
      To which, besides their own demean,[1]
The late-past frosts tributes of pleasures bring.
            Grief melts away
            Like snow in May,

---

[1] Demeanor.

As if there were no such cold thing.
Who would have thought my shrivl'd heart
Could have recover'd greenness? It was gone
Quite under ground; as flowers depart
To see their mother-root, when they have blown;[2]
Where they together
All the hard weather
Dead to the world, keep house unknown.
These are thy wonders, Lord of power,
Killing and quickning, bringing down to hell
And up to heaven in an hour;
Making a chiming of a passing-bell.[3]
We say amiss,
This or that is:
Thy word is all, if we could spell.
O that I once past changing were,
Fast in thy Paradise, where no flower can wither!
Many a spring I shoot up fair,
Off'ring[4] at heav'n, growing and groaning thither:
Nor doth my flower
Want a spring-shower,
My sins and I joining together:
But while I grow in a straight line,
Still upwards bent, as if heav'n were mine own,
Thy anger comes, and I decline:
What frost to that? what pole is not the zone,
Where all things burn,
When thou dost turn,
And the least frown of thine is shown?

---

[2] Bloomed.
[3] A single bell ringing to mark a death.
[4] Aiming.

And now in age I bud again,
After so many deaths I live and write;
I once more smell the dew and rain,
And relish versing: O my only light,
It cannot be
That I am her
On whom thy tempests fell all night.
These are thy wonders, Lord of love,
To make us see we are but flowers that glide:
Which when we once can find and prove,
Thou hast a garden for us, where to bide.
Who would be more,
Swelling through store,[5]
Forfeit their Paradise by their pride.

Affliction (II)

Kill me not every day,
Thou Lord of life; since Thy one death for me
Is more than all my deaths can be,
Though I in broken pay,
Die over each hour of Methusalem's stay.

If all men's tears were let
Into one common sewer, sea, and brine;
What were they all, compared to Thine?
Wherein if they were set,
They would discolour Thy most bloody sweat.

---

[5] Possessions.

Thou art my grief alone,
Thou Lord conceal it not;   and as Thou art
All my delight, so all my smart:
Thy cross took up in one,
By way of imprest, all my future moan.

Thomas Carew

(1595–1640)

Thomas Carew (pronounced "Carry") was an English Cavalier poet (Cavalier poets supported King
Charles I during the English Civil War rather than the
Puritans on the Parliamentarian side; much of their
poetry is light in style and secular in subject) as well as a
courtier and soldier. He studied at Cambridge. Carew
worked for Sir Dudley Carleton, a diplomat, until he was
dismissed for slander. He had trouble finding another
job, but eventually found a position with Edward Herbert, Baron Herbert of Cherbury. Then he worked for
King Charles I and became a favorite of the queen's
because he kept quiet about her affair with Lord St.
Albans. Around 1630 Carew became a taster to the king
and made friendships with the poets Sir John Suckling
and Ben Jonson. John Donne, whose celebrity as a
court-preacher lasted until his death in 1631, was very
influential for Carew. In fact he had an almost servile
admiration for Donne.

Carew's first poem was published in 1622 and in the
early 1620s he became part of Jonson and his circle.
Carew wrote sensual, direct lyrics. His poetry was sexu-
ally explicit for its time and he was believed to be a libertine (a freethinker unrestrained by moral or sexual
strictures), however he translated psalms and wrote a
celebrated elegy in honor of Donne's important role in
English poetry, "An Elegy on the Death of the Dean of
St. Paul's Dr. John Donne." His metrical style was influ-

enced by Jonson, while his imagery was influenced by Donne, but shows more lucidity. He was one of the earliest professional Cavalier songwriters (John Wilmot, Earl of Rochester was a later example), poets who took scandalous incidents at court and created delicate poems with pure melodies from them. He also wrote verse criticism about his peers.

Song. To My Inconstant Mistress

When thou, poor excommunicate
    From all the joys of love, shalt see
The full reward and glorious fate
    Which my strong faith shall purchase me,
    Then curse thine own inconstancy.

A fairer hand than thine shall cure
    That heart, which thy false oaths did wound;
And to my soul a soul more pure
    Than thine shall by Love's hand be bound,
    And both with equal glory crown'd.

Then shalt thou weep, entreat, complain
    To Love, as I did once to thee;
When all thy tears shall be as vain
    As mine were then, for thou shalt be
    Damned for thy false apostacy.[1]

---

[1] Apostacy usually refers to giving up one's religious beliefs, but here it used to describe abandoning faithfulness in love.

JAMES SHIRLEY

(1596–1666)

JAMES SHIRLEY was a popular English playwright and poet who is no longer well-known. He was born in London and educated at Oxford. His first poem was published in 1618. After he converted to Roman Catholicism he moved to London in 1625 and became a prolific writer for the stage. He produced more than thirty tragedies and comedies including *Love Tricks*, *The Maid's Revenge*, and *Hyde Park*. He established himself as a leading playwright of the Caroline stage, the period between 1625 and 1649 coinciding with the reign of Charles I. In 1640 he became the King's Men dramatist, writing for court audiences. The Puritan edict of 1642, which called for the closing of all theaters, put an end to his career.

Shirley was influenced by the work of Francis Beaumont and John Fletcher. He is said to have died along with his second wife from exposure during the Great Fire of London. He developed a new kind of comedy noted for its refinement, wit, and intellect. He is considered a forerunner to Restoration drama. His plays are full of satire and double entendres.

DEATH THE LEVELLER[1]

The glories of our blood and state
  Are shadows, not substantial things;[2]
There is no armour against Fate;[3]
  Death lays his icy hand on kings:
      Sceptre and Crown
      Must tumble down,
  And in the dust be equal made
With the poor crookèd scythe and spade.

Some men with swords may reap the field,
  And plant fresh laurels where they kill:
But their strong nerves at last must yield;
  They tame but one another still:
      Early or late
      They stoop to fate,
And must give up their murmuring breath
When they, pale captives, creep to death.

The garlands wither on your brow,
  Then boast no more your mighty deeds!
Upon Death's purple altar now
  See where the victor-victim bleeds.
      Your heads must come
      To the cold tomb:
Only the actions of the just
Smell sweet and blossom in their dust.

---

[1] This poem deals with death as an equalizer or a dealer of justice.
    Whether rich or poor, every person succumbs to death, thus
    death levels or settles the score. There have been many poems
    written about this subject.

[2] The splendors of life are not important; they are illusion.

[3] There is no escape from death; death can't be defended against.

EDMUND WALLER

(1607–1687)

EDMUND WALLER was an English poet and orator from a wealthy background. He served as a member of parliament for both James I and Charles I. His speeches for parliament were admired greatly. In 1631 Waller secretly married a well-off ward of the Court of Aldermen and was heavily fined for this offense. She died three years later. Around 1635 he fell in love with Lady Dorothy Sidney, the eldest daughter of Robert Sidney, 2nd Earl of Leicester. She rejected him and married someone else. Waller was arrested for an obscure plot against Parliament and in favor of the king. He recanted and was released from the Tower of London but forced into exile. Waller remarried and published his poetry in 1645. Many of his lyrics had already been set to music. In 1651 Waller was allowed back to England. In 1661 Waller rejoined the House of Commons where he was known for his tolerance.

Waller was a celebrated poet in his lifetime. He worked on refining the heroic couplet, which was later perfected by John Dryden and Alexander Pope. He was highly regarded in the 18th century. Dryden stated that Waller "first made writing easily an art" and the poet and wit Alexander Pope called him "the most celebrated lyric poet that ever England produced." Waller is now known mainly for his lyrics "Go, Lovely Rose" and "On a Girdle."

Go, Lovely Rose

Go lovely rose!
Tell her that wastes her time and me,
That now she knows,
When I resemble[1] her to thee,
How sweet and fair she seems to be.

Tell her that's young,
And shuns to have her graces spied,
That hadst thou sprung
In deserts, where no men abide,
Thou must have uncommended died.

Small is the worth
Of beauty from the light retired:
Bid her come forth,
Suffer herself to be desired,
And not blush so to be admired.

Then die, that she
The common fate of all things rare
May read in thee;
How small a part of time they share
That are so wondrous sweet and fair!

---

[1] Compare.

JOHN MILTON

(1608–1674)

JOHN MILTON is one of the most important poets of the English language. He was also a historian, scholar, pamphleteer, and civil servant for the Puritan Commonwealth. He is most famous for *Paradise Lost*, which is generally regarded as the greatest epic poem in English. Born in London, he studied at Cambridge where he penned his noted poem "On the Morning of Christ's Nativity." During the English Civil War he supported Oliver Cromwell and wrote anti-royalist tracts, including an argument defending the execution of King Charles I. Milton became a foreign secretary for the English government in 1649. After the restoration of the monarchy in 1660 he was arrested and his books were burned, but then he was granted a general pardon and lived quietly. Milton's blindness became almost total by 1652, although he was still able to faintly make out light. From then on he dictated his work to secretaries, which included the poet Andrew Marvell. *Paradise Lost* (1667) is the story of Satan's rebellion and defeat and the fall of Adam and Eve. Although the work was inspired by the Bible, it is work of powerful imagination that relates the war in heaven, the fall of the rebel angels, the creation, the fall of man, Satan's final defeat, and the formation of Christ's kingdom. His other noted writings include *Paradise Regained* (1671) about Christ's triumph over Satan's temptations, the tragic drama *Samson Agonistes*, the masque *Comus* (1637), and his defense of free speech (although he made exceptions for libel, pornography, blasphemy and sedition) *Areopagiticaz* (1644).

Milton wrote eighteen sonnets in English and five in Italian, including "On His Blindness" and "On His Deceased Wife" (this sonnet is a memorial to his second wife, Kathrine Woodcock, who died in childbirth). His sonnets are considered masterpieces of the form and are sometimes referred to as Miltonic sonnets, because although he employed the Petrarchan or Italian sonnet rhyme scheme, he left out the "volte" or change in perspective that occurs between the octet and sestet. In 1645, *Poems* was published, which included noted lyrics such as "On a May Morning," and "At a Solemn Musick," as well as sonnets, elegies, masques, odes, hymns, and epigrams. "Lycidas," one of his most celebrated poems is a pastoral elegy that mourns a drowned friend and schoolmate.

In terms of literary influence, Milton's work has reverberated down through the centuries and deeply influence poets such as John Dryden, Alexander Pope (who satirized some aspects of *Paradise Lost* in *The Rape of the Lock*) John Keats, and Alfred, Lord Tennyson. Samuel Taylor Coleridge praised Milton's writing in his critical work, while William Blake and Percy Bysshe Shelley were greatly inspired by the portrayal in *Paradise Lost* of Satan as a rebel and saw him as a kind of romantic hero. William Wordsworth wrote, "Milton . . . shouldst be living at this hour."

from LYCIDAS[1]

Yet once more, O ye laurels, and once more,
Ye myrtles brown, with ivy never sere,[2]
I come to pluck your berries harsh and crude,[3]
And with forced fingers rude
Shatter[4] your leaves before the mellowing year.
Bitter constraint, and sad occasion dear,
Compels me to disturb your season due;
For Lycidas[5] is dead, dead ere his prime,
Young Lycidas, and hath not left his peer.
Who would not sing for Lycidas? He knew
Himself to sing, and build the lofty rhyme.
He must not float upon his wat'ry bier
Unwept, and welter[6] to the parching wind,
Without the meed[7] of some melodious tear.[8]

---

[1] "Lycidas" (1638) is a pastoral elegy about the death of Milton's
friend and schoolmate Edward King., who was a teacher at
Cambridge and died on a voyage to Ireland. It laments King as a
shepherd-poet and grapples with difficult questions about the
ways of God.
[2] "Never sere" means never withered. Laurel is associated with
Apollo, myrtle with Venus, and ivy with Bacchus.
[3] Not yet ripe.
[4] Scatter.
[5] A common name in ancient Greek pastorals.
[6] Roll about.
[7] Token of honor.
[8] Poetic synonym for elegy.

Begin then, Sisters of the sacred well,[9]
That from beneath the seat of Jove doth spring,
Begin, and somewhat loudly sweep the string.
~~Hence with denial vain, and coy excuse,~~
So may some gentle Muse
With lucky words favour my destined urn,
And as he passes turn
And bid fair peace be to my sable shroud.

For we were nursed upon the selfsame hill,
Fed the same flock by fountain, shade, and rill.
Together both, ere the high lawns appeared
Under the opening eyelids of the morn,
We drove a-field, and both together heard
What time the gray-fly winds her sultry horn,
Batt'ning[10] our flocks with the fresh dews of night,
Oft till the star[11] that rose, at ev'ning, bright
Toward heav'n's descent had sloped his west'ring wheel.
Meanwhile the rural ditties were not mute,
Tempered to th' oaten flute;[12]
Rough Satyrs[13] danced, and Fauns with cloven heel
From the glad sound would not be absent long;
And old Damoetas[14] loved to hear our song.

---

[9] Following in Greek and Roman tradition, Milton evokes the muses to begin his lament. The sisters are the nine muses, daughters of Zeus and Mnemosyne (memory). Their sacred well is called Aganippe on Mount Helicon.

[10] Feeding or fattening

[11] Venus or Hesperus, the evening star.

[12] A flute used by Pan that is traditionally associated with shepherds.

[13] Mythical goat-men famous for their lustiness.

[14] A traditional pastoral name. It probably refers to one of King's colleagues at Cambridge.

But O! the heavy change now thou art gone,
Now thou art gone and never must return!
Thee, Shepherd, thee the woods, and desert caves,
With wild thyme and the gadding[15] vine o'ergrown,
And all their echoes mourn.
The willows and the hazel copses green
Shall now no more be seen
Fanning their joyous leaves to thy soft lays.
As killing as the canker[16] to the rose,
Or taint-worm to the weanling[17] herds that graze,
Or frost to flowers that their gay wardrobe wear
When first the white thorn[18] blows:[19]
Such, Lycidas, thy loss to shepherd's ear.

---

[15] Unruly or wandering.
[16] A cankerworm is a garden pest that feeds on a flower and pro-
ducers canker in its blossom.
[17] "Taint-worms" are intestinal parasites thought to infect young
calves or "weanlings."
[18] Hawthorn.
[19] Blossoms.

ON HIS BLINDNESS[20]

When I consider how my light is spent
~~Ere half my days in this dark world and wide,~~
   And that one talent which is death to hide,
   Lodged with me useless, though my soul more bent
To serve therewith my Maker, and present
   My true account, lest He returning chide,
   'Doth God exact day labor, light denied?'
I fondly[21] ask. But Patience to prevent
That murmur soon replies, 'God doth not need
   Either man's work or his own gifts. Who best
   Bear his mild yoke, they serve him best. His state
Is kingly: thousands at his bidding speed,
   And post o'er land and ocean without rest;
   They also serve who only stand and wait.'

---

[20] This famous sonnet is the first poem in which Milton refers to
his blindness. The Miltonic sonnet consists of a Petrarchan sonnet rhyme scheme without the volte or turn between the octet
and sestet, which gives the poem a monolithic structure.

[21] Foolishly.

ANNE BRADSTREET

(c. 1612–1672)

ANNE BRADSTREET is both the first published American poet and the first published American woman writer. She was born Anne Dudley in Northamptonshire, England into a cultured Puritan family. Anne was remarkably learned for a woman at the time. She married Simon Bradstreet when she was sixteen and later both her father and husband were appointed governors of the Massachusetts Bay Colony (an English settlement on the east coast of North America around Salem and Boston). Anne emigrated to America in 1630 with her husband and parents during a time when many Puritans left England. The Bradstreets settled in Ipswich and later Andover. They had eight children and a very harmonious marriage.

Bradstreet's work was based on observations of the world around her and focused on domestic and spiritual themes. She was influenced by Guillaume du Bartas, a 16th-century French poet who was popular at the time. Her first work was published in 1650 when her brother-in-law, Reverend John Woodbridge, went to England and printed *The Tenth Muse*, without Bradstreet's knowledge, to show that a religious, educated woman could raise the position of wife and mother. In her poem "Prologue," Bradstreet pleads the case for women writers to be read but does not challenge the superior position of men in society: "Let Greeks be Greeks, and Women what they are./ Men have precedency and still excel;/It is but vain unjustly to wage war./Men can do best, and

Women know it well./Preeminence in all and each is yours;/Yet grant some small acknowledgement of ours." Bradstreet had a library of over 800 books that were ruined when her home burned in 1666. *Contemplations* was written for her family and not published until the mid-1800s. These later poems show her total acceptance of Puritanism and her spiritual growth, as well as personal responses to childbirth and the death of a grandchild. For some time Bradstreet's poetry was considered chiefly of historical interest, but during the 20th century she won critical acclaim for her verse.

Before the Birth of One of Her Children

All things within this fading world hath end,
Adversity doth still our joys attend;
No ties so strong, no friends so dear and sweet,
But with death's parting blow are sure to meet.
The sentence past is most irrevocable,
A common thing, yet oh, inevitable.
How soon, my Dear, death may my steps attend,
How soon't may be thy lot to lose thy friend,
We both are ignorant, yet love bids me
These farewell lines to recommend to thee,
That when the knot's untied that made us one,
I may seem thine, who in effect am none.
And if I see not half my days that's due,
What nature would, God grant to yours and you;
The many faults that well you know I have
Let be interred in my oblivious grave;

If any worth or virtue were in me,
Let that live freshly in thy memory
And when thou feel'st no grief, as I no harmes,
Yet love thy dead, who long lay in thine arms,
And when thy loss shall be repaid with gains
Look to my little babes, my dear remains.
And if thou love thyself, or loved'st me,
These O protect from stepdame's injury.
And if chance to thine eyes shall bring this verse,
With some sad sighs honor my absent hearse;
And kiss this paper for thy dear love's sake,
Who with salt tears this last farewell did take.

OLD AGE

My memory is short, and braine is dry.
My Almond-tree (gray haires) doth flourish now,
And back, once straight, begins apace to bow.
My grinders now are few, my sight doth faile
My skin is wrinkled, and my cheeks are pale.
No more rejoyce, at musickes pleasant noyse.

To my Dear and Loving Husband[1]

If ever two were one, then surely we.
If ever man were lov'd by wife, then thee.
If ever wife was happy in a man,
Compare with me, ye women, if you can.
I prize thy love more than whole Mines of gold
Or all the riches that the East[2] doth hold.
My love is such that Rivers cannot quench,
Nor ought but love from thee give recompetence.
Thy love is such I can no way repay.
The heavens reward thee manifold, I pray.
Then while we live, in love let's so persever[3]
That when we live no more, we may live ever.

---

[1] Anne Bradstreet's husband was Simon Bradstreet whom she married when she was sixteen. They had a strong, happy marriage.
[2] The East Indies.
[3] The accent is probably on the second syllable.

Samuel Butler

(1612–1680)

Samuel Butler was an English poet and satirist most remembered for his satirical poem, *Hudibras*, about the folly of religious hypocrisy. The poem ridiculed the excesses of puritanism and Butler employed couplets of rhymed eight syllable lines to heighten the humor. Butler was born in Worcestershire, the son of a farmer. He was a page for the Countess of Kent while young and later he worked as a clerk for a number of Puritan justices. He began writing *Hudibras* around 1658 and worked on the poem for about twenty years. The first part of the poem was published in December 1662 and the other two parts in 1664 and 1678. King Charles II was an admirer of Butler's *Hudibras* and gave Butler an annual pension. *Hudibras* is a significant piece of satire and wit that inspired many imitations. The work is influenced by the satirical poems of John Skelton and by Miguel de Cervantes' novel *Don Quixote*. Despite the popularity of *Hudibras*, Butler died in poverty and neglect. Most of his other writings were not published until 1759 and the term "hudibrastic" (after Butler's *Hudibras*) came to mean deliberate, humorous, badly rhymed, and poorly rhythmic couplets.

HYPOCRISY[1]

Hypocrisy will serve as well
To propogate a church as zeal;
As persecution and promotion
Do equally advance devotion:
So round white stones will serve, they say,
As well as eggs to make hens lay.

---

[1] This poem is an epigram: a concise, clever poem on a single topic. In this epigram Butler wittily excoriates the disingenuousness he believes inherent to religion.

RICHARD CRASHAW

(c. 1613–1649)

Richard Crashaw, an English metaphysical poet who converted to Catholicism, is renowned for his ardent religious poetry. His father was a Puritan minister who presided at Mary, Queen of Scots' execution and whose writings showed virulently anti-Catholic sentiments. Crashaw studied at Cambridge where he became sympathetic to the Catholic Church. He published his first book of Latin verse in 1634, a year after George Herbert's metaphysical masterpiece *Temple* was published. Crashaw taught at Cambridge and became friends with the poet Abraham Cowley around 1638. In 1644, during the English Civil War, Crashaw left for France after being ousted from his position at Cambridge because he was a Catholic sympathizer. Crashaw converted to Catholicism, fully embracing the religion he had long been drawn to, shortly after fleeing England. Abraham Cowley discovered Crashaw living in poverty in Paris in 1646. Cowley then introduced him to King Charles I's wife, Queen Henrietta Maria, who sent Crashaw to Rome where he became an attendant to a cardinal and later was made a canon of a church in Loretto, Italy. When he died of a fever, a suspicion lingered that he was poisoned.

Crashaw's poetry is notable for its combination of mysticism and lush sensuousness. His verse was inspired by Marino, an Italian poet, and by Italian and Spanish mystics. While he was exiled a friend published his religious and secular verse in the book *Steps to the Temple*

133

(1646). Crashaw was also noted for his music, painting, and engraving during his lifetime. Cowley wrote an elegy in praise of Crashaw. Crashaw's poetry is full of fanciful imagery, some of which is incredibly striking, others of which are notably clumsy. There is an intense, almost morbid passion in his writing. His well-known poem, "A Hymn to the Name and Honor of the Admirable Saint Teresa," shows the idiosyncrasies of his style, which have been likened to Italian and Spanish baroque art.

from A HYMN TO THE NAME AND HONOUR OF THE ADMIRABLE SAINT TERESA[1]

Love, thou are absolute, sole Lord
Of life and death. To prove the word,
We'll now appeal to none of all
Those thy old soldiers, great and tall,
Ripe men of martyrdom, that could reach down
With strong arms their triumphant crown:
Such as could with lusty breath
Speak loud, unto the face of death,
Their great Lord's glorious name; to none
Of those whose spacious bosoms spread a throne
For love at large to fill. Spare blood and sweat:
We'll see Him take a private seat,

---

[1] Saint Teresa was an important Spanish mystic who lived from 1515 to 1582. She was a principal figure in the Counter Reformation (the Roman Catholic response to the Protestant revolution) and successfully reawakened religious spirit in Spain that then spread to other countries. She was canonized in 1622.

And make His mansion in the mild
And milky soul of a soft child.
Scarce has she learnt to lisp a name
Of martyr, yet she thinks it shame
Life should so long play with that breath
Which spent can buy so brave a death.
She never undertook to know
What death with love should have to do.
Nor has she e'er yet understood
Why, to show love, she should shed blood;
Yet, though she cannot tell you why,
She can love, and she can die.
Scarce has she blood enough to make
A guilty sword blush for her sake;
Yet has a heart dares hope to prove
How much less strong is death than love. . . .

On Marriage

I would be married, but I'd have no wife,
I would be married to a single life.

RICHARD LOVELACE

(1618–1657)

RICHARD LOVELACE was an English Cavalier poet, nobleman, and devoted Royalist. Born in Kent, his father was a knight. Lovelace studied at Oxford. He was imprisoned for a short time in 1642 after presenting a petition to restore the bishops (a way of strengthening the monarchy) to Parliament. During the English Civil War he fought with the French army in support of the monarchy and when he returned to England he was again imprisoned briefly in 1648 by Oliver Cromwell's Commonwealth government. He spent his wealth on supplies for the Royalist forces and died impoverished soon after. His brother published Lovelace's poetry posthumously. Lovelace wrote numerous Lucasta poems—love poems dedicated to Lucy Sacheverell. He is now known for his often quoted lyric poems, "To Althea, from Prison" and "To Lucasta, Going to the Wars."

To Lucasta,[1] Going to the Wars

Tell me not, sweet, I am unkind,
    That from the nunnery
Of thy chaste breast and quiet mind
    To war and arms I fly.

True, a new mistress now I chase,
    The first foe in the field;
And with a stronger faith embrace
    A sword, a horse, a shield.

Yet this inconstancy is such
    As you too shall adore;
I could not love thee, dear, so much,
    Loved I not honour more.

---

[1] Lovelace wrote many poems to "Lucasta," or Lucy Sacheverell,
    who married someone else after she mistakenly thought
    Lovelace was killed in the Battle of Dunkirk in 1646. Lovelace
    also referred to her as Lux Casta.

ANDREW MARVELL

(1621–1678)

ANDREW MARVELL was a renowned English meta-physical poet and an important critic of the 17th century (although he was not celebrated as a great lyric poet until T.S. Eliot wrote an essay about Marvell in 1921). His father was an Anglican minister and Marvell grew up in Hull. He studied at Cambridge and while the English Civil War raged, he traveled through continental Europe. Back in England he became Thomas Fairfax's daughter's tutor. Fairfax was the retired general of the Parliamentary army, which fought against the monarchists. During his three years as tutor he wrote much of his non-satiric verse. Marvell began assisting Milton in the post of Latin secretary to Cromwell in 1657. He was elected to Parliament in 1659. In 1660 King Charles II took the throne, but despite such a political turmoil, Marvell managed to remain in favor and he helped to keep John Milton from being imprisoned and possibly executed for his anti-monarchical writings. Marvell was also friends with the metaphysical poet Richard Lovelace. Marvell continued serving in Parliament until his death. He went on diplomatic trips to Holland and Russia. He died in poverty.

Marvell contributed a prefatory poem to the second edition of Milton's *Paradise Lost*. He wrote anonymous satires criticizing the monarchy and defending Puritan rebels but he declared that he was not a dissenter himself. "To His Coy Mistress" is Marvell's most well-known poem and it's theme is to make the most of time while you can, in the tradition of Christopher Marlowe's "The Passionate Shepherd to His Love." "To His Coy Mistress" is one of the most famous carpe diem seduction poems in the English language. The lines "But at my back I always hear/Time's wingèd chariot hurrying near" are particularly famous. Marvell's poetry is noted for its irony and the alienation expressed even in his romantic lyrics where he often shows mixed feelings about sexual love.

TO HIS COY MISTRESS[1]

Had we but world enough, and time,
This coyness, lady, were no crime.
We would sit down and think which way
To walk, and pass our long love's day;
Thou by the Indian Ganges' side
Shouldst rubies[2] find; I by the tide
Of Humber[3] would complain. I would
Love you ten years before the Flood;

---

[1] Like Christopher Marlowe's "The Passionate Shepherd to His Love" and Robert Herrick's "To the Virgins, to Make Much of Time," the theme of this poem is to make the most of life before one dies and more specifically, the poem urges the woman he desires to not put off having sex because before too long she'll be in the grave. This poem shouldn't be taken merely at face value, however, Marvell is also satirizing the conventions of the seduction poem, filling it with some unsettling imagery like "Worms shall try/That long preserv'd Virginity" and "am'rous birds of prey" who will "tear our Pleasures with rough strife." The speaker's longing for his hesitant lady is mixed with aversion at the prospect of mortality.

[2] Rubies are talismans that preserve virginity.

[3] A river that runs through Marvell's hometown, Hull.

And you should, if you please, refuse
Till the conversion of the Jews.[4]
My vegetable love should grow
Vaster than empires, and more slow.
An hundred years should go to praise
Thine eyes, and on thy forehead gaze;
Two hundred to adore each breast,
But thirty thousand to the rest;
An age at least to every part,
And the last age should show your heart.
For, lady, you deserve this state,[5]
Nor would I love at lower rate.
      But at my back I always hear
Time's wingèd chariot hurrying near;
And yonder all before us lie
Deserts of vast eternity.
Thy beauty shall no more be found,
Nor, in thy marble vault, shall sound
My echoing song; then worms shall try
That long preserv'd virginity,
And your quaint[6] honour turn to dust,
And into ashes all my lust.
The grave's a fine and private place,
But none I think do there embrace.
      Now therefore, while the youthful hue
Sits on thy skin like morning dew,
And while thy willing soul transpires[7]
At every pore with instant fires,

---

[4] Traditionally, the conversion of Jews to Christianity is supposed to occur at the end of the world.

[5] Dignity.

[6] Too subtle.

[7] Breathes out.

Now let us sport us while we may;
And now, like am'rous birds of prey,
Rather at once our time devour,
Than languish in his slow-chapp'd[8] power.
Let us roll all our strength, and all
Our sweetness, up into one ball;
And tear our pleasures with rough strife
Thorough the iron gates of life.
Thus, though we cannot make our sun
Stand still, yet we will make him run.

The Fair Singer[9]

To make a final conquest of all me,
Love did compose so sweet an enemy,
In whom both beauties to my death agree,
Joining themselves in fatal harmony;
That while she with her eyes my heart does bind,
She with her voice might captivate my mind.

I could have fled from one but singly fair,
My disentangled soul itself might save,
Breaking the curled trammels of her hair.
But how should I avoid to be her slave,
Whose subtle art invisibly can wreath
My fetters of the very air I breathe?

---

[8] Slow-jawed or slowly devouring.
[9] This poem is about dueling lovers. In it the man is captivated by
the woman through her charmed voice and beauty despite his
struggle against falling in love. The terms of the struggle are
couched in terms of war: "enemy," "fighting," "forces,"
"victory," etc.

It had been easy fighting in some plain,
Where victory might hang in equal choice,
But all resistance against her is vain,
Who has th'advantage both of eyes and voice,
And all my forces needs must be undone,
She having gained both the wind and sun.

THE MOWER TO THE GLO-WORMS[10]

i

Ye living Lamps, by whose dear light
The Nightingale does sit so late,
And studying all the Summer-night,
Her matchless Songs does meditate;

ii

Ye Country Comets, that portend
No War, nor Princes funeral,
Shining unto no higher end
Then to presage the Grasses fall;

---

[10] In Marvell's time, a mower cut grass or grain with a scythe or
sickle. Marvell wrote four Mower poems. They are variants on
pastoral poems—instead of a shepherd Marvell uses a mower.
Along with "Damon the Mower" and "The Mower's Song," this
poem expresses disatisfaction with Juliana, a shepherdness who
has spurned the mower's advances. Despite the beautiful lights of
the fireflies or glo-worms Damon will not be consoled. Marvell
is poking a little fun at the mower's despondency over unrequited love—Damon revels a little too much in his own pathos,
saying "I shall never find my home."

iii

Ye Glo-worms, whose officious Flame
To wandring Mowers shows the way,
That in the Night have lost their aim,
And after foolish Fires do stray;

iv

Your courteous Lights in vain you wast,
Since Juliana here is come,
For She my Mind hath so displac'd
That I shall never find my home.

Henry Vaughan

(1622–1695)

Henry Vaughan was a Welsh metaphysical poet whose work drew on his appreciation of nature and mysticism. Vaughan was born in Breconshire, Wales and lived there for much of his life. He identified himself as a Silurist, taking literary inspiration from his local surroundings. The Silures were an ancient and powerful Celtic tribe of south Wales that resisted being conquered during the Roman invasion of Britain. Vaughan studied at Oxford, but did not graduate, and later became a doctor. He was an esteemed physician for most of his life. He was also a supporter of he monarchy during the English Civil War. Vaughan's poetry was inspired by his spiritual beliefs and love for the natural world, as well as, the metaphysical poet George Herbert. Vaughan influenced the romantic poet William Wordsworth, among other poets. His poetry celebrates communion with nature and spirituality. He published a number of books of poetry. His most important volume was *Silex Scintillans*, published in two parts in 1650 and 1655.

PEACE

My soul, there is a country
    Far beyond the stars,
Where stands a wingèd sentry
    All skillful in the wars:
There, above noise and danger,
    Sweet Peace sits crown'd with smiles,
And One born in a manger
    Commands the beauteous files.
He is thy gracious Friend,
    And—O my soul awake!—
Did in pure love descend,
    To die here for thy sake.
If thou canst get but thither,
    There grows the flower of Peace,
The Rose that cannot wither,
    Thy fortress, and thy ease.
Leave then thy foolish ranges;[1]
    For none can thee secure,
But One, who never changes,
    Thy God, thy life, thy cure.

---

[1] Wanderings, travels.

Margaret Cavendish,
Duchess of Newcastle

(1623–1673)

Margaret Cavendish was a prolific writer who wrote poetry, fiction, plays, memoirs, and works of scientific and philosophical speculation. She published her first of many books of poetry in 1653, *Poems and Fancies*. She was a noted iconoclast who believed that education would benefit women. One of her most well known works is a utopian fantasy called *The Blazing World* (1668), which posits that infinite worlds exist and that society should be based on Platonic love (derived from the concept in Plato's *Symposium* and *Phaedras* of a chaste but passionate love that brings people closer to wisdom and virtue) a concept that the poet Katherine Philips shared and that was popular in the court of Queen Henrietta Maria, King Charles I's French wife. She met her husband, William Newcastle in 1645. She was a Royalist who accompanied Queen Henrietta Maria to France during the English Civil War. She published a biography of the life of her husband in 1667.

Love and Poetry

O love, how thou art tired out with rhyme!
Thou art a tree whereon all poets clime;
And from they branches every one takes some
Of thy sweet fruit, which Fancy feeds upon.
But now thy tree is left so bare and poor,
That they can scarcely gather one plumb more.

JOHN BUNYAN

(1628–1688)

JOHN BUNYAN was an English preacher and the most important allegorical Puritan writer of the 17th century, famous for his seminal work *The Pilgrim's Progress*. Bunyan grew up in a fairly well-to-do family and was educated through his teenage years. He became a tinker like his father before him. During the English Civil War he fought on the side of the parliamentary forces. He joined the army in 1644 at age sixteen. In 1646 he married a devout woman and had four children. His wife died around 1655, leaving Bunyan with four motherless children to care for until he remarried. He became an unlicensed deacon in 1657 after joining the Baptist church, publishing his first two works, *Some Gospel Truths Opened* and *Vindication of Gospel Truths*. In 1660 he was imprisoned for twelve years for being a religious dissenter and preaching the Gospel without permission. While in jail he wrote an autobiography, *The Holy City* (published in 1666.) He wrote other work in prison, including a poem called "Prison Meditations," which responded to a letter of encouragement he received. After his release he became a licensed preacher and was again thrown in jail for half a year in 1675 where he wrote *The Pilgrim's Progress*, which became the most read English book until the 20th century and is probably the most renowned Christian allegory ever published. Bunyan continued writing and publishing. He died from a chill in 1688.

Of Man by Nature[1]

From God he's a Back slider,
Of Ways, he loves the wider;
With Wickedness a Sider,
More Venom than a Spider.
In Sin he's a Confider,
A Make-bate[2], and Divider;
Blind Reason is his Guider,
The Devil is his Rider.

The Shepherd Boy Sings in the Valley of Humiliation

He that is down needs fear no fall,
    He that is low, no pride;
He that is humble ever shall
    Have God to be his guide.

I am content with what I have,
    Little be it or much:
And, Lord, contentment still I crave,
    Because Thou savest such.

Fullness to such a burden is
    That go on pilgrimage:
Here little, and hereafter bliss,
    Is best from age to age.

---

[1] This poem was published in *A Book for Boys and Girls* in 1701,
    thirteen years after Bunyan's death.
[2] A troublemaker.

149

Upon Time and Eternity

Eternity is like unto a Ring.
Time, like to Measure, doth it self extend;
Measure commences, is a finite thing.
The Ring has no beginning, middle, end.

JOHN DRYDEN

(1631–1700)

JOHN DRYDEN was the Poet Laureate of England during the Restoration and one of the greatest literary figures of that era. In literary circles the time period became known as the Age of Dryden. As well as being a famed poet, he was also a playwright, literary critic, and translator. Born in Aldwinkle, Northamptonshire, he was the son of a country gentleman and studied at Cambridge. He settled in London around 1657 and although he first got attention for his commemoration of the death of Oliver Cromwell, *Heroic Stanzas* (1659), Dryden honored the restoration of King Charles II with his *Astraea Redux*. Charles named him Poet Laureate in 1668. He lost his laureateship with the accession of King William III, or the Prince of Orange, who reigned as king of Britain from 1689 to 1702. Even after losing his court patronage, Dryden was still a formidable figure in the literary scene. He wrote nearly thirty comedies, tragedies, and dramatic operas, including *The Conquest of Granada* (2 parts, 1670–1671), *Marriage A-la-Mode* (1672), *Aureng-Zebe* (1675), and *All for Love* (1677). In 1668 he published a book of dramatic criticism, *Of Dramatick Poesie* or *An Essay of Dramatic Poesy*.

Dryden's poetry is notable for being mainly written in heroic couplets. Two of Dryden's most well-known poems are "Absalom and Achitophel" and "Mac Flecknoe." "Absalom and Achitophel" is a political satire based on the Biblical story of David and Absalom. "Mac Flecknoe" (written around 1676, published in

1682) is a satire about the poet Thomas Shadwell who was also prominent at the time. In it, Dryden envisions Flecknoe as the ruler of the "realms of Nonsense" who appoints Shadwell as his successor right before his death. He also wrote many translations of Latin poetry, among them Virgil's *Aeneid* and notable Pindaric odes (an ode in the form used by the Greek poet Pindar) including "Alexander's Feast" and "Ode to the Memory of Mrs. Anne Killigrew."

from MAC FLECKNOE

All human things are subject to decay,
And, when fate summons, monarchs must obey.
This Flecknoe[1] found, who, like Augustus, young
Was called to empire, and had governed long;
In prose and verse was found without dispute,
Through all the realms of Nonsense, absolute.
This agèd prince, now flourished in peace,
And blessed with issue of a large increase,
Worn out with business, did at length debate
To settle the succession of the state;
And, pondering which of all his sons was fit
To reign, and wage immortal war with wit,
Cried,—"'Tis resolved! for nature pleads, that he
Should only rule, who most resembles me.

---

[1] Flecknoe refers to the English priest, poet, and dramatist Richard Flecknoe (c. 1600–c. 1678).

Shadwell[2] alone my perfect image bears,
Mature in dulness[3] from his tender years;
Shadwell alone, of all my sons, is he,
Who stands confirmed in full stupidity.
The rest to some faint meaning make pretence,
But Shadwell never deviates into sense;
Some beams of wit on other souls may fall,
Strike through, and make a lucid interval;
But Shadwell's genuine night admits no ray,
His rising fogs prevail upon the day.
Besides, his goodly fabric fills the eye,
And seems designed for thoughtless majesty;
Thoughtless as monarch oaks, that shade the plain,
And, spread in solemn state, supinely reign.
Heywood and Shirley[4] were but types of thee,
Thou last great prophet of tautology!
Even I, a dunce of more renown than they,
Was sent before but to prepare the way;
And, coarsely clad in Norwich drugget, came
To teach the nation in thy greater name."

---

[2] Thomas Shadwell (1642-1692), a poet who considered himself the poetic heir to Ben Jonson. It is possible that the disagreement between Shadwell and Dryden was partly based on the fact that Shadwell believed Dryden underestimated Jonson. In addition, they had opposing political beliefs. Dryden was a strong supporter of the Staurt monarchy and Shadwell was a Whig.

[3] Every epic hero has a defining trait (usually a positive one) and Shadwell's is dullness—Dryden mocks the heroic epic by giving his protagonist a negative trait as his one virtue. To belittle Shadwell he raises him to greatness in order to show the discrepancy between the Shadwell of the poem and the actual man.

[4] Refers to the playwright-poets Thomas Heywood (c. 1575–1650) and James Shirley (1596-1666).

Fair Iris I Love, and Hourly I Die[5]

Fair Iris I love, and hourly I die,
But not for a lip, nor a languishing eye:
She's fickle and false, and there we agree,
For I am as false and as fickle as she.
We neither believe what either can say;
And, neither believing, we neither betray.
'Tis civil to swear, and say things of course;
We mean not the taking for better or worse.
When present, we love; when absent, agree:
I think not of Iris, nor Iris of me.
The legend of love no couple can find,
So easy to part, or so equally join'd.

---

[5] This poem (sometimes known as "Song from Amphitryon") is
from Act IV, scene I of *Amphitryon*.

KATHERINE PHILIPS

(1632–1664)

KATHERINE PHILIPS was an Anglo-Welsh poet known for her intense friendships and the poems she wrote about them. Her father, John Fowler, was a Presbyterian cloth merchant. Katherine was educated at boarding school and at fifteen moved to Wales upon her mother's remarriage. Philips became a Royalist, breaking with Presbyterians tradition. In 1647 she married James Philips, a Welsh member of Parliament from 1653 to 1662. It appears they had a strong marriage apart from political differences that she wrote about in her poems: Katherine supported the monarchy, while James supported Oliver Cromwell. Her home became a center of the "Society of Friendship." The society she created was a group connected by coterie names and belief in the prevalent concept of Platonic love or intimate relationships that transcend physical desire. The idea of Platonic love was popular in the court of Queen Henrietta Maria. Philips was known as "Orinda" and she was admired and respected by poets such as Abraham Cowley and Henry Vaughan. She circulated her poetry through Wales, London, and Dublin in manuscript form. She moved to Dublin in 1662 to join her friend Anne Owen (the "Lucasia" of Philips' poems) and became an important court figure where she further established herself as a writer by translating plays. In 1664 an unauthorized collection of her poems was published and then withdrawn. Soon after Philips died of small pox at age thirty-three. Three years after her death, her more than 100 poems were officially published.

Against Love

Hence Cupid! with your cheating toys,
Your real griefs, and painted joys,
Your pleasure which itself destroys.
Lovers like men in fevers burn and rave,
And only what will injure them do crave.
Men's weakness makes love so severe,
They give him power by their fear,
And make the shackles which they wear.
Who to another does his heart submit,
Makes his own idol, and then worships it.
Him whose heart is all his own,
Peace and liberty does crown,
He apprehends no killing frown.
He feels no raptures which are joys diseased,
And is not much transported, but still pleased.

Sir George Etherege

(1635–1691)

GEORGE ETHEREGE was a Restoration playwright noted for having pioneered the comedy of manners. He studied law and probably traveled to France where it is possible that he saw some of Moliere's early comedies. He wrote three very successful plays. His first play was produced in 1664, *The Comical Revenge; or, Love in a Tub* and his second, *She Would if She Could,* in 1668. The latter play is all about flirtation and it introduced a new kind of literature to the stage. His writing is full of wit, spirit, and immoral goings-on. Etherege himself lived a life of frivolity and associated with other noble wits of the time. William Congreve continued the tradition in his plays. *The Man of Mode or, Sir Fopling Flutter* (1676), Etherege's final play, is renowned for creating the character of the fop.

Song from Love in a Tub[1]

If she be not as kind as fair,
    But peevish and unhandy,
Leave her, she's only worth the care
    Of some spruce Jack-a-dandy.
I would not have thee such an ass,
Hadst thou ne'er so much leisure,
To sigh and whine for such a lass
    Whose pride's above her pleasure.

---

[1] This poem is from Etherege's play *The Comical Revenge; or, Love in a Tub* (1664).

EDWARD TAYLOR

(c. 1642–1729)

EDWARD TAYLOR was an American poet and Puritan clergyman. He was born in Leicestershire, England and became a teacher with Puritan sympathies. Taylor emigrated in 1668 to America. In 1671 he graduated from Harvard Divinity School and for the rest of his life he worked as a Congregational minister in Westfield, Massachusetts. A colleague of famous American Puritans such as Increase Mather and Charles Chauncy, he also corresponded with divines (theologians) in England. He was a passionate Calvinist who believed he had a mystical communion with Jesus. His strongest poems show a similarity to English metaphysical poetry. Taylor's work was not published until the early 20th century. He is considered the leading colonial American poet whose poems are inspired by his devout spiritual sensibility.

Upon a Wasp Chilled with Cold[1]

The bear that breathes the northern blast
Did numb, torpedo-like, a wasp
Whose stiffened limbs encramped, lay bathing
In Sol's warm breath and shine as saving,
Which with her hands she chafes and stands
Rubbing her legs, shanks, thighs, and hands.
Her pretty toes, and fingers' ends
Nipped with this breath, she out extends
Unto the sun, in great desire
To warm her digits at that fire.
Doth hold her temples in this state
Where pulse doth beat, and head doth ache.
Doth turn, and stretch her body small,
Doth comb her velvet capital.
As if her little brain pan were
A volume of choice precepts clear.
As if her satin jacket hot
Contained apothecary's shop
Of nature's receipts, that prevails
To remedy all her sad ails,
As if her velvet helmet high
Did turret rationality.

---

[1] Taylor closely observes a chilled wasp and notices how she is
warmed by the sun and brought into wondrous flight. Taylor
longs to bask in the light of God's grace and have his soul spiri-
tually awakened just as the wasp was physically warmed. The
extended metaphor of the wasp is used by Taylor to praise God
and illustrate the goodness that eminates from God.

She fans her wing up to the wind
As if her pettycoat were lined,
With reason's fleece, and hoists sails
And humming flies in thankful gales
Unto her dun curled palace hall
Her warm thanks offering for all.
Lord, clear my misted sight that I
May hence view Thy divinity,
Some sparks whereof thou up dost hasp
Within this little downy wasp
In whose small corporation we
A school and a schoolmaster see,
Where we may learn, and easily find
A nimble spirit bravely mind
Her work in every limb: and lace
It up neat with a vital grace,
Acting each part though ne'er so small
Here of this fustian animal.
Till I enravished climb into
The Godhead on this ladder do,
Where all my pipes inspired upraise
An heavenly music furred with praise.

Aphra Behn

(1640–1689)

Aphra Behn (née Johnson) was an English poet, playwright, and novelist during the Restoration era who is considered to be one of the first professional women authors writing in English. She was a very productive writer of amatory fiction, a genre of literature popular during the late 17th century. An early predecessor of the romance novel, amatory fiction was written by women, for women, and its subject was sexual love. Behn was known for being part of "The Fair Triumvirate of Wit," along with two other women writers who all had a reputation for scandalous writing. Behn was criticized for her feminist writing and occasionally imprisoned for it.

Born in Kent, it is thought that her father was a barber and her mother was a wet nurse. Behn probably had some educational opportunities and it is likely she went to South America in 1663 when her father was appointed to a military post. She married a Dutch merchant, Hans Behn, in 1664 and evidence suggests that he died in the plague that swept London in 1665. In the 1660s, Behn served as a spy for King Charles II in Belgium (Charles had just gained the throne after Cromwell's rule) to find out information in the war against Holland. Under the code name "Astrea," Behn learned about plans to destroy the English fleet—which did happen in June 1667. It seems as though Charles never paid for her work and she was briefly in debtor's prison in 1668.

Her first play was produced by 1670, *The Forced Marriage*, and was followed by many successful plays, including *The Amorous Prince; or, The Curious Husband* (1671); *The Dutch Lover* (1673); *Abdelazer, or, The Moor's Revenge* (1676); and her most popular play, *The Rover; or, the Banish'd Cavaliers*. Behn's plays were usually about thwarted love and seduction Her most renowned literary work was the novel *Oroonoko; or, The Royal Slave*. She also penned *The Lucky Chance; or, An Alderman's Bargain* (1686); *The Fair Jilt; or, The History of Prince Tarquin and Miranda* (1686); and *The History of the Nun; or, The Fair Vow-Breaker* (1686). To earn a living Behn also translated Latin and French and adapted *Aesop's Fables*. About her poetry, Behn asserted that she wanted the "Masculine Part the Poet in me" to be taken seriously and she wrote in verse genres considered suitable only to men—erotic, social, and political poetry. Behn's health deteriorated in the late 1680s and in an elegy to the poet Edmund Waller she wrote that she was one "who by Toils of Sickness, am become/Almost as near as thou art to a Tomb." She died in April 1689 and was buried in Westminster Abbey. Virginia Woolf declared that "all women together ought to let flowers fall upon the tomb of Aphra Behn . . . for it was she who earned them the right to speak their minds."

LOVE ARMED[1]

Love in Phantastique Triumph sat,
Whilst Bleeding hearts about him flow'd,
For whom fresh pays he did create,
And strange Tyrannick pow'r he shew'd;
From thy bright Eyes he took his fires,
Which round about in sport he hurl'd;
But 'twas from mine he took desires,
Enough t'undoe the Amorous world.

From me he took his sighs and tears,
From thee his pride and cruelty;
From me his languishments and fears,
And ev'ry killing Dart from thee:
Thus thou, and I, the God have arm'd,
And set him up a Deity,
But my poor heart alone is harm'd,
Whilst thine the Victor is, and free.

---

[1] "Love Armed" is also known as "Song from Abdelazar." It is from Behn's play, *Abdelazar, or the Moor's Revenge* (1677). The play opens with this song while the character of Abdelazer sits gloomily with his head in his hands. This poem was reprinted in *Poems on Several Occasions* in 1684.

LIBERTINE[2]

A thousand martyrs I have made,
       All sacrificed to my desire,
A thousand beauties have betray'd
       That languish in resistless fire:
The untamed heart to hand I brought,
And fix'd the wild and wand'ring thought.

I never vow'd nor sigh'd in vain,
       But both, tho' false, were well received;
The fair are pleased to give us pain,
       And what they wish is soon believed:
And tho' I talk'd of wounds and smart,
Love's pleasures only touch'd my heart.

Alone the glory and the spoil
       I always laughing bore away;
The triumphs without pain or toil,
       Without the hell the heaven of joy;
And while I thus at random rove
Despise the fools that whine for love.

---

[2] "Libertine" is sometimes titled by its first line, "A Thousand Martyrs I Have Made."

John Wilmot,
Earl of Rochester

(1647–1680)

John Wilmot, the 2nd Earl of Rochester, was an English poet and courtier, as well as one of the most infamous, decadent figures of the Restoration period. Born in Oxfordshire, his father was a landowner and Royalist general while his mother was from a well-known Puritan family. Wilmot inherited his title when he was eleven, attended Oxford at thirteen, and finished up his education by traveling through France and Italy. He was one of the principal wits of King Charles II's court, though he fell out of favor several times because of his recklessness. He married an heiress and fought in naval battles with distinction. Wilmot was influenced by John Donne, and his poetry was known for its sharp wit, polish, and lewdness. Some of his most popular poems are "Satyre Against Mankind" and "Epitaph on King Charles II." Most of his poetry was only published under his own name posthumously. Towards the end of his life Wilmot had a religious conversion, renouncing his notorious libertine adventures and ordering his "profane" writing to be burned.

To This Moment a Rebel

To this moment a rebel I throw down my arms,
Great Love, at first sight of Olinda's bright charms.
Make proud and secure by such forces as these,
You may now play the tyrant as soon as you please.

When Innocence, Beauty, and Wit do conspire
To betray, and engage, and inflame my Desire,
Why should I decline what I cannot avoid?
And let pleasing Hope by base Fear be destroyed?

Her innocence cannot contrive to undo me,
Her beauty's inclined, or why should it pursue me?
And Wit has to Pleasure been ever a friend,
Then what room for Despair, since Delight is Love's
    end?

There can be no danger in sweetness and youth,
Where Love is secured by good nature and truth;
On her beauty I'll gaze and of pleasure complain
While every kind look adds a link to my chain.

'Tis more to maintain than it was to surprise,
But her Wit leads in triumpth the slave of her eyes;
I beheld, with the loss of my freedom before,
But hearing, forever must serve and adore.

Too bright is my Goddess, her temple too weak:
Retire, divine image! I feel my heart break.
Help, Love! I dissolve in a rapture of charms
At the thought of those joys I should meet in her arms.

Epitaph on Charles II[1]

Here lies a great and mighty King,
Whose promise none relied on;
He never said a foolish thing,
Nor ever did a wise one.

---

[1] This joking epigram (a short, witty poem expressing a single thought) was written while King Charles II was still alive and he is alleged to have answered, "That is true; for my words are my own, but my actions are those of my ministers."

Mary, Lady Chudleigh

(1656–1710)

MARY, LADY CHUDLEIGH was a poet and a devout Anglican who was self-educated. She challenged traditional gender roles. Her poem "To the Ladies" from *Poems on Several Occasions,* published in 1703, puts forth a feminist argument for wives to be treated as equals and not as servants in marriage. She also wrote *The Female Advocate; or, A Plea for the Just Liberty of the Tender Sex and Particularly of Married Women.*

To the Ladies

Wife and servant are the same,
But only differ in the name:
For when that fatal knot is tied,
Which nothing, nothing can divide:
When she the word obey has said,[1]
And man by law supreme has made,
Then all that's kind is laid aside,
And nothing left but state[2] and pride:
Fierce as an Eastern prince he grows,
And all his innate rigour shows:

---

[1] This refers to the traditional marriage ceremony in which the wife promises "to love, honor, and obey" her husband while in return the husband promises "to love, honor, and cherish" his wife.

[2] Dignity.

Then but to look, to laugh, or speak,
Will the nuptial contract break.
Like mutes she signs alone must make,
And never any freedom take:
But still be governed by a nod,
And fear her husband as a God:
Him still must serve, him still obey,
And nothing act, and nothing say,
But what her haughty lord thinks fit,
Who with the power, has all the wit.
Then shun, oh! shun that wretched state,
And all the fawning flatt'rers hate:
Value your selves, and men despise,
You must be proud, if you'll be wise.

ANNE FINCH,
COUNTESS OF WINCHILSEA

(1661–1720)

A<small>NNE</small> F<small>INCH</small> (née Kingsmill) was a poet and one of the most noted women writers in English literary society around the turn of the 18th century. She was one of the earliest women poets in England to be published. Born in Sydmonton, she was an attendant to the Duchess of York in the court of King Charles II. She married the 4th Earl of Winchilsea, Heneage Finch, in 1684. They were both forced to leave the court when King James II was deposed. She was a friend of Jonathan Swift and Alexander Pope, along with other important literary figures of her time. "The Spleen," a Pindaric ode (a form of ode used by the Greek poet and dramatist Pindar, consisting of a three part structure containing a strophe, an antistrophe, and an epode, which echoes the three movements of the chorus in Greek drama) was one of her most popular poems. She published only one collection of poems during her lifetime, *Miscellany Poems Written by a Lady*, in 1713. *The Poems of Anne, Countess of Winchilsea* was published in 1903 and recently a manuscript with fifty-three unpublished poems was discovered. As an aristocratic woman Finch received mockery for her work but also great praise. William Wordsworth was an enthusiast of Finch's nature poetry.

On Myselfe

Good Heav'n, I thank thee, since it was design'd
I shou'd be fram'd, but of the weaker kinde,
That yet, my Soul, is rescu'd from the Love
Of all those Trifles, which their Passions move.
Pleasures, and Praise, and Plenty have with me
But their just value. If allow'd they be,
Freely, and thankfully as much I tast,
As will not reason, or Religion wast.
If they're deny'd, I on my selfe can Live,
And slight those aids, unequal chance does give.
When in the Sun, my wings can be display'd,
And in retirement, I can bless the shade.

MATTHEW PRIOR

(1664–1721)

MATTHEW PRIOR was an English poet and diplomat. He had a long diplomatic career, starting with becoming secretary to the embassy at the Hague in 1697. During Queen Anne's rule, Prior became a Tory, and in 1711 he went to Paris as a secret agent and helped conclude peace negotiations. Thus the treaty of Utrecht (1713) was popularly called "Matt's Peace." When King George I took the throne, Prior's political career was over and he was imprisoned by the Whigs for two years (1715–16). Prior is known for his light, satirical poetry, especially two lengthy satires *Alma* and *Solomon* published in 1718. He collaborated with Charles Montagu to write a burlesque of Dryden's *The Hind and the Panther*, which was titled *The Country Mouse and the City Mouse*.

Prior's poetry often deals with the hypocrisy of current social conventions and he uses ironic realism to explore themes of love and youth and beauty.

CUPID MISTAKEN

As after noon, one summer's day,
Venus[1] stood bathing in a river;
Cupid[2] a-shooting went that way,
New strung his bow, new fill'd his quiver.

---

[1] The Roman goddess of love and beauty.
[2] Venus's son, the god of love.

With skill he chose his sharpest dart:
With all his might his bow he drew:
Swift to his beauteous parent's heart
The too well-guided arrow flew.

I faint! I die! the Goddess cry'd:
O cruel, could'st thou find none other,
To wreck thy spleen on? Parricide!
Like Nero,[3] thou hast slain thy mother.

Poor Cupid sobbing scarce could speak;
Indeed, Mamma, I did not know ye:
Alas! how easy my mistake?
I took you for your likeness, Cloe.[4]

A True Maid[5]

No, no; for my virginity,
When I lose that, says Rose, I'll die:
Behind the elms last night, cried Dick,
Rose, were you not extremely sick?

---

[3] Nero was the fifth emperor of Rome who allegedly murdered his
    mother, Agrippina.
[4] Chloe is a nymph from Greek mythology, as well as shepherdess
    in a famous love story by the ancient Greek writer Longus.
[5] This poem mocks the sexual hypocrisy of the supposedly chaste
    Rose. Although female "purity" was often praised in poetry of the
    period, the virtue of virginity was equally mocked and challenged
    in verse. Here Prior turns the courtly verse of poets such as
    Thomas Wyatt on its head and uses a typical courting pair, Dick
    and Rose, to offer a less idealized look at love and honor. "The
    True Maid" may have inspired William Blake's "The Sick Rose."

JONATHAN SWIFT

(1667–1745)

JONATHAN SWIFT was an Irish writer renowned for his satirical prose and poetry, and considered the principle prose satirist in the English language. He was also a clergyman, essayist, and political pamphleteer. He is considered the most significant prose satirist in the English language and is especially famous for *Gulliver's Travels* (1726) and "A Modest Proposal" (1729). He is less remembered for his poetry. His satire was written in two different styles, the Horatian and the Juvenalian. Swift published his work anonymously or under different pseudonyms such as Lemuel Gulliver, Isaac Bickerstaff, and M.B. Drapier.

Born in Dublin, he attended Kilkenny School, where the poet and playwright William Congreve was also a student, and then studied at Trinity College where he received a B.A. and an M.A. Because of religious violence, Swift, a Protestant, left Ireland and became secretary to a retired diplomat, Sir William Temple, at Moor Park, near London. Here he met Esther Johnson, the "Stella" of his noted poems and *Journal to Stella* (1710–1713), which consists of letters about his reactions to current events. Swift was ordained in the Anglican church in 1695 and in 1713 was awarded the deanery of St. Patrick's Cathedral, Dublin. His first major work, *A Tale of a Tub* (1704), satirizes religion and learning. Much of Swift's writing is dedicated to exposing England's unfair treatment of Ireland. His ironic tract "A Modest Proposal" recommends reducing Irish poverty by butchering children and selling them as food to wealthy English landlords. *Gulliver's Travels*, seemingly the story of the protagonist's meetings with various races and societies, reflects Swift's vision of humanity's precarious position between brutishness and reason.

STELLA'S BIRTHDAY
MARCH 13, 1719

Stella[1] this day is thirty-four,
(We shan't dispute a year or more:)
However, Stella, be not troubled,
Although thy size and years are doubled,
   Since first I saw thee at sixteen,[2]
The brightest virgin on the green;
So little is thy form declin'd;
Made up so largely in thy mind.

   Oh, would it please the gods to split
Thy beauty, size, and years, and wit;
No age could furnish out a pair
Of nymphs so graceful, wise, and fair;
With half the lustre of your eyes,
With half your wit, your years, and size.

---

[1] The real "Stella" was Esther Johnson (1680-1728). Swift composed poems for her birthday every year from 1719 until her death. They had a lifelong friendship. (There were rumors that Swift was secretly married to Esther Johnson but there is no proof of this.) Swift also wrote *Journal to Stella*.

[2] When Swift was secretary to Sir William Temple at Moor Park he first met "Stella." Often he refers to her age erroneously in his poems. They met when she was eight and he twenty-two and he taught her how to write.

And then, before it grew too late,
How should I beg of gentle Fate,
(That either nymph might have her swain,)
To split my worship too in twain.

OYSTERS

Charming oysters I cry:
My masters, come buy,
So plump and so fresh,
So sweet is their flesh,
No Colchester[3] oyster
Is sweeter and moister:
Your stomach they settle,
And rouse up your mettle:
They'll make you a dad
Of a lass or a lad;
And madam your wife
They'll please to the life;
Be she barren, be she old,
Be she slut, or be she scold,
Eat my oysters, and lie near her,
She'll be fruitful, never fear her.

THE MORAL

Rebukes are easy from our betters,
From men of quality and letters;
But when low dunces will affront,
What man alive can stand the brunt?

---

[3] The Colchester oyster is the native oyster of Britain and is considered to be of finer taste than other varieties of oyster.

WILLIAM CONGREVE

(1670–1729)

WILLIAM CONGREVE was a Restoration poet and playwright best remembered for his satirical *The Way of the World*, which is considered a masterpiece of Restoration comedy. Born in Bardsey, Yorkshire, he attended Kilkenny School, where the satirist Jonathan Swift was also a student, and went on to study at Trinity College, Dublin. Congreve became a young disciple of the playwright and poet John Dryden. His first major play was *The Old Bachelour* in 1693. He followed it with *The Double-Dealer* in 1693, *Love for Love* in 1695 and *The Way of the World* in 1700. Congreve's work greatly influenced the English comedy of manners with its witty dialogue, ironic portrayal of fashionable society, and ribaldry. His plays have been compared to Oscar Wilde's for their wit and mastery of language. He also wrote many poems and translations, as well as a tragedy, *The Mourning Bride* (1697). Congreve held various minor political positions and was friends with Swift, Alexander Pope, and the French writer, Voltaire. Congreve is known for the famous quotes, "Heaven has no rage like love to hatred turned,/Nor hell a fury like a woman scorned" and "Music hath charms to soothe a savage beast," which both come from his play *The Mourning Bride*.

A Hue and Cry after Fair Amoret

Fair Amoret[1] is gone astray—
    Pursue and seek her, ev'ry lover;
I'll tell the signs by which you may
    The wand'ring Shepherdess discover.

Coquette and coy at once her air,
    Both studied, tho' both seem neglected;
Careless she is, with artful care,
    Affecting to seem unaffected.

With skill her eyes dart ev'ry glance,
    Yet change so soon you'd ne'er suspect them,
For she'd persuade they wound by chance,
    Tho' certain aim and art direct them.

She likes herself, yet others hates
    For that which in herself she prizes;
And, while she laughs at them, forgets
    She is the thing that she despises.

---

[1] In Greek mythology Amoret was brought up by the goddess of
  Venus in her courts of love. Amoret is the personification of
  young, virginal, desirable womanhood. Amoret also came to men
  an amorous girl or woman; a wanton.

ISAAC WATTS

(1674–1748)

ISAAC WATTS was an English poet and Nonconformist minister who is considered to be the "Father of English Hymnody." He was born in Southhampton, England and his father was imprisoned many times for not adhering to the mandates of the Church of England. Watts was a Nonconformist, a term used after the 1662 Act of Uniformity to refer to an English subject belonging to a non-Anglican church. He became the pastor of a large Congregational church in London but his poor health stopped him from spending much time on his ministerial duties. Watts wrote over 750 hymns, including setting most of the psalms into English meter. Benjamin Franklin brought Watts' psalms and hymns to the United States.

AGAINST IDLENESS AND MISCHIEF[1]

How doth the little busy bee
    Improve each shining hour,
And gather honey all the day
    From every opening flower!

How skillfully she builds her cell!
    How neat she spreads the wax!
And labours hard to store it well
    With the sweet food she makes.

In works of labour or of skill,
    I would be busy too;
For Satan finds some mischief still
    For idle hands to do.

In books, or work, or healthful play,
    Let my first years be passed,
That I may give for every day
    Some good account at last.

---

[1] This poem was published in 1715 in *Divine Songs for the Use of Children.* Lewis Carroll famously parodied Watts's poem in *Alice in Wonderland.*with the poem that begins "How doth the little crocodile/Improve his shining tail,/And pour the waters of the Nile/On every golden scale!"

JOHN GAY

(1687–1732)

JOHN GAY was an English poet and playwright who's most renowned work was *The Beggar's Opera*. The 1728 play was set to music and its characters, including Polly Peachum and Captain Macheath, became famous. Gay grew up in Barnstaple, England and after leaving grammar school was apprenticed to a silk merchant in London, but he didn't last long in that line of work. He started writing and became a good friend of Alexander Pope, to whom he dedicated his *Rural Sports* in 1713. After Pope's prompting, the next year Gay wrote *The Shepherd's Week*, a satire of the pastoral genre. Gay continued writing and publishing and in 1720 his *Poems on Several Occasions* was printed. He had many patrons but lost all his money in a bad investment. He soon recovered his losses with the help of his friends and patrons. In 1727 he wrote his well-known *Fifty-one Fables in Verse* for Prince William. He hoped to gain court favor through his verse but when he was offered the post of Gentleman Usher to Princess Louisa, he turned it down.

Gay's *The Beggar's Opera* was performed in 1728. Its anti-heroes, Peachum and Macheath represented a famous highwayman, Jonathan Wild, and a house burglar, Jack Sheppard. But Peachum also represented Sir Robert Walpole, the British statesman who served under King George I and II and was considered the first unofficial Prime Minister of England. John Gay was buried in Westminster Abbey, and in addition to an epitaph by Pope, his tomb is inscribed with his own satiric couplet:

"Life is a jest, and all things show it, / I thought so once, and now I know it."

He that Tastes Woman[1]

Man may escape from rope and gun;
Nay, some have out-liv'd the doctor's pill;
Who takes a woman must be undone,
That basilisk[2] is sure to kill.
The fly that sips treacle is lost in the sweets,
So he that tastes woman, woman, woman,
He that tastes woman, ruin meets.

---

[1] This poem is from *The Beggar's Opera*.

[2] The mythic basilisk was considered the king of the serpents, supposedly produced by the egg of a cock hatching under toads or snakes. According to myth, basilisks were highly deadly: they would either burn someone up just by approaching him or could cause someone to die of horror by staring him in the eye.

If Lawyer's Hand is Fee'd[3]

A fox may steal your hens, sir,
A whore your health and pence, sir,
Your daughter rob your chest, sir,
Your wife may steal your rest, sir,
A thief your goods and plate.

But this is all but picking,
With rest, pence, chest and chicken;
It ever was decreed, sir,
If lawyer's hand is fee'd, sir,
He steals your whole estate.

---

[3] This poem is from *The Beggar's Opera*. Peachum sings this verse
after he finds out that his daughter, Polly, has secretly married
Captain Macheath.

Henry Carey

(c. 1687–1743)

Henry Carey was an English poet and musician, as well as a writer of burlesque plays (comedies that rely on imitation that is distorted and exaggerated in coarser, broader ways than parody). Carey was born illegitimately and it is unknown who his father was, although it is possible that it was George Savile, Marquess of Halifax. His mother is thought to have been a teacher. Carey taught music at various schools, but mainly made a living from his writing. He was influenced by the essayist and politician Joseph Addison. Carey is most known now for his satirical poems and his ballads such as "Sally in Our Alley," which was published in *The Musical Century* (1737), a volume of Carey's poems set to music. His poem "Namby-Pamby" mocks the writing style of the poet Ambrose Phillips and is considered valuable as an early example of a nursery rhyme. He has been accredited by some as the author of "God Save the King," England's National Anthem, although authorship has not been confirmed. His most complete volume of poems is *Poems on Several Occasions*, published in 1729. At the age of fifty-six, a poverty-stricken Carey hanged himself and left behind his wife and four children.

The Man-hater, a Song

I

What's Man, but a perfidious Creature,
Of an inconstant, fickle Nature,
Deceitful, and Conceited too,
Boasting of more than he can do?

II

Beware, ye heedless Nymphs, beware,
For Men will Lye, and Fawn, and Swear;
But, when they once have gain'd the Prize,
Good Heav'ns! How they will Tyranize!

The Woman Hater, a Song

I

What's a Woman but a Name,
A pretty, empty, Gaudy Frame,
Full of Nonsense, full of Pride,
Full of Talk, and Naught beside?

II

Beateous as Angels is her Face,
She moves with more than Humane Grace,
But who can prove, or who can find
One single Beauty in her Mind?

ALEXANDER POPE

(1688–1744)

ALEXANDER POPE was one of the greatest English writers of the 18th century and was known as "The Wicked Wasp of Twickenham" for his biting literary satires. Pope dominated the literary scene of the Augustan period. (The Augustan period refers to the first half of the 18th century when many political and satirical works were being written. King George I of England envisioned himself as Caesar Augustus, the Roman Emperor.) Pope wrote most of his poetry in heroic couplets and his mastery of that form is considered unparalleled. Born in London, Pope had little formal education because he suffered from anti-Catholic restrictions at a time when Protestants ruled England. He educated himself through extensive reading and began writing poetry as a teenager. His first published work, *Essay on Criticism* (1711), established Pope as a significant poetic voice. His patron was the poet William Walsh and Pope became a celebrity in London literary circles.

The Rape of the Lock (1712–1714) is a mock epic that exposes the lives of the aristocratic class of the times. He uses heroic verse to diminish the grandness of the epic. Pope also satirizes female vanity in his poem. Its narrative is about the cutting off of a lock of Miss Arabella Fermor's hair without permission by Robert, Lord Petre, which leads to a falling out between two distinguished Catholic families—a true event. In the poem Fermor is represented as Belinda and Lord Petre as the Baron, and the petty bickering of the families is elevated to the epic world of the gods. His other work includes the devastating satire *The Dunciad* (1728–42), *Moral Essays* (1731–35) and *Essay on Man* (1733). Additionally he translated Homer's the *Iliad*. He is the source of many commonly-used (and often unattributed) quotes, including: "To err is human, to forgive divine," "A little learning is a dangerous thing," and "For fools rush in where angels fear to tread."

from THE RAPE OF THE LOCK

What dire offence from am'rous causes springs,
What mighty contests rise from trivial things,
I sing—This verse to CARYL, Muse![1] is due:
This, ev'n Belinda[2] may vouchsafe to view:
Slight is the subject, but not so the praise,
If She inspire, and He approve my lays.

Say what strange motive, Goddess![3] could compel
A well-bred Lord t' assault a gentle Belle?
O say what stranger cause, yet unexplor'd,
Could make a gentle Belle reject a Lord?
In tasks so bold, can little men engage,
And in soft bosoms dwells such mighty Rage?

---

[1] John Caryl was a friend of Pope's and it was he that suggested that Pope write this poem about the silliness of the quarrel between an acquaintance of Caryl's, Lord Petre, and the Fermor family, after Petre cut off a lock of Arabella Fermor's hair. Pope is addressing Caryl as if he were a muse.

[2] Belinda represents Arabella Fermor. In poetry the name Belinda is associated with gentleness.

[3] Pope again invokes Caryl as a muse.

Sol[4] thro' white curtains[5] shot a tim'rous ray,
And oped those eyes that must eclipse the day:
Now lap-dogs give themselves the rousing shake,
And sleepless lovers, just at twelve, awake:
Thrice rung the bell, the slipper knock'd the ground,
And the press'd watch[6] return'd a silver sound.
Belinda still her downy pillow prest,
Her guardian SYLPH[7] prolong'd the balmy rest:
'Twas He had summon'd to her silent bed
The morning-dream that hover'd o'er her head;
A Youth more glitt'ring than a Birth-night Beau,[8]
 (That ev'n in slumber caus'd her cheek to glow)
Seem'd to her ear his winning lips to lay,
And thus in whispers said, or seem'd to say.

---

[4] The sun.

[5] Refers to the curtains of Belinda's bed.

[6] A kind of clock. Pressing a button on it caused a bell to sound the
current hour or quarter hour.

[7] A fairy or sprite.

[8] Evening celebration of a royal person's birthday.

The Dying Christian to His Soul

Vital spark of heav'nly flame,
Quit, oh, quit, this mortal frame!
Trembling, hoping, ling'ring, flying,
Oh, the pain, the bliss of dying!
Cease, fond Nature, cease thy strife,
And let me languish into life!

Hark! they whisper; Angels say,
Sister Spirit, come away.
What is this absorbs me quite,
Steals my senses, shuts my sight,
Drowns my spirits, draws my breath?
Tell me, my Soul! can this be Death?

The world recedes; it disappears;
Heav'n opens on my eyes; my ears
With sounds seraphic ring:
Lend, lend your wings! I mount! I fly!
O Grave! where is thy Victory?
O Death! where is thy Sting?

Lady Mary Wortley Montague

(1689–1762)

Lady Mary Wortley Montague was an aristocratic English poet and prose writer known in particular for her correspondence. She married Edward Wortley Montague in 1712. He became the ambassador to Turkey in 1716. When they returned to England she worked at educating the public about the importance of inoculation to prevent smallpox, which she learned from Turkish medical practice. Back in England Lady Montague herself suffered from smallpox and her brother died from the disease. She inoculated her own daughter and brought the medical practice of inoculation to Western Europe.

Epithalamium

Since you, Mr. H**d, will marry black Kate,
Accept of good wishes for that blessed state:
May you fight all the day like a dog and a cat,
And yet ev'ry year produce a new brat.
Fal la!

May she never be honest—you never be sound;
May her tongue like a clapper be heard a mile round;
Till abandon'd by joy, and deserted by grace,
You hang yourselves both in the very same place.
Fal la!

A Summary of Lord Lyttleton's Advice to a Lady[1]

Be plain in dress, and sober in your diet,
In short, my deary, kiss me! and be quiet.

---

[1] Lord George Lyttleton was a poet, politician, and patron of the arts.

JAMES THOMSON

(1700–1748)

JAMES THOMSON was a Scottish poet and playwright whose most famous work was the long poem "The Seasons." Educated at the University of Edinburgh where he began publishing poetry, Thomson moved to London in 1725. In London he became a tutor and met prominent literary men such as Alexander Pope and John Gay. Lord George Lyttelton became Thomson's patron and after his death was his literary executer.

"The Seasons," a poem in blank verse, was published in four parts, starting with "Winter," which was immediately popular. Thomson followed with "Summer," "Spring," and lastly "Autumn." The thoughtful images of nature were juxtaposed against the urbane, polished poetry of Pope. "The Seasons" (1726–1730) and "The Castle of Indolence" (1748) are both examples of poems that foreshadow Romanticism, particularly the poetry of Thomas Gray and William Cowper. In "Liberty" (1735–36) Thomson pays tribute to Britain. A masque he co-wrote contains his celebrated ode "Rule Britannia," which was set to music.

from RULE BRITANNIA[1]

When Britain first at Heav'n's command
   Arose from out the azure main;
This was the charter of the land,
   And guardian angels sang this strain:
     Rule, Britannia! Britannia, rule the waves:
     Britons never shall be slaves.

The nations not so blest as thee,
   Shall in their turns to tyrants fall;
While thou shalt flourish great and free,
   The dread and envy of them all.
     Rule, Britannia! Britannia, rule the waves:
     Britons never shall be slaves.

Still more majestic shalt thou rise,
   More dreadful from each foreign stroke;
As the loud blast that tears the skies,
   Serves but to root thy native oak.
     Rule, Britannia! Britannia, rule the waves:
     Britons never shall be slaves.

---

[1] James Thomson's patriotic poem was written for the masque
Alfred. Thompson co-wrote the masque with David Mallet to
commemorate the accession of King George I and the birthday
of Princess Augusta. It was set to music by Thomas Arne in
1740.

SAMUEL JOHNSON

(1709–1784)

SAMUEL JOHNSON, often referred to as Dr. Johnson, is one of the greatest literary figures in 18th century England. He was a poet, critic, essayist, biographer, and lexicographer. His criticism of English literature is considered to be among the finest. He was also a famous wit and prose writer. (Dr. Johnson is known in philosophy for his "refutation" of Bishop Berkeley's idealism—when told by his biographer that Berkeley's theory of idealism couldn't be argued against, Johnson kicked a stone and stated, "I refute it thus!") Born in Lichfield, Staffordshire, he was the son of a bookseller and briefly studied at Oxford. He moved to London and started writing for periodicals. In 1775 he produced his monumental *Dictionary of the English Language*, the first distinguished English dictionary, which made him famous. His *Lives of the Most Eminent English Poets*, 10 vol. (1779–1781), was an important critical work. Renowned as a brilliant conversationalist, he helped found the Literary Club. His contemporary, James Boswell wrote a biography of Johnson, *Life of Samuel Johnson* (1791), that is one of the most celebrated biographies of all time. Other works by Johnson include the moral romance *Rasselas* (1759), his essays for *The Rambler* (1750–52) and *The Idler* (1758–60), as well as an eight-volume edition of the works of William Shakespeare.

Johnson published his master poem, *The Vanity of Human Wishes*, in 1749. It was the first work he published under his own name. Its subject is the futility of the human pursuit of greatness and happiness, and critics have debated whether it reflects pessimism or hope for redemption. The poem imitates one of the Latin poet Juvenal's satires, but instead of emphasizing the social and political themes, it concerns itself with moral questions.

ONE AND TWENTY

Long-expected one and twenty
Ling'ring year at last has flown,
Pomp and pleasure, pride and plenty
Great Sir John, are all your own.

Loosen'd from the minor's tether,
Free to mortgage or to sell,
Wild as wind, and light as feather
Bid the slaves of thrift farewell.

Call the Bettys, Kates, and Jenneys
Ev'ry name that laughs at care,
Lavish of your Grandsire's guineas,
Show the spirit of an heir.

All that prey on vice and folly
Joy to see their quarry fly,
Here the gamester light and jolly
There the lender grave and sly.

Wealth, Sir John, was made to wander,
Let it wander as it will;
See the jocky, see the pander,
Bid them come, and take their fill.

When the bonny blade carouses,
Pockets full, and spirits high,
What are acres? What are houses?
Only dirt, or wet or dry.

If the Guardian or the Mother
Tell the woes of willful waste,
Scorn their counsel and their pother,
You can hang or drown at last.

from THE VANITY OF HUMAN WISHES

Let Observation with extensive View,
Survey Mankind, from *China* to *Peru*;
Remark each anxious Toil, each eager Strife,
And watch the busy Scenes of crouded Life;
Then say how Hope and Fear, Desire and Hate,
O'er spread with Snares the clouded Maze of Fate,
Where wav'ring Man, betray'd by vent'rous Pride,
To tread the dreary Paths without a Guide;
As treach'rous Phantoms in the Mist delude,
Shuns fancied Ills, or chases airy Good.
How rarely Reason guides the stubborn Choice,
Rules the bold Hand, or prompts the suppliant Voice,
How Nations sink, by darling Schemes oppres'd,
When Vengeance listens to the Fool's Request.

Fate wings with ev'ry Wish th' afflictive Dart,
Each Gift of Nature, and each Grace of Art,
With fatal Heat impetuous Courage glows,
With fatal Sweetness Elocution flows,
Impeachment stops the Speaker's pow'rful Breath,
And restless Fire precipitates on Death.

But scarce observ'd the Knowing and the Bold,
Fall in the gen'ral Massacre of Gold;
Wide-wasting Pest! that rages unconfin'd,
And crouds with Crimes the Records of Mankind,
For Gold his Sword the Hireling Ruffian draws,
For Gold the hireling Judge distorts the Laws;
Wealth heap'd on Wealth, nor Truth nor Safety buys,
The Dangers gather as the Treasures rise.

Let Hist'ry tell where rival Kings command,
And dubious Title shakes the madded Land,
When Statutes glean the Refuse of the Sword,
How much more safe the Vassal than the Lord,
Low sculks the Hind beneath the Rage of Pow'r,
And leaves the *bonny Traytor* in the *Tow'r*,
Untouch'd his Cottage, and his Slumbers sound,
Tho' Confiscation's Vulturs clang around.

The needy Traveller, serene and gay,
Walks the wild Heath, and sings his Toil away.
Does Envy seize thee? crush th' upbraiding Joy,
Encrease his Riches and his Peace destroy,
New Fears in dire Vicissitude invade,
The rustling Brake alarms, and quiv'ring Shade,
Nor Light nor Darkness bring his Pain Relief,

One shews the Plunder, and one hides the Thief.

Yet still the gen'ral Cry the Skies assails
And Gain and Grandeur load the tainted Gales;
Few know the toiling Statesman's Fear or Care,
Th' insidious Rival and the gaping Heir.

Once more, *Democritus*, arise on Earth,
With chearful Wisdom and instructive Mirth,
See motley Life in modern Trappings dress'd,
And feed with varied Fools th' eternal Jest:
Thou who couldst laugh where Want enchain'd
    Caprice,
Toil crush'd Conceit, and Man was of a Piece;
Where Wealth unlov'd without a Mourner dy'd;
And scarce a Sycophant was fed by Pride;
Where ne'er was known the Form of mock Debate,
Or seen a new-made Mayor's unwieldy State;
Where change of Fav'rites made no Change of Laws,
And Senates heard before they judg'd a Cause;
How wouldst thou shake at *Britain*'s modish Tribe,
Dart the quick Taunt, and edge the piercing Gibe?
Attentive Truth and Nature to descry,
And pierce each Scene with Philosophic Eye.
To thee were solemn Toys or empty Shew,
The Robes of Pleasure and the Veils of Woe:
All aid the Farce, and all thy Mirth maintain,
Whose Joys are causeless, or whose Griefs are vain.

JUPITER HAMMON

(1711–c. 1806)

JUPITER HAMMON was a poet and a slave, and the first African American writer to publish in the United States. He is considered one of the founders of African American literature. Hammon's poetry deals with the subjects of race, slavery, and white injustice. All of his work draws heavily on Christian motifs. His writing was edited by white patrons and probably approved by them. He published *Evening Thought* in 1760, *An Essay on the Ten Virgins* in 1779, *A Winter Piece* in 1782, *An Evening's Improvement* in 1783, and *An Address to the Negroes in the State of New York* in 1787. Hammon received an unusually extensive education for a slave on the Long Island Lloyd Manor Estate from Nehemiah Bull, a Harvard graduate. Hammon was able to read in the Lloyd library and write his poetry there. Hammon gave a speech to the African Society in 1786, when he was 76 years old, in which he famously said, "If we should ever get to Heaven, we shall find nobody to reproach us for being black, or for being slaves."

from AN ADDRESS TO MISS PHILLIS WHEATLEY[1]

Miss Wheatly; pray give leave to express as follows:

O, come you pious youth: adore
The wisdom of thy God.
In bringing thee from distant shore,
To learn His holy word.

Thou mightst been left behind,
Amidst a dark abode;
God's tender Mercy still combin'd,
Thou hast the holy word.

Fair wisdom's ways are paths of peace,
And they that walk therein,
Shall reap the joys that never cease,
And Christ shall be their king.

God's tender mercy brought thee here,
tost o'er the raging main;
In Christian faith thou hast a share,
Worth all the gold of Spain.

---

[1] Hammon wrote this poem in 1778 to Phillis Wheatley, the first African-American woman writer to be published in the United States. Wheatley was sold into slavery as a child and was made to convert to Christianity. Like Hammon, she embraced the Christian religion in her life and writing.

While thousands tossed by the sea,
And others settled down,
God's tender mercy set thee free,
From dangers still unknown.

That thou a pattern still might be,
To youth of Boston town,
The blessed Jesus thee free,
From every sinful wound.

The blessed Jesus, who came down,
Unveil'd his sacred face,
To cleanse the soul of every wound,
And give repenting grace.

That we poor sinners may obtain
The pardon of our sin;
Dear blessed Jesus now constrain,
And bring us flocking in.

Come you, Phillis, now aspire,
And seek the living God,
So step by step thou mayst go higher,
Till perfect in the word.

While thousands mov'd to distant shore,
And others left behind,
The blessed Jesus still adore,
Implant this in thy mind.

Thou hast left the heathen shore;
Thro' mercy of the Lord,
Among the heathen live no more,
Come magnify thy God.

I pray the living God may be,
The sheperd of thy soul;
His tender mercies still are free,
His mysteries to unfold.

Thou, Phillis, when thou hunger hast,
Or pantest for thy God;
Jesus Christ is thy relief,
Thou hast the holy word.

The bounteous mercies of the Lord,
Are hid beyond the sky,
And holy souls that love His word,
Shall taste them when they die.

THOMAS GRAY

(1716–1771)

THOMAS GRAY was one of the most distinguished English poets of his age. Born in London, he was educated at Eton and Cambridge. In 1739 he went on a tour of the Continent with Horace Walpole (who would become Prime Minister) but they had an argument in Italy and Gray returned to England in 1741. He then continued his studies at Cambridge, where he lived in seclusion, studying Greek and writing melancholy, wistful poems. He was not a prolific writer but he was the most distinguished poet of his day. In 1768 he became a professor of history and modern languages, but he never taught. Gray remained shy and sensitive throughout his life. He was offered the position of Poet Laureate in 1757, but turned it down.

Gray's first important poems, written in 1742, include "To Spring," "On a Distant Prospect of Eton College" (noted for the often quoted statement "where ignorance is bliss, 'tis folly to be wise"), the humorous "Ode on the Death of a Favourite Cat, Drowned in a Tub of Gold Fishes," and "Sonnet on the Death of Mr. Richard West." Thomas Gray's most famous poem, "Elegy Written in a Country Churchyard" (1751), is a meditation on death. It was tremendously popular during its time and the lines "Some mute, inglorious Milton here may rest,/Some Cromwell guiltless of his country's blood" are particularly well-known. After that poem's tremendous success, Gray's subsequent poems (In 1757, Walpole published his Pindaric odes, "The Progress of

Poesy" and "The Bard.") met with a disappointing
response and he almost entirely stopped writing.

ELEGY WRITTEN IN A COUNTRY CHURCHYARD[1]

The Curfew tolls the knell of parting day,
The lowing herd wind slowly o'er the lea,
The plowman homeward plods his weary way,
And leaves the world to darkness and to me.

Now fades the glimmering landscape on the sight,
And all the air a solemn stillness holds,
Save where the beetle wheels his droning flight,
And drowsy tinklings lull the distant folds;

Save that from yonder ivy-mantled tow'r
The moping owl does to the moon complain
Of such as, wand'ring near her secret bow'r,
Molest her ancient solitary reign.

Beneath those rugged elms, that yew-tree's shade,
Where heaves the turf in many a mould'ring heap,
Each in his narrow cell for ever laid,
The rude Forefathers of the hamlet sleep.

---

[1] This poem is a meditation upon a life that never gained wordly
fame or recognition. More specifically, it's a contemplation on
someone who had had the opportunity to express fully his or her
gifts and talents. The speaker of the poem is drawn into contemplation by the sight of a rural graveyard.

The breezy call of incense-breathing Morn,
The swallow twitt'ring from the straw-built shed,
The cock's shrill clarion, or the echoing horn,
No more shall rouse them from their lowly bed.

For them no more the blazing hearth shall burn,
Or busy housewife ply her evening care:
No children run to lisp their sire's return,
Or climb his knees the envied kiss to share.

Oft did the harvest to their sickle yield,
Their furrow oft the stubborn glebe has broke:
How jocund did they drive their team afield!
How bow'd the woods beneath their sturdy stroke!

Let not Ambition mock their useful toil,
Their homely joys, and destiny obscure;
Nor Grandeur hear with a disdainful smile
The short and simple annals of the poor.

The boast of heraldry, the pomp of pow'r,
And all that beauty, all that wealth e'er gave,
Awaits alike th' inevitable hour:
The paths of glory lead but to the grave.

Nor you, ye Proud, impute to These the fault,
If Memory o'er their Tomb no Trophies raise,
Where through the long-drawn aisle and fretted vault
The pealing anthem swells the note of praise.

Can storied urn or animated bust
Back to its mansion call the fleeting breath?
Can Honour's voice provoke the silent dust,
Or Flatt'ry soothe the dull cold ear of death?

Perhaps in this neglected spot is laid
Some heart once pregnant with celestial fire;
Hands, that the rod of empire might have sway'd,
Or waked to ecstasy the living lyre.

But Knowledge to their eyes her ample page
Rich with the spoils of time did ne'er unroll;
Chill Penury repress'd their noble rage,
And froze the genial current of the soul.

Full many a gem of purest ray serene
The dark unfathom'd caves of ocean bear:
Full many a flower is born to blush unseen,
And waste its sweetness on the desert air.

Some village Hampden that with dauntless breast
The little tyrant of his fields withstood,
Some mute inglorious Milton here may rest,
Some Cromwell guiltless of his country's blood.

Th' applause of list'ning senates to command,
The threats of pain and ruin to despise,
To scatter plenty o'er a smiling land,
And read their history in a nation's eyes,

Their lot forbade: nor circumscribed alone
Their glowing virtues, but their crimes confined;
Forbade to wade through slaughter to a throne,
And shut the gates of mercy on mankind,

The struggling pangs of conscious truth to hide,
To quench the blushes of ingenuous shame,
Or heap the shrine of Luxury and Pride
With incense kindled at the Muse's flame.

Far from the madding crowd's ignoble strife,
Their sober wishes never learn'd to stray;
Along the cool sequester'd vale of life
They kept the noiseless tenor of their way.

Yet ev'n these bones from insult to protect
Some frail memorial still erected nigh,
With uncouth rhymes and shapeless sculpture deck'd,
Implores the passing tribute of a sigh.

Their name, their years, spelt by th' unletter'd muse,
The place of fame and elegy supply:
And many a holy text around she strews,
That teach the rustic moralist to die.

For who, to dumb Forgetfulness a prey,
This pleasing anxious being e'er resign'd,
Left the warm precincts of the cheerful day,
Nor cast one longing ling'ring look behind?

On some fond breast the parting soul relies,
Some pious drops the closing eye requires;
Ev'n from the tomb the voice of Nature cries,
Ev'n in our Ashes live their wonted Fires.

For thee, who, mindful of th' unhonour'd dead,
Dost in these lines their artless tale relate;
If chance, by lonely contemplation led,
Some kindred spirit shall inquire thy fate,

Haply some hoary-headed Swain may say,
'Oft have we seen him at the peep of dawn
Brushing with hasty steps the dews away
To meet the sun upon the upland lawn.

'There at the foot of yonder nodding beech
That wreathes its old fantastic roots so high,
His listless length at noontide would he stretch,
And pore upon the brook that babbles by.

'Hard by yon wood, now smiling as in scorn,
Mutt'ring his wayward fancies he would rove,
Now drooping, woeful wan, like one forlorn,
Or crazed with care, or cross'd in hopeless love.

'One morn I miss'd him on the custom'd hill,
Along the heath and near his fav'rite tree;
Another came; nor yet beside the rill,
Nor up the lawn, nor at the wood was he;

'The next with dirges due in sad array
Slow through the church-way path we saw him borne.
Approach and read (for thou canst read) the lay
Graved on the stone beneath yon aged thorn:'

THE EPITAPH[2]

Here rests his head upon the lap of Earth
A Youth to Fortune and to Fame unknown.
Fair Science frown'd not on his humble birth,
And Melancholy mark'd him for her own.

Large was his bounty, and his soul sincere,
Heav'n did a recompense as largely send:
He gave to Mis'ry all he had, a tear,
He gain'd from Heav'n ('twas all he wish'd) a friend.

No farther seek his merits to disclose,
Or draw his frailties from their dread abode,
(There they alike in trembling hope repose,)
The bosom of his Father and his God.

---

[2] This epitaph is most likely for Gray's friend, the poet Richard West.

OLIVER GOLDSMITH

(1728–1774)

OLIVER GOLDSMITH was an Irish poet, novelist, playwright, and doctor known for leading a dissolute life. His father became rector of the parish at Kilkenny West when Goldsmith was young. When he was eight years old Goldsmith contracted smallpox that left him disfigured for life. He studied law and theology at Trinity College in Dublin and then went on to study medicine at the University of Edinburgh but never earned a degree. He traveled through Europe and then lived in London as an apothecary's assistant. He liked to live extravagantly and gamble, and he was constantly in debt. To earn money, Goldsmith worked as a hack writer (a writer for hire, paid by the word not for the quality of his writing), churning out work for London publishers. He also wrote literary works that earned him the praise of Samuel Johnson. Goldsmith and Johnson, along with the painter Joshua Reynolds, founded "The Club," which would meet once a week in Soho. Horace Walpole, writer, politician, and the son of the British Prime Minister Robert Walpole, nicknamed Goldsmith the "Inspired Idiot." Goldsmith is said to have failed to immigrate to America because he missed the ferry he was due to travel on. There is a monument to Goldsmith in Westminster Abbey with an epitaph written by Samuel Johnson.

Goldsmith is especially noted for his 1766 novel, *The Vicar of Wakefield*, his plays *The Good-natur'd Man* (1768) and *She Stoops to Conquer* (written in 1771 and first performed in 1773), and for his long pastoral poem *The Deserted Village* (1770), which was written in remembrance of his brother and draws on memories of his childhood home of Lissoy.

WHEN LOVELY WOMAN STOOPS TO FOLLY[1]

When lovely woman stoops to folly,
And finds too late that men betray,
What charm can soothe her melancholy,
What art can wash her guilt away?

The only art her guilt to cover,
To hide her shame from every eye,
To give repentance to her lover
And wring his bosom, is—to die.

---

[1] This well-known poem was first published in the novel, *The Vicar of Wakefield*, in 1776. T.S. Eliot quotes Goldsmith's opening line in his epic poem "The Waste Land."

THOMAS PAINE

(1737–1809)

THOMAS PAINE was an Anglo-American writer and radical political theorist most famous for writing his enormously popular pamphlet *Common Sense* in 1776, as well as *The Rights of Man* (published in two parts in 1791 and 1792) and for *The Age of Reason* (published in two parts in 1794 and 1795). Paine came to America in 1774 from England and advocated change through revolution rather than reform. He promoted democracy throughout his writings.

His poem, "Liberty Tree," in support of the American Revolution, was widely read among his contemporaries. In the first part of the poem Paine writes that the Liberty Tree was transferred from a celestial home and planted deep in American soil. In the second part of the poem Paine writes of America's selfless support of British interests ("Her battles they fought, without having a groat") until the tyranny of British "King, Commons, and Lords" tried to cut down the Liberty Tree. In the last lines Paine exhorts the believers in liberty to unite in freedom's defense.

LIBERTY TREE[1]

In a chariot of light from the regions of day,
The Goddess of Liberty came;
Ten thousand celestials directed the way,
And thither conducted the dame,
This fair budding branch, from the garden above,
Where millions with millions agree;
She bro't in her hand, as a pledge of her love,
The plant she call'd Liberty Tree.

This celestial exotic struck deep in the ground,
Like a native it flourish'd and bore;
The fame of its fruit, drew the nations around,
To seek out its peaceable shore.
Unmindful of names or distinction they came,
For freemen like brothers agree:
With one sprit endow'd, they one friendship pursued,
And their temple was *Liberty Tree*.

---

[1] This poem was originally printed in *Pennsylvania Magazine*, July, 1775. Later the subtitle "A Song, Written Early in the American Revolution" was added to "Liberty Tree," but when it was first published not everyone was aware that there was a revolution going on.

Beneath this fair branch, like the patriarchs of old,
Their bread, in contentment they eat;
Unwearied with trouble, of silver or gold,
~~Or the cares of the grand and the great.~~
With timber and tar, they old England supplied,
Supported her power on the seas;
Her battles they fought, without having a groat,[2]
For the honor of *Liberty Tree*.

But hear, O ye swains,[3] ('tis a tale the most profane)
How all they tyrannical powers,
King, Commons, and Lords[4] are uniting amain,
To cut down this guardian of ours;
From the east to the west, blow the trumpet to arms,
Thro' the land let the sound of it flee,
Let the far and the near, all unite with a cheer,
In defense of our *Liberty Tree*.

---

[2] An English silver coin worth four pennies.

[3] Young men.

[4] After the American Revolution, Paine revised the poem to be more universal and changed "King, Commons, and Lords" to the more general "Kingcraft and Priestcraft." Since the outcome of America's fate was now certain, the revised poem no longer ended in a call to battle but triumphantly: "Fell Discord, dire torment of gods and of men,/Attacks the celestial decree,/With snake-twisted locks she creeps out/from her den,/To strike at our Liberty Tree./Ye gods who preside o'er the empire of man,/Dispers'd o'er the face of the globe,/Look cheerfully down and survey thine own plan,/And spare not, if wanted, the probe./Bid Concord descend from thy charming/abodes,/Bid Discord and Jealousy flee,/And then in a bumper of nectar, ye gods,/Drink health to our Liberty Tree."

Anna Laetitia Barbauld

(1743–1825)

ANNA LAETITIA BARBAULD (née Aikin) was an English poet. She learned the classics and modern languages from her father, a teacher, and his colleagues. Barbauld's first poetry collection, *Poems* (1773), was reprinted five times by 1777. She married Rochemont Barbauld, a Nonconformist clergyman who suffered from a mental disease that grew more and more violent and eventually forced him to be confined. He committed suicide in 1808. Before his death they founded a boys' school and Samuel Johnson lamented the waste of Barbauld's literary talent on "small beer." However, this work led Barbauld to publish *Lessons for Children* and *Hymns in Prose*. She had many literary friends, including Joanna Baillie, Sir Walter Scott, William Wordsworth, and Samuel Taylor Coleridge. Like many of her contemporaries, Barbauld incorporated poetry into her friendships— writing poems to celebrate a gift or refer to a game. But at the same time, she aimed her writing at more serious political ends, including expressing her abolitionist views. William Wordsworth called her "the first of our literary women."

The Rights of Women

Yes, injured Woman! Rise, assert thy right!
Woman! too long degraded, scorned, oppressed;
O born to rule in partial Law's despite,
Resume they native empire o'er the breast!

Go forth arrayed in panoply divine;
That angel pureness which admits no stain;
Go, bid proud Man his boasted rule resign,
And kiss the golden specter of thy reign.

Go, gird thyself with grace; collect thy store
Of bright artillery glancing from afar;
Soft melting tones thy thundering cannon's roar,
Blushes and fears thy magazine of war.

Thy rights are empire: urge no meaner claim—
Felt, not defined, and if debated, lost;
Like sacred mysteries, which withheld from fame,
Shunning discussion, are revered the most.

Try all that wit and art suggest to bend.

from WASHING DAY

The Muses are turned gossips; they have lost
The buskined step, and clear high-sounding phrase,
Language of gods. Come then, domestic Muse,
In slipshod measure loosely prattling on
Of farm or orchard, pleasant curds and cream,
Or drowning flies, or shoe lost in the mire
By little whimpering boy, with rueful face;
Come, Muse, and sing the dreaded Washing Day.

Hannah More

(1745–1833)

Hannah More was an English writer of religious and ethical works, and a social reformer. She attended her sisters' school for girls in Bristol and later taught there. At 22 she was engaged to a wealthy older man, William Turner. They never married but Turner gave her enough money to make her financially independent. More wrote popular treatises about the need to educate the poor. She created clubs for women and was a member of the Blue Stockings Society—an informal women's social and educational movement—along with Elizabeth Montagu and other literary women of the time. She also was a patron of the working class poet Ann Yearsley until they had a falling out. More wrote two plays, *Percy* (1777) and *Fatal Falsehood* (1779), as well as a treatise *Thoughts on the Importance of the Manners of the Great to General Society* in 1788 and a popular religious novel *Coelebs in Search of a Wife* in 1808.

from Slavery, a Poem

If heaven has into being deign'd to call
Thy light, O LIBERTY! to shine on all;
Bright intellectual Sun! why does thy ray
To earth distribute only partial day?
Since no resisting cause from spirit flows
Thy penetrating essence to opose;
No obstacles by Nature's hand imprest,

Thy subtle and ethereal beams arrest;
Nor motion's laws can speed thy active course,
Nor strong repulsion's pow'rs obstruct thy force;
Since there is no convexity in MIND,
Why are thy genial beams to parts confin'd?
While the chill North with thy bright ray is blest,
Why should fell darkness half the South invest?
Was it decreed, fair Freedom! at thy birth,
That thou shou'd'st ne'er irradiate *all* the earth?
While Britain basks in thy full blaze of light,
Why lies sad Afric quench'd in total night?

 Thee only, sober Goddess! I attest,
In smiles chastis'd, and decent graces drest.
Not that unlicens'd monster of the crowd,
Whose roar terrific bursts in peals so loud,
Deaf'ning the ear of Peace: fierce Faction's tool;
Of rash Sedition born, and mad Misrule;
Whose stubborn mouth, rejecting Reason's rein,
No strength can govern, and no skill restrain;
Whose magic cries the frantic vulgar draw
To spurn at Order, and to outrage Law;
To tread on grave Authority and Pow'r,
And shake the work of ages in an hour:
Convuls'd her voice, and pestilent her breath,
She raves of mercy, while she deals out death:
Each blast is fate; she darts from either hand
Red conflagration o'er th' astonish'd land;
Clamouring for peace, she rends the air with noise,
And to reform a part, the whole destroys.

 O, plaintive Southerne![1] whose impassion'd strain
So oft has wak'd my languid Muse in vain!

---

[1] Thomas Southerne wrote the popular play *Oroonoko: A Tragedy*
 (1696), adapted from a short novel by the well-known playwright
 Aphra Behn. It is a tragic story about Oroonoko, the grandson of

Now, when congenial themes her cares engage,
She burns to emulate thy glowing page;
Her failing efforts mock her fond desires,
She shares thy feelings, not partakes thy fires.
Strange pow'r of song! the strain that warms the heart
Seems the same inspiration to impart;
Touch'd by the kindling energy alone,
We think the flame which melts us is our own;
Deceiv'd, for genius we mistake delight,
Charm'd as we read, we fancy we can write.

    Tho' not to me, sweet Bard, thy pow'rs belong
Fair Truth, a hallow'd guide! inspires my song.
Here Art wou'd weave her gayest flow'rs in vain,
For Truth the bright invention wou'd disdain.
For no fictitious ills these numbers flow,
But living anguish, and substantial woe;
No individual griefs my bosom melt,
For millions feel what Oronoko[2] felt:
Fir'd by no single wrongs, the countless host
I mourn, by rapine dragg'd from Afric's coast.

    Perish th'illiberal thought which wou'd debase
The native genius of the sable race!

---

  an African king, and his love for Imoinda, the daughter of the
  king's general. Both Oroonoko and Imoinda are sold as slaves and
  end up in Surinam, an English colony in the West Indies.
  Oroonoko organizes a slave uprising but he is captured. Imoinda
  kills herself rather than endure life without Oroonoko and
  Oroonoko is publicly executed. The Dutch then take over the
  colony and slaughter all the slaves involved in the revolt.
[2] More refers to the title character of Southerne's play, Oroonoko,
  as a symbol of the horror and tragedy of slavery.

ANNA SEWARD

(1747–1809)

ANNA SEWARD was an English poet who was cele-brated in her time as the "Swan of Litchfield" and was a major figure in the intellectual circles of Litchfield. She was one of the most famous English women poets of her day. Born in Eyam, Derbyshire, her father, Thomas Seward, was a rector with literary interests who edited the works of the Elizabethan playwrights Beaumont and Fletcher. Anna's three siblings all died and the family then adopted Honora Sneyd. Honora and Anna became very close companions. In 1750 Thomas Seward became Canon of Litchfield Cathedral and the family moved into Bishop's Palace where Anna remained for most of her life. Seward was educated at home and encouraged in her writing of poetry by her father and her father's friend Erasmus Darwin (a poet, physician, botanist and the grandfather of Charles Darwin). However, Anna's mother didn't approve of her poetry and after her mother died she became caretaker to her ailing father.

When Honora Sneyd married, Anna felt it as a per-sonal loss and wrote many sonnets decrying the loss of her friendship. They had become estranged, but when Sneyd died in 1780, Seward deeply lamented her death and continued to write poems about their friendship for the rest of her life. Romantic friendships were accepted during Seward's time and it is not known whether Seward's passion towards Sneyd indicated lesbian feel-ings towards her adopted sister.

Seward's poetry was conventional in style, but deeply

felt and unconventional in content. She published some work in *Gentleman's Magazine* under the pseudonym "Benvolio" and was engaged in literary debates with other writers of the time. In 1784 she published a sentimental and poetic novel, *Louisa*.

ELEGY
Written at the Sea-side,
and Addressed to Miss Honora Sneyd

I write, Honora,[1] on the sparkling sand!—
The envious waves forbid the trace to stay:
Honora's name again adorns the strand!
Again the waters bear their prize away!
So Nature wrote her charms upon thy face,
The cheek's light bloom, the lip's envermeil'd dye,
And every gay, and every witching grace,
That Youth's warm hours, and Beauty's stores supply.
But Time's stern tide, with cold Oblivion's wave,
Shall soon dissolve each fair, each fading charm;
E'en Nature's self, so powerful, cannot save
Her own rich gifts from this o'erwhelming harm.
Love and the Muse can boast superior power,
Indelible the letters they shall frame;
They yield to no inevitable hour,
But will on lasting tablets write thy name.

---

[1] Honora Sneyd was Anna Seward's adopted sister. She was nine years younger than Seward and lived with her family for thirteen years. Honora and Anna were very close. Although they experienced a rift when Honora was married, when Honora died of tuburculosis, Anna deeply mourned her death and continued writing poems about her for thirty years.

CHARLOTTE SMITH

(1749–1806)

CHARLOTTE SMITH was an English Romantic poet and novelist. She was raised by her father in comfort and formally educated. At fifteen she married Benjamin Smith, the dissolute son of the wealthy director of the East India Company. In 1783 the couple were imprisoned for debt. While still in prison she printed the first volume of *Elegiac Sonnets, and Other Essays*, which was successful. She wrote ten novels and was able to support her family with the money she earned from publication. Her novels are considered to be somewhat Gothic in style. Gothic literature was a precursor to horror fiction and it contained psychological and physical terror, mystery, madness, and the supernatural. Her writing influenced Jane Austen and Charles Dickens. Charlotte Smith was very interested in social conditions and politics, especially the French Revolution.

Sonnet III: To a Nightingale[1]

Poor melancholy bird—that all night long
Tell'st to the Moon, thy tale of tender woe;
From what sad cause can such sweet sorrow flow,
And whence this mournful melody of song?

Thy poet's musing fancy would translate
What mean the sounds that swell thy little breast,
When still at dewy eve thou leav'st thy nest,
Thus to the listening night to sing thy fate!

Pale Sorrow's victims wert thou once among,
Tho' now releas'd in woodlands wild to rove?
Say—hast thou felt from friends some cruel wrong,
Or diedst thou—pmartyr of disastrous love?
Ah! songstress sad! that such my lot might be,
To sigh and sing at liberty—like thee!

---

[1] John Keats wrote his famous "Ode to a Nightingale" partly in
response to this poem.

LADY ANNE LINDSAY

(1750–1825)

Lady Anne Lindsay was a Scottish artist, travel and letter writer best known for her popular ballad "Auld Robin Gray." The daughter of Sir James Lindsay, 5th Earl of Balcarres, she married Andrew Barnard in 1793. Barnard was the son of the Bishop of Limerick and Lady Anne helped her husband obtain the position of colonial secretary of the Cape of Good Hope (South Africa). They traveled there in 1797. Andrew Barnard returned to Scotland in 1794, but Lady Anne stayed in South Africa until 1802. Her journal entries, letters, and drawings were published as a book, *South Africa A Century Ago*, in 1901. Lady Anne was an accomplished artist and some of her drawings and oil paintings were included in published accounts of life in the 18th and 19th centuries.

Lady Anne wrote "Auld Robin Gray" in 1772 and Reverend William Leeves set it to music. Alfred, Lord Tennyson was inspired to write his 1864 poem "Enoch Arden" in response to Lady Anne's ballad. She did not claim authorship of the poem until two years before her death in a letter she wrote to Sir Walter Scott. Scott edited the poem and published it through the Bannatyne Club, a press he founded to print rare works of Scottish interest.

AULD ROBIN GRAY

WHEN the sheep are in the fauld,[1] and the kye[2] at
    hame,
And a' the warld to rest are gane,
The waes o' my heart fa' in showers frae my e'e,
While my gudeman lies sound by me.

Young Jamie lo'ed me weel, and sought me for his bride;
But saving a croun he had naething else beside:
To make the croun a pund, young Jamie gaed to sea;
And the croun and the pund were baith for me.

He hadna been awa' a week but only twa,
When my father brak his arm, and the cow was stown[3]
    awa;
My mother she fell sick,—and my Jamie at the sea—
And auld Robin Gray came a-courtin' me.

My father couldna work, and my mother couldna spin;
I toil'd day and night, but their bread I couldna win;
Auld Rob maintain'd them baith, and wi' tears in his e'e
Said, 'Jennie, for their sakes, O, marry me!'

My heart it said nay; I look'd for Jamie back;
But the wind it blew high, and the ship it was a wrack;
His ship it was a wrack—Why didna Jamie dee?
Or why do I live to cry, Wae 's me?

---

[1] Fold.
[2] Cows.
[3] Stolen.

My father urged me sair: my mother didna speak;
But she look'd in my face till my heart was like to break:
They gi'ed him my hand, tho' my heart was in the sea;
Sae auld Robin Gray he was gudeman to me.

I hadna been a wife a week but only four,
When mournfu' as I sat on the stane at the door,
I saw my Jamie's wraith,[4]—for I couldna think it he,
Till he said, 'I'm come hame to marry thee.'

O sair, sair did we greet,[5] and muckle[6] did we say;
We took but ae kiss, and we tore ourselves away:
I wish that I were dead, but I'm no like to dee;
And why was I born to say, Wae 's me!

I gang like a ghaist, and I carena to spin;
I daurna think on Jamie, for that wad be a sin;
But I'll do my best a gude wife aye to be,
For auld Robin Gray he is kind unto me.

[4] Ghost.
[5] Weep.
[6] Much.

Richard Brinsley Sheridan

(1751–1816)

Richard Brinsley Sheridan was a highly successful Irish playwright, as well as a poet and politician. Born in Dublin, his father was a theater manager, actor, and elocution teacher, while his mother was a writer who died when her son was 15. Sheridan was supposed to study law but instead eloped and moved to London to write for the stage. His first play, *The Rivals*, was a huge success. It was performed in 1775 at Covent Garden. In 1776 Sheridan became a co-owner and director of the Drury Lane Theatre. His fame continued to grow with his second comic masterpiece, *The School for Scandal* in 1777. The play is considered one of the best comedies of manners in the English language. Both *The Rivals* and *The School for Scandal* were influenced by Restoration comedy and satirize the materialism and hypocrisy of fashionable society. Sheridan, sponsored by Georgiana, Duchess of Devonshire, became a member of Parliament in 1780. He was a masterful public speaker and became a leading figure in the Whig political party. He used his oratorical skills to support the French Revolution. He remained in parliament until 1812. When the Drury Lane Theatre burned down in 1809, Sheridan was ruined financially and became imprisoned for debt in 1813. In 1816 Sheridan was buried in Westminster Abbey's Poets' Corner. His great-nephew was the well-known ghost story writer Sheridan le Fanu.

If a Daughter You Have[1]

If a daughter you have, she's the plague of your life,
No peace shall you know, tho' you've buried your wife,
At twenty she mocks at the duty you taught her,
O, what a plague is an obstinate daughter.
Sighing and whining,
Dying and pining,
O, what a plague is an obstinate daughter.

When scarce in their teens, they have wit to perplex us,
With letters and lovers for ever they vex us,
While each still rejects the fair suitor you've brought her,
O, what a plague is an obstinate daughter.
Wrangling and jangling,
Flouting and pouting,
O, what a plague is an obstinate daughter.

---

[1] This poem was originally published in *The Duenna*, a comic opera, in 1775.

Thomas Chatterton

(1752–1770)

Thomas Chatterton was an English poet honored as a brilliant, doomed literary hero by Romantic and Pre-Raphaelite poets such as John Keats and Samuel Taylor Coleridge (both of whom wrote poems about Chatterton). The son of a poor Bristol teacher who died before Chatterton was born, Chatterton started forging poems—called the "Rowley Poems"—at the age of twelve, claiming they were copies of 15th century manuscripts. In 1768 he published the forgeries in a local magazine under the false pretense that these were medieval poems found among old papers in the Church of St. Mary Redcliff. Chatterton sent several poems to the writer and politician Horace Walpole who enjoyed the poems until he found out that they were fakes. Walpole then ended all correspondence with Chatterton. In 1770 Chatterton went to London and attempted without much success to sell his poems to magazines. He wasn't willing to borrow or beg for money and when he was close to starvation he killed himself at the age of seventeen by ingesting poison (arsenic).

Chatterton was both a skilled imitator as well as an original poet who juxtaposed 15th century vocabulary with modern rhythms in masterful poems such as "Ælla." Romantic writers celebrated Chatterton as a precocious literary genius who wrote beautiful medieval-inspired poetry and died tragically young. Although at the time of his death he received little notice, he is now considered one of the heralds of Romantic poetry.

Song from Ælla[1]

O sing unto my roundelay,[2]
O drop the briny tear with me;
Dance no more at holyday,
Like a running river be:
My love is dead,
Gone to his death-bed
All under the willow-tree.

Black his cryne[3] as the winter night,
White his rode[4] as the summer snow,
Red his face as the morning light,
Cole he lies in the grave below:
My love is dead,
Gone to his death-bed
All under the willow-tree.

Sweet his tongue as the throstle's[5] note,
Quick in dance as thought can be,

---

[1] Chatterton passed off this poem as a 15th century work by
  Thomas Rowley. Chatterton falsely claimed to have found this
  poem and others in an old Bristol church. In Greek mythology
  Ælla was an Amazon warrior killed by Hercules during his quest
  for Hippolyta's girdle. The word also means "whirlwind" in
  Greek.
[2] A roundelay is a poem or song with a regularly repeated refrain.
  In Chatterton's poem the lines "Gone to his death-bed/All under
  the willow-tree" are repeated at the end of every stanza.
[3] Hair.
[4] Complexion.
[5] A thrush.

Deft his tabor,[6] cudgel stout;
O he lies by the willow-tree!
My love is dead,
~~Gone to his death-bed~~
All under the willow-tree.

Hark! the raven flaps his wing
In the brier'd dell below;
Hark! the death-owl loud doth sing
To the nightmares, as they go:
My love is dead,
Gone to his death-bed
All under the willow-tree.

See! the white moon shines on high;
Whiter is my true-love's shroud:
Whiter than the morning sky,
Whiter than the evening cloud:
My love is dead,
Gone to his death-bed
All under the willow-tree.

Here upon my true-love's grave
Shall the barren flowers be laid;
Not one holy saint to save
All the coldness of a maid:
My love is dead,
Gone to his death-bed
All under the willow-tree.

.   .   .

---

[6] A small drum.

ANN YEARSLEY

(1752–1806)

Ann Yearsley was a working-class English poet and novelist also known as "Lactilla" and "the Poetical Milkwoman of Bristol." She was born in Bristol to John and Anne Cromartie. Yearsley worked as a milkwoman like her mother before her. She married John Yearsley, a laborer, in 1774 and they had six children. When the family was near starvation she would read the works of Virgil and Milton.

Yearsley would buy slops from the poet Hannah More's cook. More discovered Yearsley's poetic talent and she arranged for publication of *Poems on Several Occasions* (1785) by organizing subscriptions. More believed that Yearsley's work "breathed the genuine spirit of poetry." The book received strong reviews and went through four printings. Eventually, More and Yearsley argued over access to the trust in which profits from her poetry were held and underlying this dispute were issues of class. Hannah More and her peers thought that "parish Sapphos" should stick to their stations. Yearsley wrote about her fight with More in an "Autobiographical narrative," which she included in a fourth edition of *Poems on Several Occasions*. Yearsley went on to publish a novel and four more volumes of poetry under the support of Frederick Hervey, 4th Earl of Bristol. Robert Southey, the poet laureate, included Yearsley in his overview of "the uneducated poets."

from A Poem on the Inhumanity of the Slave-Trade[1]

Bristol,[2] thine heart hath throbb'd to glory.—Slaves,
E'en Christian slaves, have shook their chains, and gaz'd
With wonder and amazement on thee. Hence
Ye grov'ling souls, who think the term I give,
Of Christian slave, a paradox! to *you*
I do not turn, but leave you to conception
Narrow; with that be blest, nor dare to stretch
Your shackled souls along the course of *Freedom*.

    Yet, Bristol, list! nor deem Lactilla's[3] soul
Lessen'd by distance; snatch her rustic thought,
Her crude ideas, from their panting state,
And let them fly in wide expansion; lend
Thine energy, so little understood
By the rude million, and I'll dare the strain
Of Heav'n-born Liberty till Nature moves
Obedient to her voice. Alas! my friend,
Strong rapture dies within the soul, while Pow'r
Drags on his bleeding victims. Custom, Law,
Ye blessings, and ye curses of mankind,
What evils do ye cause? We feel enslaved,

---

[1] Ann Yearsley contributed to the anti-slavery debate in England
with this celebrated poem that was published in 1788. Yearsley's
mentor, Hannah More, had previously written a poem on the
same subject and with the same title. Some people saw Yearsley's
poem as trying to compete with More's poem.

[2] The port city of Bristol played a major part in the transatlantic
slave trade of the 17th and 18th centuries. Bristol ships took tens
of thousands of slaves from West Africa to the Caribbean.

[3] Yearsley was sometimes known as Lactilla.

Yet move in your direction. Custom, thou
Wilt preach up filial piety; thy sons
Will groan, and stare with impudence at Heav'n,
As if they did abjure the act, where Sin
Sits full on Inhumanity; the church
They fill with mouthing, vap'rous sighs and tears,
Which, like the guileful crocodile's, oft fall,
Nor fall, but at the cost of human bliss.

      Custom, thou hast undone us! led us far
From God-like probity, from truth, and heaven.
  But come, ye souls who feel for human woe,
Tho' drest in savage guise! Approach, thou son,
Whose heart would shudder at a father's chains,
And melt o'er thy lov'd brother as he lies
Gasping in torment undeserv'd. Oh, sight
Horrid and insupportable! far worse
Than an immediate, an heroic death;
Yet to this sight I summon thee. Approach,
Thou slave of avarice, that canst see the maid
Weep o'er her inky fire! Spare me, thou God
Of all-indulgent Mercy, if I scorn
This gloomy wretch, and turn my tearful eye
To more enlighten'd beings. Yes, my tear
Shall hang on the green furze, like pearly dew
Upon the blossom of the morn. My song
Shall teach sad Philomel a louder note,
When Nature swells her woe. O'er suff'ring *man*
My soul with sorrow bends! Then come, ye few
Who feel a more than cold, material essence;
Here ye may vent your sighs, till the bleak North
Find its adherents aided. —Ah, no more!

PHILLIS WHEATLEY

(1753–1784)

PHYLLIS WHEATLEY was the first African American woman writer to be published in the United States. She was kidnapped from Africa (present-day Senegal) and brought to America. At age eight, she was sold as a slave to John Wheatly, a Boston merchant. The Wheatley family taught her to read and write in English and Latin. Around age fourteen, Phillis Wheatley started writing poetry, and she developed her style along the lines of Alexander Pope and other Neo-classical poets. Her poetry was first published in 1773 in *Poems on Various Subjects, Religious and Moral.* The book was published in England and it made her famous in Europe. She traveled to England where she was greatly admired. Wheatley became a free woman in 1773, marrying a free black grocer who subsequently left her. She then worked as a servant until she died in poverty at the young age of thirty-one. The second volume of poetry that she was working on was never found. Wheatley's poetry is concerned with religion and morality, and utilizes Christian imagery and themes. She is considered by some to be the first important black writer in America.

On Being Brought from Africa to America[1]

'Twas mercy brought me from my *Pagan* land,
Taught my benighted soul to understand
That there's a God, that there's a *Saviour* too:
Once I redemption neither sought nor knew,
Some view our sable race with scornful eye,
"Their colour is a diabolic die."
Remember, *Christians*, *Negroes*, black as *Cain*,
May be refin'd, and join th' angelic train.

To His Excellency General Washington

Celestial choir! enthron'd in realms of light,
Columbia's scenes of glorious toils I write.
While freedom's cause her anxious breast alarms,
She flashes dreadful in refulgent arms.
See mother earth her offspring's fate bemoan,
And nations gaze at scenes before unknown!
See the bright beams of heaven's revolving light
Involved in sorrows and the veil of night!
The goddess comes, she moves divinely fair,
Olive and laurel binds her golden hair;
Wherever shines the native of the skies,
Unnumber'd charms and recent graces rise.
Muse! bow propitious while my pen relates
How pour her armies through a thousand gates,

---

[1] This is one of the few poems in which Wheatley writes about her own life and being a slave.

As when Eolus heaven's fair face deforms,
Enwrapp'd in tempest and a night of storms;
Astonish'd ocean feels the wild uproar,
The refluent surges beat the sounding shore;
Or thick as leaves in Autumn's golden reign,
Such, as so many, moves the warriors's train.
In bright array they seek the work of war,
Where high unfurl'd the ensign waves in air.
Shall I to Washington their praise recite?
Enough thou know'st them in the fields of fight.
Thee, first in peace and honours,—we demand
The grace and glory of thy martial band.
Fam'd for thy valour, for thy virtues more,
Hear every tongue thy guardian aid implore!
One century scarce perform'd its destined round,
When Gallic powers Columbia's fury found;
And so may you, whoever dares disgrace
The land of freedom's heaven-defended race!
Fix'd are the eyes of nations on the scales,
For in their hopes Columbia's arm prevails.
Anon Britannia droops the pensive head,
While round increase the rising hills of dead.
Ah! cruel blindness to Columbia's state!
Lament thy thirst of boundless power too late.
Proceed, great chief, with virtue on thy side,
Thy ev'ry action let the goddess guide.
A crown, a mansion, and a throne that shine,
With gold unfading, WASHINGTON! be thine.

WILLIAM BLAKE

(1757–1827)

WILLIAM BLAKE is one of the most celebrated English poets and visionaries, as well as a precursor to the Romantic poets. Born the son of a draper, Blake grew up in London, and spent most of his life there. He started writing poems as a child, many of them inspired by religious visions of angels and prophets. He taught himself art by studying the Renaissance masters. Blake become apprenticed to an engraver and learned how to put his poems and drawings together on etchings. In 1779 he began studying art at London's Royal Academy and in 1784 he opened up his printing shop. He self-published his work and survived on small commissions, never gaining much recognition from the London art world. His work was rejected by the public, but he had a profound influence on the Romantic literary movement.

In his writing Blake posits his belief in the need for a personal connection with God and concentrates on the themes of the fall of humankind and possible redemption. He celebrates love and liberty in his verse and rejects the reductive, rationalist philosophy used to justify the inequalities brought about by the Industrial Revolution. His most famous collection of poetry is the final 1794 version of *Songs of Innocence and Experience* (previously published separately as Songs of Innocence in 1789 and Songs of Experience in 1794), which is written from a child's perspective and contains some of his most popular poems including "The Tiger," "Infant Joy," "The Sick Rose," "London," and "The Lamb." Blake also published *The Book of Thel* (1789), *The Marriage of Heaven and Hell* (1793), *Milton* (1804–1808), and *Jerusalem* (1804–1820), his third major work on the fall and redemption of humanity. Blake was called insane for his imaginative work and for his unconventional views, and he lived near poverty and died neglected. He is now one of the most revered poets in English literature, celebrated for his original and visionary body of work in which God and spirituality was an expression of the human and reality was indivisible from imagination.

THE LAMB[1]

Little lamb, who made thee?
    Does thou know who made thee,
Gave thee life, and bid thee feed
By the stream and o'er the mead;
Gave thee clothing of delight,
Softest clothing, woolly, bright;
Gave thee such a tender voice,
Making all the vales rejoice?
    Little lamb, who made thee?
    Does thou know who made thee?

    Little lamb, I'll tell thee;
    Little lamb, I'll tell thee:
He is called by thy name,
For He calls Himself a Lamb.
He is meek, and He is mild,
He became a little child.

---

[1] "The Lamb" was published in *Songs of Innocence*.

I a child, and thou a lamb,
We are called by His name.
    Little lamb, God bless thee!
    Little lamb, God bless thee!

THE TIGER[2]

Tiger, tiger, burning bright
In the forests of the night,
What immortal hand or eye
Could frame thy fearful symmetry?

In what distant deeps or skies
Burnt the fire of thine eyes?
On what wings dare he aspire?[3]
What the hand dare seize the fire?[4]

And what shoulder and what art
Could twist the sinews of thy heart?
And, when thy heart began to beat,
What dread hand and what dread feet?

---

[2] "The Tiger" or "The Tyger" was published in *Songs of Experience*. The poems in this collection show an understanding of the cruelty and injustice that exists in the world as a result not of fate, but of people's actions.

[3] This line refers to the Greek myth of Icarus who, despite his father Dedalus's warning, flew too close to the sun and drowned in the sea after his wax wings melted.

[4] This line refers to the Greek myth of Prometheus, a Titan (an elder god who predated Zeus and the other Olympian gods) who stole fire to give to mortals against Zeus's wishes. As punishment Zeus chained him to a mountain with an eagle tearing at his liver.

What the hammer? What the chain?
In what furnace was thy brain?
What the anvil? What dread grasp
Dare its deadly terrors clasp?

When the stars threw down their spears,[5]
And water'd heaven with their tears,
Did He smile His work to see?
Did He who made the lamb make thee?

Tiger, tiger, burning bright
In the forests of the night,
What immortal hand or eye
Dare frame thy fearful symmetry?

THE SICK ROSE[6]

O Rose thou art sick!
The invisible worm,
That flies in the night,
In the howling storm,

---

[5] This line refers to the original battle in heaven when Satan and
other angels rebelled against God.

[6] "The Sick Rose" was published in The Songs of Experience. The
poem is most commonly seen as about the protection of Rose's
virginity but some critics see the poem as a response to Matthew
Prior's poem "A True Maid." Thus "the dark secret love"
destroying Rose would be her own sexual experience which she
tries to cover up.

Has found out thy bed
Of crimson joy;
And his dark secret love
Does thy life destroy.

from JERUSALEM[7]

And did those feet in ancient time
Walk upon England's mountains green?
And was the holy Lamb of God
On England's pleasant pastures seen?

And did the Countenance Divine
Shine forth upon our clouded hills?
And was Jerusalem builded here
Among these dark Satanic Mills?[8]

Bring me my bow of burning gold!
Bring me my arrows of desire!
Bring me my spear! O clouds, unfold!
Bring me my chariot of fire!

---

[7] "Jerusalem" is an excerpt to the preface of one of Blake's
prophetic books, *Milton*. In this poem Jerusalem represents a
place where commerce, imperialism, and war don't exist. Blake's
prophetic books are grounded in the real world, but often appear
obscure because they are ordered by the poet's own mythology,
drawn from the work of Swedenborg, Jacob Boehme, and other
mystical sources.

[8] "Satanic Mills" refer to mills in London that produced iron and
steel for war purposes. Blake abhorred the inequities that the
Industrial Revolution brought to people's social and economic
lives.

I will not cease from mental fight,
Nor shall my sword sleep in my hand,
Till we have built Jerusalem
In England's green and pleasant land.

ENGLAND! AWAKE! AWAKE! AWAKE!

England! awake! awake! awake!
Jerusalem[9] thy Sister calls!
Why wilt thou sleep the sleep of death
And close her from thy ancient walls?

Thy hills and valleys felt her feet
Gently upon their bosoms move:
Thy gates beheld sweet Zion's[10] ways:
Then was a time of joy and love.

And now the time returns again:
Our souls exult, and London's towers
Receive the Lamb of God to dwell
In England's green and pleasant bowers.

---

[9] Here as in the poem "Jerusalem," the city Jerusalem stands as an emblem of republican ideals.

[10] A synonym for the city of Jerusalem.

Mary Robinson

(1758–1800)

MARY DARBY ROBINSON was an English poet, novelist, actor, playwright, editor, feminist, translator, and journalist known as the "English Sappho." Robinson is considered an important woman writer of the late 18th century. She is also noted for playing the role of Perdita, the heroine of Shakespeare's *A Winter Tale*, in 1779. During her performance she came to the attention of the current Prince of Wales, later King George IV of Great Britain. She became his first mistress but the affair ended in 1781 and she supported herself mostly through her writing. She wrote a sonnet sequence *Sappho and Phaon* in 1796.

Sonnet XXXIII: To a Sigh[1]

Oh Sigh! thou steal'st, the herald of the breast,
The lover's fears, the lover's pangs to tell;
Thou bid'st with timid grace the bosom swell,
Cheating the day of joy, the night of rest!
Oh! lucid Tears! with eloquence confest,
Why on my fading cheek unheeded dwell,
Meek, as the dew-drops on the flowret's bell
By ruthless tempests to the green-sod prest.
Fond sigh be hush'd! congeal, O! slighted tear!
Thy feeble pow'rs the busy Fates control!
Or if thy crystal streams again appear,
Let them, like Lethe's, oblivion roll:
For Love the tyrant plays, when hope is near,
And she who flies the lover, chains the soul!

---

[1] This is the 38th sonnet in the sequence *Sappho and Phaon.* It deals
with the Greek poet being abandoned by her lover as recorded
by Ovid.

Robert Burns

(1759–1796)

ROBERT BURNS is considered by many to be the national poet of Scotland and has become a cultural icon. He was also a pioneer of the Romantic movement. One of the most lauded poets and lyricists of Scotland, Burns had a love of Scottish songs, and is probably best known for the lyrics to "Auld Lang Syne," famous throughout the English-speaking world. Burns wrote in Scots, English, and a light highland dialect. He is the most read Scots poet and his use of Scottish dialect would have been understood by a larger audience than Scottish people. He wrote in English to make political and social commentary. Collecting folk songs from all over Scotland, he often revised or adapted them. After Burns's death, he became an inspiration to the liberalism and socialism political movements. He has had a very strong influence on Scottish literature.

Known as the Bard of Ayrshire, or in Scotland simply as the Bard, he was born in Alloway, South Ayrshire, the son of a poor farmer. Burns was educated in literature and started writing poetry when he was a teenager. When his father died in 1784, Burns tried to make a living as a farmer, but he had more luck with his poetry. He published *Poems, Chiefly in the Scottish Dialect* in Kilmarnock in 1786, in order to raise money to emigrate to Jamaica. The volume was successful and Burns decided to stay in Scotland where he had gained a reputation as a poet. He toured the country, published another edition in Edinburgh (1787) and joined James Johnson in publishing *The Scots Musical Museum*, a collection of Scottish folk songs. Burns is credited with collecting, revising and adapting hundreds of traditional songs, and his original poems brought international attention to Scottish language and culture. Despite his early death at the age of thirty-seven, Burns produced a huge body of work, including the popular Scot anthem "Scots Wha Hae" and the poem "A Red, Red Rose." "Rabbie" Burns is still considered Scotland's best-loved poet.

AULD LANG SYNE[1]

For auld lang syne,[2] my dear,
For auld lang syne,
We'll tak a cup of kindness yet,
For auld lang syne!

Should auld acquaintance be forgot,
And never brought to mind?
Should auld acquaintance be forgot,
And auld lang syne?

And surely ye'll be your pint-stowp,[3]
And surely I'll be mine,
And we'll tak a cup o kindness yet,
For auld lang syne!

---

[1] This song is traditionally sung at New Year's.
[2] "Auld Lang Syne" means old long ago.
[3] Pay for.

We twa[4] hae run about the braes,[5]
And pou'd[6] the gowans[7] fine,
But we've wander'd monie a weary fit,
Sin auld lang syne.

We twa hae paidl'd[8] in the burn[9]
Frae[10] morning[11] sun till dine,[12]
But[13] seas between us braid[14] hae[15] roar'd
Sin auld lang syne.

And there's a hand my trusty fiere,[16]
And gie's a hand o thine,
And we'll tak a right guid-willie waught,[17]
For auld lang syne.

---

[4] Two.
[5] Hillsides.
[6] Pulled.
[7] Daisies.
[8] Waded.
[9] Stream.
[10] From.
[11] Noon.
[12] Dinnertime.
[13] Without.
[14] Broad.
[15] Have.
[16] Companion.
[17] Goodwill drink.

A Red, Red Rose

O, my Luve's like a red, red rose,
That's newly sprung in June.
O, my Luve's like a melodie
That's sweetly play'd in tune.

As fair as thou, my bonnie lass,
So deep in luve am I;
And I will love thee still, my dear,
Till a' the seas gang dry.

Till a' the seas gang[18] dry, my dear,
And the rocks melt wi' the sun:
I will love thess till, my dear,
While the sands o' life shall run:

And fare thee well, my only luve!
And fare thee weel, a while!
And I will come again, my luve,
Tho' it ware ten thousand mile.

---

[18] Go.

Scots Wha Hae[19]

Scots, wha hae[20] wi Wallace bled,
Scots, wham Bruce has aften led,
Welcome to your gory bed
Or to victorie!
Now's the day, and now's the hour:
See the front o' battle lour,
See approach proud Edward's power—
Chains and slaverie!

Wha will be a traitor knave?
Wha can fill a coward's grave?
Wha sae base as be a slave?—
Let him turn, and flee!
Wha for Scotland's King and Law
Freedom's sword will strongly draw,
Freeman stand, or Freeman fa',
Let him follow me!

By Oppression's woes and pains,
By your sons in servile chains,
We will drain your dearest veins,
But they shall be free!
Lay the proud usurpers low!
Tyrants fall in every foe!
Liberty's in every blow!—
Let us do, or die!

---

[19] "Scots Wha Hae" was the unofficial Scottish national anthem for
many years.
[20] Have.

JANET LITTLE

(1759–1813)

JANET LITTLE was a Scottish poet known as "the Scotch Milkmaid." She had only a little education before becoming the servant of a local clergyman. Little loved to read and by 1788 gained a small reputation as a "rustic poetess." She then applied for a job working for Mrs. Frances Dunlop who was a friend of the renowned poet Robert Burns. Little became a milkmaid for Mrs. Dunlop's daughter, Mrs. Henri, and Mrs. Dunlop wrote to Burns about her skill as a poet. Burns was at first cautious, but then advised Mrs. Dunlop where to send Janet Little's poems for publication.

In 1792 Little published *The Poetical Works of Janet Little, The Scottish Milkmaid* and among the subscribers to her book were Robert Burns and Mrs. Dunlop. Janet Little supposedly made 50 pounds from the book. She married a widower with five children, John Richmond, after Mrs. Henri left the area. Little was a religious dissenter—she did not follow the doctrines of the Church of England—and some of her poems about religion were published after her death.

Given to a Lady Who Asked Me to Write a Poem

In royal Anna's[1] golden days,
Hard was the task to gain the bays:
Hard was it then the hill to climb;
Some broke a neck, some lost a limb.
The vot'ries for poetic fame,
Got aff decrepit, blind, an' lame:
Except that little fellow Pope,[2]
Few ever then got near its top:
An' Homer's[3] crutches he may thank,
Or down the brae he'd got a clank.
    Swift, Thomson, Addison, an' Young[4]
Made Pindus[5] echo to their tongue,
In hopes to please a learned age;
But Doctor Johnston,[6] in a rage,
Unto posterity did shew
Their blunders great, their beauties few.
But now he's dead, we weel may ken;
For ilka dunce maun hae a pen,

---

[1] Queen Anne (1665–1714) was the daughter of King James II. She supported the overthrow of her father in favor of her sister, Mary, and brother-in-law, William. William and Mary gained the throne and when they died, Anne became queen. None of Anne's children survived into adulthood and so she was the last Stuart monarch. She was succeeded by George I in 1714.

[2] The great 18th century poet Alexander Pope.

[3] The ancient Greek poet of the *Iliad* and the *Odyssey*.

[4] The 18th century poets Jonathan Swift, James Thompson, Joseph Addison, and Edward Young.

[5] Pindar was an ancient Greek poet.

[6] The poet and critic Samuel Johnson, also refered to as Dr. Johnson.

To write in uncouth rhymes;
An' yet forsooth they please the times.

    A ploughman chiel, Rab Burns[7] his name,
Pretends to write; an' thinks nae shame
To souse his sonnets on the court;
An' what is strange, they praise him for't.
Even folks, wha're of the highest station,
Ca' him the glory of our nation.

    But what is more surprising still,
A milkmaid[8] must tak up her quill;
An' she will write, shame fa' the rabble!
That think to please wi' ilka bawble.
They may thank heav'n, auld Sam's asleep:[9]
For could he ance but get a peep,
He, wi' a vengeance wad them sen'
A' headlong to the dunces' den.

---

[7] The Scottish Bard Robert Burns.
[8] The poet is referring to herself.
[9] Refers to Samuel Johnson's death.

Mary Lamb

(1764–1847)

MARY LAMB was an English poet and prose writer who collaborated with her younger brother Charles Lamb, the renowned essayist and poet. She suffered from mental illness, probably bipolar disorder. She also had a breakdown while caring for the family and during a bout of insanity in 1796, at the age of thirty-one, she killed her invalid mother with a carving knife. Charles kept Mary from being institutionalized but she had to be kept under constant supervision. Charles became her legal guardian after their father died.

Charles and Mary Lamb collaborated on the children's book *Tales from Shakespeare*, published in 1807. The book was a very popular adaptation of Shakespeare's plays for children. Charles and Mary collaborated on many successful books for children. Mary published *Mrs. Leicester's School*, an epistolary work, which the poet Samuel Coleridge highly praised. The book deals with motherless and orphaned girls. While Mary continued to suffer periods of mental illness throughout her life, she and her brother were at the center of literary life in London. When Charles died in 1834 from an infected wound, she grew increasingly frail, but lived on in the care of family and at times in an asylum. She was buried next to her brother upon her death. Mary Lamb's solo work is no longer read much today although *Tales from Shakespeare* remains in print.

A Child[1]

A child's a plaything for an hour;[2]
~~Its pretty tricks we try~~
For that or for a longer space—
    Then tire, and lay it by.

But I knew one that to itself
    All seasons could control;
That would have mock'd the sense of pain
    Out of a grieved soul.

Thou straggler into loving arms,
    Young climber-up of knees,
When I forget thy thousand ways
    Then life and all shall cease.

---

[1] This poem was attributed to Mary's brother, Charles Lamb, by
E.V. Lucas III who edited *The Works of Charles and Mary Lamb*,
which was published in 1903. Because Charles and Mary's poetry
was published as collaborations there was confusion about who
was the individual author of a poem.

[2] Mary Lamb is known for the quote, "A child is fed with milk and
praise."

JOHN QUINCY ADAMS

(1767–1848)

JOHN QUINCY ADAMS was the sixth president of the United States, as well as a lawyer and diplomat. The son of John Adams (the first vice president and second president of the United States) and Abigail Adams, although not renowned for his verse, he was an earnest reader and writer of poetry. He read three chapters of the Bible every morning and completed his reading of the entire Bible each year. Adams wrote hymns, versifications of the Psalms, and secular poetry, as well as translating poems into English. His long poem, *Dermot MacMorrogh or the Conquest of Ireland* was not well received by the critics. A collection of Adams's verse, *Poems of Religion and Society*, was edited and published posthumously in 1848 by Senators Thomas Hart Benton and John Davis. Adams once wrote, "Could I have chosen my own genius and condition, I would have made myself a great poet."

To the Sun-Dial

Thou silent herald of Time's silent flight!
Say, could'st thou speak, what warning voice were thine?
Shade, who canst only show how others shine!
Dark, sullen witness of resplendent light
In day's broad glare, and when the noontide bright
Of laughing fortune sheds the ray divine,
Thy ready favors cheer us—but decline
The clouds of morning and the gloom of night.
Yet are thy counsels faithful, just, and wise;
They bid us seize the moments as they pass—
Snatch the retrieveless sunbeam as it flies,
Nor lose one sand of life's revolving glass—
Aspiring still, with energy sublime,
By virtuous deeds to give eternity to Time.

James Hogg

(1770–1835)

JAMES HOGG was a Scottish poet, novelist, and shepherd known as the Ettrick Shepherd who wrote both in English and Scots. (He was born on the same day as the great Scottish poet Robert Burns—January 25th, 1770.) He had little formal education and went to work as a cowherd when his father, a tenant farmer, went bankrupt. Religion and oral folk traditions were important parts of Hogg's upbringing. In his early twenties, while working as a shepherd, he became interested in literature and began to write songs and poems. He had work published in *The Scots Magazine*. In 1810 Hogg moved to Edinburgh to try to earn his living as a writer, but three years later he returned to shepherding in Selkirkshire. He continued to publish and had tempestuous ties with the literary figures of Edinburgh, including his mentor Sir Walter Scott. Scott was an admirer of Hogg's poetry and included some of Hogg's poems in Scott's *Border Minstrelsy*.

CALEDONIA[1]

Caledonia! thou land of the mountain and rock,
Of the ocean, the mist, and the wind—
Thou land of the torrent, the pine, and the oak,
Of the roebuck,[2] the hart, and the hind;
Though bare are thy cliffs, and though barren thy glens,
Though bleak thy dun islands appear,
Yet kind are the hearts, and undaunted the clans,
That roam on these mountains so drear!

A foe from abroad, or a tyrant at home,
Could never thy ardour restrain;
The marshall'd array of imperial Rome
Essay'd thy proud spirit in vain!
Firm seat of religion, of valour, of truth,
Of genius unshackled and free,
The muses have left all the vales of the south,
My loved Caledonia, for thee!

Sweet land of the bay and wild-winding deeps
Where loveliness slumbers at even,
While far in the depth of the blue water sleeps
A calm little motionless heaven!
Thou land of the valley, the moor, and the hill,
Of the storm and the proud rolling wave—
Yes, thou art the land of fair liberty still,
And the land of my forefathers' grave!

---

[1] Caledonia is the Latin name for the northern area of Great
   Britain, given by the Roman Empire. In English and Scots Caledonia is used as a romantic, poetic name for Scotland.
[2] A roebuck, also called a roe deer, is a species of small deer found
   in Europe and Asia.

WILLIAM WORDSWORTH

(1770–1850)

WILLIAM WORDSWORTH was Poet Laureate of England and one of the foremost English Romantic poets. He was highly influenced by the ideals of the French Revolution. Along with Samuel Taylor Coleridge and Robert Southey he was known as one of the Lake Poets since he lived in the Lake District of England. Born in Cockermouth, he studied at Cambridge and then traveled in France during the Revolution. When he returned to England he met Coleridge and they collaborated on the seminal work *Lyrical Ballads* in 1789, which launched the Romantic movement and contained Coleridge's "The Rime of the Ancient Mariner" and Wordsworth's "Tintern Abbey," a contemplation on humanity and nature inspired by the ruins of the ancient church. Critics initially were dismissive of Wordsworth's poetry and political views but in later years he was regarded as the principal voice of the Romantic movement.

His other works include *Poems in Two Volumes* (1807) and *The Excursion* (1814). He was Poet Laureate of England from 1843 until his death in 1850. His autobiographical epic, "The Prelude," which he worked on for over forty years, was published by his wife after his death. Wordsworth corresponded frequently with the London poet and essayist Charles Lamb, who preferred city life, and he had a close relationship with his younger sister, Dorothy, who was an accomplished writer herself. Wordsworth praises her in "Tintern Abbey."

Wordsworth had a daughter, Caroline, with a woman he met in France, and in 1802 he married his childhood friend, Mary Hutchinson.

Among Wordsworth's most remembered verse are "Daffodils," "The Solitary Reaper," "Resolution and Independence," "The Rainbow," and the Lucy Poems, written about a girl who died uncelebrated by the world but who the poet feels great love for. The Lucy Poems include "She Dwelt Among the Untrodden Ways," "Strange Fits of Passion Have I Known," "Three Years She Grew," "A Slumber Did My Spirit Seal," "Lucy Gray," and "I Traveled Among Unknown Men." Wordsworth's celebrated ode "Intimations of Immortality," was published in 1807 and it contains the noted lines "Though nothing can bring back the hour/Of splendour in the grass, of glory in the flower." For Wordsworth there is no separation between man and the natural world, and nature becomes a symbol for the mind of God. Wordsworth was a deeply earnest thinker and his poetry expresses tenderness and a love of simplicity.

I Wandered Lonely as a Cloud[1]

I wandered lonely as a cloud
That floats on high o'er vales and hills,
When all at once I saw a crowd,
A host, of golden daffodils;
Beside the lake, beneath the trees,
Fluttering and dancing in the breeze.

Continuous as the stars that shine
And twinkle on the milky way,
They stretched in never-ending line
Along the margin of a bay:
Ten thousand saw I at a glance,
Tossing their heads in sprightly dance.

The waves beside them danced, but they
Out-did the sparkling leaves in glee;
A poet could not be but gay,
In such a jocund company!
I gazed—and gazed—but little thought
What wealth the show to me had brought:

For oft, when on my couch I lie
In vacant or in pensive mood,
They flash upon that inward eye

---

[1] This poem is sometimes referred to by the title "Daffodils."
   Wordsworth was inspired to write this poem in part because of a
   description in his sister Dorothy's journal, which reads, "I never
   saw daffodils so beautiful . . . some rested their heads . . . the rest
   tossed and reeled and danced, and seemed as if they verily
   laughed with the wind . . . they looked so gay, ever glancing,
   ever changing."

Which is the bliss of solitude;[2]
And then my heart with pleasure fills,
And dances with the daffodils.

from LINES COMPOSED A FEW MILES ABOVE TINTERN ABBEY

Five years have past; five summers, with the length
Of five long winters! and again I hear
These waters, rolling from their mountain-springs
With a soft inland murmur. Once again
Do I behold these steep and lofty cliffs,
That on a wild secluded scene impress
Thoughts of more deep seclusion; and connect
The landscape with the quiet of the sky.
The day is come when I again repose
Here, under this dark sycamore, and view
These plots of cottage ground, these orchard tufts,
Which at this season, with their unripe fruits,
Are clad in one green hue, and lose themselves
'Mid groves and copses. Once again I see
These hedgerows, hardly hedgerows, little lines
Of sportive wood run wild; these pastoral farms,
Green to the very door; and wreaths of smoke
Sent up, in silence, from among the trees!
With some uncertain notice, as might seem
Of vagrant dwellers in the houseless woods,
Or of some Hermit's cave, where by his fire
The Hermit sits alone.

---

[2] Wordsworth noted that he believed "They flash upon that inward
eye / Which is the bliss of solitude" were the greatest two lines
in the poem and that they were written by his wife.

These beauteous forms,
Through a long absence, have not been to me
As is a landscape to a blind man's eye;
But oft, in lonely rooms, and 'mid the din
Of towns and cities, I have owed to them,
In hours of weariness, sensations sweet,
Felt in the blood, and felt along the heart;
And passing even into my purer mind,
With tranquil restoration:—feelings too
Of unremembered pleasure; such, perhaps,
As have no slight or trivial influence

On that best portion of a good man's life,
His little, nameless, unremembered, acts
Of kindness and of love. Nor less, I trust,
To them I may have owed another gift,
Of aspect more sublime; that blessed mood,
In which the burthen of the mystery,
In which the heavy and the weary weight
Of all this unintelligible world,
Is lightened:—that serene and blessed mood,
In which the affections gently lead us on—
Until, the breath of this corporeal frame
And even the motion of our human blood
Almost suspended, we are laid asleep
In body, and become a living soul;
While with an eye made quiet by the power
Of harmony, and the deep power of joy,
We see into the life of things.

She Dwelt among the Untrodden Ways

She[3] dwelt among the untrodden ways
Beside the springs of Dove,
A Maid whom there were none to praise
And very few to love:

A violet by a mossy stone
Half hidden from the eye!
Fair as a star, when only one
Is shining in the sky.

She lived unknown, and few could know
When Lucy ceased to be;
But she is in her grave, and, oh,
The difference to me![4]

---

[3] "She" refers to Lucy who is the subject of a group of
   Wordsworth's poems written mostly in 1798-99. Lucy has never
   been identified as a real person. She probably exists as a creation
   of the poet's imagination and is perhaps partly based on
   Wordsworth's sister Dorothy, whom he was very close to.
[4] "She Dwelt among the Untrodden Ways" is similar in theme to
   Thomas Gray's "Elegy Written in a Country Churchyard." It
   deals with the death of a person who was not valued or known
   by larger society, but sorely missed by the poet.

A Slumber Did my Spirit Seal[5]

A slumber did my spirit seal;
I had no human fears:
She seemed a thing that could not feel
The touch of earthly years.

No motion has she now, no force;
She neither hears nor sees;
Rolled round in earth's diurnal course
With rocks, and stones, and trees.

---

[5] Samuel Taylor Coleridge wrote about this poem in a letter in
    1799, noting: "Some months ago Wordsworth transmitted to
    me a most sublime Epitaph . . . Most probably, in some
    gloomier moment he had fancied the moment in which his
    Sister might die."

Sir Walter Scott

(1771–1832)

S IR WALTER SCOTT was a famous and prolific Scottish poet, novelist, biographer, historian, and publisher, especially celebrated for his historical novels and tales of chivalry. Some of his famous titles include *Ivanhoe*, *Rob Roy*, *The Lady of the Lake*, *Waverley*, and *The Heart of Midlothian*. Born in Edinburgh, he went to high school there and learned French, German, Italian, Latin, and Spanish. Scott was attracted from his youth to legends and history. He became a lawyer and was made sheriff-deputy of Selkirkshire. He started his literary career translating German ballads into English. He also translated Goethe. Scott edited *Minstrels of the Scottish Border* (two volumes, 1802 and 1803), a collection of Scottish ballads for which he supplied notes and introductions. His first major poem, *The Lay of the Last Minstrel* appeared in 1805 and was followed by successful narrative and lyric poems, as well as ballads, including 1808's *Marmion* (which contains the often quoted lines "Oh! what a tangled web we weave/When first we practice to deceive!") and *The Lady of the Lake* (1810). His first novel, *Waverley* (1814), was an immediate success. Scott was one of the first authors to have a truly international career. He had readers from Europe, North America, and Australia who loved his vivid storytelling ability. Scott received honorary degrees from Cambridge and Oxford. He worked as a court clerk and died of apoplexy on June 9, 1832.

Hunter's Song

The toils are pitched, and the stakes are set,
Ever sing merrily, merrily;
The bows they bend, and the knives they whet,
Hunters live so cheerily.

It was a stag, a stag of ten,
Bearing its branches sturdily;
He came silently down the glen,
Ever sing hardily, hardily.

It was there he met with a wounded doe,
She was bleeding deathfully;
She warned him of the toils below,
O so faithfully, faithfully!

He had an eye, and he could heed,
Ever sing so warily, warily;
He had a foot, and he could speed—
Hunters watch so narrowly.

THE ROVER'S ADIEU

A WEARY lot is thine, fair maid,
    A weary lot is thine!
To pull the thorn thy brow to braid,
    And press the rue for wine.
A lightsome eye, a soldier's mien,
    A feather of the blue,
A doublet of the Lincoln green—
    No more of me ye knew,
        My Love!
No more of me ye knew.

'This morn is merry June, I trow,
    The rose is budding fain;
But she shall bloom in winter snow
    Ere we two meet again.'
—He turn'd his charger as he spake
    Upon the river shore,
He gave the bridle-reins a shake,
    Said 'Adieu for evermore,
        My Love!
And adieu for evermore.'

DOROTHY WORDSWORTH

(1771–1855)

DOROTHY WORDSWORTH, William Wordsworth's sister, is known for her Romantic poetry and journal writing although she did not consider herself a poet and had no intention in becoming a famous author. She once wrote that, "I should detest the idea of setting myself up as an author." However Dorothy did write prodigiously, including approximately thirty poems, journals and travel accounts. Many of her poems reflect on or engage with her brother's poems. William was also inspired by Dorothy's writing and by his affection for her. In his famous "Tintern Abbey," he writes of Dorothy: "Of this fair river; thou my dearest Friend, / My dear, dear Friend; and in thy voice I catch / The language of my former heart, and read / My former pleasures in the shooting lights / Of they wild eyes [. . .] / My dear, dear Sister!" William Wordsworth published some of Dorothy's poems in his own volumes. Her travel book *Recollections of a Tour Made in Scotland* was not published until 1873 and *The Grasmere Journal* was not published until 1933, after the children's book author and illustrator Beatrix Potter discovered it.

Dorothy Wordsworth lived with her brother for most of her life and never married. For the last twenty years of her life she was an invalid and became prematurely senile.

To a Butterfly

Stay near me—do not take thy flight!
A little longer stay in sight!
Much converse do I find I thee,
Historian of my infancy!
Float near me; do not yet depart!
Dead times revive in thee:
Thou bring'st, gay creature as thou art!
A solemn image to my heart,
My father's family!

Oh! pleasant, pleasant were the days,
The time, when, in our childish plays,
My sister Emmeline and I
Together chased the butterfly!
A very hunter did I rush
Upon the prey:—with leaps and spring
I followed on from brake to bush;
But she, God love her, feared to brush
The dust from off its wings.

Floating Island

Harmonious powers with nature work
On sky, earth, river, lake and sea;
Sunshine and storm, whirlwind and breeze,
All in one duteous task agree.

Once did I see a slip of earth
By throbbing waves long undermined,
Loosed from its hold—*how* no one knew,
But all might see it float, obedient to the wind;

Might see it from the verdant shore
Dissevered float upon the lake,
Float with its crest of trees adorned
On which the warbling birds their pastime take.

Food shelter, safety, there they find;
There berries ripen, flowerets bloom;
There insects live their lives and die—
A peopled *world* it is, in size a tiny room.

And thus through many season's space
This little island may survive,
But nature (though we mark her not)
Will take away, may cease to give.

Perchance when you are wandering forth
Upon some vacant sunny day
Without an object, hope, or fear,
Thither your eyes may turn—the isle is passed away.

Buried beneath the glittering lake,
Its place no longer to be found,
Yet the lost fragments shall remain
To fertilize some other ground.

Mary Tighe

(1772–1810)

Mary Tighe was an Irish Romantic poet famous in her day for *Psyche, or the Legend of Love*, as well as for her influence on the poetry of John Keats. Born in Dublin, Tighe had a strict religious upbringing and became a poet at the age of seventeen. She married her cousin Henry Tighe when she was twenty-one and their marriage was not a happy one. The couple moved to London and Tighe met Thomas Moore and other literary figures. Her first publication was her epic poem *Psyche* was published in 1805. *Psyche* was an allegorical poem written in Spenserian stanzas and made up of six cantos. A new edition of *Psyche* was published a year after Mary Tighe's death, along with previously unpublished poems. It was this volume that made her into a popular literary figure. Keats became one of her admirers and paid tribute to her in his poem "To Some Ladies." Felicia Hemans also wrote a poetic tribute to her in "The Grave of a Poetess."

from Psyche, or the Legend of Love[1]

Much wearied with her long and dreary way,
And now with toil and sorrow well nigh spent,
Of sad regret and wasting grief the prey,

---

[1] This poem is inspired by the Greek myth of Psyche. John Keats was influenced by Tighe's poem in his "Ode to Psyche."

Fair Psyche[2] through untrodden forests went,
To lone shades uttering oft a vain lament.
And oft in hopeless silence sighing deep,
As she her fatal error did repent,
While dear remembrance bade her ever weep,
And her pale cheek in ceaseless showers of sorrow steep.

Amid the thick covert of that woodland shade,
A flowery bank there lay undressed by art,
But of the mossy turf spontaneous made;
Here the young branches shot their arms athwart,
And wove the bower so thick in every part,
That the fierce beams of Phoebus[3] glancing strong
Could never through the leaves their fury dart;
But the sweet creeping shrubs that round it throng,
Their loving fragrance mix, and trail their flowers along.

And close beside a little fountain play'd,
Which through the trembling leaves all joyous shone,
And with the cheerful birds sweet music made,
Kissing the surface of each polish'd stone
As it flowed past: sure as her favourite throne
Tranquillity might well esteem the bower,
The fresh and cool retreat have called her own,
A pleasant shelter in the sultry hour,
A refuge from the blast, and angry tempest's power.

---

[2] In Greek myth Psyche was one of the most beautiful mortals.
Aphrodite, the goddess of love, was jealous of Psyche and
wanted her son, Eros, to make her fall in love with a hideous
man. However, Eros pricked his finger on his own arrow and
thus fell in love with Psyche himself. He hid her away but Psyche was still persecuted by Aphrodite and contemplated suicide.
Eventually Zeus made Psyche immortal and allowed Eros to
marry her. Psyche became the personification of soul.

[3] Phoebus was Apollo, the Greek god of the sun.

Wooed by the soothing silence of the scene
Here Psyche stood, and looking round, lest aught
Which threaten'd danger near her might have been,
Awhile to rest her in that quiet spot
She laid her down, and piteously bethought
Herself on the sad changes of her fate,
Which in so short a space so much had wrought,
And now had raised her to such high estate,
And now had plunged her low in sorrow desolate.

Oh! how refreshing seemed the breathing wind
To her faint limbs! and while her snowy hands
From her fair brow her golden hair unbind,
And of her zone unloose the silken bands,
More passing bright unveiled her beauty stands;
For faultless was her form as beauty's queen,
And every winning grace that Love demands,
With mild attempered dignity was seen
Play o'er each lovely limb, and deck her angel mien.

Though solitary now, dismay'd, forlorn,
Without attendant through the forest rude,
The peerless maid of royal lineage born
By many a royal youth had oft been wooed;
Low at her feet full many a prince had sued,
And homage paid unto her beauty rare;
But all their blandishments her heart withstood;
And well might mortal suitor sure despair,
Since mortal charms were none which might with hers
  compare.

.   .   .

SAMUEL TAYLOR COLERIDGE

(1772–1834)

SAMUEL TAYLOR COLERIDGE was a renowned English poet, critic, and philosopher, as well as a co-founder of the Romantic Movement in England. Coleridge and his close friend, the poet William Wordsworth, started the Romantic Movement with their collaboration on *Lyrical Ballads*, published in 1798. Born in Devonshire, he was the tenth child in the family and when his father died in 1782, he was sent to Christ's Hospital as a charity case. There he showed an impressive knowledge of the classics and an amazing ability to memorize literature. While studying at Cambridge, Coleridge met Robert Southey, the future Poet Laureate of England. Coleridge and Southey became friends and in 1795 Coleridge married Sara Fricker, the sister of Southey's fiancée. His productive period lasted from 1795 to 1802 and despite his health problems, he produced great work, including "The Eolian Harp," which was published in his *Poems on Various Subjects* (1796). The poem combines lyrical description with philosophical meditation.

Coleridge's most celebrated poem is probably "The Rime of the Ancient Mariner" (first published in *Lyrical Ballads* along with three other poems by Coleridge), a lengthy poem about a sailor who kills an albatross and thus curses himself and his ship. The poem is about the themes of sin and punishment, and redemption through suffering and coming to understand nature. It includes the famous lines "Water, water, every where/Nor any drop to drink." His other noted work includes "Kubla

Khan," which he supposedly wrote subconsciously during a dream, the Gothic "Christabel," a long narrative poem, "The Nightingale," and "Dejection: An Ode." In the latter two poems Coleridge explores the relationship between mind and nature and finds that consciousness can't obtain its feeling from nature, nor can it instill nature with its own feeling. His major work of prose is his *Biographia Literaria*. Coleridge's personal life was tumultuous and he suffered from melancholia and opium addiction.

from THE RIME OF THE ANCIENT MARINER[1]

PART I

It is an ancient Mariner,
And he stoppeth one of three.
'By thy long grey beard and glittering eye,
Now wherefore stopp'st thou me?

The bridegroom's doors are opened wide,
And I am next of kin;
The guests are met, the feast is set:
Mayst hear the merry din.'

He holds him with his skinny hand,
"There was a ship," quoth he.
'Hold off! unhand me, grey-beard loon!'
Eftsoons his hand dropped he.

---

[1] There are many different interpretations of this poem. Some critics believe that it is a metaphor for original sin with the subsequent remorse of the mariner and the rain seen as a baptism.

He holds him with his glittering eye—
The Wedding-Guest stood still,
And listens like a three years' child:
The Mariner hath his will.

The Wedding-Guest sat on a stone:
He cannot choose but hear;
And thus spake on that ancient man,
The bright-eyed Mariner.

"The ship was cheered, the harbour cleared,
Merrily did we drop
Below the kirk, below the hill,
Below the lighthouse top.

The sun came up upon the left,
Out of the sea came he!
And he shone bright, and on the right
Went down into the sea.

Higher and higher every day,
Till over the mast at noon—"
The Wedding-Guest here beat his breast,
For he heard the loud bassoon.

The bride hath paced into the hall,
Red as a rose is she;
Nodding their heads before her goes
The merry minstrelsy.

The Wedding-Guest he beat his breast,
Yet he cannot choose but hear;
And thus spake on that ancient man,
The bright-eyed Mariner.

"And now the storm-blast came, and he
Was tyrannous and strong:
He struck with his o'ertaking wings,
And chased us south along.

With sloping masts and dipping prow,
As who pursued with yell and blow
Still treads the shadow of his foe,
And foward bends his head,
The ship drove fast, loud roared the blast,
And southward aye we fled.

And now there came both mist and snow,
And it grew wondrous cold:
And ice, mast-high, came floating by,
As green as emerald.

And through the drifts the snowy clifts
Did send a dismal sheen:
Nor shapes of men nor beasts we ken—
The ice was all between.

The ice was here, the ice was there,
The ice was all around:
It cracked and growled, and roared and howled,
Like noises in a swound!

At length did cross an Albatross,
Thorough the fog it came;
As it had been a Christian soul,
We hailed it in God's name.

It ate the food it ne'er had eat,
And round and round it flew.
The ice did split with a thunder-fit;
The helmsman steered us through!

And a good south wind sprung up behind;
The Albatross did follow,
And every day, for food or play,
Came to the mariner's hollo!

In mist or cloud, on mast or shroud,
It perched for vespers nine;
Whiles all the night, through fog-smoke white,
Glimmered the white moonshine."

'God save thee, ancient Mariner,
From the fiends that plague thee thus!—
Why look'st thou so?'—"With my crossbow
I shot the Albatross."

Part II

"The sun now rose upon the right:
Out of the sea came he,
Still hid in mist, and on the left
Went down into the sea.

And the good south wind still blew behind,
But no sweet bird did follow,
Nor any day for food or play
Came to the mariners' hollo!

And I had done a hellish thing,
And it would work 'em woe:
For all averred, I had killed the bird
That made the breeze to blow.
Ah wretch! said they, the bird to slay,
That made the breeze to blow!

Nor dim nor red, like God's own head,
The glorious sun uprist:
Then all averred, I had killed the bird
That brought the fog and mist.
'Twas right, said they, such birds to slay,
That bring the fog and mist.

The fair breeze blew, the white foam flew,
The furrow followed free;
We were the first that ever burst
Into that silent sea.

Down dropped the breeze, the sails dropped down,
'Twas sad as sad could be;
And we did speak only to break
The silence of the sea!

All in a hot and copper sky,
The bloody sun, at noon,
Right up above the mast did stand,
No bigger than the moon.

Day after day, day after day,
We stuck, nor breath nor motion;
As idle as a painted ship
Upon a painted ocean.

Water, water, every where,
And all the boards did shrink;
Water, water, every where,
Nor any drop to drink.

The very deep did rot: O Christ!
That ever this should be!
Yea, slimy things did crawl with legs
Upon the slimy sea.

About, about, in reel and rout
The death-fires danced at night;
The water, like a witch's oils,
Burnt green, and blue, and white.

And some in dreams assured were
Of the Spirit that plagued us so;
Nine fathom deep he had followed us
From the land of mist and snow.

And every tongue, through utter drought,
Was withered at the root;
We could not speak, no more than if
We had been choked with soot.

Ah! well-a-day! what evil looks
Had I from old and young!
Instead of the cross, the Albatross
About my neck was hung."

FROST AT MIDNIGHT[2]

The Frost performs its secret ministry,
Unhelped by any wind. The owlet's cry
Came loud,—and hark, again! loud as before.
The inmates of my cottage, all at rest,
Have left me to that solitude, which suits
Abstruser musings: save that at my side
My cradled infant slumbers peacefully.
'Tis calm indeed! so calm, that it disturbs
And vexes meditation with its strange
And extreme silentness. Sea, hill, and wood,
With all the numberless goings-on of life,
Inaudible as dreams! the thin blue flame

---

[2] This poem was composed in 1798. The speaker of "Frost at Midnight" is generally thought to be Coleridge himself, and the poem is a personal statement about the common themes of Romanticism: the effect of nature on the imagination, the relationship between children and the natural world, the contrast between the freedom of the present country setting and the city, and the association between adulthood and childhood as they are linked in adult memory.

Lies on my low-burnt fire, and quivers not;
Only that film, which fluttered on the grate,
Still flutters there, the sole unquiet thing.
Methinks its motion in this hush of nature
Gives it dim sympathies with me who live,
Making it a companionable form,
Whose puny flaps and freaks the idling Spirit
By its own moods interprets, every where
Echo or mirror seeking of itself,
And makes a toy of Thought.

But O! how oft,
How oft, at school, with most believing mind,
Presageful, have I gazed upon the bars,
To watch that fluttering stranger! and as oft
With unclosed lids, already had I dreamt
Of my sweet birthplace, and the old church-tower,
Whose bells, the poor man's only music, rang
From morn to evening, all the hot Fair-day,
So sweetly, that they stirred and haunted me
With a wild pleasure, falling on mine ear
Most like articulate sounds of things to come!
So gazed I, till the soothing things, I dreamt,
Lulled me to sleep, and sleep prolonged my dreams!
And so I brooded all the following morn,
Awed by the stern preceptor's face, mine eye
Fixed with mock study on my swimming book:
Save if the door half opened, and I snatched
A hasty glance, and still my heart leaped up,
For still I hoped to see the stranger's face,
Townsman, or aunt, or sister more beloved,
My playmate when we both were clothed alike!

Dear Babe, that sleepest cradled by my side,
Whose gentle breathings, heard in this deep calm,
Fill up the interspersed vacancies
And momentary pauses of the thought!
My babe so beautiful! it thrills my heart
With tender gladness, thus to look at thee,
And think that thou shalt learn far other lore,
And in far other scenes! For I was reared
In the great city, pent mid cloisters dim,
And saw nought lovely but the sky and stars.
But thou, my babe! shalt wander like a breeze
By lakes and sandy shores, beneath the crags
Of ancient mountain, and beneath the clouds,
Which image in their bulk both lakes and shores
And mountain crags: so shalt thou see and hear
The lovely shapes and sounds intelligible
Of that eternal language, which thy God
Utters, who from eternity doth teach
Himself in all, and all things in himself.
Great universal Teacher! he shall mould
Thy spirit, and by giving make it ask.

Therefore all seasons shall be sweet to thee,
Whether the summer clothe the general earth
With greenness, or the redbreast sit and sing
Betwixt the tufts of snow on the bare branch
Of mossy apple-tree, while the nigh thatch
Smokes in the sun-thaw; whether the eave-drops fall
Heard only in the trances of the blast,
Or if the secret ministry of frost
Shall hang them up in silent icicles,
Quietly shining to the quiet Moon.

Kubla Khan[3]

In Xanadu did Kubla Khan
A stately pleasure-dome decree:
Where Alph, the sacred river, ran
Through caverns measureless to man
Down to a sunless sea.

So twice five miles of fertile ground
With walls and towers were girdled round:
And there were gardens bright with sinuous rills,
Where blossomed many an incense-bearing tree;
And here were forests ancient as the hills,
Enfolding sunny spots of greenery.

But oh! that deep romantic chasm which slanted
Down the green hill athwart a cedarn cover!
A savage place! as holy and enchanted
As e'er beneath a waning moon was haunted
By woman wailing for her demon-lover!
And from this chasm, with ceaseless turmoil seething,
As if this earth in fast thick pants were breathing,
A mighty fountain momently was forced:
Amid whose swift half-intermitted burst
Huge fragments vaulted like rebounding hail,
Or chaffy grain beneath the thresher's flail:

---

[3] Coleridge claims that this poem was inspired by an opium-induced dream. It's full title is "Kubla Khan, or a Vision in a Dream. A Fragment." The poem takes its title from the Mongolian emperor Kublai Khan of the Yuan dynasty and the poem opens at Xanadu, or Shangdu, Kublai Khan's summer palace. It was written in 1797 and first published in 1816.

And 'mid these dancing rocks at once and ever
It flung up momently the sacred river.
Five miles meandering with a mazy motion
Through wood and dale the sacred river ran,
Then reached the caverns measureless to man,
And sank in tumult to a lifeless ocean:
And 'mid this tumult Kubla heard from far
Ancestral voices prophesying war!

The shadow of the dome of pleasure
Floated midway on the waves;
Where was heard the mingled measure
From the fountain and the caves.
It was a miracle of rare device,
A sunny pleasure-dome with caves of ice!

A damsel with a dulcimer
In a vision once I saw:
It was an Abyssinian maid,
And on her dulcimer she played,
Singing of Mount Abora.
Could I revive within me
Her symphony and song,
To such a deep delight 'twould win me
That with music loud and long
I would build that dome in air,
That sunny dome! those caves of ice!
And all who heard should see them there,
And all should cry, Beware! Beware!
His flashing eyes, his floating hair!
Weave a circle round him thrice,
And close your eyes with holy dread,

For he on honey-dew hath fed
And drunk the milk of Paradise.

from DEJECTION: AN ODE[4]

Late, late yestreen I saw the new moon,
With the old moon in her arms;
And I fear, I fear, my master dear!
We shall have a deadly storm.
(Ballad of Sir Patrick Spence)

I

Well! If the Bard was weather-wise, who made
The grand old ballad of Sir Patrick Spence,
This night, so tranquil now, will not go hence
Unroused by winds, that ply a busier trade
Than those which mould yon cloud in lazy flakes,
Or the dull sobbing draft, that moans and rakes
Upon the strings of this Aeolian lute,
Which better far were mute.
For lo! the New-moon winter-bright!
And overspread with phantom light,
(With swimming phantom light o'erspread
But rimmed and circled by a silver thread)
I see the old Moon in her lap, foretelling
The coming-on of rain and squally blast.

---

[4] "Dejection: An Ode" was first written in a letter in April 1802 to
Sara Hutchinson. The poem was revised—shortened, refined,
and made less intimate—for publication in the *Morning Post* in
October of the same year.

And oh! that even now the gust were swelling,
And the slant night-shower driving loud and fast!
Those sounds which oft have raised me, whilst they
    awed,
And sent my soul abroad,
Might now perhaps their wonted impulse give,
Might startle this dull pain, and make it move and live!

II

A grief without a pang, void, dark, and drear,
A stifled, drowsy, unimpassioned grief,
Which finds no natural outlet, no relief,
In word, or sigh, or tear—
O Lady! in this wan and heartless mood,
To other thoughts by yonder throstle wooed,
All this long eve, so balmy and serene,
Have I been gazing on the western sky,
And its peculiar tint of yellow green:
And still I gaze—and with how blank an eye!
And those thin clouds above, in flakes and bars,
That give away their motion to the stars;
Those stars, that glide behind them or between,
Now sparkling, now bedimmed, but always seen:
Yon crescent Moon, as fixed as if it grew
In its own cloudless, starless lake of blue;
I see them all so excellently fair,
I see, not feel, how beautiful they are!

THOMAS CAMPBELL

(1774–1844)

THOMAS CAMPBELL was a Scottish poet who is most remembered for his patriotic war poetry such as "Ye Mariners of England," "Hohenlinden," and "The Battle of the Baltic." He was born in Glasgow and studied at the University of Glasgow where he won prizes for classics and writing verse. Six months after Wordsworth's *Lyrical Ballads* was published in 1799, Campbell published *The Pleasures of Hope*, a long political poem written in couplets. It was quite successful. In 1800 he went abroad and while finding refuge from war in a Scottish monastery in Germany he wrote some of his greatest lyric poems. Campbell was praised for his patriotic verse and it won him a pension from the British government. He also wrote long narrative poems, but they were less popular. *Gertrude of Wyoming* is notable for being the first long poem about life in America by a British author. Campbell wrote professionally for newspapers and encyclopedias as well as writing poetry.

YE MARINERS OF ENGLAND[1]

Ye Mariners of England
That guard our native seas!
Whose flag has braved a thousand years
The battle and the breeze!
Your glorious standard launch again
To match another foe;
And sweep through the deep,
While the stormy winds do blow!
While the battle rages loud and long
And the stormy winds do blow.

The spirits of your fathers
Shall start from every wave—
For the deck it was their field of fame,
And Ocean was their grave:
Where Blake[2] and mighty Nelson[3] fell
Your manly hearts shall glow,
As ye sweep through the deep,
While the stormy winds do blow!
While the battle rages loud and long
And the stormy winds do blow.

---

[1] This poem was inspired by Campbell's viewing of the British fleet that took part in the battle of Copenhagen, which he saw when traveling back to England in 1800.

[2] Robert Blake was one of the most famous English admirals of the 17th century.

[3] Horatio Nelson was a famous English admiral who lost his life in the Battle of Trafalgar during the Napoleonic Wars in 1805.

Britannia needs no bulwarks,
No towers along the steep;
Her march is o'er the mountain-waves,
Her home is on the deep.
The thunders from her native oak
She quells the floods below,
As they roar on the shore,
When the stormy winds do blow!
When the battle rages loud and long,
And the stormy winds do blow.

The meteor flag of England
Shall yet terrific burn;
Till danger's troubled night depart
And the star of peace return.
Then, then, ye ocean-warriors!
Our song and feast shall flow
To the fame of your name,
When the storm has ceased to blow!
When the fiery fight is heard no more,
And the storm has ceased to blow.

ROBERT SOUTHEY

(1774–1843)

ROBERT SOUTHEY was poet laureate of Britain for thirty years, an influential Romantic poet who was friends with Samuel Taylor Coleridge, as well as William and Dorothy Wordsworth, but whose reputation now is much diminished. He was considered the leader of the Lake Poets, who included Wordsworth, Coleridge, and Charles Lamb.

Southey was born in Bristol, the son of a draper. He studied at Oxford where he became friends with Coleridge and began writing poems and plays with rebellious themes. Coleridge married Southey's wife's sister, probably at Southey's instigation. Byron lambasted Southey's work, rhyming his name with "mouthey."

Southey's short lyrics and ballads are now considered his most successful work, including poems such as "My Days Among the Dead are Past," "The Battle of Blenheim," "The Inchcape Rock," and "The Holly Tree." Lewis Carroll parodied Southey's poem "The Old Man's Complaints" in his poem "You are Old Father William."

My Days Among the Dead Are Past[1]

My days among the Dead are past;
    Around me I behold,
Where'er these casual eyes are cast,
    The mighty minds of old:
My never-failing friends are they,
With whom I converse day by day.

With them I take delight in weal
    And seek relief in woe;
And while I understand and feel
    How much to them I owe,
My cheeks have often been bedew'd
With tears of thoughtful gratitude.

My thoughts are with the Dead; with them
    I live in long-past years,
Their virtues love, their faults condemn,
    Partake their hopes and fears;
And from their lessons seek and find
Instruction with an humble mind.

My hopes are with the Dead; anon
    My place with them will be,
And I with them shall travel on
    Through all Futurity;
Yet leaving here a name, I trust,
That will not perish in the dust.

---

[1] This poem is often known as "His Books."

Jane Austen

(1775–1817)

J ANE AUSTEN was a renowned English novelist, famous for her six classic novels: *Sense and Sensibility*, *Pride and Prejudice*, *Mansfield Park*, *Emma*, *Northanger Abbey*, and *Persuasion*. Austen also wrote poetry, most of it light verse. The daughter of a clergyman, Austen spent the first twenty-five years of her life living in a Hampshire vicarage. It is here that she wrote her first three novels, *Pride and Prejudice*, *Sense and Sensibility*, and *Northanger Abbey*, but they were not published until much later. When Jane's father retired in 1801, the family moved to Bath and then Southhampton, finally settling at Chawton Cottage close by Alton, Hampshire. She sold *Northanger Abbey*, a satire of the gothic romantic novel, for ten pounds in 1803, but the publisher never printed the book and her family bought back the rights so that it was published in 1818 after Austen's death. *Persuasion* was also published posthumously. The novels published in Austen's lifetime were *Sense and Sensibility* (1811), *Pride and Prejudice* (1813), *Mansfield Park* (1814), and *Emma* (1816).

Jane received little literary attention in her lifetime as her name did not appear on any of her title pages and only her friends knew of her authorship. However Sir Walter Scott, one of her influences, praised her work, saying "That young lady has a talent for describing the involvements of feelings and characters of ordinary life which is to me the most wonderful I ever met with." Others criticized her. Charlotte Bronte complained

"What sees keenly, speaks aptly, moves flexibly, it suits her to study: but what throbs fast and full, though hidden, what the blood rushes through, what is the unseen seat of life and the sentient target of death—this Miss Austen ignores… Jane Austen was a complete and most sensible lady, but a very incomplete and rather insensible (not *senseless*) woman." Today Austen's novels are noted for the ironic wit they display in evoking society of the time. Jane compared her work to that of a miniaturist and focused on middle and upper class characters, poking fun at their silliness, their vanity, and their pretentiousness in her comedies of manners.

OH! MR. BEST, YOU'RE VERY BAD

Oh! Mr. Best, you're very bad
~~And all the world shall know it;~~
Your base behaviour shall be sung
By me, a tunefull Poet.—
You used to go to Harrowgate
Each summer as it came,
And why I pray should you refuse
To go this year the same?—

The way's as plain, the road's as smooth,
The Posting not increased;
You're scarcely stouter than you were,
Not younger Sir at least.—

If e'er the waters were of use
Why now their use forego?
You may not live another year,
All's mortal here below.—

It is your duty Mr Best
To give your health repair.
Vain else your Richard's pills will be,
And vain your Consort's care.

But yet a nobler Duty calls
You now towards the North.
Arise ennobled—as Escort
Of Martha Lloyd stand forth.

She wants your aid—she honours you
With a distinguished call.
Stand forth to be the friend of her
Who is the friend of all.—

Take her, and wonder at your luck,
In having such a Trust.
Her converse sensible and sweet
Will banish heat and dust.—

So short she'll make the journey seem
You'll bid the Chaise stand still.
T'will be like driving at full speed
From Newb'ry to Speen hill.—

Convey her safe to Morton's wife
And I'll forget the past,
And write some verses in your praise
As finely and as fast.

But if you still refuse to go
I'll never let your rest,
Buy haunt you with reproachful song
Oh! wicked Mr. Best!—

CHARLES LAMB

(1775–1834)

CHARLES LAMB (pseudonym Elia) was a renowned English essayist, letter-writer, and critic, as well as a poet and the brother of the poet and writer Mary Lamb, whom he collaborated and lived with for most of his life. Lamb worked as a clerk for the East India Company from 1792 to 1825. Charles Lamb became the legal guardian of his sister in 1796 after Mary killed their ailing mother with a kitchen knife in one of her fits of mental illness.

Lamb was best known for the autobiographical essays he wrote under the pen name Elia for *London Magazine*. The essays were collected in *Essays of Elia* in 1823 and in *The Last Essays of Elia* in 1833. Lamb is also considered one of the finest English letter writers in which he included incisive literary criticism. With his sister, he collaborated on the popular *Tales from Shakespeare*, as well as several poetry collections. Lamb became friends with Samuel Taylor Coleridge. "The Old Familiar Faces" remains Lamb's most well known poem.

THE OLD FAMILIAR FACES

I have had playmates, I have had companions[1]
In my days of childhood, in my joyful school-days;
All, all are gone, the old familiar faces.

I have been laughing, I have been carousing,
Drinking late, sitting late, with my bosom cronies;
All, all are gone, the old familiar faces.

I loved a Love once, fairest among women:
Closed are her doors on me, I must not see her—
All, all are gone, the old familiar faces.

I have a friend, a kinder friend has no man:
Like an ingrate, I left my friend abruptly;
Left him, to muse on the old familiar faces.

Ghost-like I paced round the haunts of my childhood,
Earth seem'd a desert I was bound to traverse,
Seeking to find the old familiar faces.

Friend of my bosom, thou more than a brother,
Why wert not thou born in my father's dwelling?
So might we talk of the old familiar faces,

How some they have died, and some they have left me,
And some are taken from me; all are departed;
All, all are gone, the old familiar faces.

---

[1] Originally this poem began with a verse that referred to the painful memory of his sister killing their mother. The beginning verse contained these two lines: "I had a mother, but she died, and left me, / Died prematurely in a day of horrors—" Even without these lines, it is clear that the terrible loss of his mother and the loss of sister to mental illness for periods of time contribute to the deep sorrow of the poem.

CLEMENT MOORE

(1779–1863)

CLEMENT CLARKE MOORE was an American Biblical Hebrew scholar and professor famous for his poem "A Visit from St. Nicholas," more commonly known today as "Twas the Night Before Christmas." Born in New York City to Benjamin Moore, a president of Columbia College, Clement Moore graduated from Columbia in 1798 after earning both a B.A. and an M.A. Moore was a professor of biblical learning at the General Theological Seminary in New York from 1821 to 1850. In 1809 he compiled a two volume Hebrew dictionary, *Hebrew and English Lexicon*. He published a volume of poetry in 1844.

"A Visit from St. Nicholas" first appeared anonymously in the Troy, New York *Sentinel* on December 23, 1823 and the original publisher hinted that Moore was the author, although he didn't name him. The poem was frequently reprinted and Moore was first given credit as the author by Charles Fenno Hoffman, the editor of *The New York Book of Poetry* in 1837. Moore's authorship has since come into question and Henry Livingston Jr. has been named as the alternative author, although there is no evidence that Livingston himself ever claimed authorship. In 2000, Don Foster, an English professor at Vassar College in Poughkeepsie, New York, published a book disputing Moore's authorship, but Foster's evidence has itself been disputed and Moore is known to have written out four copies of the poem in his later life. One copy is at the Huntington Library in San Marino, California, and it is dated March

24, 1856. Another copy is with the New York Historical Society, written in 1862, while a third copy is at the Strong Museum in Rochester, New York, and a fourth copy is owned by a private gallery.

A Visit from St. Nicholas[1]

'Twas the night before Christmas, when all through the
   house
Not a creature was stirring, not even a mouse;
The stockings were hung by the chimney with care,
In hopes that St. Nicholas soon would be there;
The children were nestled all snug in their beds,
While visions of sugar-plums danced in their heads;
And Mama in her 'kerchief, and I in my cap,
Had just settled our brains for a long winter's nap;
When out on the lawn there arose such a clatter,
I sprang from the bed to see what was the matter.
Away to the window I flew like a flash,
Tore open the shutters and threw up the sash.
The moon on the breast of the new-fallen snow,
Gave the lustre of mid-day to objects below,
When, what to my wondering sight should appear,
But a miniature sleigh, and eight tiny reindeer,
With a little old driver, so lively and quick,
I knew in a moment it must be St. Nick.
More rapid than eagles his coursers they came,
And he whistled, and shouted, and called them by name;
"Now, Dasher! now, Dancer! now, Prancer and Vixen!
On, Comet! on, Cupid! on, Donder and Blitzen!

---

[1] More commonly known today as "Twas the Night Before Christmas."

To the top of the porch! to the top of the wall!
Now dash away! dash away! dash away all!"
As dry leaves that before the wild hurricane fly,
When they meet with an obstacle, mount to the sky;
So up to the house-top the coursers they flew,
With the sleigh full of Toys, and St. Nicholas too.
And then, in a twinkling, I heard on the roof,
The prancing and pawing of each little hoof—
As I drew in my head, and was turning around,
Down the chimney St. Nicholas came with a bound.
He was dressed all in fur, from his head to his foot,
And his clothes were all tarnished with ashes and soot;
A bundle of Toys he had flung on his back,
And he look'd like a pedlar just opening his pack.
His eyes—how they twinkled! his dimples how merry!
His cheeks were like roses, his nose like a cherry!
His droll little mouth was drawn up like a bow,
And the beard of his chin was as white as the snow;
The stump of a pipe he held tight in his teeth,
And the smoke it encircled his head like a wreath;
He had a broad face and a little round belly,
That shook when he laughed, like a bowlfull of jelly.
He was chubby and plump, a right jolly old elf,
And I laughed when I saw him, in spite of myself;
A wink of his eye and a twist of his head,
Soon gave me to know I had nothing to dread;
He spoke not a word, but went straight to his work,
And fill'd all the stockings; then turned with a jerk,
And laying his finger aside of his nose,
And giving a nod, up the chimney he rose;
He sprang to his sleigh, to his team gave a whistle,
And away they all flew like the down of a thistle.
But I heard him exclaim, ere he drove out of sight,
"Happy Christmas to all, and to all a good night."

Francis Scott Key

(1779–1843)

Francis Scott Key was an American poet and lawyer famous for writing the lyrics to the "Star Spangled Banner," which became the official national anthem of The United States in 1931. Key was thirty-five when he wrote the poem after American soldiers bravely defended Fort McHenry during the British attack on September 13, 1814. Key wrote the poem to correspond to the meter of the English drinking song "To Anacreon in Heaven." Key was born to a prominent Maryland family and went on to practice law in Georgetown, Maryland. He appeared before the United States Supreme Court numerous times. Deeply religious, Key was involved in the Episcopal church, and although he was opposed to the war, he served in it for a short period. Key was sailing on a truce ship to meet the British fleet and negotiate a prisoner of war release for a doctor when he witnessed the British attack on Fort McHenry. After the war, Key became a United States District Attorney and continued his work with the church, writing several hymns. Key wrote about his inspiration for his "Star Spangled Banner:" "Then, in that hour of deliverance, my heart spoke. Does not such a country, and such defenders of their country, deserve a song?"

The Star Spangled Banner[1]

Oh, say can you see, by the dawn's early light,
What so proudly we hailed at the twilight's last
  gleaming?
Whose broad stripes and bright stars, through the
  perilous fight,
O'er the ramparts we watched, were so gallantly
  streaming?
And the rockets' red glare, the bombs bursting in air,
Gave proof through the night that our flag was still
  there.
O say, does that star-spangled banner yet wave
O'er the land of the free and the home of the brave?

On the shore, dimly seen through the mists of the
  deep,
Where the foe's haughty host in dread silence reposes,
What is that which the breeze, o'er the towering steep,
As it fitfully blows, half conceals, half discloses?
Now it catches the gleam of the morning's first beam,
In full glory reflected now shines on the stream:
'Tis the star-spangled banner! O long may it wave
O'er the land of the free and the home of the brave.

---

[1] This poem is also known as "The Defence of Fort McHenry" and
"Stars and Stripes Forever."

And where is that band who so vauntingly swore
That the havoc of war and the battle's confusion
A home and a country should leave us no more?
Their blood has wiped out their foul footstep's
    pollution.
No refuge could save the hireling and slave
From the terror of flight, or the gloom of the grave:
And the star-spangled banner in triumph doth wave
O'er the land of the free and the home of the brave.

Oh! thus be it ever, when freemen shall stand
Between their loved homes and the war's desolation!
Blest with victory and peace, may the heaven-rescued
    land
Praise the Power that hath made and preserved us a
    nation.
Then conquer we must, when our cause it is just,
And this be our motto: "In God is our trust."
And the star-spangled banner in triumph shall wave
O'er the land of the free and the home of the brave!

ANN TAYLOR

(1782–1866)

ANN TAYLOR was an English poet, children's book author, and hymn writer famous for having collaborated with her younger sister Jane on the words for the song "Twinkle, Twinkle, Little Star." The sisters first published the poem in 1806 as "The Star" in *Rhymes for the Nursery*. Born in London, the Taylor sisters grew up in Colchester, England in a literary household. Their father was an engraver and minister and their mother was a writer. In 1804 Ann and Jane co-wrote *Original Poems for Infant Minds* and in 1808 followed up with *Hymns for Infant Minds*. Both Ann's and Jane's work often contained gentle moral lessons about how to behave. Ann married Reverend Joseph Gilbert in 1813. She continued writing poems, hymns, essays, and letters and remained dedicated to prison reform and the anti-slavery movement.

Ann Taylor died on December 20, 1866 and she is attributed with this quotation about death: "So, while their bodies moulder here/Their souls with God himself shall dwell,—/But always recollect, my dear,/That wicked people go to hell." Some of Anne Taylor's most popular poems include "Baby Dance," "My Mother," and "Meddlesome Matty."

The Star[1]

Twinkle, twinkle, little star,
How I wonder what you are!
Up above the world so high,
Like a diamond in the sky.

When the blazing sun is gone,
When he nothing shines upon,
Then you show your little light,
Twinkle, twinkle, all the night.

Then the trav'ller in the dark,
Thanks you for your tiny spark,
He could not see which way to go,
If you did not twinkle so.

In the dark blue sky you keep,
And often thro' my curtains peep,
For you never shut your eye,
Till the sun is in the sky.

'Tis your bright and tiny spark,
Lights the trav'ller in the dark:
Tho' I know not what you are,
Twinkle, twinkle, little star.

---

[1] Known today as "Twinkle, Twinkle, Little Star," this poem was
written by Ann and Jane Taylor and first published in 1806.

THE BABY'S DANCE

Dance little baby, dance up high,
Never mind baby, mother is by;
Crow and caper, caper and crow,
There little baby, there you go;
Up to the ceiling, down to the ground,
Backwards and forwards, round and round;
Dance little baby, and mother shall sing,
With the merry coral, ding, ding, ding.

JANE TAYLOR

(1783–1824)

JANE TAYLOR was an English poet, children's book author, and hymn writer famous for having collaborated with her older sister Ann on the words for the song "Twinkle, Twinkle, Little Star." The sisters first published the poem in 1806 as "The Star" in *Rhymes for the Nursery.* Jane was twenty-three at the time. Born in London, the Taylor sisters grew up in Colchester, England in a literary household. Their father was an engraver and minister and their mother was a writer. In 1804 Ann and Jane co-wrote *Original Poems for Infant Minds* and in 1808 followed up with *Hymns for Infant Minds.* Because their work was published together there has been confusion over authorship.

Both Ann's and Jane's work often contained gentle moral lessons about how to behave. Jane went on to publish a novel, *Display* (1814), *Essays in Rhyme* (1816), and *Correspondence between a mother and her daughter at school* (1817), which she collaborated on with her mother. She also wrote many essays, plays, stories, poems, and letters which were never published during her lifetime. After Jane Taylor died from cancer, her brother collected much of her writing and published it in *The Writings of Jane Taylor, In Five Volumes.*

Come and Play in the Garden

Little sister, come away,
And let us in the garden play,
For it is a pleasant day.

On the grass-plat let us sit,
Or, if you please, we'll play a bit,
And run about all over it.

But the fruit we will not pick,
For that would be a naughty trick,
And very likely make us sick.

Nor will we pluck the pretty flowers
That grow about the beds and bowers,
Because you know they are not ours.

We'll take the daisies, white and red,
Because mamma has often said
That we may gather then instead.

And much I hope we always may
Our very dear mamma obey,
And mind whatever she may say.

LEIGH HUNT

(1784–1859)

L EIGH HUNT (James Henry Leigh Hunt) was an English poet, essayist, journalist, and critic who is mainly known for his light verse and essays. He was also one of the first admirers of John Keats and Percy Bysshe Shelley. Hunt's home was a meeting place for eminent writers such as William Hazlitt, Charles Lamb, Keats, and Shelley. In 1808 he founded the *Examiner* with his brother. It was a liberal weekly paper and the brothers were jailed for two years for the publication of a scathing article on the prince regent. From jail they continued editing the journal. Hunt joined Shelley and Byron in Italy and tried to establish a radical political journal called the *Liberal*, but it only lasted from 1822 to 1823. Hunt contributed articles to the *Indicator*, the *Tatler*, and *Leigh Hunt's London Journal*. Hunt's biggest contribution to literature was his critical insight and his discovery of poets such as Keats, Shelley, Robert Browning, and Alfred Tennyson. He also nurtured Hazlitt, Lamb, Walter Savage Landor, and Charles Dickens.

His most famous lyrics are "Jenny Kissed Me, " "The Glove and the Lions," and "Abou Ben Adhem," while his only noted long poem is "The Story of Rimini." He wrote an autobiography in 1850 as well as a novel and several plays. "Abou Ben Adhem" includes the line that became Hunt's epitaph: "Write me as one who loves his fellow men."

JENNY KISSED ME[1]

Jenny[2] kiss'd me when we met,
Jumping from the chair she sat in;
Time, you thief, who love to get
Sweets into your list, put that in!
Say I'm weary, say I'm sad,
Say that health and wealth have miss'd me,
Say I'm growing old, but add,
Jenny kiss'd me.

---

[1] This poem was first published in the *Monthly Chronicle*, November 1838.

[2] "Jenny Kissed Me" is a rondeau inspired by Thomas Carlyle's wife, Jane Welsh Carlyle. She was a poet and letter writer known for her wit and charm.

LADY CAROLINE LAMB

(1785–1828)

LADY CAROLINE LAMB (nee Ponsonby) was an English novelist and poet best known for her turbulent love affair with Lord Byron. She was born to Lord Duncannon and Lady Henrietta and her childhood nickname "Caro" remained with her throughout her life. Lamb has been quoted as calling Lord Byron "mad bad and dangerous to know." She was twenty-seven, married to the politician William Lamb, and Byron was twenty-four when they met in 1812. He was just starting to become famous for publishing *Childe Harolde's Pilgrimage* and their affair lasted around four months until Byron broke it off suddenly. The affair was public and serious, almost resulting in elopement. Lamb was heartbroken. After the affair Lamb wrote her first book, a gothic novel, *Glenarvon*, published in 1816, and followed up with two more novels, *Graham Hamilton* in 1822 and *Ada Reiss* in 1823. Lamb and her husband separated when Lamb was forty.

If a Dark Wretch e'er Stray'd

If a dark wretch e'er stray'd,
~~Worse than the first fell slayer,~~
'Tis he that wooes a maid,
To rifle and betray her!
For wealth may be retriev'd,
And friends long doom'd to sever,
But the fond heart deceiv'd,
Hath lost its peace for ever!

Thomas Love Peacock

(1785–1866)

Thomas Love Peacock was an English poet and novelist most remembered for his satirical work. He and Percy Bysshe Shelley were very close friends and influenced each other's writing. (Peacock became Shelley's literary executor after Shelley's untimely death.) Peacock worked for the East India Company from 1819 to 1856, and for the last twenty years he was its chief examiner. His novels are known for parodying the intellectual pretenses of the time. His most successful novel, *Nightmare Abbey*, published in 1818, satirizes the English Romantic movement. The book includes characters based on Coleridge, Byron, and Shelley. Some of his other novels are *Headlong Hall* (1816), *Maid Marian* (1822), and *Crotchet Castle* (1831). Peacock's strongest poems (lyrics and drinking songs) can be found spread through his novels.

Rich & Poor; or Saint & Sinner

The poor man's sins are glaring;
In the face of ghostly warning
  He is caught in the fact
  Of an overt act—
Buying greens on a Sunday morning.

The rich man's sins are hidden
In the pomp of wealth and station;
   And escape the sight
   Of the children of light,
Who are wise in their generation.

The rich man has a kitchen,
And cooks to dress his dinner;
   The poor who would roast
   To the baker's must post,
And thus becomes a sinner.

The rich man has a cellar,
And a ready butler by him;
   The poor man must steer
   For his pint of beer
Where the saint can't choose but to spy him.

The rich man's painted windows
Hide the concerts of the quality;
   The poor can but share
   A crack'd fiddle in the air,
Which offends all sound morality.

The rich man is invisible
In the crowd of his gay society;
   But the poor man's delight
   Is a sore in the sight,
And a stench in the nose of piety.

Caroline Bowles Southey

(1787–1854)

CAROLINE BOWLES SOUTHEY was an English Romantic poet. Born in Buckland, England, the daughter of a navy captain, Caroline sent her poem "Ellen Fitzarthur: A Metrical Tale" to the Poet Laureate Robert Southey early in her career. Southey wrote back, "You have the eye, the ear, and the heart of a poetess. . . ." They became good friends and planned to work together on a long poem about Robin Hood, however the poem was never completed. Bowles married Southey four years before he died, becoming his second wife. She is considered by literary critics to be an important writer who has been neglected in comparison to her male peers. Among her books she published a novel, *Chapters on Churchyards*, a verse satire, *The Cat's Tail*, a verse autobiography, *The Birth-day*, and a dramatic monologue, *Tales of the Factories*. Caroline Bowles is most known for her correspondence with Southey.

To Death

Come not in terrors clad, to claim
    An unresisting prey:
Come like an evening shadow, Death!
  So stealthily, so silently!
And shut mine eyes, and steal my breath;
   Then willingly, O willingly,
     With thee I'll go away!

What need to clutch with iron grasp
    What gentlest touch may take?
What need with aspect dark to scare,
  So awfully, so terribly,
The weary soul would hardly care,
  Call'd quietly, call'd tenderly,
    From thy dread power to break?

'Tis not as when thou markest out
    The young, the blest, the gay,
The loved, the loving—they who dream
  So happily, so hopefully;
Then harsh thy kindest call may seem,
  And shrinkingly, reluctantly,
    The summon'd may obey.

But I have drunk enough of life—
    The cup assign'd to me
Dash'd with a little sweet at best,
  So scantily, so scantily—
To know full well that all the rest
  More bitterly, more bitterly,
    Drugg'd to the last will be.

And I may live to pain some heart
    That kindly cares for me:
To pain, but not to bless. O Death!
  Come quietly—come lovingly—
And shut mine eyes, and steal my breath;
  Then willingly, O willingly,
    I'll go away with thee!

George Gordon,
Lord Byron

(1788–1824)

George Gordon, Lord Byron is one of the most highly respected English Romantic poets. He was known as a highly romantic figure (flamboyant, rebellious, handsome, brooding) as well as a noted satirist. Lord Byron embodied Romanticism. Born with a clubfoot and painfully aware of it, he unexpectedly inherited his title and estates when he was ten years old. He studied at Cambridge and at twenty-one traveled around Europe. *Childe Harold's Pilgramage* (1812–1818) is a poetic travelogue expressing sorrow and disillusionment. The poem brought him literary fame while his complicated personality and scandalous love affairs brought him further attention. Byron lived near Geneva and wrote *Manfred* (1817), a poetic drama whose "Byronic hero" was modeled after himself and reflects Byron's own frustrations and guilt, brooding about some darkness in his past. The long, satirical, picaresque poem *Don Juan* (1819–1824), written in ottava rima, is unfinished at 17 cantos. Byron wrote numerous works, including verse tales and poetic dramas. He fought in the Greek war for independence and died there of a fever, which made him a Greek national hero.

SHE[1] WALKS IN BEAUTY

She walks in beauty, like the night
    Of cloudless climes and starry skies;
And all that 's best of dark and bright
    Meet in her aspect and her eyes:
Thus mellow'd to that tender light
    Which heaven to gaudy day denies.
One shade the more, one ray the less,
    Had half impair'd the nameless grace
Which waves in every raven tress,
    Or softly lightens o'er her face;
Where thoughts serenely sweet express
    How pure, how dear their dwelling-place.

And on that cheek, and o'er that brow,
    So soft, so calm, yet eloquent,
The smiles that win, the tints that glow,
    But tell of days in goodness spent,
A mind at peace with all below,
    A heart whose love is innocent!

---

[1] "She" refers to Mrs. Wilmot, Byron's cousin. He met her at a
party where she was wearing a black mourning dress.

PROMETHEUS[2]

Titan![3] to whose immortal eyes
    The sufferings of mortality,
    Seen in their sad reality,
Were not as things that gods despise;
What was thy pity's recompense?
A silent suffering, and intense;
The rock, the vulture, and the chain,
All that the proud can feel of pain,
The agony they do not show,
The suffocating sense of woe,
    Which speaks but in its loneliness,
And then is jealous lest the sky
Should have a listener, nor will sigh
    Until its voice is echoless.

Titan! to thee the strife was given
    Between the suffering and the will,
    Which torture where they cannot kill;
And the inexorable Heaven,
And the deaf tyranny of Fate,
The ruling principle of Hate,
Which for its pleasure doth create
The things it may annihilate,
Refus'd thee even the boon to die:

---

[2] In Greek mythology, Prometheus gave the gift of fire to man in
    defiance of Zeus and in punishment he was chained to a moun-
    tain and fed to a vulture. Aeschylus's *Prometheus Bound* was one
    of Byron's favorite books.
[3] In Greek mythology the Titans were a faction of Saturn, who was
    replaced as chief god by Zeus, his son. The Titans were popular
    symbols of resistance to tyranny in 19th century England.

The wretched gift Eternity
Was thine—and thou hast borne it well.
All that the Thunderer wrung from thee
Was but the menace which flung back
On him the torments of thy rack;
The fate thou didst so well foresee,
But would not to appease him tell;
And in thy Silence was his Sentence,
And in his Soul a vain repentance,
And evil dread so ill dissembled,
That in his hand the lightnings trembled.

Thy Godlike crime was to be kind,
   To render with thy precepts less
   The sum of human wretchedness,
And strengthen Man with his own mind;
But baffled as thou wert from high,
Still in thy patient energy,
In the endurance, and repulse
   Of thine impenetrable Spirit,
Which Earth and Heaven could not convulse,
A mighty lesson we inherit:
Thou art a symbol and a sign
   To Mortals of their fate and force;
Like thee, Man is in part divine,
   A troubled stream from a pure source;
And Man in portions can foresee
His own funereal destiny;
His wretchedness, and his resistance,
And his sad unallied existence:
To which his Spirit may oppose
Itself—and equal to all woes,

And a firm will, and a deep sense,
Which even in torture can descry
    Its own concenter'd recompense,
Triumphant where it dares defy,
And making Death a Victory.

We'll Go No More A-Roving

So we'll go no more a-roving
So late into the night,
Though the heart be still as loving,
And the moon be still as bright.

For the sword outwears its sheath,
And the soul wears out the breast,
And the heart must pause to breathe,
And love itself have a rest.

Though the night was made for loving,
And the day returns too soon,
Yet we'll go no more a-roving
By the light of the moon.

from CHILDE HAROLD: CANTO THE THIRD[4]

I

Is thy face like thy mother's, my fair child![5]
Ada! sole daughter of my house and heart?
When last I saw thy young blue eyes they smil'd,
    And then we parted—not as now we part,
    But with a hope.—
              Awaking with a start,
    The waters heave around me; and on high
    The winds lift up their voices: I depart,
    Whither I know not; but the hour's gone by,
When Albion's[6] lessening shores could grieve or
    glad mine eye.

II

Once more upon the waters! yet once more!
And the waves bound beneath me as a steed
That knows his rider. Welcome to their roar!
Swift be their guidance, wheresoe'er it lead!
Though the strain'd mast should quiver as a reed,
And the rent canvas fluttering strew the gale,
Still must I on; for I am as a weed,
Flung from the rock, on Ocean's foam to sail
Where'er the surge may sweep, or tempest's breath
    prevail.

---

[4] Byron published the first two cantos in 1812. Canto the Third was written in May and June of 1816. Childe (an archaic title once given to the eldest son of a nobleman) Harold takes the same journey that Byron had just taken. It is hard to distinguish the pilgrim of the poem from Byron himself.

[5] Byron's daughter Ada was born in December, 1815 and he had not seen her since she was five weeks old.

[6] Albion is a poetically archaic name for England.

Sarah Josepha Hale

(1788–1879)

Sarah Josepha Hale (née Buell) was an American poet and novelist, famous for her popular children's poem "Mary's Lamb." She also helped Thanksgiving become a national holiday through petitioning President Abraham Lincoln and was the first woman editor of a magazine. She married David Hale in 1813 and they had five children. Her husband died in 1822 and Hale started on her literary career as a widow trying to support her family. She edited the *Ladies' Magazine* from 1828 to 1837 and then *Godey's Lady's Book* from 1837 to 1877. She edited a volume of poetry by women writers called *The Ladies Wreath* in 1837. Her celebrated poem "Mary's Lamb" was published in her *Poems for Our Children* (1830).

Mary's Lamb[1]

Mary had a little lamb,
Its fleece was white as snow;
And everywhere that Mary went,
The lamb was sure to go.

He followed her to school one day—
That was against the rule;
It made the children laugh and play,
To see a lamb at school.

---

[1] This poem is based on a real event from Hale's childhood.

So the teacher turned him out,
But still he lingered near,
And waited patiently about,
Till Mary did appear.

Then he ran to her, and laid
His head upon her arm,
As if he said, "I'm not afraid—
You'll keep me from all harm."

"What makes the lamb love Mary so?"
The eager children cry.
"Oh, Mary loves the lamb, you know,"
The teacher did reply.

Percy Bysshe Shelley

(1792–1822)

Percy Bysshe Shelley was one of the most prominent Romantic poets. Some of his best lyrics include "Ode to the West Wind," "To a Skylark" and "The Cloud. The heir to estates from his grandfather and the son of a member of Parliament, Shelley was a rebellious radical. He got expelled from Oxford in 1811 for refusing to admit that he wrote *The Necessity of Atheism*. Shelley saw himself as a reformer. Shelley wanted to free humanity and "purify life of its misery and evil." He believed in personal freedom, including freedom in love, and he brought these ideas to his poetry. He was influenced by the philosophical writing of William Godwin and fell in love with his daughter, Mary Wollstonecraft Godwin, who later became the famed author of *Frankenstein*. His first major poem was *Queen Mab* (1813) a utopian epic expressing his progressive political beliefs. Shelley eloped to France with Mary while married to Harriet Westbrook, and when she committed suicide in 1816, he and Mary were married and moved to Italy in 1818. Away from England, Shelley focused more on his poetry and composed some of his best poetry, including the lyric drama *Prometheus Unbound* in 1820. Shelley was lost at sea at age thirty, presumed drowned, while sailing off the coast of Italy during a storm leaving his last poem, *The Triumph of Life*, unfinished.

To the Moon: A Fragment

I

Art thou pale for weariness
    Of climbing Heaven, and gazing on the earth,
Wandering companionless
    Among the stars that have a different birth,—
      And ever changing, like a joyless eye
      That finds no object worth its constancy?

II

Thou chosen sister of the Spirit,
    That gazes on thee till in thee it pities . . .

Ode to the West Wind

I

O wild West Wind, thou breath of Autumn's being,
Thou, from whose unseen presence the leaves dead
Are driven, like ghosts from an enchanter fleeing,

Yellow, and black, and pale, and hectic red,
Pestilence-stricken multitudes: O thou,
Who chariotest to their dark wintry bed

The winged seeds, where they lie cold and low,
Each like a corpse within its grave, until
Thine azure sister of the Spring shall blow

Her clarion o'er the dreaming earth, and fill
(Driving sweet buds like flocks to feed in air)
With living hues and odors plain and hill:

Wild Spirit, which art moving everywhere;
Destroyer and preserver; hear, oh, hear!

II

Thou on whose stream, 'mid the steep sky's
    commotion,
Loose clouds like earth's decaying leaves are shed,
Shook from the tangled boughs of Heaven and Ocean,

Angels of rain and lightning: there are spread
On the blue surface of thine aery surge,
Like the bright hair uplifted from the head

Of some fierce Maenad, even from the dim verge
Of the horizon to the zenith's height,
The locks of the approaching storm. Thou dirge

Of the dying year, to which this closing night
Will be the dome of a vast sepulchre,
Vaulted with all thy congregated might

Of vapors, from whose solid atmosphere
Black rain, and fire, and hail will burst: oh, hear!

III

Thou who didst waken from his summer dreams
The blue Mediterranean, where he lay,
Lulled by the coil of his crystalline streams,

Beside a pumice isle in Baiae's bay,
And saw in sleep old palaces and towers
Quivering within the wave's intenser day,

All overgrown with azure moss and flowers
So sweet, the sense faints picturing them! Thou
For whose path the Atlantic's level powers

Cleave themselves into chasms, while far below
The sea-blooms and the oozy woods which wear
The sapless foliage of the ocean, know

Thy voice, and suddenly grow gray with fear,
And tremble and despoil themselves: oh, hear!

IV

If I were a dead leaf thou mightest bear;
If I were a swift cloud to fly with thee;
A wave to pant beneath thy power, and share

The impulse of thy strength, only less free
Than thou, O uncontrollable! If even
I were as in my boyhood, and could be

The comrade of thy wanderings over Heaven,
As then, when to outstrip thy skiey speed
Scarce seemed a vision; I would ne'er have striven

As thus with thee in prayer in my sore need.
Oh, lift me as a wave, a leaf, a cloud!
I fall upon the thorns of life! I bleed!

A heavy weight of hours has chained and bowed
One too like thee: tameless, and swift, and proud.

V

Make me thy lyre, even as the forest is:
What if my leaves are falling like its own!
The tumult of thy mighty harmonies

Will take from both a deep, autumnal tone,
Sweet though in sadness. Be thou, Spirit fierce,
My spirit! Be thou me, impetuous one!

Drive my dead thoughts over the universe
Like withered leaves to quicken a new birth!
And, by the incantation of this verse,

Scatter, as from an unextinguished hearth
Ashes and sparks, my words among mankind!
Be through my lips to unawakened earth

The trumpet of a prophecy! O Wind,
If Winter comes, can Spring be far behind?

Ozymandias

I met a traveller from an antique land
Who said: 'Two vast and trunkless legs of stone
Stand in the desert. Near them, on the sand,
Half sunk, a shattered visage lies, whose frown,
And wrinkled lip, and sneer of cold command,
Tell that its sculptor well those passions read
Which yet survive, stamped on these lifeless things,
The hand that mocked them and the heart that fed.
And on the pedestal these words appear—
"My name is Ozymandias,[1] king of kings:
Look on my works, ye Mighty, and despair!"
Nothing beside remains. Round the decay
Of that colossal wreck, boundless and bare
The lone and level sands stretch far away.'

Song to the Men of England

Men of England, wherefore plough
For the lords who lay ye low?
Wherefore weave with toil and care
The rich robes your tyrants wear?

Wherefore feed and clothe and save,
From the cradle to the grave,
Those ungrateful drones who would
Drain your sweat—nay, drink your blood?

---

[1] Greek name for the Egyptian king Rameses II.

Wherefore, Bees of England, forge
Many a weapon, chain, and scourge,
That these stingless drones may spoil
The forced produce of your toil?

Have ye leisure, comfort, calm,
Shelter, food, love's gentle balm?
Or what is it ye buy so dear
With your pain and with your fear?

The seed ye sow another reaps;
The wealth ye find another keeps;
The robes ye weave another wears;
The arms ye forge another bears.

Sow seed,—but let no tyrant reap;
Find wealth,—let no imposter heap;
Weave robes,—let not the idle wear;
Forge arms, in your defence to bear.

Shrink to your cellars, holes, and cells;
In halls ye deck another dwells.
Why shake the chains ye wrought? Ye see
The steel ye tempered glance on ye.

With plough and spade and hoe and loom,
Trace your grave, and build your tomb,
And weave your winding-sheet, till fair
England be your sepulchre!

Good-Night

Good-night? ah! no; the hour is ill
Which severs those it should unite;
Let us remain together still,
Then it will be good night.

How can I call the lone night good,
Though thy sweet wishes wing its flight?
Be it not said, thought, understood—
Then it will be—good night.

To hearts which near each other move
From evening close to morning light,
The night is good; because, my love,
They never say good-night.

JOHN CLARE

(1793–1864)

JOHN CLARE was an English Romantic poet famous for
his nature poems. During his day he was known as
"the Northamptonshire Peasant Poet." The son of a
poor farm worker, Clare was born in Northampton in
1793 and had little formal education or contact with
books. He was inspired by folk ballads and James
Thompson's poem *The Seasons*. His first book, *Poems
Descriptive of Rural Life and Scenery*, was printed by John
Keats's publishers in 1820. The book was successful and
Clare became known as a "ploughman poet" in the vein
of Robert Burns. However, his subsequent volumes,
including *The Shepherd's Calendar* (1827) and *The Rural
Muse* (1835), did not sell well. In 1837, the increasingly
delusional Clare was confined to an asylum where he
briefly escaped after four years. He was declared insane
and spent the rest of his years in another asylum where
he wrote much of his best poetry. Clare's work has
inspired many poets, including the contemporary American poet John Ashbury.

I AM![1]

I am! yet what I am none cares or knows,
My friends forsake me like a memory lost;

---

[1] This poem was written while John Clare was committed to the
Northampton County Asylum. It is believed that these are the
last lines he ever wrote.

I am the self-consumer of my woes,
They rise and vanish in oblivious host,
Like shades in love and death's oblivion lost;
And yet I am! and live with shadows tost

Into the nothingness of scorn and noise,
Into the living sea of waking dreams,
Where there is neither sense of life nor joys,
But the vast shipwreck of my life's esteems;
And e'en the dearest—that I loved the best—
Are strange—nay, rather stranger than the rest.

I long for scenes where man has never trod;
A place where woman never smil'd or wept;
There to abide with my creator, God,
And sleep as I in childhood sweetly slept:
Untroubling and untroubled where I lie;
The grass below—above the vaulted sky.

ALL NATURE HAS A FEELING

All nature has a feeling: woods, fields, brooks
Are life eternal: and in silence they
Speak happiness beyond the reach of books;
There's nothing mortal in them; their decay
Is the green life of change; to pass away
And come again in blooms revivified.
Its birth was heaven, eternal it its stay,
And with the sun and moon shall still abide
Beneath their day and night and heaven wide.

Felicia Dorothea Hemans

(1793–1835)

Felicia Dorothea Hemans (née Browne) was an English poet and hymnist who was admired by Percy Shelley. "Casabianca," based on a tragedy that occurred when Hemans was five years old, is one of her most remembered poems. Modern poets have written responses to "Casabianca," including the 20th century poet Elizabeth Bishop's short poem of the same title.

Felicia married Captain Hemans in 1812 and they had five sons. Hemans wrote prolifically while her children were young. She was influenced by the poetry of Lord Byron who praised her poem "The Restoration of the Works of Art to Italy" (1816) to his publisher. In 1818 Captain Hemans left for Rome and never saw his wife again, although they did correspond through letters. It seems that they had a private agreement to separate. Hemans was left with five children all less than six years old and she had to support herself by living with her mother in Wales. Hemans wrote many poems showing her love for Wales, most strongly in her collection *Welsh Melodies*.

Dirge

Calm on the bosom of thy God,
    Fair spirit, rest thee now!
E'en while with ours thy footsteps trod,
    His seal was on thy brow.

Dust, to its narrow house beneath!
    Soul, to its place on high!
They that have seen thy look in death
    No more may fear to die.

Casabianca[1]

The boy stood on the burning deck
  Whence all but he had fled;
The flame that lit the battle's wreck
  Shone round him o'er the dead.

Yet beautiful and bright he stood,
  As born to rule the storm;
A creature of heroic blood,
  A proud, though childlike form.

---

[1] This poem is also known by its first line, "The Boy Stood on the Burning Deck." It commemerates the death of the thirteen-year-old boy, Casabianca, who was the son of the Admiral of the ship the "Orient." During the Battle of the Nile, the ship caught fire and Casabianca stayed at his post even after all the gun posts had been abandoned. He died in the explosion that occurred when the flames reached the gun powder. The battle took place on August 1, 1798. Admiral Nelson ended up defeating the French fleet in Aboukir Bay.

The flames roll'd on . . . he would not go
  Without his father's word;
That father, faint in death below,
  His voice no longer heard.

He call'd aloud . . . "Say, father,say
  If yet my task is done!"
He knew not that the chieftain lay
  Unconscious of his son.

"Speak, father!" once again he cried
  "If I may yet be gone!"
And but the booming shots replied,
  And fast the flames roll'd on.

Upon his brow he felt their breath,
  And in his waving hair,
And looked from that lone post of death,
  In still yet brave despair;

And shouted but one more aloud,
  "My father, must I stay?"
While o'er him fast, through sail and shroud
  The wreathing fires made way,

They wrapt the ship in splendour wild,
  They caught the flag on high,
And stream'd above the gallant child,
  Like banners in the sky.

There came a burst of thunder sound . . .
  The boy-oh! where was he?
Ask of the winds that far around
  With fragments strewed the sea.

With mast, and helm, and pennon fair,
  That well had borne their part;
But the noblest thing which perished there
  Was that young faithful heart.[2]

---

[2] In 1946, the renowned 20th century American poet Elizabeth
  Bishop wrote a response to Hemans's poem, also titling it
  "Casabianca."

WILLIAM CULLEN BRYANT

(1794–1878)

WILLIAM CULLEN BRYANT was a renowned American Romantic poet, lawyer, and journalist. He is considered by some to be the greatest American poet of the early 19th century and is famous for his nature poetry. Born in Cummington, Massachusetts, his parents were both from prominent families whose ancestors came to America on the *Mayflower*. Bryant was introduced to poetry in his father's large library and developed his love of the New England countryside as a boy. At the age of seventeen he wrote "Thanatopsis," which is considered one of his best poems. He wrote a good deal of his most celebrated poems before the age of twenty-one. Bryant was educated at Williams College and then went on to study law. He worked as a lawyer in Massachusetts until 1825 when he married and moved to New York City. He became a journalist for the *New York Review* and then the *New York Evening Post*. He eventually became associate editor of the latter paper and from 1829 until his death he was editor-in-chief and part owner. Bryant also became known as a defender of human rights and a proponent of free trade, abolition, and other reforms. Some of Bryant's best known poems are "To a Waterfowl," "Green River," "Inscription for the Entrance to a Wood," and "The Yellow Violet."

To a Waterfowl[1]

Whither, 'midst falling dew,
While glow the heavens with the last steps of day,
Far, through their rosy depths, dost thou pursue
Thy solitary way?

Vainly the fowler's eye
Might mark thy distant flight to do thee wrong,
As, darkly painted on the crimson sky,
Thy figure floats along.

Seek'st thou the plashy brink
Of weedy lake, or marge of river wide,
Or where the rocking billows rise and sink
On the chafed ocean side?

There is a Power whose care
Teaches thy way along that pathless coast,—
The desert and illimitable air,—
Lone wandering, but not lost.

All day thy wings have fann'd
At that far height, the cold thin atmosphere:
Yet stoop not, weary, to the welcome land,
Though the dark night is near.

---

[1] The speaker of "To a Waterfowl" becomes inspired watching a
water bird flying high in the sky. It turns into a moment that
reveals mysterious divine guidance.

And soon that toil shall end,
Soon shalt thou find a summer home, and rest,
And scream among thy fellows; reed shall bend
Soon o'er thy sheltered nest.

Thou'rt gone, the abyss of heaven
Hath swallowed up thy form; yet, on my heart
Deeply hath sunk the lesson thou hast given,
And shall not soon depart.

He, who, from zone to zone,
Guides through the boundless sky thy certain flight,
In the long way that I must tread alone,
Will lead my steps aright.

The Murdered Traveler

When spring, to woods and wastes around,
Brought bloom and joy again,
The murdered traveller's bones were found,
Far down a narrow glen.

The fragrant birch, above him, hung
Her tassels in the sky;
And many a vernal blossom sprung,
And nodded careless by.

The red-bird warbled, as he wrought
His hanging nest o'erhead,
And fearless, near the fatal spot,
Her young the partridge led.

But there was weeping far away,
And gentle eyes, for him,
With watching many an anxious day,
Were sorrowful and dim.

They little knew, who loved him so,
The fearful death he met,
When shouting o'er the desert snow,
Unarmed, and hard beset;—

Nor how, when round the frosty pole
The northern dawn was red,
The mountain wolf and wild-cat stole
To banquet on the dead;

Nor how, when strangers found his bones,
They dressed the hasty bier,
And marked his grave with nameless stones,
Unmoistened by a tear.

But long they looked, and feared, and wept,
Within his distant home;
And dreamed, and started as they slept,
For joy that he was come.

So long they looked—but never spied
His welcome step again,
Nor knew the fearful death he died
Far down that narrow glen.

MUTATION

They talk of short-lived pleasure—be it so—
Pain dies as quickly: stem, hard-featured pain
Expires, and lets her weary prisoner go.
The fiercest agonies have shortest reign;
And after dreams of horror, comes again
The welcome morning with its rays of peace.
Oblivion, softly wiping out the stain,
Makes the strong secret pangs of shame to cease.
Remorse is virtue's root; its fair increase
Are fruits of innocence and blessedness:
Thus joy, o'erborne and bound, doth still release
His young limbs from the chains that round him press.
Weep not that the world changes—did it keep
A stable changeless state, 'twere cause indeed to weep.

JOHN KEATS

(1795–1821)

JOHN KEATS, BORN IN LONDON, was one of the foremost
Romantic poets. He was very influenced by the poetry
of John Milton, Edmund Spenser, and William Shakespeare and often felt himself under the shadow of their
work. His poetry was not appreciated during his lifetime
and he received critical attacks on his work, more because
of politics than for artistic reasons. By the middle of the
19th century, Keats's poetry became fully appreciated. He
produced his best work toward the end of his short life,
including a series of odes that are among the most beloved
in English poetry.

His father was a hostler or stableman, who fell off a
horse and died when Keats was a young child. His
mother remarried but then left her second husband and
moved into her mother's house with her four children.
His mother then died of tuberculosis and his grand-
mother appointed guardians who removed Keats from
school, where he was developing a love for literature, to
apprentice him to a surgeon. He then became a student
at a hospital while devoting time to studying literature.
Keats took care of his brother, Tom, until he too suc-
cumbed to tuberculosis. John moved in to his friend's
house and fell in love with his neighbor, Fanny Brawne.
The love affair was not a happy one.

Spenser's *The Faerie Queene* inspired his first poem,
"Imitation of Spenser." Keats became friends with the
poet and editor Leigh Hunt who published Keats's first
poem in 1816. His first book came out in 1817, *Poems*,

and it was not reviewed well. September 1818 to September 1819 is called the Great Year among Keats scholars because he was so productive and wrote his most celebrated poems including "Ode to Psyche," "Ode on a Grecian Urn," "Ode to a Nightingale," "Ode on Melancholy," and "To Autumn." Keats was also inspired by the young poet Thomas Chatterton, who was beloved among the Romantics for his brilliant and tragic life. Keats's poetry is characterized by elaborate vocabulary and sensual imagery. He also coined the term *negative capability*, which means to dwell in a place of uncertainty where multiple meanings are possible and fact and reason do not interfere with the authority of the imagination. Oscar Wilde famously wrote of Keats: "that godlike boy, the real Adonis of our age[. . .] In my heaven he walks eternally with Shakespeare and the Greeks."

To Autumn[1]

Season of mists and mellow fruitfulness,
    Close bosom-friend of the maturing sun;
Conspiring with him how to load and bless
    With fruit the vines that round the thatch-eves run;
To bend with apples the moss'd cottage-trees,

---

[1] Keats wrote this poem after walking through meadows in Winchester, England on an autumn evening in 1819. In the poem Keats describes the tastes, sights, and sounds of fall.

And fill all fruit with ripeness to the core;
    To swell the gourd, and plump the hazel shells
With a sweet kernel; to set budding more,
And still more, later flowers for the bees,
Until they think warm days will never cease,
    For Summer has o'er-brimm'd their clammy cells.

Who hath not seen thee oft amid thy store?
    Sometimes whoever seeks abroad may find
Thee sitting careless on a granary floor,
    Thy hair soft-lifted by the winnowing wind;
Or on a half-reap'd furrow sound asleep,
    Drows'd with the fume of poppies, while thy hook
      Spares the next swath and all its twined flowers:
And sometimes like a gleaner thou dost keep
    Steady thy laden head across a brook;
    Or by a cyder-press, with patient look,
      Thou watchest the last oozings hours by hours.

Where are the songs of Spring? Ay, where are they?
    Think not of them, thou hast thy music too,—
While barred clouds bloom the soft-dying day,
    And touch the stubble-plains with rosy hue;
Then in a wailful choir the small gnats mourn
    Among the river sallows, borne aloft
      Or sinking as the light wind lives or dies;
And full-grown lambs loud bleat from hilly bourn;
    Hedge-crickets sing; and now with treble soft
    The red-breast whistles from a garden-croft;
      And gathering swallows twitter in the skies.

La Belle Dame Sans Merci[2]

I

O, WHAT can ail thee, wretched wight,
    Alone and palely loitering;
The sedge is wither'd from the lake,
    And no birds sing.

II

Ah, what can ail thee, wretched wight,
    So haggard and so woe-begone?
The squirrel's granary is full,
    And the harvest's done.

III

I see a lily on thy brow,
    With anguish moist and fever dew;
And on thy cheek a fading rose
    Fast withereth too.

IV

I met a lady in the meads
    Full beautiful, a faery's child;
Her hair was long, her foot was light,
    And her eyes were wild.

---

[2] Keats took the title from a poem by Alain Chartier (the court poet of Charles VI and Charles VII of France), however Keats's ballad has nothing to do with the Chartier poem. He draws on the imagery of a medieval world of enchantment and knight-errantry to write about a love that is not a blessing but a curse—the lover is reduced to a wastrel. In its simplest narrative the poem is about a man deceived by a woman's love.

V

I set her on my pacing steed,
    And nothing else saw all day long;
For sideways would she lean, and sing
    A faery's song.

VI

I made a garland for her head,
    And bracelets too, and fragrant zone;
She look'd at me as she did love,
    And made sweet moan.

VII

She found me roots of relish sweet,
    And honey wild, and manna dew;
And sure in language strange she said,
    I love thee true.

VIII

She took me to her elfin grot,
    And there she gaz'd and sighed deep,
And there I shut her wild sad eyes—
    So kiss'd to sleep.

IX

And there we slumber'd on the moss,
    And there I dream'd, ah woe betide,
The latest dream I ever dream'd
    On the cold hill side.

X

I saw pale kings, and princes too,
    Pale warriors, death-pale were they all;
Who cry'd—"La belle Dame sans merci
    Hath thee in thrall!"

XI

I saw their starv'd lips in the gloam
    With horrid warning gaped wide,
And I awoke, and found me here
    On the cold hill side.

XII

And this is why I sojourn here
    Alone and palely loitering,
Though the sedge is wither'd from the lake,
    And no birds sing.

ODE TO A NIGHTINGALE[3]

My heart aches, and a drowsy numbness pains
    My sense, as though of hemlock I had drunk,
Or emptied some dull opiate to the drains
    One minute past, and Lethe-wards had sunk:
'Tis not through envy of thy happy lot,
    But being too happy in thine happiness,—

---

[3] This poem was written in May, 1819, in a garden of an Inn in
   Hampstead. In it Keats explores negative capability, nature, and
   mortality. The poem was in part inspired by the 1818 death of
   his brother from tuberculosis.

That thou, light-winged Dryad[4] of the trees
    In some melodious plot
Of beechen green, and shadows numberless,
    Singest of summer in full-throated ease.

O, for a draught of vintage! that hath been
    Cool'd a long age in the deep-delved earth,
Tasting of Flora and the country green,
    Dance, and Provençal song, and sunburnt mirth!
O for a beaker full of the warm South,
    Full of the true, the blushful Hippocrene,[5]
        With beaded bubbles winking at the brim,
            And purple-stained mouth;
    That I might drink, and leave the world unseen,
        And with thee fade away into the forest dim:

Fade far away, dissolve, and quite forget
    What thou among the leaves hast never known,
The weariness, the fever, and the fret
    Here, where men sit and hear each other groan;
Where palsy shakes a few, sad, last gray hairs,
    Where youth grows pale, and spectre-thin, and dies;
        Where but to think is to be full of sorrow
            And leaden-eyed despairs,
    Where Beauty cannot keep her lustrous eyes,
        Or new Love pine at them beyond to-morrow.

Away! away! for I will fly to thee,
    Not charioted by Bacchus and his pards,

---

[4] A wood nymph.
[5] In Greek mythology, Hippocrene is a fountain on Mount Helicon, Greece, sacred to the Muses and regarded as a source of poetic inspiration.

But on the viewless wings of Poesy,
    Though the dull brain perplexes and retards:
Already with thee! tender is the night,
    And haply the Queen-Moon is on her throne,
        Cluster'd around by all her starry Fays;
          But here there is no light,
    Save what from heaven is with the breezes blown
        Through verdurous glooms and winding
            mossy ways.

I cannot see what flowers are at my feet,
    Nor what soft incense hangs upon the boughs,
But, in embalmed darkness, guess each sweet
    Wherewith the seasonable month endows
The grass, the thicket, and the fruit-tree wild;
    White hawthorn, and the pastoral eglantine;
        Fast fading violets cover'd up in leaves;
          And mid-May's eldest child,
    The coming musk-rose, full of dewy wine,
        The murmurous haunt of flies on summer eves.

Darkling I listen; and, for many a time
    I have been half in love with easeful Death,
Call'd him soft names in many a mused rhyme,
    To take into the air my quiet breath;
        Now more than ever seems it rich to die,
    To cease upon the midnight with no pain,
        While thou art pouring forth thy soul abroad
          In such an ecstasy!
    Still wouldst thou sing, and I have ears in vain—
        To thy high requiem become a sod.

Thou wast not born for death, immortal Bird!
    No hungry generations tread thee down;
The voice I hear this passing night was heard
    In ancient days by emperor and clown:
Perhaps the self-same song that found a path
        Through the sad heart of Ruth, when, sick for home,
           She stood in tears amid the alien corn;
           The same that oft-times hath
    Charm'd magic casements, opening on the foam
        Of perilous seas, in faery lands forlorn.

Forlorn! the very word is like a bell
    To toll me back from thee to my sole self!
Adieu! the fancy cannot cheat so well
    As she is fam'd to do, deceiving elf.
Adieu! adieu! thy plaintive anthem fades
    Past the near meadows, over the still stream,
        Up the hill-side; and now 'tis buried deep
        In the next valley-glades:
    Was it a vision, or a waking dream?
        Fled is that music:—Do I wake or sleep?

ODE ON MELANCHOLY[6]

NO, no, go not to Lethe,[7] neither twist
    Wolf's-bane, tight-rooted, for its poisonous wine;
Nor suffer thy pale forehead to be kiss'd
    By nightshade, ruby grape of Proserpine;[8]

---

[6] This is a fragmentary poem that seems to have no proper beginning—Keats discarded the first stanza. In the poem he expresses
his experience of the alternating emotions of joy and pain.

[7] In Greek myth, the river of forgetfulness or oblivion that runs
through Hades.

[8] This refers to the red berries of the deadly nightshade plant.

Make not your rosary of yew-berries,
Nor let the beetle, nor the death-moth be
Your mournful Psyche,[9] nor the downy owl
A partner in your sorrow's mysteries;
For shade to shade will come too drowsily,
And drown the wakeful anguish of the soul.

But when the melancholy fit shall fall
Sudden from heaven like a weeping cloud,
That fosters the droop-headed flowers all,
And hides the green hill in an April shroud;
Then glut thy sorrow on a morning rose,
Or on the rainbow of the salt sand-wave,
Or on the wealth of globed peonies;
Or if thy mistress some rich anger shows,
Emprison her soft hand, and let her rave,
And feed deep, deep upon her peerless eyes.

She dwells with Beauty—Beauty that must die;
And Joy, whose hand is ever at his lips
Bidding adieu; and aching Pleasure nigh,
Turning to poison while the bee-mouth sips:
Ay, in the very temple of Delight
Veil'd Melancholy has her sovran shrine,
Though seen of none save him whose
strenuous tongue
Can burst Joy's grape against his palate fine;
His soul shalt taste the sadness of her might,
And be among her cloudy trophies hung.

---

[9] In Greek myth, Psyche was a young woman who loved and was
loved by Eros and was united with him after Aphrodite's jealousy
was overcome. She then became the personification of the soul.

ODE ON A GRECIAN URN[10]

THOU still unravish'd bride of quietness,
~~Thou foster-child of silence and slow time,~~
Sylvan[11] historian, who canst thus express
    A flowery tale more sweetly than our rhyme:
What leaf-fring'd legend haunts about thy shape
      Of deities or mortals, or of both,
          In Tempe or the dales of Arcady?[12]
    What men or gods are these? What maidens loth?
What mad pursuit? What struggle to escape?
          What pipes and timbrels?[13] What wild
            ecstasy?

---

[10] This poem was first published in January, 1820, and it is believed that it was inspired by seeking a Greek exhibit that included the Elgin Marbles at the British Museum. "Ode on a Grecian Urn" explores Keats's idea of negative capability—there is much uncertainty in the poem including who the figures on the urn are, what they are doing, and where they are going. It is unclear whether the poem promotes the beauty and truth of the urn or if there is anything of real worth in the ephemeral world. The sight of an ancient object leads the poet to meditate on ancient life and worship as well as the more abstract concept of the relation of art to life. Keats writes of the difference between life, which is real but decays, and art, which because it isn't real gains permanent beauty and the heightened vividness of imagination. The famous last two lines keep the poem a mystery with the speaker both admiring and criticizing the figures on the urn who are forever passionate but will never get to consummate their moment.

[11] Wooded.

[12] Arcady or Arcadia was an ancient, isolated, bucolic location in Greece, which represents paradise.

[13] Similar to a tambourine.

Heard melodies are sweet, but those unheard
    Are sweeter; therefore, ye soft pipes, play on;
Not to the sensual ear, but, more endear'd,
    Pipe to the spirit ditties of no tone:
Fair youth, beneath the trees, thou canst not leave
    Thy song, nor ever can those trees be bare;
        Bold Lover, never, never canst thou kiss,
Though winning near the goal yet, do not grieve;
    She cannot fade, though thou hast not thy bliss,
        For ever wilt thou love, and she be fair!

Ah, happy, happy boughs! that cannot shed
    Your leaves, nor ever bid the Spring adieu;
And, happy melodist, unwearied,
    For ever piping songs for ever new;
More happy love! more happy, happy love!
    For ever warm and still to be enjoy'd,
        For ever panting, and for ever young;
All breathing human passion far above,
    That leaves a heart high-sorrowful and cloy'd,
        A burning forehead, and a parching tongue.

Who are these coming to the sacrifice?
    To what green altar, O mysterious priest,
Lead'st thou that heifer lowing at the skies,
    And all her silken flanks with garlands drest?
What little town by river or sea shore,
    Or mountain-built with peaceful citadel,
        Is emptied of this folk, this pious morn?
And, little town, thy streets for evermore
    Will silent be; and not a soul to tell
        Why thou art desolate, can e'er return.

O Attic shape! Fair attitude! with brede
    Of marble men and maidens overwrought,
With forest branches and the trodden weed;
    Thou, silent form, dost tease us out of thought
As doth eternity: Cold Pastoral!
    When old age shall this generation waste,
        Thou shalt remain, in midst of other woe
Than ours, a friend to man, to whom thou say'st,
      "Beauty is truth, truth beauty,p—that is all
        Ye know on earth, and all ye need to know."

Sojourner Truth

(1797–1883)

Sojourner Truth was an African American abolition-ist, women's rights advocate, preacher, and lecturer. A slave in New York until she was freed through the New York Gradual Abolition Act in 1827, she was born Isabella Baumfree and her first language was Dutch. In 1843 she believed that God called on her to travel, or sojourn, around the country and preach the truth of the Bible. Thus, she believed that God named her Sojourner Truth. Sojourner Truth wrote a memoir of her life that was published in 1850. Her most famous speech, which became known as "Ain't I a Woman?" was put into poetic form and recited at the Ohio Women's Rights Convention in 1851. Before she became known as an abolitionist she was a follower of "The Kingdom of Matthias," an evangelical cult. In 1870, Truth tried to get land grants from the government to give to former slaves. She pursued the project for seven years without success. She met with President Ulysses S. Grant while in Washington, D.C. Truth kept speaking around the country about abolition, women's rights, prison reform, and against capital punishment. Some of her supporters were William Lloyd Garrison, Lucretia Mott, and Susan B. Anthony. Truth died at her home in Battle Creek, Michigan. Her last words were "Be a follower of the Lord Jesus."

Ain't I a Woman?

That man over there say
        a woman needs to be helped into carriages
and lifted over ditches
        and to have the best place everywhere.
Nobody ever helped me into carriages
    or over mud puddles
        or gives me a best place. . .
And ain't I a woman?
        Look at me
Look at my arm!
        I have plowed and planted
and gathered into barns
        and no man could head me. . .
And ain't I a woman?
    I could work as much
and eat as much as a man—
    when I could get to it—
and bear the lash as well
    and ain't I a woman?
I have born 13 children
        and seen most all sold into slavery
and when I cried out a mother's grief
        none but Jesus heard me. . .
and ain't I a woman?
        that little man in black there say
a woman can't have as much rights as a man
        cause Christ wasn't a woman
Where did your Christ come from?
        From God and a woman!
Man had nothing to do with him!

If the first woman God ever made
was strong enough to turn the world
          upside down, all alone
together women ought to be able to turn it
          rightside up again.

Thomas Hood

(1798–1845)

Thomas Hood was an English poet and editor best known for his comic verse. Born in London, his father was a bookseller, and Thomas became apprenticed to an engraver in 1818. He became an editor at the *London Magazine* in 1821 and was then introduced to the literary figures of the day such as the poets Charles Lamb, Henry Cary, and John Clare. Hood took over the *Comic Annual*, a publication that caricatured current events. He also published his poetry in various magazines and became a regular contributor to the *Athenaeum*, which was started in 1828.

Hood was renowned for his wit and his use of puns. Although he was known for his humorous poetry, he also wrote serious verse which showed his empathy for the poor and solemn views of the condition of workers in society, such as in "The Song of the Shirt" (1843), "Song of the Labourer," and "The Bridge of Sighs." Hood himself suffered from poverty and ill-health. His compassionate poetry served as models for many writers concerned with social protest. Another concern during Hood's time was grave-digging and the selling of corpses. He wrote about this in a number of poems. In one poem he writes: "Don't go to weep upon my grave,/And think that there I be./They haven't left an atom there/Of my anatomie." His other noted poems include "The Dream of Eugene Aram" (1829) and "The Plea of the Midsummer Fairies."

GOLD!

Gold! Gold! Gold! Gold!
Bright and yellow, hard and cold
Molten, graven, hammered and rolled,
Heavy to get and light to hold,
Hoarded, bartered, bought and sold,
Stolen, borrowed, squandered, doled,
Spurned by young, but hung by old
To the verge of a church yard mold;
Price of many a crime untold.
Gold! Gold! Gold! Gold!
Good or bad a thousand fold!
How widely it agencies vary,
To save—to ruin—to curse—to bless—
As even its minted coins express:
Now stamped with the image of Queen Bess,
And now of a bloody Mary.

from THE SONG OF THE SHIRT

With fingers weary and worn,
With eyelids heavy and red,
A woman sat, in unwomanly rags,
Plying her needle and thread
Stitch! stitch! stitch!
In poverty, hunger, and dirt,
And still with a voice of dolorous pitch
She sang the "Song of the Shirt."

"Work! work! work!
While the cock is crowing aloof!
And work   work   work,
Till the stars shine through the roof!
It's Oh! to be a slave
Along with the barbarous Turk,
Where woman has never a soul to save,
If this is Christian work!

"Work   work   work
Till the brain begins to swim;
Work   work   work
Till the eyes are heavy and dim!
Seam, and gusset, and band,
Band, and gusset, and seam,
Till over the buttons I fall asleep,
And sew them on in a dream!

"Oh, Men, with Sisters dear!
Oh, Men, with Mothers and Wives!
It is not linen you're wearing out,
But human creatures' lives!
Stitch   stitch   stitch,
In poverty, hunger, and dirt,
Sewing at once with a double thread,
A Shroud as well as a Shirt.

But why do I talk of Death?
That Phantom of grisly bone,
I hardly fear its terrible shape,
It seems so like my own
It seems so like my own,
Because of the fasts I keep;
Oh, God! that bread should be so dear,
And flesh and blood so cheap!

"Work   work   work!
My Labour never flags;
And what are its wages? A bed of straw,
A crust of bread   and rags.
That shatter'd roof   and this naked floor
A table   a broken chair
And a wall so blank, my shadow I thank
For sometimes falling there!

"Work   work   work!
From weary chime to chime,
Work   work   work!
As prisoners work for crime!
Band, and gusset, and seam,
Seam, and gusset, and band,
Till the heart is sick, and the brain benumb'd,
As well as the weary hand.

WILLIAM BARNES

(1801–1886)

WILLIAM BARNES was an English poet, clergyman, teacher, philologist, and folklorist who influenced many Victorian poets, especially Thomas Hardy, and is most remembered for his use of dialect. Like Hardy, Barnes was born in Dorset. His father was a farmer. Barnes studied theology at Cambridge, becoming a clergyman in 1848. For the first part of his career Barnes was a teacher and then became a rector in 1862 until his death. He started publishing poetry in 1833 in local newspapers. Renowned for his three volume series of *Poems of Rural Life in the Dorset Dialect* published in 1844, 1857, and 1862, the work was compiled in a single volume in 1879. "The Wife A-Lost" and "My Orcha'd in Linden Lea" (set to music by Ralph Vaughan Williams) are considered among his best poetry, which showed much fondness for the people and countryside of Dorset. His lyric poems use warm, unadorned language to celebrate nature, life, and love. His 1854 work, *Philological Grammar*, showed Barnes great affection for the study of languages (he knew over 70 languages including Hebrew, Persian, and Hindustani). Barnes wrote more than eight hundred poems during his lifetime. In addition, Barnes printed over two hundred engravings.

Hardy wrote his poem "The Last Signal" for Barnes after his death and published Barnes's selected poetry in 1908. Barnes also greatly influenced the Victorian poets Alfred, Lord Tennyson and Gerard Manley Hopkins. Unfortunately, because Barnes wrote in dialect that is considered less accessible than modern English, he is not read widely today.

ZUMMER AN' WINTER

When I led by zummer streams
The pride o' Lea, as naighbours thought her,
While the zun, wi' evenen beams,
Did cast our sheades athirt the water;
Winds a-blowen,
Streams a-flowen,
Skies a-glowen,
Tokens ov my jay zoo fleeten,
Heightened it, that happy meeten.

Then, when maid an' man took pleaces,
Gay in winter's Chris'mas dances,
Showen in their merry feaces
Kindly smiles an' glisnen glances;
Stars a-winken,
Day a-shrinken,
Sheades a-zinken,
Brought anew the happy meeten,
That did meake the night too fleeten.

SARA COLERIDGE

(1802–1850)

SARA COLERIDGE was an English poet and translator, and the only daughter of Samuel Taylor Coleridge. She wrote verse for her children, which was very popular. Born in Keswick, she and her family lived with Robert Southey and his wife (Mrs. Coleridge's sister) and the Wordsworths were their neighbors. Southey guided her education and she read Greek and Latin classics, as well as learning French, German, Italian and Spanish. In 1822 Sara published *Account of the Abipones*, a translation of three books by Martin Dobrizhoffer, a Roman Catholic missionary. After being engaged for seven years, Sara married her cousin, Henry Nelson Coleridge. They lived in a cottage in Hampstead with their two children. In 1834 Coleridge published her *Pretty Lessons in Verse for Good Children; with some Lessons in Latin in Easy Rhyme*. The book was very successful. She then published *Phantasmion, a Fairy Tale* (1837), her longest original work. The songs in the volume were praised by the poet and critic Leigh Hunt and other literary figures. When her husband died in 1843, Coleridge had the job of editing her father's work. She also added some of her own writing. Shortly before she died she wrote an autobiography for her daughter. It was published in 1873 along with some of her letters as *Memoirs and Letters of Sara Coleridge*. Sara Coleridge is known more for her writings about her father and the other Lake Poets than for her own poetry. However, since more of her poetry has recently been published, this could change.

O Sleep, My Babe

O sleep, my babe, hear not the rippling wave,
Nor feel the breeze that round thee ling'ring strays
    To drink thy balmy breath,
    And sigh one long farewell.

Soon shall it mourn above thy wat'ry bed,
And whisper to me, on the wave-beat shore,
    Deep murm'ring in reproach,
    Thy sad untimely fate.

Ere those dear eyes had open'd on the light,
In vain to plead, thy coming life was sold,
    O waken'd but to sleep,
    Whence it can wake no more!

A thousand and a thousand silken leaves
The tufted beech unfolds in early spring,
    All clad in tenderest green,
    All of the self-same shape:

A thousand infant faces, soft and sweet,
Each year sends forth, yet every mother views
    Her last not least beloved
    Like its dear self alone.

No musing mind hath ever yet foreshaped
The face to-morrow's sun shall first reveal,
    No heart hath e'er conceived
    What love that face will bring.

O sleep, my babe, nor heed how mourns the gale
To part with thy soft locks and fragrant breath,
    As when it deeply sighs
      O'er autumn's latest bloom.

Letitia Elizabeth Landon

(1802–1838)

L ETITIA ELIZABETH LANDON (commonly known by her initials L. E. L.) was a successful English poet and novelist who died at the age of thirty-six from an accidental overdose of prussic acid. Born in London, Landon began contributing to the *Literary Gazette* in the 1820s and eventually became co-editor of the paper. Her first book of poetry was published in 1820, *The Fate of Adelaide*. She published other books of poetry, which soon received acclaim. She also wrote several novels, and *Ethel Churchill* (1837) is considered her strongest piece of fiction. Landon's writing is characterized by romantic sentiment and gentle melancholy. In 1838 she married George Maclean, governor of the Gold Coast (now Ghana), and their brief, unhappy marriage was ended within a few months by her death from prussic acid. Various editions of her *Poetical Works* have been published since her death.

SECRETS

Life has dark secrets; and the hearts are few
That treasure not some sorrow from the world—
A sorrow silent, gloomy, and unknown,
Yet coloring the future from the past.
We see the eye subdued, the practiced smile,
The word well weighed before it pass the lip,
And know not of the misery within:
Yet there it works incessantly, and fears
The time to come; for time is terrible,
Avenging, and betraying.

THE POWER OF WORDS

'Tis a strange mystery, the power of words!
Life is in them, and death. A word can send
The crimson color hurrying to the cheek.
Hurrying with many meanings; or can turn
The current cold and deadly to the heart.
Anger and fear are in them; grief and joy
Are on their sound; yet slight, impalpable:—
A word is but a breath of passing air.

RALPH WALDO EMERSON

(1803–1882)

RALPH WALDO EMERSON was an American writer, poet, philosopher, essayist, and lecturer, as well as one of the leading spokesmen for Transcendentalism. He was known as the "Sage of Concord" and is a major figure in American literature. His father, William Emerson, was the minister of the First Unitarian Church in Boston. At Harvard he began writing his renowned *Journal* and he went on to Harvard Divinity School where he was licensed to preach. In 1829 he became pastor of the Old North Church in Boston and married Ellen Tucker. Her death from tuberculosis in 1831 affected Emerson deeply. In 1832 he retired from his position as pastor because of differences in religious views with his congregation. He went to Europe where he met Thomas Carlyle and the two became close friends. He also met Coleridge and Wordsworth and they prompted Emerson's interest in transcendental thought. Transcendentalism emphasized the intuitive and spiritual above the empirical and material and stressed the role of divinity in nature.

Emerson settled in Concord, Massachusetts in 1834 and remarried a year later to Lydia Jackson. During the 1830s Emerson began his career as a writer and lecturer, and in 1836 he anonymously published his essay *Nature* that set forth the principles of Transcendentalism such as a belief in the mystical unity of nature. In 1838 he spoke at the Harvard divinity school and said one could only find redemption in one's soul. In 1840 Emerson and others started *The Dial*, a magazine that promoted the ideas of Transcendentalism. Henry David Thoreau contributed to the magazine and became Emerson's most famous disciple. He lived with Emerson for two years. In 1847 Emerson published his first poetry collection. He always regarded himself as essentially a poet. Some of his most noted poems are "Threnody," "Brahma," "The Problem," "The Rhodora," and the "The Concord Hymn." However, it was his lectures that made Emerson famous and he profoundly influenced American thought through his lecturing and writing.

BERRYING

"May be true what I had heard,
Earth's a howling wilderness
Truculent with fraud and force,"
Said I, strolling through the pastures,
And along the riverside.
Caught among the blackberry vines,
Feeding on the Ethiops sweet,
Pleasant fancies overtook me:
I said, "What influence me preferred
Elect to dreams thus beautiful?"
The vines replied, "And didst thou deem
No wisdom to our berries went?"

Concord Hymn

By the rude bridge that arched the flood,
Their flag to April's breeze unfurled,
Here once the embattled farmers stood,
And fired the shot heard round the world.

The foe long since in silence slept;
Alike the conqueror silent sleeps;
And Time the ruined bridge has swept
Down the dark stream which seaward creeps.

On this green bank, by this soft stream,
We set to-day a votive stone;
That memory may their deed redeem,
When, like our sires, our sons are gone.

Spirit, that made those heroes dare
To die, or leave their childern free,
Bid Time and Nature gently spare
The shaft we raise to them and thee.

THE SNOW-STORM

Announced by all the trumpets of the sky,
Arrives the snow, and, driving o'er the fields,
Seems nowhere to alight: the whited air
Hides hills and woods, the river, and the heaven,
And veils the farmhouse at the garden's end.
The sled and traveler stopped, the courier's feet
Delayed, all friends shut out, the housemates sit
Around the radiant fireplace, enclosed
In a tumultuous privacy of storm.

Come see the northwind's masonry.
Out of an unseen quarry evermore
Furnished with tile, the fierce artificer
Curves his white bastions with projected roof
Round every wayward stake, or tree, or door.
Speeding, the myriad-handed, his wild work
So fanciful, so savage, nought cares he
For number or proportion. Mockingly,
On coop or kennel he hangs Parian wreaths;
A swan-like form invests the hidden thorn;
Fills up the farmer's lane from wall to wall,
Maugre the farmer sighs; and, at the gate,
A tapering turret overtops the work.
And when his hours are numbered, and the world
Is all his own, retiring, as he were not,
Leaves, when the sun appears, astonished Art
To mimic in slow structures, stone by stone,
Built in an age, the mad wind's night-work,
The frolic architecture of snow.

WILLIAM LLOYD GARRISON

(1805–1879)

WILLIAM LLOYD GARRISON was an American poet, reformer, journalist, and leading abolitionist who helped shape the anti-slavery movement when he co-founded the American Anti-Slavery Society and published the newspaper *The Liberator* from 1831 to 1865. Born in Newburyport, Massachusetts, Garrison became an outspoken writer and editor for the abolition movement and other social causes. Garrison had a particular interest in poetry, which he considered to be "naturally and instinctively on the side of liberty." He used his poetry as a tool to raise emotional sentiment for the anti-slavery movement. He collected his works in 1843 in the book *Sonnets and Other Poems*.

Freedom for the Mind

High walls and huge the body may confine,
And iron grates obstruct the prisoner's gaze,
And massive bolts may baffle his design,
And vigilant keepers watch his devious ways:
Yet scorns the immortal mind this base control!
No chains can bind it, and no cell enclose:
Swifter than light, it flies from pole to pole,
And, in a flash, from earth to heaven it goes!
It leaps from mount to mount—from vale to vale
It wanders, plucking honeyed fruits and flowers;
It visits home, to hear the fireside tale,
Or in sweet converse pass the joyous hours.
'T is up before the sun, roaming afar,
And, in its watches, wearies every star!

ELIZABETH BARRETT BROWNING

(1806–1861)

ELIZABETH BARRETT BROWNING was of the most respected women English poets of the Victorian era. In fact, Browning is considered to be one of the greatest female poets writing in English. Her mostly lyric poetry champions the suffering and oppressed. She first published a book of poems and a translation of Aeschylus's *Prometheus Bound* anonymously, and then went on to publish *The Seraphim and Other Poems* in 1838 under her own name. Although she was an invalid who was fearful of meeting strangers she became known in literary circles. Elizabeth's literary success drew the attention of the poet Robert Browning and they met and fell in love. She married Browning secretly in 1846 despite her poor health and in defiance of her tyrannical father. They lived in Florence at Casa Guidi for their fifteen year marriage. One of Elizabeth's most renowned works is *Sonnets from the Portuguese*, a collection of love sonnets that she disguised as a translation. Published in 1850, she wrote the poems during her courtship with Robert Browning. In 1857 she published *Aurora Leigh*, a blank-verse novel about Margaret Fuller, a journalist, critic, and women's rights activist. It was a hugely ambitious work and a popular success.

To George Sand, A Desire[1]

Thou large-brained woman and large-hearted man,
Self-called George Sand! whose soul, amid the lions
Of thy tumultuous senses, moans defiance
And answers roar for roar, as spirits can:
I would some mild miraculous thunder ran
Above the applauded circus, in appliance
Of thine own nobler nature's strength and science,
Drawing two pinions, white as wings of swan,
From thy strong shoulders, to amaze the place
With holier light ! that thou to woman's claim
And man's, mightst join beside the angel's grace
Of a pure genius sanctified from blame
Till child and maiden pressed to thine embrace
To kiss upon thy lips a stainless fame.

---

[1] Browning was an admirer of the French Romantic novelist and
feminist, George Sand (a pseudonym for Armandine Aurore
Lucille Dupin), who was also known for her numerous love
affairs, including one with Frédéric Chopin.

The Poet and the Bird

Said a people to a poet—'Go out from among us
  straightway!
While we are thinking earthly things, thou singest of
  divine.
There's a little fair brown nightingale, who, sitting in
  the gateways
Makes fitter music to our ears than any song of thine!'

The poet went out weeping—the nightingale ceased
  chanting;
'Now, wherefore, O thou nightingale, is all thy
  sweetness done?'
I cannot sing my earthly things, the heavenly poet
  wanting,
Whose highest harmony includes the lowest under
  sun.'

The poet went out weeping,—and died abroad, bereft
  there—
The bird flew to his grave and died, amid a thousand
  wails:—
And, when I last came by the place, I swear the music
  left there
Was only of the poet's song, and not the nightingale's.

from THE PORTUGUESE SONNETS[2]
XLIII 43. "How do I love thee?
Let me count the ways"

How do I love thee? Let me count the ways.
I love thee to the depth and breadth and height
My soul can reach, when feeling out of sight
For the ends of Being and ideal Grace.
I love thee to the level of everyday's
Most quiet need, by sun and candlelight.
I love thee freely, as men strive for Right;
I love thee purely, as they turn from Praise.
I love thee with the passion put to use
In my old griefs, and with my childhood's faith.
I love thee with a love I seemed to lose
With my lost saints,—I love thee with the breath,
Smiles, tears, of all my life!—and, if God choose,
I shall but love thee better after death.

---

[2] This sonnet is one of Elizabeth Barrett Browning's most popular
poems and its opening lines are some of the most famous in
English poetry.

HENRY WADSWORTH LONGFELLOW

(1807–1882)

HENRY WADSWORTH LONGFELLOW was one of the most famous and popular American poets of the 19th century as well as an educator and linguist. Longfellow was one of the Fireside Poets (also called the Schoolroom or Household Poets) along with Oliver Wendell Holmes, James Russell Lowell, John Greenleaf Whittier, and William Cullen Bryant. The Fireside Poets were the first group of American poets to rival British poets in popularity in both England and the United States. They adhered to poetic conventions of form, meter, and rhyme, which made their poetry particularly suitable for memorization and recitation in schools and at home, where it was a source of entertainment for families gathered around the fire.

At the peak of his career, Longfellow's popularity was as great as Alfred, Lord Tennyson's in England and America. He is most remembered for his long narrative poems including *Evangeline* (1847), *The Song of Hiawatha* (1855), *The Courtship of Miles Standish* (1858), and *Tales of a Wayside Inn* (1863), which included "Paul Revere's Ride." His best-known shorter poems include "The Village Blacksmith," "Excelsior," "The Wreck of the Hesperus," "A Psalm of Life," and "A Cross of Snow." Longfellow was not involved in the religious and social issues of his time except for abolition. His poetry was idealistic, patriotic, sentimental, and moralizing. While these characteristics made Longfellow popular in the 19th century, they led to a decline in his reputation in the

20th century. He also used unusual rhythms to evoke the American past. A noted translator, in 1867 he published a translation of Dante's *Divine Comedy*. Longfellow was the first American poet to be honored with a bust in Westminster Abbey's Poet's Corner.

Paul Revere's Ride

Listen, my children, and you shall hear
Of the midnight ride of Paul Revere,
On the eighteenth of April, in Seventy-five;
Hardly a man is now alive
Who remembers that famous day and year.

He said to his friend, "If the British march
By land or sea from the town to-night,
Hang a lantern aloft in the belfry arch
Of the North Church tower as a signal light,—
One, if by land, and two, if by sea;
And I on the opposite shore will be,
Ready to ride and spread the alarm
Through every Middlesex village and farm,
For the country folk to be up and to arm."
Then he said, "Good night!" and with muffled oar
Silently rowed to the Charlestown shore,
Just as the moon rose over the bay,
Where swinging wide at her moorings lay
The Somerset, British man-of-war;
A phantom ship, with each mast and spar
Across the moon like a prison bar,
And a huge black hulk, that was magnified
By its own reflection in the tide.

Meanwhile, his friend, through alley and street,
Wanders and watches with eager ears,
Till in the silence around him he hears
The muster of men at the barrack door,
The sound of arms, and the tramp of feet,
And the measured tread of the grenadiers,
Marching down to their boats on the shore.

.   .   .

It was twelve by the village clock,
When he crossed the bridge into Medford town.
He heard the crowing of the cock,
And the barking of the farmer's dog,
And felt the damp of the river fog,
That rises after the sun goes down.

It was one by the village clock,
When he galloped into Lexington.
He saw the gilded weathercock
Swim in the moonlight as he passed,
And the meeting-house windows, blank and bare,
Gaze at him with a spectral glare,
As if they already stood aghast
At the bloody work they would look upon.

It was two by the village clock,
When he came to the bridge in Concord town.
He heard the bleating of the flock,
And the twitter of birds among the trees,
And felt the breath of the morning breeze

Blowing over the meadows brown.
And one was safe and asleep in his bed
Who at the bridge would be first to fall,
Who that day would be lying dead,
Pierced by a British musket-ball.

You know the rest. In the books you have read,
How the British Regulars fired and fled, —
How the farmers gave them ball for ball,
From behind each fence and farm-yard wall,
Chasing the red-coats down the lane,
Then crossing the fields to emerge again
Under the trees at the turn of the road,
And only pausing to fire and load.

So through the night rode Paul Revere;
And so through the night went his cry of alarm
To every Middlesex village and farm, —
A cry of defiance and not of fear,
A voice in the darkness, a knock at the door,
And a word that shall echo forevermore!
For, borne on the night-wind of the Past,
Through all our history, to the last,
In the hour of darkness and peril and need,
The people will waken and listen to hear
The hurrying hoof-beats of that steed,
And the midnight message of Paul Revere.

THE CROSS OF SNOW

In the long, sleepless watches of the night,
    A gentle face — the face of one long dead —
    Looks at me from the wall, where round its head
    The night-lamp casts a halo of pale light.
Here in this room she died; and soul more white
    Never through martyrdom of fire was led
    To its repose; nor can in books be read
    The legend of a life more benedight.
There is a mountain in the distant West
    That, sun-defying, in its deep ravines
    Displays a cross of snow upon its side.
Such is the cross I wear upon my breast
    These eighteen years, through all the changing
        scenes
    And seasons, changeless since the day she died.

JOHN GREENLEAF WHITTIER

(1807–1892)

JOHN GREENLEAF WHITTIER was an American poet, abolitionist, and reformer who was a member of the Fireside Poets. The Fireside Poets (also called the Schoolroom or Household Poets) included Oliver Wendell Holmes, James Russell Lowell, Henry Wadsworth Longfellow, and William Cullen Bryant. The Fireside Poets were the first group of American poets to rival British poets in popularity in both England and the United States. They adhered to poetic conventions of form, meter, and rhyme, which made their poetry particularly suitable for memorization and recitation in schools and at home, where it was a source of entertainment for families gathered around the fire.

Born on a farm near Haverhill, Massachusetts to poor Quaker parents, he had little formal education. When he was fourteen he discovered Robert Burns's poetry and began writing poems. The abolitionist William Lloyd Garrison published one of Whittier's poems in his paper, the *Newburyport Free Press*. Garrison encouraged him to continue his schooling, which Whittier did while having his poems published in local papers. He went on to edit various journals and in 1833 he published his ardent anti-slavery essay "Justice and Expediancy." His anti-slavery poems include "The Yankee Girl," "The Slavery-Ships," "The Hunters of Men," "Massachusetts to Virginia," and "Ichabod." He also wrote ballads and narrative poems that were popular and include ""John

Underhill," "Maud Muller," "Telling the Bees," "The Barefoot Boy," "Snow-Bound" and "My Psalm."

Ichabod

So fallen! so lost! the light withdrawn
Which once he wore!
The glory from his gray hairs gone
Forevermore!

Revile him not, the Tempter hath
A snare for all;
And pitying tears, not scorn and wrath,
Befit his fall!

Oh, dumb be passion's stormy rage,
When he who might
Have lighted up and led his age,
Falls back in night.

Scorn! would the angels laugh, to mark
A bright soul driven,
Fiend-goaded, down the endless dark,
From hope and heaven!

Let not the land once proud of him
Insult him now,
Nor brand with deeper shame his dim,
Dishonored brow.

But let its humbled sons, instead,
From sea to lake,
A long lament, as for the dead,
In sadness make.

Of all we loved and honored, naught
Save power remains;
A fallen angel's pride of thought,
Still strong in chains.

All else is gone; from those great eyes
The soul has fled:
When faith is lost, when honor dies,
The man is dead!

Then, pay the reverence of old days
To his dead fame;
Walk backward, with averted gaze,
And hide the shame!

EDWARD FITZGERALD

(1809–1883)

E DWARD FITZGERALD was an English poet, scholar, and translator who is famous for his translation of *The Rubaiyat of Omar Khayyam*. The translation was published anonymously in 1859 and was unnoticed until Dante Gabriel Rossetti helped make it famous. Revised editions came out in 1868, 1872, and 1879. Fitzgerald's *Rubaiyat* became one of the most popular poems in English although its popularity is now on the decline. It is actually an adaptation rather than a translation of the poem by the 11th century Persian poet Omar Khayyam. Fitzgerald's version retains the spirit of the original, which expresses a philosophy that a person should live life to the fullest. Probably the most famous stanza of the poem is "A Book of Verses underneath the Bough,/A Jug of Wine, a Loaf of Bread—and Thou/Beside me singing in the Wilderness—/O, Wilderness were Paradise enow!" Among Fitzgerald's other works are *Euphranor* (1851), a Platonic dialogue, and *Polonius* (1852), a collection of aphorisms.

from THE RUBAIYAT OF OMAR KHAYYAM

I

A book of Verses underneath the Bough,
A Jug of Wine, a Loaf of Bread—and Thou
    Beside me singing in the Wilderness—
O, Wilderness were Paradise enow!

Some for the Glories of This World; and some
Sigh for the Prophet's Paradise to come;
     Ah, take the Cash, and let the Credit go,
Nor heed the rumble of a distant Drum!

Look to the blowing Rose about us—'Lo,
Laughing,' she says, 'into the world I blow,
     At once the silken tassel of my Purse
Tear, and its Treasure on the Garden throw.'

And those who husbanded the Golden grain
And those who flung it to the winds like Rain
     Alike to no such aureate Earth are turn'd
As, buried once, Men want dug up again.

II

Think, in this batter'd Caravanserai
Whose Portals are alternate Night and Day,
     How Sultán after Sultán with his Pomp
Abode his destined Hour, and went his way.

They say the Lion and the Lizard keep
The Courts where Jamshyd gloried and drank deep:
     And Bahrám, that great Hunter—the wild Ass
Stamps o'er his Head, but cannot break his Sleep.

I sometimes think that never blows so red
The Rose as where some buried Caesar bled;
     That every Hyacinth the Garden wears
Dropt in her Lap from some once lovely Head.

And this reviving Herb whose tender Green
Fledges the River-Lip on which we lean—
    Ah, lean upon it lightly! for who knows
From what once lovely Lip it springs unseen!

Ah, my Beloved, fill the Cup that clears
TO-DAY of past Regrets and Future Fears:
    To-morrow!—Why, To-morrow I may be
Myself with Yesterday's Sev'n thousand Years.

For some we loved, the loveliest and the best
That from his Vintage rolling Time hath prest,
    Have drunk their Cup a Round or two before,
And one by one crept silently to rest.

And we, that now make merry in the Room
They left, and Summer dresses in new bloom,
    Ourselves must we beneath the Couch of Earth
Descend—ourselves to make a Couch—for whom?

Ah, make the most of what we yet may spend,
Before we too into the Dust descend;
    Dust unto Dust, and under Dust to lie,
Sans Wine, sans Song, sans Singer, and—sans End!

Oliver Wendell Holmes

(1809–1894)

Oliver Wendell Holmes was a practicing doctor who wrote witty essays, biographies, and novels as well as poetry. He was also a member of the Fireside Poets along with Henry Wadsworth Longfellow, John Greenleaf Whittier, James Russell Lowell, and William Cullen Bryant. Born in Cambridge Massachusetts, Holmes was from a distinguished New England family. He studied at Harvard Medical School and went to Paris for two years where he learned new approaches to medicine. From 1838 to 1840 Holmes taught anatomy at Dartmouth College. He married in 1840 and returned to practicing medicine. He also became a professor of anatomy and physiology at Harvard Medical School and later served as dean. He was noted for being an excellent teacher and lecturer. Among his best-known poems are "The Deacon's Masterpiece," "The Last Leaf," "The Chambered Nautilus," "My Aunt," "The Moral Bully," and "Brother Jonathan's Lament for Sister Caroline."

Old Ironsides[1]

Ay, tear her tattered ensign down!
Long has it waved on high,
And many an eye has danced to see
That banner in the sky;
Beneath it rung the battle shout,
And burst the cannon's roar;—
The meteor of the ocean air
Shall sweep the clouds no more!

Her deck, once red with heroes' blood,
Where knelt the vanquished foe,
When winds were hurrying o'er the flood
And waves were white below,
No more shall feel the victor's tread,
Or know the conquered knee;—
The harpies of the shore shall pluck
The eagle of the sea!

Oh, better that her shattered hulk
Should sink beneath the wave;
Her thunders shook the mighty deep,
And there should be her grave;

---

[1] Holmes tackled contemporary politics in this poem. The frigate *Constitution* (popularly called *Old Ironsides*) had a warm place in the American imagination for winning a famous sea battle against an English ship during the War of 1812. When Holmes heard that the Secretary of the Navy had recommended that the *Constitution* be taken apart, he immediately wrote this poem. "Old Ironsides" became a battle cry around the nation and the ship was rebuilt instead of being dismantled.

Nail to the mast her holy flag,
Set every threadbare sail,
And give her to the God of storms,—
The lightning of the gale!

THE CHAMBERED NAUTILUS[2]

This the ship of pearl, which, poets feign,
Sails the unshadowed main,—
The venturous bark that flings
On the sweet summer wind its purpled wings
In gulfs enchanted, where the Siren[3] sings,
And coral reefs lie bare,
Where the cold sea-maids rise to sun their streaming
    hair.

Its webs of living gauze no more unfurl;
Wrecked is the ship of pearl!
And every chambered cell,
Where its dim dreaming life was wont to dwell,
As the frail tenant shaped his growing shell,
Before thee lies revealed,—
Its irised ceiling rent, its sunless crypt unsealed!

---

[2] The chambered (or pearly) nautilus is a type of mollusk found in
   the Indian and Pacific oceans. It has a spiral, pearly-lined shell
   with air-filled chambers. As the nautilus grows it secretes larger
   chambers, sealing off the old ones. The animal lives in the
   largest and newest chamber of the spiral shell.

[3] In Greek mythology, there are three Sirens who were the daughters of the river god Achelous and were part human and part
   bird. In the *Odyssey*, the Sirens' enchanted voices could lure
   sailors to their deaths and so Odysseus had his crew fill their ears
   with wax to avoid temptation.

Year after year beheld the silent toil
That spread his lustrous coil;
Still, as the spiral grew,
He left the past year's dwelling for the new,
Stole with soft step its shining archway through,
Built up its idle door,
Stretched in his last-found home, and knew the old no
    more.

Thanks for the heavenly message brought by thee,
Child of the wandering sea,
Cast from her lap, forlorn!
From thy dead lips a clearer note is born
Than ever Triton[4] blew from wreathèd horn!
While on mine ear it rings,
Through the deep caves of thought I hear a voice that
    sings:—

Build thee more stately mansions, O my soul,
As the swift seasons roll!
Leave thy low-vaulted past!
Let each new temple, nobler than the last,
Shut thee from heaven with a dome more vast,
Till thou at length art free,
Leaving thine outgrown shell by life's unresting sea!

---

[4] Triton is a Greek god of the sea. The son of Poseidon, his upper
   body is human and his lower body is the tail of a fish. Subsequent legends spoke of multiple Tritons who rode the sea on
   horses and blew trumpets of conch shells.

EDGAR ALLAN POE

(1809–1849)

EDGAR ALLAN POE is a celebrated American short story writer, critic, and poet of the 19th century most known for his tales of psychological horror. He is considered one of the most original writers in American literature and is also known as the father of the detective story. Orphaned when he was three years old, he lived with his godfather, John Allan, who took Poe to Europe where he started his schooling. Upon returning the United States, he entered the University of Virginia in 1826. He was an adept scholar in classical and romance languages, but was forced to leave after only eight months because he was fighting with his godfather over his gambling debts. Poe published his first book, *Tamerlane and Other Poems* in 1827, and followed it with two more volumes of poetry, but none of these books attracted attention. In 1836 Poe married Virginia Clemm who was thirteen years old. They moved to New York City and then to Philadelphia and back to New York where he worked on the *Evening Mirror* and then edited and owned the *Broadway Journal*. It was Poe's 1845 publication *The Raven and Other Poems*, which won him international literary fame. Poe's wife died in 1847 and in 1849 he was about to get remarried when he became involved in a drinking binge in Baltimore and died a few days later.

Poe had a fascination with intense beauty, violent horror, and death. His sense of the world of dreams contributed to his greatness as a writer. Such compelling stories as "The Masque of the Red Death" and "The Fall of the House of Usher" involve the reader in a world that is at once beautiful and grotesque, real and fantastic. His poems, including "To Helen," "The Raven," "The City in the Sea," "The Bells," and "Annabel Lee," are rich with musical phrases, as well as sensuous and scary images. "The Murders in the Rue Morgue" and "The Purloined Letter" are two of his finest detective stories. Poe influenced such diverse authors as Algernon Swinburne, Alfred, Lord Tennyson, Fyodor Dostoyevsky, Sir Arthur Conan Doyle, and the French Symbolist poets.

The Raven[1]

Once upon a midnight dreary, while I pondered weak
  and weary,
Over many a quaint and curious volume of forgotten
  lore,
While I nodded, nearly napping, suddenly there came a
  tapping,
As of some one gently rapping, rapping at my chamber
  door.
"'Tis some visitor,' I muttered, 'tapping at my chamber
  door—
Only this, and nothing more.'

---

[1] First published on January 29, 1845 in the *New York Evening Mirror*, this narrative poem is noted for its musicality, stylized language, and macabre, supernatural atmosphere. It tells of the mysterious visit of a raven who speaks to a distraught lover and traces the lover's descent into insanity. Poe's most famous poem, its publication made him famous in his day and it remains one of the most recognized poems in English literature.

Ah, distinctly I remember it was in the bleak
    December,
And each separate dying ember wrought its ghost upon
    the floor.
Eagerly I wished the morrow;—vainly I had sought to
    borrow
From my books surcease of sorrow—sorrow for the
    lost Lenore—
For the rare and radiant maiden whom the angels
    named Lenore—
Nameless here for evermore.

And the silken sad uncertain rustling of each purple
    curtain
Thrilled me—filled me with fantastic terrors never felt
    before;
So that now, to still the beating of my heart, I stood
    repeating
''Tis some visitor entreating entrance at my chamber
    door—
Some late visitor entreating entrance at my chamber
    door;—
This it is, and nothing more,'

Presently my soul grew stronger; hesitating then no
    longer,
'Sir,' said I, 'or Madam, truly your forgiveness I
    implore;
But the fact is I was napping, and so gently you came
    rapping,

And so faintly you came tapping, tapping at my
    chamber door,
That I scarce was sure I heard you'—here I opened
    wide the door;—
Darkness there, and nothing more.

Deep into that darkness peering, long I stood there
    wondering, fearing,
Doubting, dreaming dreams no mortal ever dared to
    dream before
But the silence was unbroken, and the darkness gave no
    token,
And the only word there spoken was the whispered
    word, 'Lenore!'
This I whispered, and an echo murmured back the
    word, 'Lenore!'
Merely this and nothing more.

Back into the chamber turning, all my soul within me
    burning,
Soon again I heard a tapping somewhat louder than
    before.
'Surely,' said I, 'surely that is something at my window
    lattice;
Let me see then, what thereat is, and this mystery
    explore—
Let my heart be still a moment and this mystery
    explore;—
'Tis the wind and nothing more!'

Open here I flung the shutter, when, with many a flirt
    and flutter,

In there stepped a stately raven of the saintly days of
    yore.
Not the least obeisance made he; not a minute stopped
    or stayed he;
But, with mien of lord or lady, perched above my
    chamber door—
Perched upon a bust of Pallas just above my chamber
    door—
Perched, and sat, and nothing more.

Then this ebony bird beguiling my sad fancy into
    smiling,
By the grave and stern decorum of the countenance it
    wore,
'Though thy crest be shorn and shaven, thou,' I said,
    'art sure no craven.
Ghastly grim and ancient raven wandering from the
    nightly shore—
Tell me what thy lordly name is on the Night's
    Plutonian shore!'
Quoth the raven, 'Nevermore.'

Much I marvelled this ungainly fowl to hear discourse
    so plainly,
Though its answer little meaning—little relevancy
    bore;
For we cannot help agreeing that no living human being
Ever yet was blessed with seeing bird above his
    chamber door—
Bird or beast above the sculptured bust above his
    chamber door,
With such name as 'Nevermore.'

But the raven, sitting lonely on the placid bust, spoke
    only,
That one word, as if his soul in that one word he did
    outpour.
Nothing further then he uttered—not a feather then he
    fluttered—
Till I scarcely more than muttered 'Other friends have
    flown before—
On the morrow will he leave me, as my hopes have
    flown before.'
Then the bird said, 'Nevermore.'

Startled at the stillness broken by reply so aptly spoken,
'Doubtless,' said I, 'what it utters is its only stock and
    store,
Caught from some unhappy master whom unmerciful
    disaster
Followed fast and followed faster till his songs one
    burden bore—
Till the dirges of his hope that melancholy burden bore
Of "Never-nevermore."'

But the raven still beguiling all my sad soul into
    smiling,
Straight I wheeled a cushioned seat in front of bird and
    bust and door;
Then, upon the velvet sinking, I betook myself to
    linking
Fancy unto fancy, thinking what this ominous bird of
    yore—

What this grim, ungainly, gaunt, and ominous bird of
    yore
Meant in croaking 'Nevermore.'

This I sat engaged in guessing, but no syllable
    expressing
To the fowl whose fiery eyes now burned into my
    bosom's core;
This and more I sat divining, with my head at ease
    reclining
On the cushion's velvet lining that the lamp-light
    gloated o'er,
But whose velvet violet lining with the lamp-light
    gloating o'er,
She shall press, ah, nevermore!

Then, methought, the air grew denser, perfumed from
    an unseen censer
Swung by Seraphim whose foot-falls tinkled on the
    tufted floor.
'Wretch,' I cried, 'thy God hath lent thee—by these
    angels he has sent thee
Respite—respite and nepenthe from thy memories of
    Lenore!
Quaff, oh quaff this kind nepenthe, and forget this lost
    Lenore!'
Quoth the raven, 'Nevermore.'

'Prophet!' said I, 'thing of evil!—prophet still, if bird or
    devil!—
Whether tempter sent, or whether tempest tossed thee
    here ashore,

Desolate yet all undaunted, on this desert land
enchanted—
On this home by horror haunted—tell me truly, I
implore—
Is there—is there balm in Gilead?—tell me—tell me, I
implore!'
Quoth the raven, 'Nevermore.'

'Prophet!' said I, 'thing of evil!—prophet still, if bird or
devil!
By that Heaven that bends above us—by that God we
both adore—
Tell this soul with sorrow laden if, within the distant
Aidenn,
It shall clasp a sainted maiden whom the angels named
Lenore—
Clasp a rare and radiant maiden, whom the angels
named Lenore?'
Quoth the raven, 'Nevermore.'

'Be that word our sign of parting, bird or fiend!' I
shrieked upstarting—
'Get thee back into the tempest and the Night's
Plutonian shore!
Leave no black plume as a token of that lie thy soul
hath spoken!
Leave my loneliness unbroken!—quit the bust above
my door!
Take thy beak from out my heart, and take thy form
from off my door!'
Quoth the raven, 'Nevermore.'

And the raven, never flitting, still is sitting, still is
    sitting
On the pallid bust of Pallas just above my chamber
    door;
And his eyes have all the seeming of a demon's that is
    dreaming,
And the lamp-light o'er him streaming throws his
    shadow on the floor;
And my soul from out that shadow that lies floating on
    the floor
Shall be lifted—nevermore!

ANNABEL LEE[2]

It was many and many a year ago,
    In a kingdom by the sea,
  That a maiden there lived whom you may know
    By the name of ANNABEL LEE;
And this maiden she lived with no other thought
    Than to love and be loved by me.

I was a child and she was a child,
    In this kingdom by the sea;
But we loved with a love that was more than love—
    I and my Annabel Lee;
With a love that the winged seraphs of heaven
    Coveted her and me.

---

[2] This poem appeared in *The International Miscellany* in 1849.
  "Annabel Lee" is generally taken to represent Poe's young wife,
  Virginia Clemm, whose death left Poe heartbroken.

And this was the reason that, long ago,
 In this kingdom by the sea,
A wind blew out of a cloud, chilling
 My beautiful Annabel Lee;
So that her highborn kinsman came
 And bore her away from me,
To shut her up in a sepulchre
 In this kingdom by the sea.

The angels, not half so happy in heaven,
 Went envying her and me—
Yes!—that was the reason (as all men know,
 In this kingdom by the sea)
That the wind came out of the cloud by night,
 Chilling and killing my Annabel Lee.

But our love it was stronger by far than the love
 Of those who were older than we—
 Of many far wiser than we—
And neither the angels in heaven above,
 Nor the demons down under the sea,
Can ever dissever my soul from the soul
 Of the beautiful Annabel Lee.

For the moon never beams without bringing me
 dreams
 Of the beautiful Annabel Lee;
And the stars never rise but I feel the bright eyes
 Of the beautiful Annabel Lee;
And so, all the night-tide, I lie down by the side
Of my darling—my darling—my life and my bride,
 In the sepulchre there by the sea,
 In her tomb by the sounding sea.

Alfred, Lord Tennyson

(1809–1892)

ALFRED, LORD TENNYSON is often considered the most celebrated English poet of the Victorian era. He became poet laureate of the United Kingdom after William Wordsworth in 1850. Born in Somersby, Lincolnshire, his father was a clergyman who suffered from depression. Tennyson started writing poetry while young and imitated the style of Lord Byron. While at Cambridge he joined a literary club and in 1830 he published *Poems, Chiefly Lyrical.* Another volume, including "The Lotus-Eaters" and "The Lady of Shalott," was published in 1832. Much of Tennyson's poetry is influenced by classical literature and mythology, such as his well-known poem "Ulysses." His poem "In Memoriam A.H.H" has a unique stanza form and was very popular and influential. The famous line, "Nature, red in tooth and claw" comes from that poem. He wrote it after his close friend Arthur Hallam died. Hallam's death also inspired lyrics that later appeared in *Maud* (1855). *Poems* (1842), including "Ulysses," "Morte d'Arthur," and "Locksley Hall," followed. Among his subsequent works are "The Charge of the Light Brigade" (1855); *Idylls of the King* (1859), an Arthurian romance; and *Enoch Arden* (1864). Tennyson was also considered a spokesman for the educated English middle class. His poems often dealt with the difficulties of an age when traditional beliefs were being called into question by science and modern progress.

The Eagle: A Fragment

He clasps the crag with crooked hands;
Close to the sun in lonely lands,
Ringed with the azure world, he stands.

The wrinkled sea beneath him crawls;
He watches from his mountain walls,
And like a thunderbolt he falls.

Break, Break, Break[1]

Break, break, break
   On thy cold grey stones, O Sea!
And I would that my tongue could utter
   The thoughts that arise in me.

O well for the fisherman's boy,
   That he shouts with his sister at play!
O well for the sailor lad,
   That he sings in his boat on the bay!

And the stately ships go on
   To their haven under the hill;
But O for the touch of a vanished hand,
   And the sound of a voice that is still!

---

[1] Tennyson wrote this poem in memory of his friend Arthur Hallam who died in 1833. He wrote that he came up with the poem "in a Lincolnshire lane at five o'clock in the morning, between blossoming hedges."

Break, break, break
 At the foot of thy crags, O Sea!
But the tender grace of a day that is dead
 Will never come back to me.

from ULYSSES[2]

It little profits that an idle king,
By this still hearth, among these barren crags,
Matched with an aged wife, I mete and dole
Unequal laws unto a savage race,
That hoard, and sleep, and feed, and know not me.
I cannot rest from travel: I will drink
Life to the lees: all times I have enjoyed
Greatly, have suffered greatly, both with those
That loved me, and alone; on shore, and when
Through scudding drifts the rainy Hyades
Vexed the dim sea: I am become a name;
For always roaming with a hungry heart
Much have I seen and known; cities of men
And manners, climates, councils, governments,
Myself not least, but honoured of them all;
And drunk delight of battle with my peers,
Far on the ringing plains of windy Troy.
I am a part of all that I have met;

---

[2] The conceit of this poem is that Ulysses (or Odysseus) is now an
 old man settled in Ithaca. His adventures long over, Ulysses is a
 bored king and contemplates going to sea again with his
 companions.

Yet all experience is an arch wherethrough
Gleams that untravelled world, whose margin fades
For ever and for ever when I move.
How dull it is to pause, to make an end,
To rust unburnished, not to shine in use!
As though to breathe were life. Life piled on life
Were all too little, and of one to me
Little remains: but every hour is saved
From that eternal silence, something more,
A bringer of new things; and vile it were
For some three suns to store and hoard myself,
And this grey spirit yearning in desire
To follow knowledge like a sinking star,
Beyond the utmost bound of human thought.

from THE LADY OF SHALOTT

PART I

On either side the river lie
Long fields of barley and of rye,
That clothe the wold and meet the sky;
And through the field the road runs by
To many-towered Camelot;
And up and down the people go,
Gazing where the lilies blow
Round an island there below,
The island of Shalott.

Willows whiten, aspens quiver,
Little breezes dusk and shiver
Through the wave that runs for ever
By the island in the river
Flowing down to Camelot.
Four grey walls, and four grey towers,
Overlook a space of flowers,
And the silent isle imbowers
The Lady of Shalott.

By the margin, willow-veiled,
Slide the heavy barges trailed
By slow horses; and unhailed
The shallop flitteth silken-sailed
Skimming down to Camelot:
But who hath seen her wave her hand?
Or at the casement seen her stand?
Or is she known in all the land,
The Lady of Shalott?

Only reapers, reaping early
In among the bearded barley,
Hear a song that echoes cheerly
From the river winding clearly,
Down to towered Camelot:
And by the moon the reaper weary,
Piling sheaves in uplands airy,
Listening, whispers "'Tis the fairy
Lady of Shalott."

ROBERT BROWNING

(1812–1889)

ROBERT BROWNING was an English Victorian poet and playwright. Born in Camberwell, England, he was raised in a family with intellectual and literary interests (they had a library of 6,000 books) and he had a notably broad education. As a child, Browning loved poetry and he wrote a book of poetry at age twelve. By fourteen he was fluent in French, Greek, Italian, and Latin. He was influenced by the Romantic poets, in particular by Percy Bysshe Shelley. At sixteen he went to University College in London but only stayed for a year. His first published poem, *Pauline*, appeared anonymously in 1833. In 1834 Browning went to Italy and it eventually became his second home. In 1837 he started writing for the stage and produced eight verse plays in nine years. *Pippa Passes*, a narrative poem, was published in 1841, and it was published again with other poems in *Bells and Pomegranates* (1846). Browning secretly married the poet Elizabeth Barrett Browning in 1846 and they lived in Italy for fifteen years. They had a very successful marriage. After Elizabeth's death he returned to England and wrote what some critics consider his masterwork, *The Ring and the Book* (1868–1869), a four-volume poem that reveals how a murder is perceived differently by various people. After this work was published Browning was celebrated as a great poet.

Many of Browning's poems are written as dramatic monologues, such as his renowned "Porphyria's Lover" and "My Last Duchess." This was the ideal medium for Browning's poetic talent. His verses paint psychological portraits that are often ironic and usually optimistic. He experimented with diction and rhythm, which made his poetry more modern in style than some of his peers.

PORPHYRIA'S LOVER[1]

The rain set early in to-night,
The sullen wind was soon awake,
It tore the elm-tops down for spite,
And did its worst to vex the lake:
I listened with heart fit to break.
When glided in Porphyria;[2] straight
She shut the cold out and the storm,
And kneeled and made the cheerless grate[3]
Blaze up, and all the cottage warm;
Which done, she rose, and from her form
Withdrew the dripping cloak and shawl,
And laid her soiled gloves by, untied
Her hat and let the damp hair fall,
And, last, she sat down by my side
And called me. When no voice replied,
She put my arm about her waist,
And made her smooth white shoulder bare,

---

[1] This poem was often published together with the poem "Johannes Agricola in Meditation" and as a pair they were usually titled "Madhouse Cells."

[2] Porphyria comes from the Greek word for purple and the word "porphyry," often used by poets, means a purple stone similar to marble.

[3] Fireplace.

And all her yellow hair displaced,
And, stooping, made my cheek lie there,
And spread, o'er all, her yellow hair,
Murmuring how she loved me—she
Too weak, for all her heart's endeavour,
To set its struggling passion free
From pride, and vainer ties dissever,
And give herself to me for ever.
But passion sometimes would prevail,
Nor could to-night's gay feast restrain
A sudden thought of one so pale
For love of her, and all in vain:
So, she was come through wind and rain.
Be sure I looked up at her eyes
Happy and proud; at last I knew
Porphyria worshipped me; surprise
Made my heart swell, and still it grew
While I debated what to do.
That moment she was mine, mine, fair,
Perfectly pure and good: I found
A thing to do, and all her hair
In one long yellow string I wound
Three times her little throat around,
And strangled her. No pain felt she;
I am quite sure she felt no pain.
As a shut bud that holds a bee,
I warily oped her lids:[4] again
Laughed the blue eyes without a stain.
And I untightened next the tress
About her neck; her cheek once more
Blushed bright beneath my burning kiss:

---

[4] Carefully opened her eyelids.

I propped her head up as before,
Only, this time my shoulder bore
Her head, which droops upon it still:
The smiling rosy little head,
So glad it has its utmost will,
That all it scorned at once is fled,
And I, its love, am gained instead!
Porphyria's love: she guessed not how
Her darling one wish would be heard.
And thus we sit together now,
And all night long we have not stirred,
And yet God has not said a word!

PIPPA'S SONG[5]

The year's at the spring,
And day's at the morn;
Morning's at seven;
The hill-side's dew-pearl'd;
The lark's on the wing;
The snail's on the thorn;
God's in His heaven—
All's right with the world!

---

[5] "Pippa's Song" is from Browning's verse play *Pippa's Passing*. Its
last two lines ("God's in His Heaven—/All's right with the
world) are especially quoted. Aldous Huxley parodied them in
Brave New World, making up the slogan "Ford's in his flivver, all's
right with the world!" (A flivver is a Ford Model T, and in Huxley's dystopian novel, Henry Ford has been deified and the
flivver becomes a stand-in for heaven.)

Life in a Love[6]

Escape me?
Never—
Beloved!
While I am I, and you are you,
So long as the world contains us both,
Me the loving and you the loth
While the one eludes, must the other pursue.
My life is a fault at last, I fear:
It seems too much like a fate, indeed!
Though I do my best I shall scarce succeed.
But what if I fail of my purpose here?
It is but to keep the nerves at strain,
To dry one's eyes and laugh at a fall,
And, baffled, get up and begin again,—
So the chace takes up one's life, that's all.
While, look but once from your farthest bound
At me so deep in the dust and dark,
No sooner the old hope goes to ground
Than a new one, straight to the self-same mark,
I shape me—
Ever
Removed!

---

[6] First published in *Men and Women* in 1855.

EDWARD LEAR

(1812–1888)

Edward Lear was an English poet, artist, and illustrator known for his nonsense verse, especially his limericks, a form that he made popular. Born in a suburb of London, he was the twentieth child of his parents and was raised by his sister Anne who was twenty-one years older than Edward. When he was fifteen they left the family home and lived together. Lear started working seriously as an illustrator and his first publication was *Illustrations of the Family of Psittacidae, or Parrots* (1830), which was compared favorably to James Audubon, the noted ornithologist and painter. Lear published *A Book of Nonsense*, a volume of limericks, in 1846. The book went through three different editions and helped popularize the form (Lear's limericks were nonsensical and had no punch line). In 1865 he published *The History of the Seven Families of the Lake Pipple-Popple* and in 1867 his most famous piece, *The Owl and the Pussy-cat*, which he wrote for the children of his patron Edward Stanley, Earl of Derby. Lear wrote many other nonsense books and they were very successful. His humorous work is characterized by an ease of verbal invention and a joy in the sound of both real and imaginary sounds.

The Owl and the Pussy-Cat

The Owl and the Pussy-Cat went to sea
    In a beautiful pea-green boat,
They took some honey, and plenty of money,
    Wrapped up in a five pound-note.
The Owl looked up to the stars above,
    And sang to a small guitar,
'O lovely Pussy! O Pussy, my love,
    What a beautiful Pussy you are,
        You are,
        You are!
    What a beautiful Pussy you are.'

Pussy said to the Owl, 'You elegant fowl,
    How charmingly sweet you sing.
O let us be married, too long have we tarried,
    But what shall we do for a ring?'
They sailed away for a year and a day,
    To the land where the Bong-tree grows,
And there in the wood a Piggy-wig stood,
    With a ring in the end of his nose,
        His nose,
        His nose!
    With a ring in the end of his nose.

'Dear Pig, are you willing, to sell for one shilling
    Your ring?' Said the Piggy, 'I will.'
So they took it away, and were married next day,
    By the Turkey who lives on the hill.

They dined on mince, and slices of quince,
    Which they ate with a runcible spoon;[1]
And hand in hand, on the edge of the sand,
    They danced by the light of the moon,
        The moon,
        The moon!
    They danced by the light of the moon.

---

[1] "Runcible spoon" is a nonsense term coined by Lear. The term
has become known as a fork-like spoon with a cutting edge. In
other poems Lear references a "runcible hat" and a "runcible
cat." The phrase "runcible spoon" is now found in most English
dictionaries.

CHARLOTTE BRONTË

(1816–1855)

CHARLOTTE BRONTE was a renowned English novelist and poet most known for her classic novel *Jane Eyre.* Charlotte was the oldest daughter of an Anglican clergyman who lived in the parsonage at Haworth, West Riding, Yorkshire. Her siblings were Emily, Anne, and Patrick, and when their mother died they were left much to themselves. They began to write about imaginary worlds they created. In 1831, Charlotte was sent to Miss Wooler's school at Roe Head and she became a teacher there in 1835. Three years later she returned home where she found that the family was in financial trouble. Patrick, a talented poet and painter on whom the family was depending, had lost three jobs and his health was ailing because of his alcoholism and opium addiction. Charlotte discovered Emily's poetry in 1845 and Anne then revealed hers, so the three sisters self–published a collection of poetry under the pseudonyms Currer, Ellis, and Acton Bell. Charlotte's novel *Jane Eyre* was accepted for publication in 1847 and met with great success for its portrayal of a woman in conflict with her natural desires and social condition in her love for her Byronic employer. The novel gave new truthfulness to Victorian fiction. During the same year, Emily's novel *Wuthering Heights* and Anne's novel *Agnes Grey* were published as a set. The identity of the sisters as authors was unknown, even to their publishers, until 1849, when Charlotte published *Shirley* and their authorship was made public. However the family was already struck by tragedy as

Patrick had died in September 1848 and Emily died of tuberculosis in December 1848. Then Anne died of tuberculosis in May 1849. Charlotte began making trips to London where she was an important literary figure. She married in 1853 but died after only a year of marriage. Charlotte Brontë was the most professional of the sisters and consciously set out to achieve financial success from literature. *Jane Eyre* is ranked among the greatest English novels.

Life

Life, believe, is not a dream
So dark as sages say;
Oft a little morning rain
Foretells a pleasant day.
Sometimes there are clouds of gloom,
But these are transient all;
If the shower will make the roses bloom,
O why lament its fall?
Rapidly, merrily,
Life's sunny hours flit by,
Gratefully, cheerily
Enjoy them as they fly!
What though Death at times steps in,
And calls our Best away?
What though sorrow seems to win,
O'er hope, a heavy sway?
Yet Hope again elastic springs,
Unconquered, though she fell;
Still buoyant are her golden wings,

Still strong to bear us well.
Manfully, fearlessly,
The day of trial bear,
For gloriously, victoriously,
Can courage quell despair!

ON THE DEATH OF ANNE BRONTË[1]

There's little joy in life for me,
And little terror in the grave;
I've lived the parting hour to see
Of one I would have died to save.

Calmly to watch the failing breath,
Wishing each sigh might be the last;
Longing to see the shade of death
O'er those belovèd features cast.

The cloud, the stillness that must part
The darling of my life from me ;
And then to thank God from my heart,
To thank Him well and fervently;

Although I knew that we had lost
The hope and glory of our life;
And now, benighted, tempest-tossed,
Must bear alone the weary strife.

---

[1] Charlotte's younger sister, Anne, died of tuberculosis in 1849.

Patrick Branwell Brontë

(1817–1848)

Patrick Branwell Brontë (known as Branwell Bronte) was an English painter and poet, as well as the only brother of the three Brontë sisters: Charlotte, Emily, and Anne. He seems to have been considered the most gifted of the four children. As children, Branwell and Charlotte worked together on poems and stories about the imaginary country Angria (Anne and Emily worked together on Gondal), and though he was very fond of writing, it was decided early on that Branwell would be a painter. He was apprenticed to a portrait painter, William Robinson, and Patrick tried himself to work as a portrait painter but was not successful at it. During his lifetime he had only a few poems published in local Yorkshire newspapers under pseudonyms. Patrick is sometimes referred to as the "forgotten" Brontë because he did not publish the way his three sisters did. In 1839 he became a tutor to two little boys but was dismissed after a scandal. He died penniless and among his last words he said, "All my life I have done nothing either great or good."

from AUGUSTA

Augusta! Though I'm far away
Across the dark blue sea,
Still eve and morn and night and day
Will I remember Thee!

And, thou I cannot see thee nigh
Or hear thee speak to me,
Thy look and voice and memory
Shall not forgotten be.

I stand upon this Island shore,
A single hour alone,
And see the Atlantic swell before
With sullen surging tone,

While high in heaven the full Moon glides
Above the breezy deep,
Unmoved by waves or winds or tides
That far beneath her sweep.

She marches through this midnight air,
So silent and divine,
With not a wreath of vapour there
To dim her silver shine.

.   .   .

Henry David Thoreau

(1817–1862)

Henry David Thoreau was a renowned American writer, philosopher, naturalist, pacifist, tax-resister, as well as one of the most important members of the Transcendental movement. Two of his most noted literary works are *Walden* and *On the Duty of Civil Disobedience.* Thoreau was a disciple and close friend of Ralph Waldo Emerson.

In 1845 Thoreau built himself a small cabin on the shore of Walden Pond, near Concord where he lived for more than two years, "living deep and sucking out all the marrow of life." Wishing to lead a life free of materialistic pursuits, he supported himself by growing vegetables and doing odd jobs in the nearby village. He devoted most of his time to observing nature, reading, and writing, and he kept a detailed journal of his observations, activities, and thoughts. It was from this journal that he later distilled his masterpiece, *Walden.* The journal, begun in 1837, was also the source of his first book, *A Week on the Concord and Merrimack Rivers* (1849). One of Thoreau's most important works, the essay "Civil Disobedience" (1849), grew out of an overnight stay in prison as a result of his refusal to pay a poll tax that supported the Mexican War, which to Thoreau represented an effort to extend slavery. Thoreau's quiet revolution in living at Walden has become a symbol of integrity and inner freedom, while his poetry and prose articulate these ideas in writing.

What's the Railroad to Me?

What's the railroad to me?
I never go to see
Where it ends.
It fills a few hollows,
And makes banks for the swallows,
It sets the sand a-blowing,
And the blackberries a-growing.

Indeed Indeed, I Cannot Tell

Indeed, indeed, I cannot tell,
Though I ponder on it well,
Which were easier to state,
All my love or all my hate.
Surely, surely, thou wilt trust me
When I say thou dost disgust me.
O, I hate thee with a hate
That would fain annihilate;
Yet sometimes against my will,
My dear friend, I love thee still.
It were treason to our love,
And a sin to God above,
One iota to abate
Of a pure impartial hate.

SMOKE

Light-winged Smoke, Icarian[1] bird,
~~Melting thy pinions in thy upward flight,~~
Lark without song, and messenger of dawn,
Circling above the hamlets as thy nest;
Or else, departing dream, and shadowy form
Of midnight vision, gathering up thy skirts;
By night star-veiling, and by day
Darkening the light and blotting out the sun;
Go thou my incense upward from this hearth,
And ask the gods to pardon this clear flame

---

[1] "Icarian" refers to the Greek myth of Icarus, in which his waxen
  wings melted when he flew too close to the sun and then he
  plunged to his death in the sea. Here, Thoreau seems not be
  referring to the specific details of the myth, but rather to the
  immense sense of flight that smoke evokes for the speaker.

EMILY BRONTË

(1818–1848)

EMILY JANE BRONTË was an English poet and novelist, best remembered today for her classic novel *Wuthering Heights*. Emily was the middle daughter of Patrick Brontë, an Anglican clergyman who lived in the parsonage at Haworth, West Riding of Yorkshire. Her siblings were Charlotte, Anne, and Patrick, and when their mother died they were left much to themselves. They began to write about imaginary worlds they created. In 1835 Emily enrolled at Miss Wooler's school at Roe Head, Mirfield where Charlotte was teaching, but she soon returned home when she became profoundly homesick and ill. After a few years as governess at Law Hill Hall in Halifax, West Yorkshire, Emily and her sisters Charlotte and Anne traveled to Brussels, Belgium in 1842. Charlotte discovered Emily's poetry in 1845 and Anne then revealed hers, so the three sisters self-published a collection of poetry under the pseudonyms Currer, Ellis, and Acton Bell. In 1847 Emily's novel *Wuthering Heights* and Anne's novel *Agnes Grey* were published as a set while Charlotte's novel *Jane Eyre* was published separately. The identity of the sisters as authors was unknown, even to their publishers, until 1849, when Charlotte published *Shirley* and their authorship was made public. However the family was already struck by tragedy as Patrick had died in September 1848. At his funeral Emily caught a cold, and her health already weakened by the harsh climate she grew up in and refusing all medical help, Emily died of tuberculosis in December 1848,. Anne died a few months later.

Emily Brontë was the undisputed genius of the family. An enigmatic, passionate personality, she produced only one novel and a slender amount of poems, yet she is ranked among the top writers of English literature. Her literary classic, *Wuthering Heights*, is the story of the intense, almost demonic, love between Catherine Earnshaw and Heathcliff. The story is chaotic, mysterious, and violent while the characters are less people than forces. It is the power of Emily Brontë's vision and the beauty of her prose that make the novel so haunting. (Although when it was first published its innovative structure confused critics and it received only mixed reviews.) In addition, some of her powerful lyrics are counted with the best of English poetry. She is especially noted for "The Prisoner," "No Coward Soul is Mine," "God of Visions," and "Remembrence," among others.

No Coward Soul is Mine

No coward soul is mine,
  No trembler in the worlds storm-troubled sphere:
    I see Heavens glories shine,
  And faith shines equal, arming me from fear.

    O God within my breast.
  Almighty, ever-present Deity!
    Life—that in me has rest,
  As I—Undying Life—have power in Thee!

Vain are the thousand creeds
That move mens hearts: unutterably vain;
    Worthless as withered weeds,
Or idlest froth amid the boundless main,

    To waken doubt in one
Holding so fast by Thine infinity;
    So surely anchored on
The steadfast Rock of immortality.

    With wide-embracing love
Thy Spirit animates eternal years,
    Pervades and broods above,
Changes, sustains, dissolves, creates, and rears.

    Though earth and man were gone,
And suns and universes ceased to be,
    And Thou wert left alone,
Every existence would exist in Thee.

    There is not room for Death,
Nor atom that his might could render void:
    Thou — Thou art Being and Breath,
And what Thou art may never be destroyed.

HOPE

Hope was but a timid friend—
She sat without my grated den
Watching how my fate would tend
Even as selfish-hearted men.

She was cruel in her fear.
Through the bars, one dreary day,
I looked out to see her there
And she turned her face away!

Like a false guard false watch keeping
Still in strife she whispered peace;
She would sing while I was weeping,
If I listened, she would cease.

False she was, and unrelenting.
When my last joys strewed the ground
Even sorrow saw repenting
Those sad relics scattered round;

Hope—whose whisper would have given
Balm to all that frenzied pain—
Stretched her wings and soared to heaven;
Went—and ne'er returned again!

If Grief for Grief Can Touch Thee

If grief for grief can touch thee,
If answering woe for woe,
If any truth can melt thee
Come to me now!

I cannot be more lonely,
More drear I cannot be!
My worn heart beats so wildly
'Twill break for thee—

And when the world despises—
When Heaven repels my prayer—
Will not mine angel comfort?
Mine idol hear?

Yes, by the tears I'm poured,
By all my hours of pain
O I shall surely win thee,
Beloved, again!

George Eliot

(1819–1880)

GEORGE ELIOT (née Mary Ann Evans) was a famous 19th century English novelist and one of the most prominent writers of the Victorian era. She used the male pen name George Eliot to ensure that her writing would be treated seriously. She grew up in a strict evangelical Protestant household, which she later rebelled against, renouncing organized religion. She was an avid reader and her first published work was a German translation of the writer D.F. Strauss's *Life of Jesus*. After her father died, Eliot became one of the editors of the *Westminster Review* and contributed articles to the publication. She became acquainted with many literary people of her day and married G. H. Lewes in 1854. The marriage was happy but not legal since Lewe's estranged wife was still alive. Lewes encouraged Eliot's writing career through her bouts with depression and her insecurities. Her most famous novels, which include *Adam Bede* (1859), *The Mill on the Floss* (1860), and *Silas Marner* (1861) are about provincial life. Her novels are serious but marked by compassion and gentle humor.

In a London Drawing Room

The sky is cloudy, yellowed by the smoke.
For view there are the houses opposite
Cutting the sky with one long line of wall
Like solid fog: far as the eye can stretch
Monotony of surface & of form
Without a break to hang a guess upon.
No bird can make a shadow as it flies,
For all is shadow, as in ways o'erhung
By thickest canvass, where the golden rays
Are clothed in hemp. No figure lingering
Pauses to feed the hunger of the eye
Or rest a little on the lap of life.
All hurry on & look upon the ground,
Or glance unmarking at the passers by
The wheels are hurrying too, cabs, carriages
All closed, in multiplied identity.
The world seems one huge prison-house & court
Where men are punished at the slightest cost,
With lowest rate of colour, warmth & joy.

Sweet Evenings Come and Go, Love

"La noche buena se viene,
La noche buena se va,
Y nosotros nos iremos
Y no volveremos mas."
— Old Villancico.[1]

Sweet evenings come and go, love,
They came and went of yore:
This evening of our life, love,
Shall go and come no more.

When we have passed away, love,
All things will keep their name;
But yet no life on earth, love,
With ours will be the same.

The daisies will be there, love,
The stars in heaven will shine:
I shall not feel thy wish, love,
Nor thou my hand in thine.

A better time will come, love,
And better souls be born:
I would not be the best, love,
To leave thee now forlorn.

---

[1] Four lines from a Spanish Christmas song "Dime niño de quien
eres." Eliot translates the lines in the first stanza of her poem.

JULIA WARD HOWE

(1819–1910)

JULIA WARD HOWE was a poet, abolitionist, social reformer, and women's rights advocate most remembered for writing the words for the patriotic "The Battle Hymn of the Republic." Besides this famous verse, Howe's other poetry is not considered of importance and she is known for her social work. Born to a wealthy family in Newport, Rhode Island, she was privately educated. In 1843 she married Samuel Gridley Howe, an educator, and they moved to Boston. Julia and her husband worked together on publishing the *Commonwealth*, which was an abolitionist newspaper. She wrote "The Battle Hymn of the Republic" in 1861 during a visit to an army camp and it was published in *The Atlantic Monthly* in February 1862. It became the semi-official Civil War song for the Union Army, making Howe famous. After the Civil War, Howe got involved in the woman suffrage movement. She co-founded and became president of the New England Woman Suffrage Association. In addition, she edited *Woman's Journal*, and in 1908 became the first woman elected to the American Academy of Arts and Letters.

The Battle Hymn of the Republic[1]

Mine eyes have seen the glory of the coming of the
    Lord;
He is trampling out the vintage where the grapes of
    wrath are stored;
He hath loosed the fateful lightning of His terrible
    swift sword;
His truth is marching on.

I have seen Him in the watch-fires of a hundred
    circling camps;
They have builded Him an altar in the evening dews
    and damps;
I can read His righteous sentence by the dim and
    flaring lamps;
His day is marching on.

I have read a fiery gospel, writ in burnished rows of
    steel:
"As ye deal with my contemners, so with you my grace
    shall deal;
Let the Hero, born of woman, crush the serpent with
    his heel,
Since God is marching on."

---

[1] Howe wrote "The Battle Hymn of the Republic" in 1861 when
she was visiting military camps near Washington with the Secretary of War during the Civil War. The poem was set to the old
folk tune also used for "John Brown's Body."

He has sounded forth the trumpet that shall never call
    retreat;
He is sifting out the hearts of men before His
    judgment-seat:
Oh, be swift, my soul, to answer Him! be jubilant, my
    feet!
Our God is marching on.

In the beauty of the lilies Christ was born across the
    sea,
With a glory in His bosom that transfigures you and
    me:
As He died to make men holy, let us die to make men
    free,
While God is marching on.

JAMES RUSSELL LOWELL

(1819–1892)

JAMES RUSSELL LOWELL was an American Romantic poet, critic, editor, satirist, diplomat, and abolitionist. Noted for his lyric poetry, Lowell was part of a group of New England authors sometimes called the Fireside Poets or the Schoolroom Poets, which included Henry Wadsworth Longfellow, John Greenleaf Whittier, and Oliver Wendell Holmes. The Fireside Poets were known for their conservative approach to poetry and the often blatant morality in their verse. This made them popular in the 19th century and less so today. However, Lowell was less conservative and a passionate abolitionists. He was also influential in stimulating the intellectual life of mid-19thcentury New Englanders.

Born in Cambridge, Massachusetts, he studied at Harvard, where he gave up law for literature. He married Maria White, a fiery abolitionist and liberal, who inspired him in his work. Lowell's *Poems* (1844, 1846), *A Fable for Critics* (1848), *The Vision of Sir Launfal* (1848), and *The Bigelow Papers* (1848) brought him considerable notice as a poet and critic. The best remembered of these are *The Bigelow Papers*, political and social lampoons written in Yankee dialect, which established his reputation as a satirist and a wit. The first of these two series of verses expressed opposition to the Mexican War, and the second supported the cause of the North in the Civil War. In 1855, Lowell became professor of modern languages at Harvard, a position he held until 1876. In addition to teaching, he served as first editor (1857–61) of the *Atlantic Monthly* and later (1864–72) of the *North American Review*. In 1877 he was appointed minister to London, where he remained until 1885. While abroad Lowell did much to increase the respect of foreigners for American letters and American institutions.

AUSPEX

My heart, I cannot still it,
Nest that had song-birds in it;
And when the last shall go,
The dreary days to fill it,
Instead of lark or linnet,
Shall whirl dead leaves and snow.

Had they been swallows only,
Without the passion stronger
That skyward longs and sings,—
Woe's me, I shall be lonely
When I can feel no longer
The impatience of their wings!

A moment, sweet delusion,
Like birds the brown leaves hover;
But it will not be long
Before their wild confusion
Fall wavering down to cover
The poet and his song.

War[1]

Ez fer war, I call it murder,—
There you hev it plain an' flat;
I don't want to go no furder
Than my Testyment fer that. . . .
They may talk o' Freedom's airy
Tell they'er pupple in the face,—
It's a grand gret cemetary
Fer the barthrights of our race;
They jest want this Californy
So's to lug new slave-states in
To abuse ye, an' scorn ye,
An' to plunder ye like sin.

---

[1] "War" is an example of one of Lowell's poems written in Yankee
dialect. Here, he satirically expresses his opposition to the Mexican War. The Mexican War (1846-1848) was a fight over land
between the United States and Mexico. The United States won
the war and annexed the states of California, Arizona, New Mexico, Nevada, Utah, and Colorado. In this poem Lowell also
voices his hatred of slavery, for the new lands intensified debates
over the extension of slavery into new territory. It brought the
Union closer to the brink of Civil War.

HERMAN MELVILLE

(1819–1891)

HERMAN MELVILLE was one of the first American novelists, as well as a poet, and essayist. His great masterpiece is now considered to be the whaling adventure novel *Moby-Dick*. During his lifetime his early novels were popular, but by the time of his death he was forgotten as a writer. In fact, *Moby-Dick*, considered a failure while Melville was alive, was partly responsible for his drop in recognition. The novel was "rediscovered" in the 20th century and is now considered a literary masterpiece.

Melville was born in New York and went to sea as a cabin boy when he was nineteen. His first trip was to England. Later he sailed on a whaling ship bound for the South Pacific (he drew on his experiences from this journey to write *Moby-Dick*). He lived among natives in the Marquesas Islands and was imprisoned in Papeete, Tahiti. Novels such as *Typee*, *Omoo*, *Mardi*, *Redburn*, and *White-Jacket* depict the life of the sailor. One of Melville's most important works was the short story "Bartleby the Scrivener." Following scathing reviews of his novel *Pierre*, publishers became wary of Melville's work. He turned to poetry, but also found that his verse was not appreciated. He died in obscurity in New York City.

The Portent[1]

Hanging from the beam,
~~Slowing swaying (such the law),~~
Gaunt the shadow on your green,
Shenandoah![2]
The cut is on the crown
(Lo, John Brown),[3]
And the stabs shall heal no more.

Hidden in the cap
Is the anguish none can draw;
So your future veils its face,
Shenandoah!
But the streaming beard is shown
(Weird John Brown),
The meteor of the war.

---

[1] "The Portent" was originally published in *Battle-Pieces and Aspects of the War*.

[2] The Shenandoah is a valley in northern Virginia between the Allegheny Mountains and the Blue Ridge, drained by the Shenandoah River. It was the sight of many battles during the American Revolution.

[3] John Brown was an infamous antislavery activist who led a raid on the armory at Harper's Ferry in Virginia, in an attempt to lead a slave rebellion on October 16, 1859. He failed and was hanged, but his actions showed how dire the rift between abolitionists and slaveholders had become.

The Maldive Shark[4]

About the Shark, phlegmatical one,
Pale sot of the Maldive sea,
The sleek little pilot-fish, azure and slim,
How alert in attendance be.
From his saw-pit of mouth, from his charnel of maw,
They have nothing of harm to dread,
But liquidly glide on his ghastly flank
Or before his Gorgonian head;
Or lurk in the port of serrated teeth
In white triple tiers of glittering gates,
And there find a haven when peril's abroad,
An asylum in jaws of the Fates!
They are friends; and friendly they guide him to prey,
Yet never partake of the treat—
Eyes and brains to the dotard lethargic and dull,
Pale ravener of horrible meat.

---

[4] "The Maldive Shark" was originally published in *John Marr and Other Sailors*. Privately printed, 1888.

John Ruskin

(1819–1900)

JOHN RUSKIN was a famous Pre-Raphaelite English art and architecture critic, essayist, social reformer, and poet who is most remembered for his contribution to art criticism and the Pre-Raphaelite Brotherhood. His most famous works include the five volume *Modern Painters* (1843–60), *The Seven Lamps of Architecture* (1849) and *The Stones of Venice* (1851). Ruskin was born in London to a well-off wine merchant and was raised in a religious and cultured family. He made many trips to the European continent and fell in the love with the natural landscapes and the works of art, especially from the medieval and Renaissance periods. He became friends with Dante Gabriel Rossetti and encouraged Rossetti's work. Ruskin is famous for having coined the term "pathetic fallacy," which refers to assigning human emotions to nonliving objects.

Trust Thou Thy Love

Trust thou thy Love: if she be proud, is she not sweet?
Trust thou thy Love: if she be mute, is she not pure?
Lay thou thy soul full in her hands, low at her feet;
Fail, Sun and Breath!—yet, for thy peace, She shall
    endure.

WALT WHITMAN

(1819–1892)

WALT WHITMAN is one of the most celebrated American poets, as well as one of the most influential and innovative. He is also one of the originators of American *free verse*, poetry that doesn't adhere to a strict metrical or rhythmic form. Born in Long Island, New York, he spent most of his young life in Brooklyn, working as a journalist and printer through the 1850s. The first edition of *Leaves of Grass* was privately printed in 1855 and consisted of 12 untitled poems, one of which was to later become famous as "Song of Myself." At first the volume did not sell well, but it became popular in literary circles in Europe and then in America. Whitman published nine editions of *Leaves of Grass* in his lifetime (the last edition was published in 1892 and is sometimes known as the Death-Bed edition). During the Civil War Whitman moved to Washington, D.C., where he served as a civil servant and volunteer nurse. There he published the poetry collections *Drum Taps* and *Sequel to Drum Taps* (1865–66), the latter containing his famous elegies for Abraham Lincoln, "Where Lilacs Last in the Dooryard Bloom'd" and "O Captain! My Captain!" In 1873 he was paralyzed after a stroke and moved to Camden, New Jersey. By the time of his death he was an international literary celebrity. His literary style was experimental, a free-verse explosion of words, in celebration of nature and the self that has since been described as the first expression of a markedly American voice.

O Captain! My Captain![1]

O Captain! my Captain! our fearful trip is done,
The ship has weather'd every rack, the prize we sought
is won,
The port is near, the bells I hear, the people all
exulting,
While follow eyes the steady keel, the vessel grim and
daring;
But O heart! heart! heart!
O the bleeding drops of red,
Where on the deck my Captain lies,
Fallen cold and dead.

O Captain! my Captain! rise up and hear the bells;
Rise up — for you the flag is flung — for you the bugle
trills,
For you bouquets and ribbon'd wreaths — for you the
shores a-crowding,
For you they call, the swaying mass, their eager faces
turning;
Here Captain! dear father!
This arm beneath your head!
It is some dream that on the deck,
You've fallen cold and dead.

---

[1] This 1865 poem is about a captain who dies just as his ship has
reached the end of a stormy and dangerous voyage. The captain
represents Abraham Lincoln, who was assassinated at Ford's
Theatre on April 14, 1865, just days after the end of the Civil
War.

My Captain does not answer, his lips are pale and still,
My father does not feel my arm, he has no pulse nor
 will,
The ship is anchor'd safe and sound, its voyage closed
 and done,
From fearful trip the victor ship comes in with object
 won;
Exult O shores, and ring O bells!
But I with mournful tread,
Walk the deck my Captain lies,
Fallen cold and dead.

I HEAR AMERICA SINGING

I hear America singing, the varied carols I hear;
Those of mechanics—each one singing his, as it should
 be, blithe and strong;
The carpenter singing his, as he measures his plank or
 beam,
The mason singing his, as he makes ready for work, or
 leaves off work;
The boatman singing what belongs to him in his
 boat—the deckhand singing on the steamboat deck;
The shoemaker singing as he sits on his bench—the
 hatter singing as he stands;
The wood-cutter's song—the ploughboy's, on his way
 in the morning,
or at the noon intermission, or at sundown;
The delicious singing of the mother—or of the young
 wife at work—or of the girl sewing or washing—
 Each singing what belongs to her, and to none else;

The day what belongs to the day—At night, the party
    of young fellows, robust, friendly,
Singing, with open mouths, their strong melodious
    songs.

When I heard the Learn'd Astronomer

When I heard the learn'd astronomer,
When the proofs, the figures, were ranged in columns
    before me,
When I was shown the charts and diagrams, to add,
    divide, and measure them,
When I sitting heard the astronomer where he lectured
    with much applause in the lecture-room,
How soon unaccountable I became tired and sick,
Till rising and gliding out I wander'd off by myself,
In the mystical moist night-air, and from time to time,
Look'd up in perfect silence at the stars.

A Clear Midnight

This is the hour, O soul, thy free flight into the
    wordless,
Away from books, away from art, the day erased, the
    lesson done,
Thee fully forth emerging, silent, gazing, pondering
    the themes thou lovest best:
Night, sleep, death, and the stars.

THE LAST INVOCATION

At the last, tenderly,
From the walls of the powerful fortress'd house,
From the clasp of the knitted locks, from the keep of
    the well-closed doors,
Let me be wafted.
Let me glide noiselessly forth;
With the key of softness unlock the locks—with a
    whisper,
Set open the doors O soul.
Tenderly—be not impatient,
(Strong is your hold, O mortal flesh,
Strong is your hold O love.)

Anne Brontë

(1820–1849)

Anne Brontë was an English poet and novelist most remembered for her novels *Agnes Grey* and *The Tenant of Wildfell Hall*. The youngest daughter of Patrick Brontë, an Anglican clergyman who lived in the parsonage at Haworth, West Riding of Yorkshire. Her siblings were Charlotte, Emily, and Patrick, and when their mother died they were left much to themselves. They began to write about imaginary worlds they created. In 1839 Anne worked for a short period as a governess to the Inghams at Blake Hall and later in same position to the Robinsons at Thorpe Green Hall from 1841 to 1845. Her brother Patrick joined her there as a tutor in 1843. Unfortunately, he fell in love for Mrs. Robinson and Anne had to leave the work which she found enjoyable. Charlotte discovered Emily's poetry in 1845 and Anne then revealed hers, so the three sisters self-published a collection of poetry under the pseudonyms Currer, Ellis, and Acton Bell. In 1847 Emily's novel *Wuthering Heights* and Anne's novel *Agnes Grey* were published as a set while Charlotte's novel *Jane Eyre* was published separately. *Agnes Grey*, about the life of a governess, was based on Anne's memories of her experience with the Inghams and Robinsons. Her second novel, *The Tenant of Wildfell Hall*, was published in 1848 and was fairly successful. It is about a young girl who marries Arthur Huntingdon, a violent drunkard, which was partially based on Anne's brother Patrick. The identity of the sisters as authors was unknown, even to their publishers, until 1849, when Charlotte published *Shirley* and their authorship was made public. However the family was already struck by tragedy as Patrick had died in September 1848. Emily died of tuberculosis in December 1848. Anne died in May 1849, also of tuberculosis. Anne's writing was considered more conservative than her two sisters' work, and her reputation as an artist has suffered in comparison to her Charlotte and Emily, however her novels have been widely praised for their realism, integrity, and moral force.

LINES COMPOSED IN A WOOD ON A WINDY DAY

My soul is awakened, my spirit is soaring
And carried aloft on the wings of the breeze;
For above and around me the wild wind is roaring,
Arousing to rapture the earth and the seas.
The long withered grass in the sunshine is glancing,
The bare trees are tossing their branches on high;
The dead leaves, beneath them, are merrily dancing,
The white clouds are scudding across the blue sky.

I wish I could see how the ocean is lashing
The foam of its billows to whirlwinds of spray;
I wish I could see how its proud waves are dashing,
And hear the wild roar of their thunder today!

MATTHEW ARNOLD

(1822–1888)

MATTHEW ARNOLD was an English cultural and literary critic and poet more famous now for his criticism than his poetry. Born in Laleham, Middlesex, he studied at Oxford. He became a school inspector, traveling through England and Wales to report on elementary and secondary schools. Arnold was a champion of universal education. He published his first poetry volume, *The Strayed Reveller*, in 1849, and soon withdrew the book, though he republished some of the poems from the volume. He did the same with *Empedocles on Etna* in 1852. Both books were not favorably reviewed. Later he was appointed Professor of Poetry at Oxford. Arnold wrote most of his best-known poetry before he was forty, and then turned to cultural and literary criticism, as well as theology (he became an agonistic as a young man and though he respected people who were committed to religion he did not share their view).

"Dover Beach" is considered his masterpiece. Written in 1867 the poem depicts a terrible world from which religious tradition has departed. The mood of the poem is mournful and reflective, which is characteristic of much of his poetry. Arnold expresses the view that love of humanity is the only defense against the darkness that is descending on the world. The poem shows a modern sensibility and some critics see Arnold as a bridge between Romanticism and Modernism. He was very influenced by Wordsworth and has been considered the third great Victorian poet after Alfred, Lord Tennyson and Robert Browning.

Dover Beach

The sea is calm to-night.
The tide is full, the moon lies fair
Upon the straits; on the French coast the light
Gleams and is gone; the cliffs of England stand;
Glimmering and vast, out in the tranquil bay.
Come to the window, sweet is the night-air!
Only, from the long line of spray
Where the sea meets the moon-blanched land,
Listen! you hear the grating roar
Of pebbles which the waves draw back, and fling,
At their return, up the high strand,[1]
Begin, and cease, and then again begin,
With tremulous cadence slow, and bring
The eternal note of sadness in.

Sophocles long ago
Heard it on the Ægaean, and it brought
Into his mind the turbid ebb and flow
Of human misery; we
Find also in the sound a thought,
Hearing it by this distant northern sea.

---

[1] "The high strand" is the upper part of a coast line.

The Sea of Faith
Was once, too, at the full, and round earth's shore
Lay like the folds of a bright girdle[2] furled.
But now I only hear
Its melancholy, long, withdrawing roar,
Retreating, to the breath
Of the night-wind, down the vast edges drear
And naked shingles[3] of the world.

Ah, love, let us be true
To one another! for the world, which seems
To lie before us like a land of dreams,
So various, so beautiful, so new,
Hath really neither joy, nor love, nor light,
Nor certitude, nor peace, nor help for pain;
And we are here as on a darkling plain
Swept with confused alarms of struggle and flight,
Where ignorant armies clash by night.

---

[2] Belt.
[3] Seashore pebbles worn by water.

PHOEBE CARY

(1824–1871)

PHOEBE CARY was an American poet. Born near Cincinnati, Ohio, she grew up on a farm and received little formal schooling, but became interested in literature at a young age. Phoebe and her older sister, Alice, both wrote poetry and published their work in magazines. Phoebe and Alice's poetry was praised by Edgar Allan Poe and John Greenleaf Whittier and so they jointly published a volume of poetry *Poems of Alice and Phoebe Carey* [sic] in 1849. Most of the poetry was Alice's and the book's small success led the sisters to move to New York City where they became regular contributors to *Harper's*, the *Atlantic Monthly*, and other magazines. Although Alice was a more acclaimed writer during their lifetime, Phoebe was later held in higher critical esteem because of her wit. Phoebe Cary went on to publish three books of poetry on her own: *Poems and Parodies* (1854), *Poems of Faith, Hope, and Love* (1868), and *Hymns for all Christians* (which Cary edited). Both sisters were active in the women's rights movement and their home became a salon for the leading literary figures of New York. Phoebe died a few months after her sister in Newport, Rhode Island.

WHEN LOVELY WOMAN[1]

When lovely woman wants a favor,
    And finds, too late, that man won't bend,
What earthly circumstance can save her
    From disappointment in the end?

The only way to bring him over
    The last experiment to try,
Whether a husband or a lover,
    If he have feeling, is, to cry!

---

[1] This is a response to Oliver Goldsmith's famous poem "When
Lovely Woman Stoops to Folly" from his play *The Vicar of
Wakefield*.

DANTE GABRIEL ROSSETTI

(1828–1882)

D ANTE GABRIEL ROSSETTI (née Gabriel Charles
Dante Rossetti) was a noted Pre-Raphaelite poet,
illustrator, and artist, as well as the brother of the poet
Christina Rossetti. His father was an Italian political
refugee and his mother was English. The Rossetti family was cultured and political and this influenced Dante,
who was born in London, a good deal. He started drawing lessons at a London school when he was fourteen
and later studied painting at the Royal Academy where
he helped found the Pre-Raphaelite Brotherhood. Rossetti linked poetry and painting, inspired by his reading
of Keats, Shakespeare, Goethe, Sir Walter Scott, Lord
Byron, Edgar Allen Poe, and William Blake. In 1854
Dante Rossetti met the art critic John Ruskin and they
became allies. Two years later the poet and artist
William Morris joined them. In 1860 Rossetti married
the writer and painter, Elizabeth Siddal. They had met
ten years before and when they married Siddal was sick
and gave birth to a stillborn child. She then died two
years later of an overdose. Rossetti had her buried with
the only complete manuscript of his poems, then had her
exhumed seven years later to retrieve his work at the
behest of his friends. He moved into a building with the
poets Algernon Swinburne and George Meredith. Then
he settled into a house with William Morris and his wife,
with whom he was in love. He collapsed in 1872, never
regaining his health fully, and lived the last ten years of
his life in solitude.

Rossetti published a collection of his poems in 1871 and the book was controversial for its eroticism, called by its critics the paragon of the "fleshly school of poetry." *The House of Life*, a complex sonnet sequence following the physical and spiritual development of an intimate relationship, is often considered Rossetti's greatest literary work. He described the sonnet form as a "moment's monument."

The Woodspurge[1]

The wind flapp'd loose, the wind was still,
Shaken out dead from tree and hill:
I had walk'd on at the wind's will,—
I sat now, for the wind was still.

Between my knees my forehead was,—
My lips, drawn in, said not Alas!
My hair was over in the grass,
My naked ears heard the day pass.

My eyes, wide open, had the run
Of some ten weeds to fix upon;
Among those few, out of the sun,
The woodspurge flower'd, three cups in one.

From perfect grief there need not be
Wisdom or even memory:
One thing then learnt remains to me,—
The woodspurge has a cup of three.

---

[1] A woodspurge is a plant with greenish yellow cup-like flowers.

LOVE-LILY

Between the hands, between the brows,
    Between the lips of Love-Lily,
A spirit is born whose birth endows
    My blood with fire to burn through me;
Who breathes upon my gazing eyes,
    Who laughs and murmurs in mine ear,
At whose least touch my colour flies,
    And whom my life grows faint to hear.

Within the voice, within the heart,
    Within the mind of Love-Lily,
A spirit is born who lifts apart
    His tremulous wings and looks at me;
Who on my mouth his finger lays,
    And shows, while whispering lutes confer,
That Eden of Love's watered ways
    Whose winds and spirits worship her.

Brows, hands, and lips, heart, mind, and voice,
    Kisses and words of Love-Lily,—
Oh! bid me with your joy rejoice
    Till riotous longing rest in me!
Ah! let not hope be still distraught,
    But find in her its gracious goal,
Whose speech Truth knows not from her thought
    Nor Love her body from her soul.

George Meredith

(1828–1909)

GEORGE MEREDITH was an English poet and novel-ist, considered one of the greatest novelists of his time. (Oscar Wilde wrote "Ah, Meredith! Who can define him? His style is chaos illumined by flashes of lightning.") Born in Portsmouth, his mother died when he was five and he was sent to school in Germany when he was fourteen. He studied law but abandoned that to become a journalist and poet. He married the widowed daughter of the poet Thomas Love Peacock in 1849. In 1851 he published *Poems*, which received some praise, including a favorable review by Alfred, Lord Tennyson. In 1858 Meredith's wife left him and their son and she died three years later. Her leaving the family inspired Meredith's first major novel, *The Ordeal of Richard Feveral*. He remarried and continued writing novels. He acted as an advisor to publishers and helped start Thomas Hardy's literary career. Later in life he returned to writing poetry, inspired by the natural world. In 1905 he took over the presidency of the Society of Authors from Tennyson and he received an Order of Merit from King Edward VII.

LUCIFER IN STARLIGHT[1]

On a starred night Prince Lucifer uprose.
Tired of his dark dominion swung the fiend
Above the rolling ball in cloud part screened,
Where sinners hugged their spectre of repose.
Poor prey to his hot fit of pride were those.
And now upon his western wing he leaned,
Now his huge bulk o'er Afric's sands careened,
Now the black planet shadowed Arctic snows.
Soaring through wider zones that pricked his scars
With memory of the old revolt from Awe,[2]
He reached a middle height, and at the stars,
Which are the brain of heaven, he looked, and sank.
Around the ancient track marched, rank on rank,
The army of unalterable law.

SONG IN THE SONGLESS

They have no song, the sedges dry,
And still they sing.
It is within my breast they sing,
As I pass by.
Within my breast they touch a string,
They wake a sigh.
There is but sound of sedges dry;
In me they sing.

---

[1] "Lucifer in Starlight" is non-traditional sonnet. It has fourteen
   lines but follows a different rhyme scheme and syllable count
   (twelve syllables per line instead of ten, except for the last line).
[2] "Awe" refers to heaven. Lucifer's rebellion against God caused
   him to lose his heavenly home and be banished into the under-
   world.

Henry Timrod

(1828–1867)

Henry Timrod was an American poet who was called "the laureate of the Confederacy" and considered one of the most gifted Southern writers of the time. Born in Charleston, South Carolina, he studied at the University of Georgia for two years but had to leave because of illness. During the Civil War he became spokesperson for the Confederacy through his poetry and articles for the *Charleston Mercury*. Later he became assistant editor of the *South Carolinian* in 1864. "Ethogenesis," his first major work was published in 1861. The aftermath of the war brought Timrod to poverty and he died of tuberculosis. He published only one volume of poems during his lifetime but his poetry was edited posthumously by his friend Paul Hamilton Hayne and published in 1873 along with a memoir. Some of Timrod's more noted poems are "Ode to the Confederate Dead at Magnolia Cemetery," "The Cotton Boll," "Charleston," and "Carolina".

CHARLESTON

Calm as that second summer which precedes
The first fall of the snow,
In the broad sunlight of heroic deeds,
The City bides the foe.

As yet, behind their ramparts stern and proud,
Her bolted thunders sleep—
Dark Sumter, like a battlemented cloud,
Looms o'er the solemn deep.

No Calpe[1] frowns from lofty cliff or scar
To guard the holy strand;
But Moultrie[2] holds in leash her dogs of war
Above the level sand.

And down the dunes a thousand guns lie couched,
Unseen, beside the flood—
Like tigers in some Orient jungle crouched
That wait and watch for blood.

Meanwhile, through streets still echoing with trade,
Walk grave and thoughtful men,
Whose hands may one day wield the patriot's blade
As lightly as the pen.

---

[1] The location of a British colony on a limestone promontory at the southern tip of Spain; strategically important because it can control the entrance of ships into the Mediterranean.

[2] William Moultrie was an American general in the American Revolution. He defeated a British attack on Sullivan's Island in Charleston Harbor in 1776, and defended Charleston again in 1779.

And maidens, with such eyes as would grow dim
Over a bleeding hound,
Seem each one to have caught the strength of him
Whose sword she sadly bound.

Thus girt without and garrisoned at home,
Day patient following day,
Old Charleston looks from roof, and spire, and dome,
Across her tranquil bay.

Ships, through a hundred foes, from Saxon lands
And spicy Indian ports,
Bring Saxon steel and iron to her hands,
And Summer to her courts.

But still, along yon dim Atlantic line,
The only hostile smoke
Creeps like a harmless mist above the brine,
From some frail, floating oak.

Shall the Spring dawn, and she still clad in smiles,
And with an unscathed brow,
Rest in the strong arms of her palm-crowned isles,
As fair and free as now?

We know not; in the temple of the Fates
God has inscribed her doom;
And, all untroubled in her faith, she waits
The triumph or the tomb.

EMILY DICKINSON

(1830–1886)

EMILY DICKINSON is one of the most renowned American poets, sometimes called "The Belle of Amherst." Born in Amherst, Massachusetts, Dickinson led an outwardly quiet life but her poetry is fiercely visceral. Her verses were short but inventive, and her themes universal: love, death, and her relationship with God and nature. Dickinson was not famous during her lifetime; she rarely left Amherst and supposedly she never left her family's property after the late 1860s. Dickinson's output was vast—over 1,700 poems in all—but only a few of her poems were published during her lifetime. Her sister Lavinia actively promoted her work after Emily's death in 1886. *Poems of Emily Dickinson* was published in 1890, and other new editions of her work appeared over the following decades. Once published, Dickinson's words found a worldwide audience, and she is now considered one of America's finest 19th century poets. Among her best-known poems are "Because I could not stop for Death" and "I cannot live with You."

280. I Felt a Funeral, in my Brain

I felt a funeral in my brain,
   And mourners, to and fro,
Kept treading, treading, till it seemed
   That sense was breaking through.

And when they all were seated,
    A service like a drum
Kept beating, beating, till I thought
    My mind was going numb

And then I heard them lift a box,
    And creak across my soul
With those same boots of lead, again.
    Then space began to toll

As all the heavens were a bell,
    And being, but an ear,
And I and Silence some strange Race
    Wrecked, solitary, here.

288. I'M NOBODY! WHO ARE YOU?

I'm Nobody! Who are you?
Are you—Nobody—Too?
Then there's a pair of us!
Don't tell! they'd advertise—you know!

How dreary—to be—Somebody!
How public—like a Frog—
To tell one's name—the livelong June—
To an admiring Bog!

712. BECAUSE I COULD NOT STOP FOR DEATH

Because I could not stop for Death,
He kindly stopped for me;
The carriage held but just ourselves
And Immortality.

We slowly drove, he knew no haste,
And I had put away
My labor, and my leisure too,
For his civility.

We passed the school where children played
At wrestling in a ring;
We passed the fields of gazing grain,
We passed the setting sun.

We paused before a house that seemed
A swelling of the ground;
The roof was scarcely visible,
The cornice but a mound.

Since then 'tis centuries; but each
Feels shorter than the day
I first surmised the horses' heads
Were toward eternity.

1129. TELL ALL THE TRUTH BUT TELL IT SLANT

Tell all the Truth but tell it slant—
Success in Circuit lies
Too bright for our infirm Delight
The Truth's superb surprise
As Lightening to the Children eased
With explanation kind
The Truth must dazzle gradually
Or every man be blind—

CHRISTINA GEORGINA ROSSETTI

(1830–1894)

CHRISTINA GEORGINA ROSSETTI was a renowned Victorian poet who was considered for the position of Poet Laureate. Her father was an Italian political refugee and her mother was English. She was born in London to a cultured and political family. Like her brother Dante Gabriele Rossetti she showed talent as a poet at a young age. Christina was schooled at home and her family were supportive of her writing—her grandfather printed the poems she wrote as a teenager on his own press. Rossetti was a devout Anglican and she turned down two suitors over religion—one suitor was Roman Catholic, the other was an atheist.

Rossetti's poetry often deals with the refusal of earthly passion in favor of spiritual devotion. Even poems such as "Goblin Market" or "The Prince's Progress" that deal with fantasy have a moral intent. Christina suffered from poor health and was an invalid by the time she was fifty. She was considered for the position of Poet Laureate, but because of her illness she could not be appointed. She continued writing, however, and published *Time Flies: A Reading Diary* (1885) and *The Face of the Deep: A Devotional Commentary on the Apocalypse* (1892). After her death, William Michael Rossetti brought out an edition of his sister's later poetry, *New Poems* (1896), and edited her *Collected Poems* (1904).

Dream Land[1]

Where sunless rivers weep
Their waves into the deep,
She sleeps a charmed sleep:
    Awake her not.
Led by a single star,
She came from very far
To seek where shadows are
    Her pleasant lot.

She left the rosy morn,
She left the fields of corn,
For twilight cold and lorn
    And water springs.
Through sleep, as through a veil,
She sees the sky look pale,
And hears the nightingale
    That sadly sings.

Rest, rest, a perfect rest
Shed over brow and breast;
Her face is toward the west,
    The purple land.
She cannot see the grain
Ripening on hill and plain;
She cannot feel the rain
    Upon her hand.

---

[1] This poem first appeared in the periodical *The Gem* in January, 1850. It was then published in Rossetti's *Poems* (1890).

Rest, rest, for evermore
Upon a mossy shore;
Rest, rest at the heart's core
   Till time shall cease:
Sleep that no pain shall wake;
Night that no morn shall break
Till joy shall overtake
   Her perfect peace.

A Daughter of Eve[2]

A fool I was to sleep at noon,
   And wake when night is chilly
Beneath the comfortless cold moon;
   A fool to pluck my rose too soon,
A fool to snap my lily.

My garden-plot I have not kept;
   Faded and all-forsaken,
I weep as I have never wept:
   Oh it was summer when I slept,
It's winter now I waken.

Talk what you please of future spring
   And sun-warm'd sweet to-morrow—
Stripp'd bare of hope and everything,
   No more to laugh, no more to sing,
I sit alone with sorrow.

---

[2] This poem was first published in *Goblin Market, The Prince's Progress, and Other Poems* (1875).

from GOBLIN MARKET[3]

Morning and evening
~~Maids heard the goblins cry:~~
Come buy our orchard fruits,
Come buy, come buy:
Apples and quinces,[4]
Lemons and oranges,
Plump unpeck'd cherries,
Melons and raspberries,
Bloom-down-cheek'd peaches,
Swart-headed mulberries,
Wild free-born cranberries,
  Crab-apples, dewberries,
Pine-apples, blackberries,
Apricots, strawberries;—
All ripe together
In summer weather,—
Morns that pass by,
Fair eves that fly;
Come buy, come buy:
Our grapes fresh from the vine,
Pomegranates full and fine,

---

[3] Rossetti's first title for the poem was "A Peep at the Goblins—To
  M. F. R." (Christina's sister, Maria Francesca Rossetti).
  Christina's brother, William Michael Rossetti, wrote that
  Christina had said the poem was a fairy story without a deeper
  symbolic meeting. However, he also went on to write that the
  poem "implies . . . that to succumb to temptation makes one a
  victim to that same continuous temptation; that the remedy does
  not always lie with oneself; and that a stronger and more righteous will may prove of avail to restore one's lost estate."
[4] A yellow-skinned fruit looks and tastes like a cross between an
  apple and a pear.

Dates and sharp bullaces,
Rare pears and greengages,
Damsons and bilberries,
Taste them and try:
Currants and gooseberries,
Bright-fire-like barberries,
Figs to fill your mouth,
Citrons from the South,
Sweet to tongue and sound to eye;
Come buy, come buy.

Evening by evening
Among the brookside rushes,
Laura bowed her head to hear,
Lizzie veiled her blushes:
Crouching close together
In the cooling weather,
With clasping arms and cautioning lips,
With tingling cheeks and finger-tips.
"Lie close," Laura said,
Pricking up her golden head:
We must not look at goblin men,
We must not buy their fruits:
Who knows upon what soil they fed
Their hungry thirsty roots?"
"Come buy," call the goblins
Hobbling down the glen.
"O! cried Lizzie, Laura, Laura,
You should not peep at goblin men."
Lizzie covered up her eyes
Covered close lest they should look;
Laura reared her glossy head,

And whispered like the restless brook:
"Look, Lizzie, look, Lizzie,
Down the glen tramp little men.
One hauls a basket,
One bears a plate,
One lugs a golden dish
Of many pounds' weight.
How fair the vine must grow
Whose grapes are so luscious;
How warm the wind must blow
Through those fruit bushes."
"No," said Lizzie, "no, no, no;
Their offers should not charm us,
Their evil gifts would harm us."
She thrust a dimpled finger
In each ear, shut eyes and ran:
Curious Laura chose to linger
Wondering at each merchant man.
One had a cat's face,
One whisked a tail,
One tramped at a rat's pace,
One crawled like a snail,
One like a wombat prowled obtuse and furry,
One like a ratel tumbled hurry-scurry.
Lizzie heard a voice like voice of doves
Cooing all together:
They sounded kind and full of loves
In the pleasant weather.

Lewis Carroll

(1832–1898)

Lewis Carroll is the pen name for the children's book writer, poet, teacher, amateur photographer, and mathematician Charles Lutwide Dodgson, famous for the children's books *Alice's Adventures in Wonderland* (1865) and *Through the Looking Glass* (1872). Carroll studied at Oxford and spent the rest of his life there, lecturing in mathematics at Oxford from 1855 to 1881. He was shy and spoke with a stammer. Although he was ordained, he did not feel up to the demanding life of a minister and remained a deacon.

He published mathematical treatises, such as *Euclid and His Modern Rivals* (1879). Today he is most renowned for his classic children's books *Alice's Adventures in Wonderland* and *Through the Looking Glass*. The books were based on stories that Carroll invented for Alice Liddell, the daughter of Henry George Liddell, dean of Christ Church College, Oxford. They were illustrated by Sir John Tenniel and his drawings remain well known. Carroll also wrote *Phantasmagoria* (1869), *Hunting of the Snark*, (1876), *Rhyme? and Reason?* (1883), and *Sylvie and Bruno* (1889). Carroll enjoyed writing humorous poetry and his most popular verse was *The Hunting of the Snark*, published in 1876.

JABBERWOCKY[1]

'Twas brillig, and the slithy toves
  Did gyre and gimble in the wabe:
All mimsy were the borogoves,
  And the mome raths outgrabe.

"Beware the Jabberwock, my son!
  The jaws that bite, the claws that catch!
Beware the Jubjub bird, and shun
  The frumious Bandersnatch!"

He took his vorpal sword in hand:
  Long time the manxome foe he sought—
So rested he by the Tumtum tree,
  And stood awhile in thought.

And, as in uffish thought he stood,
  The Jabberwock, with eyes of flame,
Came whiffling through the tulgey wood,
  And burbled as it came!

One, two! One, two! And through and through
  The vorpal blade went snicker-snack!
He left it dead, and with its head
  He went galumphing back.

---

[1] This poem is from *Through the Looking-Glass*, 1872. "Jabberwocky"
is a famous example of a nonsense poem in which Carroll
invented his own words.

"And, has thou slain the Jabberwock?
  Come to my arms, my beamish boy!
O frabjous day! Callooh! Callay!'
  He chortled in his joy.

'Twas brillig, and the slithy toves
  Did gyre and gimble in the wabe;
All mimsy were the borogoves,
  And the mome raths outgrabe!

How Doth the Little Crocodile[2]

How doth the little crocodile
Improve his shining tail,
And pour the waters of the Nile
On every golden scale!

How cheerfully he seems to grin,
How neatly spreads his claws,
And welcomes little fishes in
With gently smiling jaws!"

---

[2] This poem is a parody of Isaac Watt's 1715 poem "Against
  Idleness and Mischief," a popular poem given to children for
  moral instruction.

WILLIAM MORRIS

(1834–1896)

WILLIAM MORRIS was a Pre-Raphaelite poet, artist, craftsman, and social reformer. He is considered the best English designer of the 19th century. While studying at Oxford, Morris gained a passionate interest in the architecture of the Middle Ages. He also was deeply inspired by his reading of the work of John Ruskin, eventually adopting the same aesthetic approach and advocacy of social progress. Morris was apprenticed to an architect when he first met Dante Gabriel Rossetti and became a member of the Pre-Raphaelite Brotherhood. Rossetti encouraged him to paint and write, and in 1858 Morris published his first book of poetry, *The Defence of Guenevere and Other Poems*. He followed up with *The Life and Death of Jason* (1867) and *The Earthly Paradise* (1868–1870). In the latter book (published in three volumes) a group of medieval Norse wanderers try to find a land without death or unhappiness. Morris's poetry was successful in his day, but is not read widely today. His impact was on the world of design and craftsmanship and he is renowned for his stained glass, carvings, carpets, wallpaper designs, and furniture, as well as for his influence on the printing industry where he created elegant type at his Kelmscott Press.

In Prison

Wearily, drearily,
Half the day long,
Flap the great banners
High over the stone;
Strangely and eerily
Sounds the wind's song,
Bending the banner-poles.

While, all alone,
Watching the loophole's spark,
Lie I, with life all dark,
Feet tether'd, hands fetter'd
Fast to the stone,
The grim walls, square-letter'd
With prison'd men's groan.

Still strain the banner-pole
Through the wind's song,
Westward the banner rolls
Over my wrong.

Algernon Charles Swinburne

(1837–1909)

ALGERNON CHARLES SWINBURNE was a celebrated
controversial poet of the Victorian era. His poetry
was concerned with such topics as sex, death, and sadomasochism. His father was an admiral, Captain Charles
Henry Swinburne, and his mother was Lady Henrietta
Swinburne. Swinburne, born in London, studied at Eton
and then Oxford. He published two plays in 1861 and
then traveled to Italy where he met the poet Walter Savage Landor and lived in Chelsea, England with the poets
Dante Gabriel Rossetti and George Meredith. His first
success was *Atalanta in Calydon*, published in 1865. His
greatest book of poems is considered the 1866 *Poems and
Ballads*, which contains noted poems such as "Dolores,"
"Hymn to Prosperine," and other dark melodic verse.
Since it contradicted Victorian principles of religion and
morality, his poetry and Swinburne himself caused a
scandal. Swinburne countered that art was for art's sake
and that his interest in sadomasochism was impersonal.
Dante and Christina Rossetti's brother William Michael
Rossetti came to his defense in Swinburne's *Poems and
Ballads: A Criticism*. Swinburne's later poetry is considered to be less original on the whole than his earlier
work. He suffered from alcoholism and his friend and
legal advisor took him away from London to care for
him in the country. Swinburne lived for thirty more
years, writing two novels and criticism of Shakespeare,
William Blake, Victor Hugo, and Elizabethan and
Jacobean drama.

Love and Sleep

Lying asleep between the strokes of night
I saw my love lean over my sad bed,
Pale as the duskiest lily's leaf or head,
Smooth-skinned and dark, with bare throat made to bite,
Too wan for blushing and too warm for white,
But perfect-coloured without white or red.
And her lips opened amorously, and said—
I wist not what, saving one word—Delight
And all her face was honey to my mouth,
And all her body pasture to mine eyes;
The long lithe arms and hotter hands than fire,
The quivering flanks, hair smelling of the south,
The bright light feet, the splendid supple thighs
And glittering eyelids of my soul's desire.

Sorrow

Sorrow, on wing through the world for ever,
Here and there for awhile would borrow
Rest, if rest might haply deliver
Sorrow.

One thought lies close in her heart gnawn thorough
With pain, a weed in a dried-up river,
A rust-red share in an empty furrow.

Hearts that strain at her chain would sever
The link where yesterday frets to-morrow:
All things pass in the world, but never
Sorrow.

Thomas Hardy

(1840–1928)

Thomas Hardy was an English novelist, short story writer, and poet of the Victorian era. He is famous for his classic novels such as *Far from the Madding Crowd* (1874), *The Mayor of Casterbridge* (1886), *Tess of the d'Ubervilles* (1891), and *Jude the Obscure* (1895). Most of his novels are set in the semi-imaginary county of Wessex and are characterized by their fatalism. He became a celebrated literary figure by the early 1900s, despite public controversy about two of his greatest works, *Tess of the d'Ubervilles* and *Jude the Obscure*. Partly because of this, he gave up writing novels and turned to poetry. Although he is generally regarded as a more accomplished novelist than poet, he stated that his first love was poetry. His first book of published poetry was *Wessex Poems and Other Verses* (1898), which included poems he had written over thirty years. Hardy continued to publish many volumes of verse including *Poems of the Past and Present*, *The Dynasts* (in three volumes), *Satires of Circumstances*, and *Collected Poems*.

Hardy's father worked as a stonemason in Dorset. His mother was very well-read and supplemented Hardy's formal education, which stopped when he was sixteen and became apprenticed to a local architect. In 1870 Hardy met Emma Lavinia Gifford and they married in 1874. They had a difficult marriage and became estranged. Still, he took her death in 1912 very hard and revisited locations in Cornwall that reminded him of their courtship. His *Poems 1912–13* explore the grief of his marriage and his wife's death. Hardy married his secretary Florence Dugdale in 1914.

Hardy is most known for his lyrics and ballads. His poetry has many champions, including the English poet Philip Larkin. The subject matter of his poetry deals with regret and disappointment in love and life, as well as mankind's struggle against the indifference to human suffering. Many of his poems deal with the unhappiness of his first marriage, his preoccupation with her sudden death, and his feelings of remorse. Various composers set Hardy's poems to music including Lee Hoiby, Benjamin Britten, Ralph Vaughan Williams, and Gustav Holst.

I Look into My Glass

I look into my glass,
And view my wasting skin,
And say, "Would God it came to pass
My heart had shrunk as thin!"

For then, I, undistrest
By hearts grown cold to me,
Could lonely wait my endless rest
With equanimity.

But Time, to make me grieve,
Part steals, lets part abide;
And shakes this fragile frame at eve
With throbbings of noontide.

THE DARKLING THRUSH[1]

I leant upon a coppice gate,
When Frost was spectre-gray,
And Winter's dregs made desolate
The weakening eye of day.
The tangled vine-stems scored the sky
Like strings of broken lyres,
And all mankind that haunted nigh
Had sought their household fires.

The land's sharp features seemed to me
The Century's corpse outleant,
Its crypt the cloudy canopy,
The wind its death-lament.
The ancient pulse of germ and birth
Was shrunken hard and dry,
And every spirit upon earth
Seemed fervorless as I.

At once a voice arose among
The bleak twigs overhead,
In a full-throated evensong
Of joy illimited.
An ancient thrush, frail, gaunt and small,
With blast-beruffled plume,
Had chosen thus to fling his soul
Upon the growing gloom.

---

[1] "The Darkling Thrush" deals with writing poetry. The poem was set to music by Lee Hoiby and became the basis for the opera *Darkling*.

So little cause for carolings
Of such ecstatic sound
Was written on terrestrial things
Afar or nigh around,
That I could think there trembled through
His happy good-night air
Some blessed Hope, whereof he knew,
And I was unaware.

THE PITY OF IT

I walked in loamy Wessex lanes, afar
From rail-track and from highway, and I heard
In field and farmstead many an ancient word
Of local lineage like "Thu bist," "Er war,"
"Ich woll," "Er sholl," and by-talk similar,
Nigh as they speak who in this month's moon gird
At England's very loins, thereunto spurred
By gangs whose glory threats and slaughters are.

Then seemed a Heart crying: "Whosoever they be
At root and bottom of this, who flung this flame
Between kin folk kin tongued even as are we,
Sinister, ugly, lurid, be their fame;
May their familiars grow to shun their name,
And their brood perish everlastingly."

A Wife in London

I—The Tragedy

She sits in the tawny vapour
    That the City lanes have uprolled,
    Behind whose webby fold on fold
Like a waning taper
    The street-lamp glimmers cold.

A messenger's knock cracks smartly,
    Flashed news is in her hand
    Of meaning it dazes to understand
Though shaped so shortly:
    He—has fallen—in the far South Land . . .

II—The Irony

'Tis the morrow; the fog hangs thicker,
    The postman nears and goes:
    A letter is brought whose lines disclose
By the firelight flicker
    His hand, whom the worm now knows:

Fresh—firm—penned in highest feather
    Page-full of his hoped return,
    And of home-planned jaunts by brake and burn
In the summer weather,
    And of new love that they would learn.

MATHILDE BLIND

(1841–1896)

MATHILDE BLIND (née Cohen) was an English poet, translator, biographer, and women's rights advocate. She was born in Mannheim, Germany. Her stepfather, the German revolutionary Karl Blind, became a political exile after taking part in failed uprisings, and the family settled in London around 1849. Blind published four volumes of poetry under the name Claude Lake, including *The Prophecy of St. Oran* in 1881, *The Heather on Fire* in 1886, *Songs and Sonnets* in 1893, and *Birds of Passage* in 1895. Blind also translated D.F. Strauss's *Old Faith and New* and wrote biographies of the English novelist George Eliot and the French revolutionary Madame Roland.

LASSITUDE

I laid me down beside the sea,
Endless in blue monotony;
The clouds were anchored in the sky,
Sometimes a sail went idling by.

Upon the shingles on the beach
Gray linen was spread out to bleach,
And gently with a gentle swell
The languid ripples rose and fell.

A fisher-boy, in level line,
Cast stone by stone into the brine:
Methought I too might do as he,
And cast my sorrows on the sea.

The old, old sorrows in a heap
Dropped heavily into the deep;
But with its sorrow on that day
My heart itself was cast away.

GERARD MANLEY HOPKINS

(1844–1889)

G ERARD MANLEY HOPKINS was one of the most innovative 19th century poets. His poems focused on God, nature, and the intensity of spiritual turmoil: both its ecstasies and its anguish. Hopkins used very few 19th century poetic conventions. He coined the term "sprung rhythm," a new way of timing stressed and unstressed syllables where the number of *stressed* syllables per line are counted instead of the number of *stressed* and *unstressed* syllables. Hopkins used this technique to create greater effects of tension and calm in his poems.

Born in Essex, England, the eldest son of a well-to-do middle-class family, he attended Oxford where he became interested in Catholicism and began a lifelong friendship with the poet Robert Bridges. Although his parents strongly opposed his conversion, he became a Jesuit and was ordained as a priest in 1887. He spent his life as a priest and a teacher. Hopkins suffered from poor health and died of typhoid fever when he was forty-four years old. During Hopkins's lifetime he was little known for his poetry. Robert Bridges edited his first volume of poetry, which was published in 1918.

Hopkins' wrote a group of sonnets often referred to as the "Terrible Sonnets," which are known for the force of their emotional anguish. "God's Grandeur" is one of the "Terrible Sonnets." Its form is that of a Petrarchan (or Italian) sonnet. Petrarchan sonnets consist of fourteen lines divided into an octet and a sestet (the beginning of the sestet marks the shift or turn in the argument of the poem). For Hopkins, the Earth in its natural state reflects God, but the rapidly growing industries of the Victorian era were marring both the outer and inner landscape of human beings ("all is seared with trade"). Economics was trumping spirituality. Hopkins believed people were becoming less sensitive to the natural world, and thus were no longer following God. He was convinced that science and religion could co-exist favorably and that the new knowledge of the way the world worked only confirmed God's existence. In "God's Grandeur" Hopkins set out to show that proof of God's beauty and grace could be found even in the midst of the "blear" and "smear" of the Industrial Age.

GOD'S GRANDEUR

THE WORLD is charged with the grandeur of God.
    It will flame out, like shining from shook foil[1];
    It gathers to a greatness, like the ooze of oil
Crushed. Why do men then now not reck[2] his rod[3]?
Generations have trod, have trod, have trod;
    And all is seared with trade; Bleared, smeared with toil;
    And wears man's smudge and shares man's smell: the soil
Is bare now, nor can foot feel, being shod[4].

And for all this, nature is never spent;
    There lives the dearest freshness[5] deep down things;
And though the last lights off the black West went

    Oh, morning, at the brown brink eastward, springs[6]—
Because the Holy Ghost over the bent
    World broods[7] with warm breast and with ah! bright wings[8].

---

[1] Hopkins compares God's power to that of electricity.
[2] Heed.
[3] "Rod" is used to mean both an electrical rod and divine authority.
[4] Wearing shoes symbolizes alienation from nature.
[5] Indicates the continual renewing power of God's creation.
[6] Morning always comes after night: another proof of God's ability to renew the world.
[7] God "broods" like a patient mother hen, protecting the world.
[8] Suggests both awe at God's grace and the joy of a newborn bird hatching out of God's tender incubation.

I Wake and Feel the Fell[9] of Dark, Not Day

I wake and feel the fell of dark, not day.
    What hours, O what black hours we have spent
    This night! what sights you, heart, saw; ways you
        went!
And more must, in yet longer light's delay.
With witness I speak this. But where I say
    Hours I mean years, mean life. And my lament
    Is cries countless, cries like dead letters sent
To dearest him that lives alas! away.

I am gall, I am heartburn. God's most deep decree
Bitter would have me taste: my taste was me;
    Bones built in me, flesh filled, blood brimmed the
        curse.
Selfyeast of spirit a dull dough sours. I see
    The lost are like this, and their scourge to be
As I am mine, their sweating selves, but worse.

---

[9] Fell refers to skin or hide of a beast with the wool or hair on; a
   pelt. It also means cruel; barbarous; fierce.

Robert Bridges

(1844–1930)

Robert Bridges was the British Poet Laureate after Alfred, Lord Tennyson and was a friend and mentor of the Victorian poet Gerard Manley Hopkins. Born in Walmer, Kent, he went to school at Eton and then Oxford. He became a doctor and worked in London hospitals until he retired in 1882. In 1884 he married and had three children. While working as a doctor, Bridges published four books of poetry, and after retirement he dedicated most of his time to writing. He published a book on Milton's prosody in 1893 and in 1905 his poetry and verse plays were published in six volumes. After Hopkins's death, Bridges edited Hopkins's collected poetry, publishing the volume in 1918. Bridges became Poet Laureate in 1913 until his death on April 21, 1930.

My Delight and Thy Delight

My delight and thy delight
Walking, like two angels white,
In the gardens of the night:

My desire and thy desire
Twinning to a tongue of fire,
Leaping live, and laughing higher;
Thro' the everlasting strife
In the mystery of life.

Love, from whom the world begun,
Hath the secret of the sun.

Love can tell and love alone,
Whence the million stars are strewn,
Why each atom knows its own,
How, in spite of woe and death,
Gay is life, and sweet is breath:

This he taught us, this we knew,
Happy in his science true,
Hand in hand as we stood
'Neath the shadows of the wood,
Heart to heart as we lay
In the dawning of the day.

EMMA LAZARUS

(1849–1887)

EMMA LAZARUS was an American poet and essayist who is most famous for her sonnet "The New Colossus," which is inscribed on a plaque on the pedestal Statue of Liberty. She was one of the first successful Jewish-American authors. Lazarus's most famous lines come from "The New Colossus:" "Give me your tired, your poor,/Your huddled masses yearning to breathe free,/The wretched refuse of your teeming shore." Born in New York City, her early poetry includes *Admetus and Other Poems* (1871) and *The Spagnoletto* (1876), a poetic drama. Infuriated by the Russian pogroms of the 1880s, she became an passionate spokeswoman for Judaism, writing many essays and the book of poems, *Songs of a Semite* (1882).

THE NEW COLOSSUS

Not like the brazen giant of Greek fame,
With conquering limbs astride from land to land;
Here at our sea-washed, sunset gates shall stand
A mighty woman with a torch, whose flame
Is the imprisoned lightning, and her name
Mother of Exiles. From her beacon-hand
Glows world-wide welcome; her mild eyes command
The air-bridged harbor that twin cities frame.
"Keep, ancient lands, your storied pomp!" cries she
With silent lips. "Give me your tired, your poor,
Your huddled masses yearning to breathe free,
The wretched refuse of your teeming shore.
Send these, the homeless, tempest-tost to me,
I lift my lamp beside the golden door!"

ALICE MEYNELL

(1850–1923)

ALICE MEYNELL (née Alice Christiana Gertrude Thompson) was an English poet and essayist who was much admired by the Victorian poets of her day, although now her reputation has diminished. John Ruskin called her poetry "perfectly heavenly" and Lord Tennyson, Dante Rossetti, and Walter de la Mare all praised her work. She was born near London but spent much of her childhood in Italy and later became a prolific and distinguished journalist and essayist. She converted to Roman Catholicism around 1868 and this was reflected in her writing. She published her first poetry collection, *Preludes*, in 1875, and went on to publish *Poems* (1893) and *Later Poems* (1902). Meynell's poetry is characterized by simplicity, gentle sorrow, religious earnestness, and the sense of time passing.

CRADLE-SONG AT TWILIGHT

The child not yet is lulled to rest.
  Too young a nurse, the slender Night
So laxly holds him to her breast
  That throbs with flight.

He plays with her, and will not sleep.
  For other playfellows she sighs;
An unmaternal fondness keep
  Her alien eyes.

ROBERT LOUIS STEVENSON

(1850–1849)

ROBERT LOUIS STEVENSON was a famous Scottish novelist, poet, and essayist. He is most remembered for his novels *Treasure Island* (1883), *Kidnapped* (1886), and *The Strange Case of Dr. Jekyll and Mr. Hyde* (1886), as well as for his children's poetry collection *A Child's Garden of Verses* (1885.) Born in Edinburgh, Scotland, he suffered from ill health in childhood and struggled his whole life against tuberculosis, which made him seek out warm climates. He studied for a career in law but never practiced. Stevenson started writing at a young age but his first popular book was *Treasure Island*, published in 1883, a swashbuckling adventure tale about the search for a pirate's buried treasure. Also exceedingly popular was his science-fiction thriller *The Strange Case of Dr. Jekyll and Mr. Hyde*. In 1889 he and his family sailed for the South Seas where he ultimately settled on the island of Upolu (now Western Samoa) in the South Pacific Ocean. The people of the island called him "Tusitala" or "teller of tales." *A Child's Garden of Verses* became one of the most influential books for children of the 19th century.

My Shadow

I have a little shadow that goes in and out with me,
And what can be the use of him is more than I can see.
He is very, very like me from the heels up to the head;
And I see him jump before me, when I jump into my
    bed.

The funniest thing about him is the way he likes to
    grow—
Not at all like proper children, which is always very
    slow;
For he sometimes shoots up taller like an india-rubber
    ball,
And he sometimes goes so little that there's none of
    him at all.

He hasn't got a notion of how children ought to play,
And can only make a fool of me in every sort of way.
He stays so close behind me, he's a coward you can see;
I'd think shame to stick to nursie as that shadow sticks
    to me!

One morning, very early, before the sun was up,
I rose and found the shining dew on every buttercup;
But my lazy little shadow, like an arrant sleepy-head,
Had stayed at home behind me and was fast asleep in
    bed.

Edwin Markham

(1852–1940)

Edwin Markham was an American poet who became famous with the publication of his poem "The Man with the Hoe." Born in Oregon City, Oregon, he grew up in California on a ranch herding sheep and riding after cattle. After studying at the University of California he became a teacher, and then a principal and superintendent of several California schools. "The Man with the Hoe" was published on January 15, 1899 in the *San Francisco Examiner* and immediately became successful. Before the year was out, Markham's first poetry collection was published, *The Man with the Hoe and Other Poems*. During Markham's lifetime the poem was printed in more than ten thousand newspapers and magazines throughout the world. The poem captured the spirit of the time with its emphasis on a person's obligation to society and its protest against the exploitation of farm labor. Markham published another popular poem, "Lincoln, The Man of the People" in *Lincoln and Other Poem* (1901). He moved to New York City after "The Man with the Hoe" was published where he lectured to labor and radical groups. Before his death in 1940, Markham received many honors as the "Dean of American Poetry." But, with the exception of his now legendary poem, lasting renown was not his, and his reputation as a poet rapidly faded.

The Man with the Hoe[1]

Bowed by the weight of centuries he leans
Upon his hoe and gazes on the ground,
The emptiness of ages in his face,
And on his back the burden of the world.
Who made him dead to rapture and despair,
A thing that grieves not and that never hopes,
Stolid and stunned, a brother to the ox?
Who loosened and let down this brutal jaw?
Whose was the hand that slanted back this brow?
Whose breath blew out the light within this brain?
Is this the Thing the Lord God made and gave
To have dominion over sea and land;
To trace the stars and search the heavens for power.
To feel the passion of Eternity?
Is this the Dream He dreamed who shaped the suns
And marked their ways upon the ancient deep?
Down all the stretch of Hell to its last gulf
There is no shape more terrible than this—
More tongued with censure of the world's blind greed—
More filled with signs and portents for the soul—
More fraught with menace to the universe.

What gulfs between him and the seraphim!
Slave of the wheel of labor, what to him
Are Plato[2] and the swing of Pleiades?[3]

---

[1] This poem was inspired by the French artist Jean-François
   Millet's well-known painting of the same name (in French
   L'homme à la houe).
[2] Plato was a famous Greek philosopher who lived from 427 B.C to
   347 B.C.
[3] The Pleiades, also known as the seven sisters or the "weeping

What the long reaches of the peaks of song,
The rift of dawn, the reddening of the rose?
Through this dread shape the suffering ages look;
Time's tragedy is in that aching stoop;
Through this dread shape humanity betrayed,
Plundered, profaned and disinherited,
Cries protest to the Judges of the World,
A protest that is also prophecy.

O masters, lords and rulers in all lands,
Is this the handiwork you give to God,
This monstrous thing distorted and soul-quenched?
How will you ever straighten up this shape;
Touch it again with immortality;
Give back the upward looking and the light;
Rebuild in it the music and the dream;
Make right the immemorial infamies,
Perfidious wrongs, immedicable woes?

O masters, lords and rulers in all lands,
How will the Future reckon with this Man?
How answer his brute question in that hour
When whirlwinds of rebellion shake the world?
How will it be with kingdoms and with kings—
With those who shaped him to the thing he is—
When this dumb Terror shall reply to God,
After the silence of the centuries?

---

sisters" are seven stars in the constellation of Taurus. In Greek
mythology, the seven daughters of Atlas and the nymph Pleione,
killed themselves in anguish after Atlas was transformed into a
mountain. In another version of the myth, Jupiter changed the
sisters into stars so that they could escape the unwanted atten-
tions of Orion.

OSCAR WILDE

(1856–1900)

OSCAR WILDE was an Irish playwright, novelist, and poet who was one of the most celebrated (as well as infamous) literary figures of his day. Most renowned for his sophisticated, witty plays as well as his own public persona (he was a noted eccentric in dress, taste, manners, and aesthetics), his life eventually ended in tragedy. Born in Dublin, his father was an eye surgeon and his mother was a literary hostess and writer. He graduated from Trinity College and then went on to study at Oxford. At Oxford he became known as a talented poet and won a prize for his poem "Ravenna." Influenced by Walter Pater and John Ruskin, Wilde believed in "art for art's sake." He published his first work, *Poems*, in 1881. The book was a success and Wilde was able to give a well-received lecture tour in the United States the following year. In 1884 he married Constance Lloyd, and they had two sons, Cyril and Vyvyan. Wilde's career took off with two collections of fairy tales, *The Happy Prince* (1888) and *The House of Pomegranates* (1892) and his famous novel *Picture of Dorian Gray* (1891). Wilde is most renowned for his plays which include *Lady Windermere's Fan* (1892), *A Woman of No Importance* (1893), *An Ideal Husband* (1895), and his masterpiece, *The Importance of Being Earnest* (1895).

Wilde became involved romantically with Lord Alfred Douglas ("Bosie") and eventually the marquess of Queensberry, Douglas's father, wrote him a note accusing him of homosexual practices. Wilde brought action for libel against the marquess and was himself charged with homosexual offenses under the Criminal Law Amendment, found guilty, and sentenced in 1895 to prison for two years. His experiences in prison inspired his most famous poem, *The Ballad of Reading Gaol* (1898). After he was released from jail, Wilde was beset by ill health and poverty, and lived in France under an assumed name until his death in 1900.

REQUIESCAT

Tread lightly, she is near
Under the snow,
Speak gently, she can hear
The daisies grow.

All her bright golden hair
Tarnished with rust,
She that was young and fair
Fallen to dust.

Lily-like, white as snow,
She hardly knew
She was a woman, so
Sweetly she grew.

Coffin-board, heavy stone,
Lie on her breast,
I vex my heart alone
She is at rest.

Peace, Peace, she cannot hear
Lyre or sonnet,
All my life's buried here,
Heap earth upon it.

AVIGNON.

To My Wife
With a Copy of My Poems

I can write no stately proem[1]
As a prelude to my lay;
From a poet to a poem
I would dare to say.

For if of these fallen petals
One to you seem fair,
Love will waft it till it settles
On your hair.

And when wind and winter harden
All the loveless land,
It will whisper of the garden,
You will understand.

---

[1] A preface.

KATHERINE LEE BATES

(1859–1929)

KATHERINE LEE BATES was an American poet who is most known for writing the words to "America the Beautiful," which was later set to music. Bates was a prolific poet and a professor of English. She attended Wellesley, graduating in 1880. She was inspired to write the poem after she journeyed to Colorado and climbed Pike's Peak.

from AMERICA THE BEAUTIFUL

O beautiful for spacious skies,
For amber waves of grain,
For purple mountain majesties
Above the fruited plain!
America! America!
God shed his grace on thee
And crown thy good with brotherhood
From sea to shining sea!

O beautiful for pilgrim feet
Whose stern impassioned stress
A thoroughfare of freedom beat
Across the wilderness!
America! America!
God mend thine every flaw,
Confirm thy soul in self-control,
Thy liberty in law!

O beautiful for heroes proved
In liberating strife.
Who more than self their country loved
And mercy more than life!
America! America!
May God thy gold refine
Till all success be nobleness
And every gain divine!

O beautiful for patriot dream
That sees beyond the years
Thine alabaster cities gleam
Undimmed by human tears!
America! America!
God shed his grace on thee
And crown thy good with brotherhood
From sea to shining sea!

O beautiful for halcyon skies,
For amber waves of grain,
For purple mountain majesties
Above the enameled plain!
America! America!
God shed his grace on thee
Till souls wax fair as earth and air
And music-hearted sea!

.   .   .

If You Could Come

My love, my love, if you could come once more
From your high place,
I would not question you for heavenly lore,
But, silent, take the comfort of your face.

I would not ask you if those golden spheres
In love rejoice,
If only our stained star hath sin and tears,
But fill my famished hearing with your voice.

One touch of you were worth a thousand creeds.
My wound is numb
Through toil-pressed, but all night long it bleeds
In aching dreams, and still you cannot come.

A.E. HOUSMAN

(1859–1936)

A. E. HOUSMAN (Alfred Edward Housman) was an English poet and scholar most famous for his poems in *A Shropshire Lad*. He studied at Oxford but left without a degree after failing his final exams. In 1892 he became a professor of Latin at University College, London, and in 1911 professor of Latin at Cambridge and fellow of Trinity College. Housman proved to be one of the finest classical scholars of his time. He produced a monumental edition of Manilius, edited Juvenal and Lucan, and wrote valuable classical studies. But he is most famous as a poet, although only two small volumes appeared during his lifetime, *A Shropshire Lad* (1896) and *Last Poems* (1922). His verse is noted for its concision, directness, and pictures of the English countryside, as well as for its mixture of humor and pathos. The passing of youth and the inevitability of death is his most common theme. His best-known poems include "When I Was One-and-twenty," "With Rue My Heart Is Laden," "To an Athlete Dying Young," and "Far in a Western Brookland."

When I Was One-and-Twenty

When I was one-and-twenty
I heard a wise man say,
"Give crowns and pounds and guineas
But not your heart away;
Give pearls away and rubies
But keep your fancy free."
But I was one-and-twenty,
No use to talk to me.

When I was one-and-twenty
I heard him say again,
"The heart out of the bosom
Was never given in vain;
'Tis paid with sighs a plenty
And sold for endless rue."
And I am two-and-twenty
And oh, 'tis true, 'tis true.

To an Athlete Dying Young

The time you won your town the race
We chaired you through the market-place;
Man and boy stood cheering by,
And home we brought you shoulder-high.

To-day, the road all runners come,
Shoulder-high we bring you home,
And set you at your threshold down,
Townsman of a stiller town.

Smart lad, to slip betimes away
From fields where glory does not stay
And early though the laurel grows
It withers quicker than the rose.

Eyes the shady night has shut
Cannot see the record cut,
And silence sounds no worse than cheers
After earth has stopped the ears:

Now you will not swell the rout
Of lads that wore their honours out,
Runners whom renown outran
And the name died before the man.

So set, before its echoes fade,
The fleet foot on the sill of shade,
And hold to the low lintel up
The still-defended challenge-cup.

And round that early-laurelled head
Will flock to gaze the strengthless dead,
And find unwithered on its curls
The garland briefer than a girl's.

EMILY PAULINE JOHNSON
(TEKAHIONWAKE)

(1861–1913)

EMILY PAULINE JOHNSON was a Canadian Native American poet who bridged her Mohawk and European background. She was a very popular poet in the late 19th and early 20th centuries.

IN THE SHADOWS

I am sailing to the leeward,
Where the current runs to seaward
    Soft and slow,
Where the sleeping river grasses
Brush my paddle as it passes
    To and fro.

On the shore the heat is shaking
All the golden sands awaking
    In the cove;
And the quaint sandpiper, winging
O'er the shallows, ceases singing
    When I move.

On the water's idle pillow
Sleeps the overhanging willow,
    Green and cool;
Where the rushes lift their burnished
Oval heads from out the tarnished
    Emerald pool.

Where the very silence slumbers,
Water lilies grow in numbers,
    Pure and pale;
All the morning they have rested,
Amber crowned, and pearly crested,
    Fair and frail.

Here, impossible romances,
Indefinable sweet fancies,
    Cluster round;
But they do not mar the sweetness
Of this still September fleetness
    With a sound.

I can scarce discern the meeting
Of the shore and stream retreating,
    So remote;
For the laggard river, dozing,
Only wakes from its reposing
    Where I float.

Where the river mists are rising,
All the foliage baptizing
    With their spray;
There the sun gleams far and faintly,
With a shadow soft and saintly,
    In its ray.

And the perfume of some burning
Far-off brushwood, ever turning
    To exhale
All its smoky fragrance dying,
In the arms of evening lying,
    Where I sail.

My canoe is growing lazy,
In the atmosphere so hazy,
    While I dream;
Half in slumber I am guiding,
Eastward indistinctly gliding
    Down the stream.

Amy Levy

(1861–1889)

A MY LEVY was an English poet, novelist, and feminist during the Victorian era. She was born into a wealthy Anglo-Jewish family. Levy studied at Newham College, Cambridge, where she was the first Jewish student. Levy did not graduate from Newham. She spent most of her life living at home where she had a close circle of literary and socialist friends, including Eleanor Marx, the daughter of Karl Marx. Writing stories, essays, and poems for magazines and newspapers, Levy eventually published three books of poetry and three novels. In 1880 she published *Xantippe and Other Verse*, her first collection of poetry. Her writings revealed her feminist concerns and her second novel, *Reuben Sachs*, dealt with Jewish identity in 19th century England. Its themes of avarice and wantonness made Levy a controversial figure, especially among London Jews. Her last book of poems, *A London Plane-Tree and Other Verse* showed the influence of the French symbolist poets. Levy traveled in Europe where she fell in love with a woman writer, however her affection was not returned. Levy wrote poetry about unrequited love for a woman, sometimes using the persona of a male speaker. Despite living a productive life, Levy had suffered from depression since childhood. Her mental illness, as well as her growing deafness, led her to commit suicide at the young age of twenty-eight by inhaling carbon monoxide fumes in her home.

In the Mile End Road[1]

How like her! But 'tis she herself,
Comes up the crowded street,
How little did I think, the morn,
My only love to meet!

Whose else that motion and that mien?
Whose else that airy tread?
For one strange moment I forgot
My only love was dead.

---

[1] This poem was published in *A London Plane-Tree and Other Verse* in 1889. In London the Mile End Road ran past the Spanish and Portuguese Jews' Hospital, as well as the first modern English Jewish cemetery.

EDITH WHARTON

(1862–1937)

EDITH WHARTON (née Edith Newbold Jones) is one of the most prominent figures in American literature. Most famous for her novels depicting New York high society, she was the first woman to win the Pulitzer Prize for her 1920 novel *The Age of Innocence*. Born in New York City into an upper-class family, she spent much of her adult life in France and did not begin her professional writing career until she was nearly forty years old. Although she had published short stories and articles in the 1890s, and in 1902 published her first novel, *The Valley of Decision*, it was her 1905 novel, *The House of Mirth* that brought her critical and popular success. Throughout her career she published over forty books, including poetry, criticism and the novel *Ethan Frome* (1911). Wharton had an unhappy marriage and after her divorce, she remained in France, but made visits to the United States to maintain her citizenship. She established two organizations for war refugees during World War I and made several visits to the French front. She received many honors from the French and Belgian governments for her contribution to the war effort. Wharton continued to write until her death on August 11, 1937. She was buried in Versailles. She is now regarded as one of the great novelists of the early 20th century and is considered as influential a writer as her longtime friend, Henry James.

Belgium[1]

La Belgique ne regrette rien[2]

Not with her ruined silver spires,
Not with her cities shamed and rent,
Perish the imperishable fires
That shape the homestead from the tent.

Wherever men are staunch and free,
There shall she keep her fearless state,
And homeless, to great nations be
The home of all that makes them great.

---

[1] Wharton was an avid supporter of France and Belgium during
World War I and took in Belgium refugees.
[2] French for "Belgium regrets nothing." Again, Wharton shows her
complete sympathies with Belgium's fight in WWI.

Life[3]

Life, like a marble block, is given to all,
A blank, inchoate mass of years and days,
Whence one with ardent chisel swift essays
Some shape of strength or symmetry to call;
One shatters it in bits to mend a wall;
One in a craftier hand the chisel lays,
And one, to wake the mirth in Lesbia's[4] gaze,
Carves it apace in toys fantastical.

But least is he who, with enchanted eyes
Filled with high visions of fair shapes to be,
Muses which god he shall immortalize
In the proud Parian's[5] perpetuity,
Till twilight warns him from the punctual skies
That the night cometh wherein none shall see.

---

[3] "Life" was published in *Scribner's Magazine* on June 15, 1894.
[4] "Lesbia" was generally considered to be the pseudonym for an aristocratic Roman women (her real name was Clodia) to whom the Roman lyric poet Catullus (84-54BC) dedicated a number of poems. However, new research suggests that "Lesbia" might not refer to an actual historical figure. The name Lesbia also suggests Lesbos Island, where the celebrated Greek poet Sappho lived.
[5] Parian is a type of marble highly valued in the ancient world for the making of sculpture.

ERNEST LAWRENCE THAYER

(1863–1940)

Ernest Lawrence Thayer was an American poet and humorous columnist most famous for his ballad "Casey at the Bat." Raised in Massachusetts, Thayer graduated magna cum laude from Harvard with a degree in philosophy in 1885. While at Harvard he edited the *Harvard Lampoon*. After college Thayer toured Europe and his college friend William Randolph Hearst (the business manager of the *Harvard Lampoon* and future newspaper mogul) hired Thayer to work as a humor columnist for the *San Francisco Examiner* where he worked for three years. The last piece he wrote for the paper was "Casey at Bat," dated June 3, 1888. This poem made Thayer famous—although it took two decades for this to happen. Thayer signed the work, "Phin." And though he recited it for his Harvard class reunion in 1895, he did not have a high opinion about the verse. Thayer contributed several more humorous poems to Hearst's New York Journal and then turned to overseeing his family's mills in Worcester, Massachusetts. In 1912 he retired and moved to Santa Barbara where he married.

"Casey at Bat" gained popularity several months after its 1888 publication when De Wolf Hopper, a popular singer, actor, and comedian of the time, performed the piece on Broadway in front of an audience that contained members of the New York Giants and the Chicago White Stockings (now the Cubs). Although there has been much speculation over whether or not the legendary town "Mudville" really exists there is no evidence that it does. Thayer claimed that he did not base "Casey" on an actual baseball player; however it is considered that the late 1880s Boston star Mike "King" Kelly was probably the model for the poem.

CASEY AT THE BAT[1]

The outlook wasn't brilliant for the Mudville nine that
  day;
The score stood four to two, with but one inning more
  to play,
And then when Cooney died at first, and Barrows did
  the same,
A pall-like silence fell upon the patrons of the game.

A straggling few got up to go in deep despair. The rest
Clung to that hope which springs eternal in the human
  breast;
They thought, "If only Casey could but get a whack at
  that—
We'd put up even money now, with Casey at the bat."

But Flynn preceded Casey, as did also Jimmy Blake,
And the former was a hoodoo, while the latter was a
  cake;
So upon that stricken multitude grim melancholy sat,
For there seemed but little chance of Casey getting to
  the bat.

---

[1] Thayer wrote "Casey at the Bat" in two hours and was paid five
  dollars for the poem. The piece first appeared on June 3, 1888,
  but it received little attention.

But Flynn let drive a single, to the wonderment of all,
And Blake, the much despisèd, tore the cover off the
ball;
And when the dust had lifted, and men saw what had
occurred,
There was Jimmy safe at second and Flynn a-hugging
third.

Then from five thousand throats and more there rose a
lusty yell;
It rumbled through the valley, it rattled in the dell;
It pounded on the mountain and recoiled upon the flat,
For Casey, mighty Casey, was advancing to the bat.

There was ease in Casey's manner as he stepped into
his place;
There was pride in Casey's bearing and a smile lit
Casey's face.
And when, responding to the cheers, he lightly doffed
his hat,
No stranger in the crowd could doubt 'twas Casey at
the bat.

Ten thousand eyes were on him as he rubbed his hands
with dirt;
Five thousand tongues applauded when he wiped them
on his shirt;
Then while the writhing pitcher ground the ball into
his hip,
Defiance flashed in Casey's eye, a sneer curled Casey's
lip.

And now the leather-covered sphere came hurtling
    through the air,
And Casey stood a-watching it in haughty grandeur
    there.
Close by the sturdy batsman the ball unheeded sped—
"That ain't my style," said Casey. "Strike one!" the
    umpire said.

From the benches, black with people, there went up a
    muffled roar,
Like the beating of the storm-waves on a stern and
    distant shore;
"Kill him! Kill the umpire!" shouted some one on the
    stand;
And it's likely they'd have killed him had not Casey
    raised his hand.

With a smile of Christian charity great Casey's visage
    shone;
He stilled the rising tumult; he bade the game go on;
He signaled to the pitcher, and once more the dun
    sphere flew;
But Casey still ignored it, and the umpire said, "Strike
    two!"

"Fraud!" cried the maddened thousands, and echo
    answered "Fraud!"
But one scornful look from Casey and the audience was
    awed.
They saw his face grow stern and cold, they saw his
    muscles strain,
And they knew that Casey wouldn't let that ball go by
    again.

The sneer has fled from Casey's lip, his teeth are
    clenched in hate;
He pounds with cruel violence his bat upon the plate.
And now the pitcher holds the ball, and now he lets it
    go.
And now the air is shattered by the force of Casey's
    blow.

Oh, somewhere in this favored land the sun is shining
    bright;
The band is playing somewhere, and somewhere hearts
    are light,
And somewhere men are laughing, and little children
    shout;
But there is no joy in Mudville—great Casey has struck
    out.

GEORGE SANTAYANA

(1863–1952)

GEORGE SANTAYANA was a Spanish poet and philosopher born in Madrid who spent much of his life in
the United States. Santayana is a principal figure in classical American philosophy. His Hispanic heritage,
shaded by his sense of being an outsider in America, captured many qualities of American life missed by insiders.
His autobiography, *Persons and Places* (1944) and only
novel, *The Last Puritan* (1936), were best-selling books.
The Last Puritan was nominated for a Pulitzer Prize.
Astonishingly, Santayana achieved this stature in American thought without being a citizen. He proudly
retained his Spanish citizenship throughout his life. Yet,
as he readily admitted, his philosophical and literary
work are to be classified as American.

There May Be Chaos Still
Around the World

There may be chaos still around the world,
This little world that in my thinking lies;
For mine own bosom is the paradise
Where all my life's fair visions are unfurled.
Within my nature's shell I slumber curled,
Unmindful of the changing outer skies,
Where now, perchance, some new-born Eros[1] flies,
Or some old Cronos[2] from his throne is hurled.
I heed them not; or if the subtle night
Haunt me with deities I never saw,
I soon mine eyelid's drowsy curtain draw
To hide their myriad faces from my sight.
They threat in vain; the whirlwind cannot awe
A happy snow-flake dancing in the flaw.

---

[1] In Greek mythology Eros was the god of love and sexual desire.
He is usually depicted as a winged boy. In Roman mythology he
is known as Cupid.

[2] In Greek mythology Cronos was the leader of the Titans (the
divine descendants of Gaia, the earth, and Uranus, the sky. Cro-
nous overthrew Uranus and ruled until he was overthrown by
his own son, Zeus.

Arthur Symons

(1865–1945)

Arthur Symons was a Welsh poet and critic who was considered one of the leading Symbolists in England. Born in Milford Haven, Wales, he was the son of a minister. His first volume of poetry, *Days and Nights*, was published in 1889. The book consisted of dramatic monologues. Symons became very influenced by French poets such as Charles Baudelaire and Verlaine. Symons also edited plays and joined the *Athenaeum* in 1891 and the *Saturday Review* in 1894.

Before the Squall

The wind is rising on the sea,
The windy white foam-dancers leap;
And the sea moans uneasily,
And turns to sleep, and cannot sleep.

Ridge after rocky ridge uplifts,
Wild hands, and hammers at the land,
Scatters in liquid dust, and drifts
To death among the dusty sand.

On the horizon's nearing line,
Where the sky rests, a visible wall,
Grey in the offing, I divine,
The sails that fly before the squall.

Rudyard Kipling

(1865–1936)

Rudyard Kipling was a renowned English novelist, short story writer, and poet who was extremely popular in his time and became quite controversial as a proponent of the British empire. Born in India Kipling is best remembered today for his children's books. His most famous work includes *The Jungle Book* (1894), *The Second Jungle Book* (1895), *Just So Stories* (1902), and *Kim* (1901). Kipling was one of the most popular writers in English during the late 19th and early 20th centuries. Considered a leading light of the short story genre, one of his most celebrated stories is "The Man Who Would Be King" (1888). His children's books remain classics. In 1907 he was the first English language writer to win the Nobel Prize for literature. Kipling was offered the British Poet Laureateship and knighthood but he declined both honors. He was praised by renowned writers such as Henry James, who called him "the most complete man of genius," and by George Orwell. However, he also came to be seen as proponent of British imperialism by Orwell and many others. His writing has been criticized for its militarism and prejudice.

Some of Kipling's most celebrated poems are "Mandalay," "Gunga Din," and "If."

If[1]

If you can keep your head when all about you
Are losing theirs and blaming it on you;
If you can trust yourself when all men doubt you,
But make allowance for their doubting too;
If you can wait and not be tired by waiting,
Or, being lied about, don't deal in lies,
Or, being hated, don't give way to hating,
And yet don't look too good, nor talk too wise;

If you can dream—and not make dreams your master;
If you can think—and not make thoughts your aim;
If you can meet with triumph and disaster
And treat those two imposters just the same;
If you can bear to hear the truth you've spoken
Twisted by knaves to make a trap for fools,
Or watch the things you gave your life to broken,
And stoop and build 'em up with wornout tools;

If you can make one heap of all your winnings
And risk it on one turn of pitch-and-toss,
And lose, and start again at your beginnings
And never breath a word about your loss;
If you can force your heart and nerve and sinew
To serve your turn long after they are gone,
And so hold on when there is nothing in you
Except the Will which says to them: "Hold on";

---

[1] "If" was published in 1895.

If you can talk with crowds and keep your virtue,
Or walk with kings—nor lose the common touch;
If neither foes nor loving friends can hurt you;
If all men count with you, but none too much;
If you can fill the unforgiving minute
With sixty seconds' worth of distance run—
Yours is the Earth and everything that's in it,
And—which is more—you'll be a Man my son!

WILLIAM BUTLER YEATS

(1865–1939)

WILLIAM BUTLER YEATS is one of the most celebrated Modernist poets. Born in Dublin, Ireland, he was a towering figure in English literature at the turn of the 20th century, not the least because of his poems and plays. He combined an immense knowledge of Irish folklore and Gaelic verse with a self-conscious flamboyance. His poetry changed decisively in the years 1909 to 1914: the otherworldly, ecstatic atmosphere of the early lyrics cleared and his work gained in directness and complexity, often dealing with political themes, though his interest in mysticism and his passion for Maud Gonne continued unabated. With *Responsibilities* (1914) and *The Wild Swans at Coole* (1917) he began the period of his highest achievement. Some of his greatest verse appears in *The Tower* (1928), *The Winding Stair* (1929), and *Last Poems* (1939). He was elected one of the first senators of the Irish Free State (1922–28), and awarded the Nobel Prize for literature in 1923. Yeats is considered by some to be the greatest English-language poet of the 20th century.

Where My Books Go

All the words that I utter,
  And all the words that I write,
Must spread out their wings untiring,
  And never rest in their flight,
Till they come where your sad, sad heart is,
  And sing to you in the night,
Beyond where the waters are moving,
  Storm-darken'd or starry bright.

Byzantium

The unpurged images of day recede;
The Emperor's drunken soldiery are abed;
Night resonance recedes, night walkers' song
After great cathedral gong;
A starlit or a moonlit dome disdains
All that man is,
All mere complexities,
The fury and the mire of human veins.
Before me floats an image, man or shade,
Shade more than man, more image than a shade;
For Hades' bobbin bound in mummy-cloth
May unwind the winding path;
A mouth that has no moisture and no breath
Breathless mouths may summon;
I hail the superhuman;
I call it death-in-life and life-in-death.
Miracle, bird or golden handiwork,
More miracle than bird or handiwork,

Planted on the star-lit golden bough,
Can like the cocks of Hades crow,
Or, by the moon embittered, scorn aloud
In glory of changeless metal
Common bird or petal
And all complexities of mire or blood.
At midnight on the Emperor's pavement flit
Flames that no faggot feeds, nor steel has lit,
Nor storm disturbs, flames begotten of flame,
Where blood-begotten spirits come
And all complexities of fury leave,
Dying into a dance,
An agony of trance,
An agony of flame that cannot singe a sleeve.
Astraddle on the dolphin's mire and blood,
Spirit after Spirit! The smithies break the flood.
The golden smithies of the Emperor!
Marbles of the dancing floor
Break bitter furies of complexity,
Those images that yet
Fresh images beget,
That dolphin-torn, that gong-tormented sea.

CRAZY JANE REPROVED

I care not what the sailors say:
All those dreadful thunder-stones,
All that storm that blots the day
Can but show that Heaven yawns;
Great Europa played the fool
That changed a lover for a bull.
Fol de rol, fol de rol.

To round that shell's elaborate whorl,
Adorning every secret track
With the delicate mother-of-pearl,
Made the joints of Heaven crack:
So never hang your heart upon
A roaring, ranting journeyman.
Fol de rol, fol de rol.

LEDA AND THE SWAN

A sudden blow: the great wings beating still
Above the staggering girl, her thighs caressed
By the dark webs, her nape caught in his bill,
He holds her helpless breast upon his breast.
How can those terrified vague fingers push
The feathered glory from her loosening thighs?
And how can body, laid in that white rush,
But feel the strange heart beating where it lies?
A shudder in the loins engenders there
The broken wall, the burning roof and tower
And Agamemnon dead.

Being so caught up,
So mastered by the brute blood of the air,
Did she put on his knowledge with his power
Before the indifferent beak could let her drop?

The Second Coming

Turning and turning in the widening gyre
The falcon cannot hear the falconer;
Things fall apart; the centre cannot hold;
Mere anarchy is loosed upon the world,
The blood-dimmed tide is loosed, and everywhere
The ceremony of innocence is drowned;
The best lack all conviction, while the worst
Are full of passionate intensity.

Surely some revelation is at hand;
Surely the Second Coming is at hand.
The Second Coming! Hardly are those words out
When a vast image out of Spiritus Mundi
Troubles my sight: somewhere in sands of the desert
A shape with lion body and the head of a man,
A gaze blank and pitiless as the sun,
Is moving its slow thighs, while all about it
Reel shadows of the indignant desert birds.
The darkness drops again; but now I know
That twenty centuries of stony sleep
Were vexed to nightmare by a rocking cradle,
And what rough beast, its hour come round at last,
Slouches towards Bethlehem to be born?

EDWIN ARLINGTON ROBINSON

(1869–1935)

EDWIN ARLINGTON ROBINSON was an American poet who won three Pulitzer Prizes for his poetry. Born in Maine, he was raised in Amesbury, Massachusetts, by a wealthy family and attended Harvard. He started writing poetry as a child. Robinson experienced many tragedies as a young man starting with his father's death. The family went bankrupt, one of his older brother's became a morphine addict (and eventually died from an overdose), and his mother suffered and died from diphtheria. Additionally, Robinson fell in love with Emma Shepherd, but because he felt that family life would distract him from his poetry he introduced her to his eldest brother and they were married. This brother provided Robinson with a monthly allowance from the family estate.

President Theodore Roosevelt read an early work by Robinson, *Children of the Night* and enjoyed it so much that he arranged for Robinson to get a job at a custom house. Robert Frost was influenced by Robinson's poetry. Robinson won the Pulitzer Prize in 1921 for his *Collected Poems*, which contained 166 poems including some of his best long and short form verses.

THE HOUSE ON THE HILL

They are all gone away,
The House is shut and still,
There is nothing more to say.

Through broken walls and gray
The winds blow bleak and shrill:
They are all gone away.

Nor is there one to-day
To speak them good or ill:
There is nothing more to say.

Why is it then we stray
Around the sunken sill?
They are all gone away,

And our poor fancy-play
For them is wasted skill:
There is nothing more to say.

There is ruin and decay
In the House on the Hill:
They are all gone away,
There is nothing more to say.

MINIVER CHEEVY

Miniver Cheevy, child of scorn,
   Grew lean while he assailed the seasons;
He wept that he was ever born,
   And he had reasons.

Miniver loved the days of old
   When swords were bright and steeds were prancing;

The vision of a warrior bold
Would set him dancing.

Miniver sighed for what was not,
And dreamed, and rested from his labors;
He dreamed of Thebes and Camelot,
And Priam's neighbors.

Miniver mourned the ripe renown
That made so many a name so fragrant;
He mourned Romance, now on the town,
And Art, a vagrant.

Miniver loved the Medici,
Albeit he had never seen one;
He would have sinned incessantly
Could he have been one.

Miniver cursed the commonplace
And eyed a khaki suit with loathing;
He missed the mediæval grace
Of iron clothing.

Miniver scorned the gold he sought,
But sore annoyed was he without it;
Miniver thought, and thought, and thought,
And thought about it.

Miniver Cheevy, born too late,
Scratched his head and kept on thinking;
Miniver coughed, and called it fate,
And kept on drinking.

EDGAR LEE MASTERS

(1868–1950)

EDGAR LEE MASTERS was an American poet famous for his *Spoon River Anthology*, published in 1915. *Spoon River Anthology* was a critical and popular triumph (no other work by Masters rivaled its success), unique in its method of having each citizen of a small town tell his or her secrets from beyond the grave. The book was also noted for bringing scandalous subject matter into American poetry.

BENJAMIN PAINTER

Together in this grave lie Benjamin Painter, attorney at
    law,
And Nig, his dog, constant companion, solace and
    friend.
Down the grey road, friends, children, men and
    women,
Passing one by one out of life, left me till I was alone
With Nig for partner, bed fellow, comrade in drink.
In the morning of life I knew aspiration and saw glory.
Then she, who survives me, snared my soul
With a snare which bled me to death,
Till I, once strong of sill, lay broken, indifferent,
Living with Nig in a room back of a dingy office.
Under my jaw-bone is snuggled the bony nose of
    Nig—
Our story is lost in silence. Go by, mad world!

Mrs. Benjamin Painter

I know that he told how I snared his soul
With a snare which bled him to death.
And all the men loved him,
And most of the women pitied him.
But suppose you are really a lady, and have delicate
     tastes,
And loathe the smell of whisky and onions.
And the rhythm of Wordsworth's "Ode" runs in your
     ears,
While he goes about from morning till night
Repeating bits of that common thing;
"Oh, why should the spirit of mortal be proud?"
And then, suppose:
You are a woman well endowed,
And the only man with whom the law and morality
Permit you to have the marital relation
Is the very man that fills you with disgust
Every time you think of it—while you think of it
Every time you see him?
That's why I drove him away from home
To live with his dog in a dingy room
Back of his office.

Minerva Jones

I am Minerva, the village poetess,
Hooted at, jeered at by the Yahoos of the street
For my heavy body, cock-eye, and rolling walk,
And all the more when "Butch" Weldy
Captured me after a brutal hunt.
He left me to my fate with Doctor Meyers;
And I sank into death, growing numb from the feet up,
Like one stepping deeper and deeper into a stream of
 ice.
Will some one go to the village newspaper,
And gather into a book the verses I wrote?—
I thirsted so for love!
I hungered so for life!

HILAIRE BELLOC

(1870–1953)

HILAIRE BELLOC was French-born English poet, historian, Catholic apologist, and essayist. A highly multi-talented writer, he is best remembered for his light verse, particularly for children, and for his cogent essays. His works include *Verses and Sonnets* (1895), *The Bad Child's Book of Beasts* (1896), *The Modern Traveller* (1898), *Mr. Burden* (1904), and *Cautionary Tales* (1907). He also wrote several historical works, including a four-volume *History of England* (1925–1931). He is noted for the humorous quotes: "I shoot the Hippopotamus with bullets made of platinum, because if I use the leaden one his hide is sure to flatten em;" "Just as there is nothing between the admirable omelet and the intolerable, so with autobiography;" and "When I am dead, I hope it may be said: His sins were scarlet, but his books were read."

Is There Any Reward?

Is there any reward?
I'm beginning to doubt it.
I am broken and bored,
Is there any reward
Reassure me, Good Lord,
And inform me about it.
Is there any reward?
I'm beginning to doubt it.

The Elephant

When people call this beast to mind,
They marvel more and more
At such a little tail behind,
So large a trunk before.

STEPHEN CRANE

(1871–1900)

STEPHEN CRANE was an American writer best remembered for his novel *The Red Badge of Courage* (1895). Crane wrote novels, short stories, and poetry. Born in Newark, New Jersey, Crane went to Syracuse University for one semester and then moved to New York City where he struggled to make a living as a writer and journalist. In 1893 he published *Maggie: A Girl of the Streets*, which was a sympathetic look at a poor girl's descent into prostitution. It was considered an important work of literary naturalism. His masterpiece, *The Red Badge of Courage*, was about the psychological confusion of a young solider during the Civil War, and it gave him an international reputation. Also in 1895, Crane published a book of poetry called *The Black Riders*. He worked as a war correspondent during the Spanish-American War and while traveling to Cuba his ship sank and he almost drowned. From this experience of surviving at sea, he wrote his well-known short story, "The Open Boat," published in 1898. His short story collections include *The Little Reigment* (1896), *The Monster* (1899), and *Wilomville Stories* (1900). In 1897, he moved to England where he became friends with the great novelists Henry James, H.G. Wells, and Joseph Conrad. He died of tuberculosis at the young age of twenty-eight. In addition to *The Black Riders*, Crane published one more book of poetry, *War is Kind*, in 1899.

Black Riders Came from the Sea

Black riders came from the sea.
There was clang and clang of spear and shield,
And clash and clash of hoof and heel,
Wild shouts and the wave of hair
In the rush upon the wind:
Thus the ride of sin.

Do Not Weep, Maiden, for War is Kind

Do not weep, maiden, for war is kind.
Because your lover threw wild hands toward the sky
And the affrighted steed ran on alone,
Do not weep.
War is kind.

Hoarse, booming drums of the regiment,
Little souls who thirst for fight,
These men were born to drill and die.
The unexplained glory flies above them,
Great is the battle-god, great, and his kingdom—
A field where a thousand corpses lie.

Do not weep, babe, for war is kind.
Because your father tumbled in the yellow trenches,
Raged at his breast, gulped and died,
Do not weep.
War is kind.

Swift blazing flag of the regiment,
Eagle with crest of red and gold,
These men were born to drill and die.
Point for them the virtue of slaughter,
Make plain to them the excellence of killing
And a field where a thousand corpses lie.

Mother whose heart hung humble as a button
On the bright splendid shroud of your son,
Do not weep.
War is kind.

JAMES WELDON JOHNSON

(1871–1938)

JAMES WELDON JOHNSON was a prominent American author, poet, and civil rights activist. He was a leading figure in the Harlem Renaissance and one of the first African-American professors at New York University. Born in Jacksonville, Florida, he attended the University of Atlanta and then Columbia. Johnson was the first African American to be admitted to the Florida bar and later was American consul, first in Venezuela and then in Nicaragua. He helped found and was secretary (1916–1930) of the National Association for the Advancement of Colored People. His novel *Autobiography of an Ex-Coloured Man* (1912), published anonymously, caused a great commotion and was republished under his name in 1927. Among his other works are the words to *Lift Every Voice and Sing* (1900), which has been called the African American national anthem, *God's Trombones* (1927), African American sermons in verse, and *Black Manhattan* (1930). He wrote songs with his brother, John Rosamond Johnson.

Lift Every Voice and Sing

Lift every voice and sing
Till earth and heaven ring,
Ring with the harmonies of Liberty;
Let our rejoicing rise
High as the listening skies,
Let it resound loud as the rolling sea.
Sing a song full of the faith that the dark past has
    taught us,
Sing a song full of the hope that the present has
    brought us.
Facing the rising sun of our new day begun,
Let us march on till victory is won.
Stony the road we trod,
Bitter the chastening rod,
Felt in the days when hope unborn had died;
Yet with a steady beat
Have not our weary feet
Come to a place for which our fathers sighed?
We have come over a way that with tears has been
    watered,
We have come, treading our path through the blood of
    the slaughtered,
Out from the gloomy past,
Till now we stand at last
Where the white gleam of our bright star is cast.
God of our weary years,
God of our silent tears,
Thou who hast brought us thus far on the way;
Thou who hast by Thy might
Led us into light,

Keep us forever in the path, we pray.
Lest our feet stray from the places, our God, where we
    met Thee,
Lest, our hearts drunk with the wine of the world, we
    forget Thee,
Shadowed beneath Thy hand,
May we forever stand.
True to our God,
True to our native land.

The Black Mammy

O whitened head entwined in turban gay,
O kind black face, O crude, but tender hand,
O foster-mother in whose arms there lay
The race whose sons are masters of the land!
It was thine arms that sheltered in their fold,
It was thine eyes that followed through the length
Of infant days these sons. In times of old
It was thy breast that nourished them to strength.

So often hast thou to thy bosom pressed
The golden head, the face and brow of snow;
So often has it 'gainst thy broad, dark breast
Lain, set off like a quickened cameo.
Thou simple soul, as cuddling down that babe
With thy sweet croon, so plaintive and so wild,
Came ne'er the thought to thee, swift like a stab,
That it some day might crush thine own black child?

Paul Laurence Dunbar

(1872–1906)

Paul Laurence Dunbar was an American writer and the first African-American to rise to national prominence as a poet. Born in Dayton, Ohio, his parents were ex-slaves. Dunbar wrote novels, plays, essays, short stories and librettos, but he is remembered for his poetry. Dunbar wrote his poetry in two different styles: the standard English of the classical poet and the contemporary dialect of the black community at the turn of the 20th century. "We Wear the Mask" and "Kindness" are examples of Dunbar's standard English poetry, while "A Negro Love Song" and "Little Brown Baby" are examples of African American dialect. Dunbar died at the young age of thirty-three.

A Negro Love Song[1]

Seen my lady home las' night,
        Jump back, honey, jump back.
Hel' huh han' an' sque'z it tight,
        Jump back, honey, jump back.
Hyeahd huh sigh a little sigh,
Seen a light gleam f'om huh eye,
An' a smile go flittin' by—
        Jump back, honey, jump back.

Hyeahd de win' blow thoo de pine,
        Jump back, honey, jump back.
Mockin'-bird was singin' fine,
        Jump back, honey, jump back.
An' my hea't was beatin' so,
When I reached my lady's do',
Dat I could n't ba' to go—
        Jump back, honey, jump back.

Put my ahm aroun' huh wais',
        Jump back, honey, jump back.
Raised huh lips an' took a tase,
        Jump back, honey, jump back.
Love me, honey, love me true?
Love me well ez I love you?
An' she answe'd, "'Cose I do"—
        Jump back, honey, jump back.

---

[1] Dunbar wrote in two distinct styles. This poem uses African-
American dialect of the turn of the 20th century.

WE WEAR THE MASK[2]

We wear the mask that grins and lies,
It hides our cheeks and shades our eyes,—
This debt we pay to human guile;
With torn and bleeding hearts we smile,
And mouth with myriad subtleties.

Why should the world be overwise,
In counting all our tears and sighs?
Nay, let them only see us, while
      We wear the mask.

We smile, but, O great Christ, our cries
To thee from tortured souls arise.
We sing, but oh the clay is vile
Beneath our feet, and long the mile;
But let the world dream otherwise,
      We wear the mask!

---

[2] "We Wear the Mask" utilizes standard English, the other style
Dunbar wrote in.

WILLA CATHER

(1873–1947)

WILLA CATHER was an American novelist, poet, and journalist. Born in Virginia, she moved with her family to Red Cloud, Nebraska, in the 1880s, living among the newly-arrived immigrants from Europe. She became a journalist, then a teacher, published a few short stories before becoming managing editor of *McClure's* and, in 1912, began writing novels full-time. She lived her later years in New York City. Her best-known novels include *My Antonia*, *O Pioneers!*, *Song of the Lark* and *Death Comes for the Archbishop*.

The Tavern[1]

In the tavern of my heart
Many a one has sat before,
Drunk red wine and sung a stave,
And, departing, come no more.
When the night was cold without,
And the ravens croaked of storm,
They have sat them at my hearth,
Telling me my house was warm.

As the lute and cup went round,
They have rhymed me well in lay;—
When the hunt was on at morn,
Each, departing, went his way.
On the walls, in compliment,
Some would scrawl a verse or two,
Some have hung a willow branch,
Or a wreath of corn-flowers blue.

Ah! my friend, when thou dost go,
Leave no wreath of flowers for me;
Not pale daffodils nor rue,
Violets nor rosemary.
Spill the wine upon the lamps,
Tread the fire, and bar the door;
So despoil the wretched place,
None will come forevermore.

---

[1] "The Tavern" was published in Cather's *April Twilights* in 1903.

Amy Lowell

(1874–1925)

AMY LOWELL was a distinguished Pulitzer Prize-winning American Modernist poet of the early 20th century whose reputation has since diminished. She was also a critic and a champion of the Imagist movement in the United States. Lowell acted as a publicist for the Imagists who included Ezra Pound, Ford Maddox Ford, and H.D. (Hilda Doolittle). Lowell was born in Brookline, Massachusetts to a distinguished Boston family—she was a relative of James Russell Lowell, poet and first editor of *Atlantic Monthly*. She was the youngest of five children and her brother became the president of Harvard. In 1910 Lowell's poem "Fixed Idea" was published in the *Atlantic Monthly* and she continued publishing poems in journals. Her first collection, *A Dome of Many Colored Glass*, was published by Houghton Mifflin in 1912. In 1915 Lowell edited and contributed to an anthology of Imagist poets. Later Lowell became interested in Japanese and Chinese poetry and had a lifelong love for John Keats. The influence of Keats can be found in her poems and she believed that he was a forbearer of Imagism. She published a biography of Keats in 1925. Also in 1925 Lowell won the Pulitzer Prize for her poetry volume *What's O'Clock*.

A LOVER[1]

If I could catch the green lantern of the firefly
I could see to write you a letter.

---

[1] This poem was originally published in *Poetry* magazine, March 1917.

Venus Transiens[2]

Tell me,
Was Venus[3] more beautiful
Than you are,
When she topped
The crinkled waves,
Drifting shoreward
On her plaited shell?
Was Botticelli's vision[4]
Fairer than mine;
And were the painted rosebuds
He tossed his lady,
Of better worth
Than the words I blow about you
To cover your too great loveliness
As with a gauze
Of misted silver?
For me
You stand poised
In the blue and buoyant air,
Cinctured by bright winds,
Treading the sunlight.
And the waves which precede you
Ripple and stir
The sands at my feet.

---

[2] "Venus Transiens" means "Venus Crossing Over." Lowell wrote it
in 1919. A stately poem, it mirrors the Renaissance awe at
female grace and beauty.

[3] Venus is the Roman goddess of love and beauty.

[4] Sandro Botticelli's famous painting "The Birth of Venus" (1485-86)
shows the goddess Venus born as a naked full-grown woman,
emerging from the sea on a shell and blown to shore by Zephyrs,
Greek gods of wind. Venus is joined by one of the Horae, god-
desses of the seasons, who hands her a flowered cloak.

GERTRUDE STEIN

(1874–1946)

GERTRUDE STEIN was an American Modernist novel-ist, critic, and poet famous for her experimental writing and her Parisian salon. Born in Allegheny, Pennsylvania to Jewish-Bavarian parents, she grew up in Vienna, Paris, and Oakland, California. Stein studied psychology at Radcliffe with the renowned philosopher William James (older brother of the novelist Henry James). William James greatly influenced Stein's writing. After studying at Johns Hopkins School of Medecine, she moved to Paris where she lived with her brother Leo, an art critic, and where she was inspired by the art-work of Paul Cezanne, Henri Matisse, George Braque and Pablo Picasso (Picasso painted her portrait). At Gertrude Stein's salon painters mixed with expatriate American writers such as Ernest Hemingway and Sherwood Anderson. Her literary and artistic criticism could make or break careers.

Picasso's Cubism influenced her volume of prose poetry from 1914, *Tender Buttons: Objects Food Rooms.* Stein was focused on illuminating the present moment, as well as playing with repetition and fragmentation. *Tender Buttons* was Stein's attempt to express the rhythm of the visible world," as she wrote in *Autobiography of Alice B. Toklas.* Her first published book was *Three Lives* in 1909 and it told the stories of three working-class women. Her most famous work of prose was 1932's *Autobiography of Alice B. Toklas,* which details her relationship with her lifelong lover Toklas. It was her only book to reach a wide audience and it was actually Stein's own autobiography. Her most famous quote is "A rose is a rose is a rose," a line from her 1913 poem "Sacred Emily," which means that things are what they are—by just uttering the name of an object, the object itself is evoked, with its attendant imagery and emotional associations.

Negligible Old Star

Negligible old star.
Pour even.
It was a sad per cent.
Does on sun day.
Watch or water.
So soon a moon or a old heavy press.

A Frightful Release[1]

A bag which was left and not only taken but turned away was not found. The place was shown to be very like the last time. A piece was not exchanged, not a bit of it, a piece was left over. The rest was mismanaged.

---

[1] This poem was originally published in 1914 in *Tender Buttons: Objects Food Rooms.*

A Long Dress[2]

What is the current that makes machinery, that makes
it crackle, what is the current that presents a long line
and a necessary waist. What is this current.
What is the wind, what is it.

Where is the serene length, it is there and a dark place
is not a dark place, only a white and red are black, only
a yellow and green are blue, a pink is scarlet, a bow is
every color. A line distinguishes it. A line just
distinguishes it.

---

[2] This poem was originally published in 1914 in *Tender Buttons:
Objects Food Rooms*.

Robert Frost

(1875–1963)

Robert Frost is one of the most widely read and celebrated American poets of the 20th century, known as the Bard of New England. He received numerous honors for his poetry including winning the Pulitzer Prize four times. Born in San Francisco, Frost lived much of his life in New England and is considered a pastoral poet whose work intimately studies the landscape and people of rural New England. He combines strong lyrical ability with philosophical contemplations. On first reading, Frost's poems often seem simple, but they are deceptively complex and often reveal a darkness of feeling not readily apparent. Frost wrote mainly in iambic meter. He was conservative politically and poetically (such as his formal meter) and this caused him to lose favor with some literary critics, however his reputation as a leading American poet has never diminished. In 1963 Frost died in Boston.

FIRE AND ICE[1]

Some say the world will end in fire,
Some say in ice.
From what I've tasted of desire
I hold with those who favor fire.
But if it had to perish twice,
I think I know enough of hate
To say that for destruction ice
Is also great
And would suffice.

MENDING WALL

Something there is that doesn't love a wall,
That sends the frozen-ground-swell under it,
And spills the upper boulders in the sun;
And makes gaps even two can pass abreast.
The work of hunters is another thing:
I have come after them and made repair
Where they have left not one stone on a stone,
But they would have the rabbit out of hiding,
To please the yelping dogs. The gaps I mean,
No one has seen them made or heard them made,
But at spring mending-time we find them there.
I let my neighbor know beyond the hill;
And on a day we meet to walk the line

---

[1] The title "Fire and Ice" contains two opposite ways of
annihilating the world—fire (passion) or ice (hatred). Frost
compares and contrasts the destructive powers of fire versus ice
in his poem. This conceit was suggested to Frost by a passage in
Canto 32 of Dante's *Inferno*. The poem was first published in
Harper's Magazine in 1920.

And set the wall between us once again.
We keep the wall between us as we go.
To each the boulders that have fallen to each.
And some are loaves and some so nearly balls
We have to use a spell to make them balance:
'Stay where you are until our backs are turned!'
We wear our fingers rough with handling them.
Oh, just another kind of outdoor game,
One on a side. It comes to little more:
There where it is we do not need the wall:
He is all pine and I am apple orchard.
My apple trees will never get across
And eat the cones under his pines, I tell him.
He only says, 'Good fences make good neighbors.'
Spring is the mischief in me, and I wonder
If I could put a notion in his head:
'*Why* do they make good neighbors? Isn't it
Where there are cows? But here there are no cows.
Before I built a wall I'd ask to know
What I was walling in or walling out,
And to whom I was like to give offense.
Something there is that doesn't love a wall,
That wants it down.' I could say 'Elves' to him,
But it's not elves exactly, and I'd rather
He said it for himself. I see him there
Bringing a stone grasped firmly by the top
In each hand, like an old-stone savage armed.
He moves in darkness as it seems to me,
Not of woods only and the shade of trees.
He will not go behind his father's saying,
And he likes having thought of it so well
He says again, 'Good fences make good neighbors.'

AFTER APPLE-PICKING

My long two-pointed ladder's sticking through a tree
Toward heaven still,
And there's a barrel that I didn't fill
Beside it, and there may be two or three
Apples I didn't pick upon some bough.
But I am done with apple-picking now.
Essence of winter sleep is on the night,
The scent of apples: I am drowsing off.
I cannot rub the strangeness from my sight
I got from looking through a pane of glass
I skimmed this morning from the drinking trough
And held against the world of hoary grass.
It melted, and I let it fall and break.
But I was well
Upon my way to sleep before it fell,
And I could tell
What form my dreaming was about to take.
Magnified apples appear and disappear,
Stem end and blossom end,
And every fleck of russet showing clear.
My instep arch not only keeps the ache,
It keeps the pressure of a ladder-round.
I feel the ladder sway as the boughs bend.
And I keep hearing from the cellar bin
The rumbling sound
Of load on load of apples coming in.
For I have had too much
Of apple-picking: I am overtired
Of the great harvest I myself desired.
There were ten thousand thousand fruit to touch,

Cherish in hand, lift down, and not let fall.
For all
That struck the earth,
No matter if not bruised or spiked with stubble,
Went surely to the cider-apple heap
As of no worth.
One can see what will trouble
This sleep of mine, whatever sleep it is.
Were he not gone,
The woodchuck could say whether it's like his
Long sleep, as I describe its coming on,
Or just some human sleep.

DUST OF SNOW

The way a crow
Shook down on me
The dust of snow
From a hemlock tree

Has given my heart
A change of mood
And saved some part
Of a day I had rued.

The Road Not Taken

Two roads diverged in a yellow wood,
And sorry I could not travel both
And be one traveler, long I stood
And looked down one as far as I could
To where it bent in the undergrowth;

Then took the other, as just as fair,
And having perhaps the better claim,
Because it was grassy and wanted wear;
Though as for that the passing there
Had worn them really about the same,

And both that morning equally lay
In leaves no step had trodden black.
Oh, I kept the first for another day!
Yet knowing how way leads on to way,
I doubted if I should ever come back.

I shall be telling this with a sigh
Somewhere ages and ages hence:
Two roads diverged in a wood, and I—
I took the one less traveled by,
And that has made all the difference.

ADELAIDE CRAPSEY

(1878–1914)

A DELAIDE CRAPSEY was an American poet. She was born in Brooklyn and spent her childhood in Rochester, New York, where her father was the rector of an Episcopal church (he was later defrocked after being put on trial for heresy). Crapsey graduated Phi Beta Kappa from Vassar College in 1901. She studied in Rome and upon returning to the United States she taught history and literature at a private school in Stamford, Connecticut. She suffered from tuberculosis and stopped teaching, traveling again to Italy, as well as England, in an attempt to restore her health. In 1911 she returned to the United States once again and became Instructor of Poetics at Smith College for two years and died a year later. Her work was published posthumously—a small press published a volume of her poetry called *Verses* in 1915 and in 1918 Alfred Knopf published her unfinished *Study of English Metrics*.

Adelaide Crapsey wrote most of her poetry during the last year of her life and she is notable for having created a new form of verse called the cinquain. She was deeply intrigued by meter and rhythm and this led her to devise the cinquain, which is an unrhymed five line form consisting of twenty-two syllables—two syllables in the first and fifth lines, four syllables in the second line, six in the third line, and eight in the fourth line. The cinquain is similar to the Japanese verse forms haiku and tanka. Crapsey found this form suited her compressed and delicate style of writing. When Crapsey's *Verses* appeared a year after her death it became very popular in literary circles and especially among younger writers. The book was enlarged and reprinted in 1922 and 1934. Carl Sandburg also championed Crapsey's work, working with the cinquain and writing a poem called "Adelaide Crapsey." Crapsey's greatest contribution to poetry was her creation of the cinquain.

THE GUARDED WOUND[1]

If it
Were lighter touch
Than petal of flower resting
On grass, oh still too heavy it were,
Too heavy!

THE WARNING[2]

Just now,
Out of the strange
Still dust . . . as strange, as still . . .
A white moth flew . . . Why am I grown
So cold?

---

[1] "The Guarded Wound" is an example of the cinquain, a delicate Japanese-style form that Adelaide Crapsey originated. Like Ezra Pound, Crapsey admired Japanese poets for their concise language and formal aesthetics.

[2] Another example of a cinquain. *Cinq* means five in French.

CARL SANDBURG

(1878–1967)

CARL SANDBURG was a celebrated American poet, journalist, historian, biographer, novelist, balladeer, and folklorist who won two Pulitzer Prizes for his poetry. He is most famous for his free verse poems honoring American people, industry, and geography. Born in Galesburg, Illinois to Swedish parents, he tried many different trades and fought in the Spanish-American War. He later moved to Chicago in 1913 where he worked as a journalist.

His first collection, *Chicago Poems*, was published in 1916. He followed up that volume with *Cornhuskers* in 1918, in which he helped make the form of the cinquain better known. Sandburg admired the poet Adelaide Crapsey and her creation of the cinquain. His next collection was *Smoke and Steel* (1920). All three of these poetry volumes show Sandburg celebrating a vision of America as an agricultural and industrial epicenter. Sandburg wrote a six-volume biography of Abraham Lincoln, published between 1926 and 1939. Sandburg uses a Whitmanesque free verse to celebrate the American worker.

Chicago[1]

Hog Butcher for the World,
Tool Maker, Stacker of Wheat,
Player with Railroads and the Nation's Freight
   Handler;
Stormy, husky, brawling,
City of the Big Shoulders:
They tell me you are wicked and I believe them, for I
   have seen your painted women under the gas lamps
   luring the farm boys.
And they tell me you are crooked and I answer: Yes, it
   is true I have seen the gunman kill and go free to kill
   again.
And they tell me you are brutal and my reply is: On the
   faces of women and children I have seen the marks
   of wanton hunger.
And having answered so I turn once more to those who
   sneer at this my city, and I give them back the sneer
   and say to them:
Come and show me another city with lifted head
   singing so proud to be alive and coarse and strong
   and cunning.
Flinging magnetic curses amid the toil of piling job on
   job, here is a tall bold slugger set vivid against the
   little soft cities;

---

[1] "Chicago" is probably Sanburg's most famous poem. Chicago was
a center of agricultural markets, commodities trading, the meat-
packing industry, and an important railroad hub. Sandburg men-
tions all of these trades in his poem. "Chicago" was originally
published in *Poetry* magazine in 1914.

Fierce as a dog with tongue lapping for action, cunning
     as a savage pitted against the wilderness,
         Bareheaded,
         Shoveling,
         Wrecking,
         Planning,
         Building, breaking, rebuilding,
Under the smoke, dust all over his mouth, laughing
     with white teeth,
Under the terrible burden of destiny laughing as a
     young man laughs,
Laughing even as an ignorant fighter laughs who has
     never lost a battle,
Bragging and laughing that under his wrist is the pulse.
     and under his ribs the heart of the people,
         Laughing!
Laughing the stormy, husky, brawling laughter of
     Youth, half-naked, sweating, proud to be Hog
     Butcher, Tool Maker, Stacker of Wheat, Player with
     Railroads and Freight Handler to the Nation.

Fog

The fog comes
on little cat feet.

It sits looking
over harbor and city
on silent haunches
and then moves on.

Bones

Sling me under the sea.
Pack me down in the salt and wet.
No farmer's plow shall touch my bones.
No Hamlet hold my jaws and speak
How jokes are gone and empty is my mouth.
Long, green-eyed scavengers shall pick my eyes,
Purple fish play hide-and-seek,
And I shall be song of thunder, crash of sea,
Down on the floors of salt and wet.
Sling me ... under the sea.

WILLIAM STANLEY BRAITHWAITE
(1878–1962)

WILLIAM STANLEY BRAITHWAITE was an African-American poet, educator, and editor who taught for over two decades at Atlanta University. Braithwaite was part of the Harlem Renaissance. Born in Boston, the second of five children, he was from a racially mixed family—on his father's side he was descended from French nobility and on his mother's side he was descended from American slaves. Braithwaite published two volumes of verse, *Lyrics of Life and Love* in 1904 and *The House of Falling Leaves* in 1908. He also edited three poetry anthologies, *The Book of Elizabethan Verse*, *The Book of Restoration Verse*, and *The Book of Georgian Verse*. He founded and edited *The Poetry Journal of Boston*.

Braithwaite was inspired by the Romantic poets, William Wordsworth and John Keats, and was especially taken with Keats's "Ode on a Grecian Urn." Upon reading the poem Braithwaite later said he entered, "into a world of magical beauty" and that this day was "a day of annunciation," for poetry became his lifelong passion. Some of his later work resembles the poetry of William Blake with its less accessible otherworldliness. He believed that poetry should be written for aesthetic reasons and not to convey social or political agendas, although he praised John Greenleaf Whittier's abolitionist poetry. His themes were generally romantic ones of life, death, nature, love, and despair. He often wrote in traditional verse forms, in particular the sonnet, and was adept at rhyme. Braithwaite felt that race did not have to

576

regulate a poet's creative impulses. He was criticized by some of his contemporaries for being embarrassed of being black and for not addressing racial self-consciousness. James Weldon Johnson wrote in *The Book of American Negro Poetry*: "As an Afroamerican poet [Braithwaite] is unique; he has written no poetry motivated or colored by race. . . . It is simply that race has not impinged upon him as it has upon other Negro poets." The 20th century African American poet Countee Cullen, whom Braithwaite admired, wrote in *Caroling Dusk: An Anthology of Verse by Negro Poets* that "American Negro poetry does not exist; only poetry written by American Negroes." He dedicated the book to Braithwaite.

Turn Me to My Yellow Leaves

Turn me to my yellow leaves,
I am better satisfied;
There is something in me grieves—
That was never born, and died.
Let me be a scarlet flame
On a windy autumn morn,
I who never had a name,
Nor from breathing image born.

From the margin let me fall
Where the farthest stars sink down,
And the void consumes me,—all
In nothingness to drown
Let me dream my dream entire,
Withered as an autumn leaf—
Let me have my vain desire,
Vain—as it is brief.

SIC VITA[1]

Heart free, hand free,
Blue above, brown under,
All the world to me
Is a place of wonder.
Sun shine, moon shine,
Stars, and winds a-blowing,
All into this heart of mine
Flowing, flowing, flowing!

Mind free, step free,
Days to follow after,
Joys of life sold to me
For the price of laughter.
Girl's love, man's love,
Love of work and duty,
Just a will of God's to prove
Beauty, beauty, beauty!

---

[1] "Sic Vita" is Latin for "Thus is Life" or "Such is Life."

VACHEL LINDSAY

(1879–1931)

NICHOLAS VACHEL LINDSAY was an American poet and visual artist. Born in Springfield, Illinois, he was the only son of Dr. Vachel Thomas Lindsay and Esther Catharine Frazee Lindsay, a teacher and artist. He began attending school when he was eight; before that his mother taught him at home. One of his most important childhood texts was Grimm's *Fairy Tales*. While at school he won several writing awards. He studied at Hiram College, the Art Institute of Chicago, and the New York School of Art.

In 1906, in an attempt to revive the oral art form, Lindsay traveled around the southern United States as a troubadour, reciting his poetry in return for food and lodging, an endeavor he described later in *A Handy Guide for Beggars*. In 1913 he gained recognition for his book *General William Booth Enters in Heaven*, which was about the founder of the Salvation Army. His other books of poetry include *Rhymes to Be Traded for Bread* (1912), *The Congo* (1914), *The Chinese Nightingale* (1917), and *Collected Poems* (1938). Lindsay's poems were noted for their strong rhythms, vibrant imagery, passion for democracy, and a romantic view of nature. His reading style was characterized by chanting, jazz rhythms, and preaching in public poetry readings. He married in 1925 and had two children. Lindsay is also noted for discovering the work of the distinguished 20th century poet Langston Hughes. Lindsay's success occurred early in his career and in his later years he lived in poverty and became mentally unstable and depressed, eventually committing suicide by drinking poison.

THE FLOWER-FED BUFFALOS

The flower-fed buffaloes of the spring
In the days of long ago,
Ranged where the locomotives sing
And the prarie flowers lie low:
The tossing, blooming, perfumed grass
Is swept away by wheat,
Wheels and wheels and wheels spin by
In the spring that still is sweet.
But the flower-fed buffaloes of the spring
Left us long ago,
They gore no more, they bellow no more:—
With the Blackfeet[1] lying low,
With the Pawnee[2] lying low.

---

[1] The Blackfeet are a Native American confederacy located on the northern Great Plains and made up of Blackfood, Blood, and Piegan tribes. Traditionally, Blackfoot life was based on nomadic buffalo hunting.

[2] The Pawnee are a Native American tribe that used to inhabit the Platte River valley in Nebraska and Kansas, and now live in north-central Oklahoma after being relocated by the United States government.

WALLACE STEVENS

(1879–1955)

WALLACE STEVENS was one of the most innovative American poets of the first half of the 20th century. His poetry was often considered obscure and highly philosophical, and it showed a brilliance of language, rhyme, and verbal music. Born in Reading, Pennsylvania, Stevens was educated in classics at Reading Boys' High School and at Harvard. While at the university he edited the *Harvard Advocate* and published some verse. After several years as a reporter in New York, Stevens entered New York Law School in 1901 and was admitted to the bar in 1904. In New York he worked for several law firms and then joined an insurance firm. He married Elsie Viola Kachel in 1909 and they moved to Hartford, Connecticut in 1916. Until his retirement, Stevens worked for the Hartford Accident and Indemnity Company, becoming Vice President in 1934.

In 1915, Stevens' poem "Peter Quince at the Clavier" was published, in which a man improvising on a clavier, thinks of his beloved and his imagination associates the sound of the music with his desire and the Biblical myth of Susanna, whose virtue was challenged. The poem uses a variety of forms including three-line unrhymed stanzas, couplet stanzas, and stanzas of varied length with irregular rhyme. Also during 1915, his poem "Sunday Morning" was published. In it, a complacent lady in a peignoir, having coffee and oranges in a sunny room, finds it possible to put off "the dark/ Encroachment of that old catastrophe," Christ's martyrdom. Instead she can unite herself with the fleeting delights of her tasteful room and the world outside.

Stevens published in many journals, having around one hundred poems in print, when his first book of poetry, *Harmonium*, was published in 1923. Stevens was forty-four. In general the book was reviewed unfavorably, but it contained some of the poetry that would become the most celebrated: "Thirteen Ways of Looking at a Blackbird," "Le Monocle de Mon Oncle," "To the One of Fictive Music," and "The Emperor of Ice Cream." A second edition of *Harmonium* came out in 1931 and Stevens followed it up in 1935 with *Ideas of Order.* He went on to publish *The Man with the Blue Guitar* (1937) and *The Auroras of Autumn* (1950). His *Collected Poems* (1954) received both the Pulitzer Prize and the National Book Award. Stevens' poetry largely explores the relationship between the imagination and reality. Although he was not widely read until his later years, he is now recognized as one of America's greatest 20th century poets.

ANECDOTE OF THE JAR[1]

I placed a jar in Tennessee,
And round it was, upon a hill.
It made the slovenly wilderness
Surround that hill.

The wilderness rose up to it,
And sprawled around, no longer wild.
The jar was round upon the ground
And tall and of a port in air.

It took dominion every where.
The jar was gray and bare.
It did not give of bird or bush,
Like nothing else in Tennessee.

from PETER QUINZE[2] AT THE CLAVIER

Just as my fingers on these keys
Make music, so the self-same sounds
On my spirit make a music, too.

Music is feeling, then, not sound;
And thus it is that what I feel,
Here in this room, desiring you,

---

[1] This poem deals with imagination imposing itself on reality, a common subject of Stevens' poetry.

[2] Peter Quinze is one of the bumbling rustics in Shakespeare's *A Midsummer Night's Dream* who put on a well-meaning but unintentionally funny play of the tragic love of Pyramus and Thisbe for the wedding of Theseus and Hippolyta.

Thinking of your blue-shadowed silk,
Is music. It is like the strain
Waked in the elders by Susanna;[3]

Of a green evening, clear and warm,
She bathed in her still garden, while
The red-eyed elders, watching, felt

The basses of their beings throb
In witching chords, and their thin blood
Pulse pizzicati[4] of Hosanna.[5]

II

In the green water, clear and warm,
Susanna lay.
She searched
The touch of springs,
And found
Concealed imaginings.
She sighed,
For so much melody.

---

[3] As told in the apocryphal book of Daniel, this virtuous wife of
  Joakim in Babylon rejected the sexual demands of two old men
  of the tribe, who then falsey accused her of being unvirtuous to
  get revenge. Daniel discovered they were lying and had them
  executed.
[4] The sound of plucked strings.
[5] Pray or save us.

Upon the bank, she stood
In the cool
Of spent emotions.
She felt, among the leaves,
The dew
Of old devotions.

She walked upon the grass,
Still quavering.
The winds were like her maids,
On timid feet,
Fetching her woven scarves,
Yet wavering.

A breath upon her hand
Muted the night.
She turned—
A cymbal crashed,
Amid roaring horns.

Angelina Weld Grimké

(1880–1958)

Angelina Weld Grimké was a poet, playwright, and civil rights activist. Her family were prominent abolitionists and civil rights activists, including her great-aunts Angelina and Sarah Grimké, and her father who was the son of a white aristocrat and an African American slave. Angelina Weld Grimké studied at the Boston Normal School of Gymnastics, graduating in 1902. She became an English teacher in Washington, D.C. In the early 1900s Grimké began to write both poems and articles expressing her concerns about racism.

Grimké was not a prolific poet. Her verse has appeared in the anthologies *Negro Poets and Their Poems* (1923), *The Poetry of the Negro* (1949), edited by the poet Langston Hughes, and *Caroling Dusk* (1927), edited by the poet Countee Cullen. Grimké concentrated on personal lyrics about isolation and desire for love. Grimké's play *Rachel,* was performed in 1916 and published in 1920. It is about a young woman who decides never to have children because of her horror at racism. Although the play received reviews that criticized its sentimentality and negativity, it is important for being one of the first American plays written by an African American writer about black issues.

At April

Toss your gay heads,
Brown girl trees;
Toss your gay lovely heads;
Shake your brown slim bodies;
Stretch your brown slim arms;
Stretch your brown slim toes.
Who knows better than we,
With the dark, dark bodies,
What it means
When April comes a-laughing and a-weeping
Once again
At our hearts?

ALFRED NOYES

(1880–1958)

Aⁿlfred Noyes was an English poet known for his traditional lyric verse and probably most remembered today for his lengthy poem "The Highwayman." He published his first book of poetry, *The Loom of Years* in 1902 while he was still at the University of Oxford. From 1914 to 1923 Noyes taught Modern English Literature at Princeton University in the United States. He is remembered for his writing dealing with patriotism and love of the sea. His later work is noteworthy for the epic trilogy *The Torch Bearers*, which focused on the progress of science through the ages. Noyes also wrote his autobiography in 1953, *Two Worlds for Memory*.

from THE HIGHWAYMAN

PART ONE

I

THE wind was a torrent of darkness among the gusty
    trees,
The moon was a ghostly galleon tossed upon cloudy
    seas,
The road was a ribbon of moonlight over the purple
    moor,
And the highwayman came riding—
           Riding—riding—
The highwayman came riding, up to the old inn-door.

II

He'd a French cocked-hat on his forehead, a bunch of
  lace at his chin,
A coat of the claret velvet, and breeches of brown doe-
  skin;
They fitted with never a wrinkle: his boots were up to
  the thigh!
And he rode with a jewelled twinkle,
                His pistol butts a-twinkle,
His rapier hilt a-twinkle, under the jewelled sky.

III

Over the cobbles he clattered and clashed in the dark
  inn-yard,
And he tapped with his whip on the shuters, but all was
  locked and barred;
He whistled a tune to the window, and who should be
  waiting there
But the landlord's black-eyed daughter,
                Bess, the landlord's daughter,
Plaiting a dark red love-knot into her long black hair.

IV

And dark in the dark old inn-yard a stable-wicket
  creaked
Where Tim the ostler listened; his face was white and
  peaked;
His eyes were hollows of madness, his hair like mouldy
  hay,
But he loved the landlord's daughter,
                The landlord's red-lipped daughter,
Dumb as a dog he listened, and he heard the robber
  say—

V

"One kiss, my bonny sweetheart, I'm after a prize to-
    night,
But I shall be back with the yellow gold before the
    morning light;
Yet, if they press me sharply, and harry me through the
    day,
Then look for me by moonlight,
            Watch for me by moonlight,
I'll come to thee by moonlight, though hell should bar
    the way."

VI

He rose upright in the stirrups; he scarce could reach
    her hand,
But she loosened her hair i' the casement! His face
    burnt like a brand
As the black cascade of perfume came tumbling over
    his breast;
And he kissed its waves in the moonlight,
           (Oh, sweet, black waves in the
                moonlight!)
Then he tugged at his rein in the moonliglt, and
    galloped away to the West.

JAMES JOYCE

(1882–1941)

JAMES JOYCE (née James Augustine Aloysius Joyce) was an Irish novelist and poet who helped found the Modernist literary movement of the 20th century along with Ezra Pound and T.S. Eliot. He is best known for his landmark novel *Ulysses* (1922) as well as for the semi-autobiographical *A Portrait of the Artist as a Young Man* (1916) and *Finnegan's Wake* (1939). His short story collection from 1914, *Dubliners*, is celebrated for its intricate portraits of Dublin life—Joyce called Dublin "the heart of all the cities of the world" and believed that "in the particular is contained the universal." Both *Ulysses* and *Finnegan's Wake* discard the traditional plot and sentence structure of the novel in preference of wordplay, stream of consciousness and interior monologue, snatches of sense perceptions woven in with the wandering daydreams of the characters. Joyce set all his major stories in Dublin where he grew up; however he left Ireland for Paris and Zurich, and after a visit to his home city in 1912 he never returned.

Joyce's reputation rests on his fiction, but his first published work was 1907's *Chamber Music*, a collection of thirty-six lyric poems. In 1938 he published his *Collected Poems*. Joyce's poetry, as opposed to his novels, does not take literature in a new direction. He does not try to be experimental in his poems and instead upholds the Romantic tradition. His poetry is not widely read and his poetic talent is considered better served in the novel form rather than straight verse. Although his poetry is not considered distinguished, his keen ear and sense of musicality is in evidence in his verse.

from CHAMBER MUSIC

"*Lean out of the window*"
V

Lean out of the window,
Goldenhair,
I hear you singing
A merry air.

My book was closed,
I read no more,
Watching the fire dance
On the floor.

I have left my book,
I have left my room,
For I heard you singing
Through the gloom.

Singing and singing
A merry air,
Lean out of the window,
Goldenhair.

"Because your voice was at my side"
XVII

Because your voice was at my side
I gave him pain,
Because within my hand I held
Your hand again.

There is no word nor any sign
Can make amend—
He is a stranger to me now
Who was my friend.

MINA LOY

(1882–1966)

MINA LOY (nee Mina Gertrude Lowy) was an English Modernist poet and visual artist who was more celebrated posthumously. Ezra Pound was a huge admirer of Loy's poetry, writing to Marianne Moore "is there anyone in America except you, Bill [William Carlos Williams] and Mina Loy who can write anything of interest in verse?" Born in London, Loy attended an art school and was influenced early in her career by Impressionism. She achieved some attention for her paintings when she lived in Paris. Her art style was given all kind of labels—Futurist, Dadaist, Surrealist, conceptualist, post-modernist, etc. In Paris Loy was a frequent participant in Gertrude Stein's salon, and she and Stein became lifelong friends.

In 1916 she moved to the United States and her reputation as an avant-garde poet preceded her. The American poet Amy Lowell refused to submit any more poetry to *Others* magazine after Loy had a poem published in the periodical. But Loy also had many champions of her work, including Pound, William Carlos Williams, Stein, T.S. Eliot, and members of the New York Dada group. In 1918 she married the poet-boxer Arthur Craven. At the end of her life Loy stated that she "never was a poet" and saw herself as a visual artist. She also became a recluse in her last years and didn't try to build a reputation for her work. Her volumes of poetry are *Lunar Baedecker [sic]* (1923) and *Lunar Baedeker & Time-Tables* (1958).

Lunar Baedeker

A silver Lucifer
serves
cocaine in cornucopia

To some somnambulists
of adolescent thighs
draped
in satirical draperies

Peris is livery
prepare
Lethe
for posthumous parvenues

Delirious Avenues
lit
with the chandelier souls
of infusoria
from Pharoah's tombstones

lead
to mercurial doomsdays
Odious oasis
in furrowed phosphorous

the eye-white sky-light
white-light district
of lunar lusts

Stellectric signs

WING SHOWS ON STARWAY
ZODIAC CAROUSEL

Cyclones
of ecstatic dust
and ashes whirl
crusaders
from hallucinatory citadels
of shattered glass
into evacuate craters

A flock of dreams
browse on Necropolis

From the shores
of oval oceans
in the oxidized Orient

Onyx-eyed Odalisques
and ornithologists
observe the flight
of Eros obsolete

And "Immortality"
mildews
in the museums of the moon

NOCTURNAL CYCLOPS
CRYSTAL CONCUBINE

Pocked with personification
the fossil virgin of the skies
waxes and wanes

E. J. PRATT

(1883–1964)

E J. PRATT was one of the most distinguished Canadian poets of the early 20th century. Born in Newfoundland, he was the son of a Methodist clergyman and Pratt was also ordained a Methodist minister, but he decided instead to teach English and psychology at the University of Toronto. He published his first poetry in 1914 and in 1923 published *Newfoundland Verse*. His 1926 collection *The Titans* includes his noted poem "The Cachalot" about a whale hunt, while his 1940 volume *Brébeuf and His Brethen*, records the martyrdom of Jesuit missionaries. His many other books included 1941's *Dunkirk*, 1947's *Behind the Log*, and 1952's *Towards the Last Spike*. He won Governor General's Literary Awards (created in 1937, they have become one of Canada's most prominent prizes) three times (1937, 1940, and 1952) and was elected in 1930 to the Royal Society of Canada. In 1940 he won the Royal Society's Lorne Pierce Medal. Pratt was also the editor of *Canadian Poetry Magazine* from 1936 to 1943. Pratt's poetry is notable for its narratives of epic events, turning away from the romantic tradition of Canadian poetry. He also created an original style in lyric poems about Newfoundland coastal and seafaring life.

THE DROWNING

The rust of hours,
  Through a year of days,
Has dulled the edge of the pain;
  But at night
  A wheel in my sleep
Grinds it smooth and keen.

  By day I remember
  A face that was lit
With the softness of human pattern;
  But at night
  It is changed in my sleep
To a bygone carved in chalk.

  A cottage inland
  Through a year of days
Has latched its doors on the sea;
  But at night
  I return in my sleep
To the cold, green lure of the waters.

WILLIAM CARLOS WILLIAMS

(1883–1963)

WILLIAM CARLOS WILLIAMS is one of the most
famous Modernist poets. Born in Rutherford,
New Jersey, he began writing poetry while a student at
Horace Mann High School, at which time he made the
decision to become both a writer and a doctor. He
received his M.D. from the University of Pennsylvania,
where he met and became friends with Ezra Pound.
Pound became a great influence in Williams's writing,
and in 1913 arranged for the London publication of
Williams's second collection, *The Tempers*. Returning to
Rutherford, where he sustained his medical practice
throughout his life, Williams began publishing in small
magazines and embarked on a productive career as a
poet, novelist, essayist, and playwright. Following
Pound, he was one of the principal poets of the Imagist
movement, though as time went on, he began to
increasingly disagree with the values put forth in the
work of Pound and especially T. S. Eliot who he felt
were too attached to European culture and traditions.
Continuing to experiment with new techniques of
meter and lineation, Williams sought to invent an
entirely fresh—and singularly American—poetic, whose
subject matter was centered on the everyday circumstances of life and the lives of common people. His
influence as a poet spread slowly during the twenties
and thirties and received increasing attention in the
1950s and 1960s as younger poets, including Allen
Ginsberg and the Beats, were impressed by the accessi-

bility of his language. His major works include *Kora in Hell* (1920), *Spring and All* (1923), *Pictures from Brueghel and Other Poems* (1962), the five-volume epic *Paterson* (1963, 1992), and *Imaginations* (1970).

THE RED WHEELBARROW

so much depends
upon

a red wheel
barrow

glazed with rain
water

beside the white
chickens.

THIS IS JUST TO SAY

I have eaten
the plums
that were in
the icebox

and which
you were probably
saving
for breakfast

Forgive me
they were delicious
so sweet
and so cold

THE YOUNG HOUSEWIFE

At ten AM the young housewife
moves about in negligee behind
the wooden walls of her husband's house.
I pass solitary in my car.

Then again she comes to the curb
to call the ice-man, fish-man, and stands
shy, uncorseted, tucking in
stray ends of hair, and I compare her
to a fallen leaf.

The noiseless wheels of my car
rush with a crackling sound over
dried leaves as I bow and pass smiling.

SARA TEASDALE

(1884–1933)

SARA TEASDALE was a successful, award-winning American poet known for her short, uncomplicated, intense lyrics. She was born in St. Louis, Missouri. Educated privately, she made many trips to Chicago, eventually becoming part of Harriet Monroe's *Poetry* magazine crowd. Her first poem was published in May 1907 in the St. Louis weekly *Reedy's Mirror*. Later that same year she published her first book of poetry, *Sonnets to Duse, and Other Poems*. She followed with *Helen of Troy, and Other Poems* in 1911. She was proposed to by poet Vachel Lindsay but married someone else in 1914. Her third collection was published in 1915, *Rivers to the Sea*. She and her husband moved to New York City the following year and in 1918 Teasdale won the Columbia University Poetry Society Prize, which was the precursor to the Pulitzer Prize. She also garnered the Poetry Society of America prize for her 1917 collection *Love Songs*. She edited two anthologies of poetry as well continued to publish her own collections. Teasdale eventually divorced her husband in 1929 and the rest of her life was spent in frail health.

Much of Teasdale's poetry is traditional in style. She wrote many quatrains and sonnets. Her later poetry grew more subtle and complex. Her last book of poetry, *Strange Victory*, is sometimes considered her best work. It was published a year after her death by suicide (she took an overdose of barbiturates) in 1934.

Coney Island

Why did you bring me here?
The sand is white with snow,
Over the wooden domes
The winter sea-winds blow—
There is no shelter near,
Come, let us go.

With foam of icy lace
The sea creeps up the sand,
The wind is like a hand
That strikes us in the face.
Doors that June set a-swing
Are bolted long ago;
We try them uselessly—
Alas, there cannot be
For us a second spring;
Come, let us go.

Central Park at Dusk

Buildings above the leafless trees
Loom high as castles in a dream,
While one by one the lamps come out
To thread the twilight with a gleam.

There is no sign of leaf or bud,
A hush is over everything—
Silent as women wait for love,
The world is waiting for the spring.

D. H. LAWRENCE

(1885–1930)

DAVID HERBERT LAWRENCE, novelist, short-story writer, poet and essayist, was born in Eastwood, Nottinghamshire, England, in 1885. Though better known as a novelist, Lawrence's first-published works (in 1909) were poems, and his poetry, especially his evocations of the natural world, have since had a significant influence on many poets on both sides of the Atlantic. His early poems reflect the influence of Ezra Pound and the Imagist movement, which reached its peak in the early teens of the twentieth century. When Pound attempted to draw Lawrence into his circle of writer-followers, however, Lawrence decided to pursue a more independent path. Many of his best-loved poems treat the physical and inner life of plants and animals; others are bitterly satiric and express his outrage at the puritanism of English society. Tremendously prolific, his work was often uneven in quality, and he was a continual source of controversy, often involved in widely-publicized censorship cases, most famously for his novel *Lady Chatterley's Lover* (1928). His collections of poetry include *Look! We Have Come Through* (1917), a collection of poems about his wife; *Birds, Beasts, and Flowers* (1923); and *Pansies* (1929), which was banned on publication in England.

PIANO

Softly, in the dusk, a woman is singing to me;
Taking me back down the vista of years, till I see
A child sitting under the piano, in the boom of the
    tingling strings
And pressing the small, poised feet of a mother who
    smiles as she sings.

In spite of myself, the insidious mastery of song
Betrays me back, till the heart of me weeps to belong
To the old Sunday evenings at home, with winter
    outside
And hymns in the cosy parlour, the tinkling piano our
    guide.

So now it is vain for the singer to burst into clamour
With the great black piano appassionato. The glamour
Of childish days is upon me, my manhood is cast
Down in the flood of remembrance, I weep like a child
    for the past.

A Youth Mowing

There are four men mowing down by the Isar;
I can hear the swish of the scythe-strokes, four
Sharp breaths taken: yea, and I
Am sorry for what's in store.

The first man out of the four that's mowing
Is mine, I claim him once and for all;
Though it's sorry I am, on his young feet, knowing
None of the trouble he's led to stall.

As he sees me bringing the dinner, he lifts
His head as proud as a deer that looks
Shoulder-deep out of the corn; and wipes
His scythe-blade bright, unhooks

The scythe-stone and over the stubble to me.
Lad, thou hast gotten a child in me,
Laddie, a man thou'lt ha'e to be,
Yea, though I'm sorry for thee.

ELINOR WYLIE

(1885–1928)

Elinor Wylie (née Elinor Morton Hoyt) was an American poet and novelist best known for the poetry collection *Nets to Catch the Wind*, published in 1921. Born in Somerville, New Jersey, Wylie was a famous beauty during her lifetime. She published the novel *Jennifer Lorne* and her second poetry collection, *Black Amour*, in 1923. Also in 1923, Wylie married the poet and editor William Rose Benét. Benét edited Wylie's collected poems in 1932 and her collected prose in 1933. He wrote a critical study of her writing in 1934.

BEAUTY

Say not of Beauty she is good,
Or aught but beautiful,
Or sleek to dove's wings of the wood
Her wild wings of a gull.

Call her not wicked; that word's touch
Consumes her like a curse;
But love her not too much, too much,
For that is even worse.

O, she is neither good nor bad,
But innocent and wild!
Enshrine her and she dies, who had
The hard heart of a child.

Ezra Pound

(1885–1975)

Ezra Weston Loomis Pound was a famous American poet known for co-founding the Imagist movement. He was also a controversial figure for his political sympathies with fascism and his anti-semitism. Born in Hailey, Idaho, he attended University of Pennsylvania for two years and got his degree at Hamilton College. After teaching for a few years at Wabash College, he traveled to Spain, Italy, and London. In 1908 he left for England and lectured in medieval Romance literature at the Regent Street Polytechnic Institute in London. His first volume of poetry, *A Lume Spento*, came out in London in 1908. It was followed by *Exultations* and *Personae* (1909), *Provenca* (1910), *Canzoni* (1911), *Ripostes* (1912), *Cathay* (1915), *Lustra* (1916), *Quia Pauper Amavi* (1918), and his early masterwork, *Hugh Selwyn Mauberley* (1920).

Portrait d'une Femme[1]

Your mind and you are our Sargasso Sea,[2]
   London has swept about you this score years
And bright ships left you this or that in fee:
   Ideas, old gossip, oddments of all things,
Strange spars of knowledge and dimmed wares of price.
   Great minds have sought you—lacking someone else.

---

[1] French for "Portrait of a Lady."
[2] An area of the North Atlantic ocean clogged with floating
   seaweed.

You have been second always. Tragical?
  No. You preferred it to the usual thing:
One dull man, dulling and uxorious,
  One average mind—with one thought less, each year.
Oh, you are patient, I have seen you sit
  Hours, where something might have floated up.
And now you pay one.   Yes, you richly pay.
  You are a person of some interest, one comes to you
And takes strange gain away:
  Trophies fished up; some curious suggestion;
Fact that leads nowhere; and a tale for two,
  Pregnant with mandrakes,[3] or with something else
That might prove useful and yet never proves,
  That never fits a corner or shows use,
Or finds its hour upon the loom of days:
  The tarnished, gaudy, wonderful old work;
Idols and ambergris[4] and rare inlays,
  These are your riches, your great store; and yet
For all this sea-hoard of deciduous things,
  Strange woods half sodden, and new brighter stuff:
In the slow float of differing light and deep,
  No! there is nothing! In the whole and all,
Nothing that's quite your own.
Yet this is you.

---

[3] Forked human-shaped plants thought to possess aphrodisiac powers and to increase fertility.

[4] A substance produced by sperm whales that is used in perfumes.

In a Station of the Metro[5]

The apparition of these faces in the crowd:
Petals on a wet, black bough

An Immortality

Sing we for love and idleness,
Naught else is worth the having.

Though I have been in many a land,
There is naught else in living.

And I would rather have my sweet,
Though rose-leaves die of grieving,

Than do high deeds in Hungary
To pass all men's believing.

---

[5] Of this haiku inspired poem, Pound wrote in 1916, "Three years ago in Paris I got out of a 'metro' train at La Concorde, and saw suddenly a beautiful face, and then another and another, and then a beautiful child's face, and then another beautiful woman, and I tried all that day to find words for what this had meant to me, and I could not find any words that seemed to me worthy, or as lovely as that sudden emotion." Pound wrote a thirty line poem and destroyed it, then a fifteen line poem and destroyed that, and a year after the initial inspiration he pared it down into his famous two line poem. Pound writes, "I dare say it is meaningless unless one has drifted into a certain vein of thought. In a poem of this sort one is trying to record the precise instant when a thing outward and objective transforms itself, or darts into a thing inward and subjective."

610

H. D.

(1886–1961)

H. D. (HILDA DOOLITTLE) was an American Modernist and Imagist poet and prose writer. Born in Bethlehem, Pennsylvania, she studied at Bryn Mawr, where she was a classmate of Marianne Moore, and later at the University of Pennsylvania where she met Ezra Pound and William Carlos Williams. She maintained lifelong friendships with Moore and Pound. In 1911 she went to travel in Europe and remained there for the rest of her life. In London, Pound introduced her into literary circles. There she met her husband, the novelist Richard Aldington. (Later her marriage became troubled when she entered into an intense, but non-sexual relationship with D.H. Lawrence. Her novel *Bid Me to Live* is about this period in her life. At some point H.D. sought analysis and became a patient of Sigmund Freud to whom she later wrote a "Tribute to Freud" as a fictionalized memoir.) With Pound's help, H.D. became one of the leaders of the Imagist movement and Harriet Monroe published some of her early poems in *Poetry* in January 1913, including "Hermes of the Ways," "Orchard," and "Epigram." H.D. gained attention from her contributions to *Poetry*. The Imagists believed in three principles: direct treatment of subject, include no word that is not essential, and follow musical phrasing rather than adhere to strict regularity in rhythm. The Imagists began publishing around 1908. Amy Lowell also became a champion of H.D's work and introduced her poetry to readers in the United States. In 1918 H.D.

met the love of her life, Bryher (born Annie Winifred Ellerman). They became lifelong companions and, although they often lived separately and Bryher married twice, they had a very loving, supportive relationship.

H.D.'s poetry is marked by economy of language, intense images, and use of classical mythology. She was not widely acclaimed during her lifetime, partly because she was so associated with the Imagist movement although her own work had grown past that label. She started to leave the boundaries of Imagism with her poem "The Walls Do Not Fall" and the first part of "Trilogy" shows her break with Imagism. It could also be that a large audience was not ready for the feminist principles expressed in her work. In all, H.D. has twelve published books of poetry, starting with *Sea Garden* (1916) and ending with *Hermetic Definition*, printed posthumously in 1972.

Leda[1]

Where the slow river
meets the tide,
a red swan lifts red wings
and darker beak,
and underneath the purple down
of his soft breast
uncurls his coral feet.

Through the deep purple
of the dying heat
of sun and mist,
the level ray of sun-beam
has caressed
the lily with dark breast,
and flecked with richer gold
its golden crest.

Where the slow lifting
of the tide,
floats into the river
and slowly drifts

---

[1] The Greek myth about Leda was a potent source for visual art
and poetry, including William Butler Yeats's famous "Leda and
the Swan," which takes a more violent approach to the myth
than H.D.'s poem, which is beautifully sensual and gentle. Leda
was the daughter of King Thestius and wife of King Tyndareus
of Sparta. Zeus fell in love with her and while she was bathing
naked in a river he seduced her in the shape of a swan. Zeus fell
into Leda's arms for her protection from a pursuing eagle. Their
consummation resulted in the hatching of two eggs. From one
egg Helen of Troy was born and from the other egg Castor and
Pollux were born.

among the reeds,
and lifts the yellow flags,
he floats
where tide and river meet.

Ah kingly kiss—
no more regret
nor old deep memories
to mar the bliss;
where the low sedge is thick,
the gold day-lily
outspreads and rests
beneath soft fluttering
of red swan wings.

THE POOL

Are you alive?
I touch you.
You quiver like a sea-fish.
I cover you with my net.
What are you—banded one?

Lethe[2]

Nor skin nor hide nor fleece
Shall cover you,
Nor curtain of crimson nor fine
Shelter of cedar-wood be over you,
Nor the fir-tree
Nor the pine.

Nor sight of whin[3] nor gorse
Nor river-yew,
Nor fragrance of flowering bush,
Nor wailing of reed-bird to waken you,
Nor of linnet,
Nor of thrush.

Nor word nor touch nor sight
Of lover, you
Shall long through the night but for this:
The roll of the full tide to cover you
Without question,
Without kiss.

---

[2] In Greek myth, Lethe is the river of forgetfulness or oblivion that
runs through Hades.
[3] A very spiny and dense evergreen shrub with fragrant golden-
yellow flowers.

SIEGFRIED SASSOON

(1886–1967)

SIEGFRIED SASSOON is an English poet famous for his bitterly satirical anti-war poems about his experience fighting in World War I. While in France he met the poets Robert Graves and Wilfred Owen. His poetry deals with the suffering of soldiers in the trenches, in hospitals, and in their homeland after they returned from battle disabled or traumatized. Sassoon's bile is aimed at those who mismanage and misunderstand war—overly patriotic civilians, hawkish politicians, military strategists in high positions, popular media, and clergymen who would identify war with godliness.

In Sassoon's "The Dug-Out," the speaker mistakes a soldier asleep in the trenches for a dead man. When he realizes the soldier is only asleep it momentarily assuages his fears, but it also highlights the fact that awareness of death is normal while sleep is almost an abnormal state. War subverts normal expectations.

Suicide in the Trenches

I KNEW a simple soldier boy
Who grinned at life in empty joy,
Slept soundly through the lonesome dark,
And whistled early with the lark.

In winter trenches, cowed and glum,
With crumps and lice and lack of rum,
He put a bullet through his brain.
No one spoke of him again.

You smug-faced crowds with kindling eye[1]
Who cheer when soldier lads march by,
Sneak home and pray you'll never know
The hell where youth and laughter go.

Dreamers[2]

Soldiers are citizens of death's gray land,
Drawing no dividend from time's to-morrows.
In the great hour of destiny they stand,
Each with his feuds, and jealousies, and sorrows.

---

[1] The last stanza of "Suicide in the Trenches" illustrates Sassoon's
poetic attacks on civilians whom he feels have no idea of the real
tragedy and ugliness of war.

[2] In this sonnet, the first eight lines are abstract while the sestet is
full of concrete observations that fully communicate the
speaker's pity for the soldiers or victims.

Soldiers are sworn to action; they must win
Some flaming, fatal climax with their lives.
Soldiers are dreamers; when the guns begin
They think of firelit homes, clean beds, and wives.

I see them in foul dug-outs, gnawed by rats,
And in the ruined trenches, lashed with rain,
Dreaming of things they did with balls and bats,
And mocked by hopeless longing to regain
Bank-holidays, and picture shows, and spats,
And going to the office in the train.

THE DUG-OUT[3]

Why do you lie with your legs ungainly huddled,
And one arm bent across your sullen, cold,
Exhausted face? It hurts my heart to watch you,
Deep-shadowed from the candle's guttering gold;
And you wonder why I shake you by the shoulder;
Drowsy, you mumble and sigh and turn your head . . .
You are too young to fall asleep for ever;
And when you sleep you remind me of the dead.

---

[3] Sassoon wrote "The Dug-Out" in July 1918. The poem is sometimes titled "The Dug-Out, St. Venant, July, 1918" and in it the
poem's speaker addresses a soldier sleeping in the trenches. Sassoon plays with the common poetic metaphor of sleep symbol-
izing death. The poem's speaker mistakes sleep for death.

Rupert Brooke

(1887–1915)

Rupert Brooke was an English poet who died during World War I at the height of his success and is particularly noted for his romantically patriotic war sonnets. He was also noted for his non-war poetry, and for his good looks of which William Butler Yeats proclaimed that Brooke was "the handsomest young man in England." Born in Rugby, Warwickshire, he won a scholarship to Cambridge where he helped start the Marlowe Society drama club and acted in plays. Brooke traveled through the United States and Canada to write travelogues for the *Westminister Gazette*, as well as several islands in the South Seas.

His poetry won acclaim and he was brought to the attention of Winston Churchill, then First Lord of the Admiralty. After turning twenty-seven he joined the Navy, serving in Antwerp and the Dardanelles where he died in 1915 of blood poisoning from an infected mosquito bite. His early fame as a poet and tragic death made Brooke an almost legendary figure. He published two volumes of poetry, *Poems* in 1911 and *1914 and Other Poems* in 1915. Brooke's optimistic poetry about the war is in sharp contrast to the disenchanted poetry of Wilfred Owen and Siegfried Sassoon.

The Soldier[1]

If I should die, think only this of me:
That there's some corner of a foreign field
That is for ever England. There shall be
In that rich earth a richer dust concealed;
A dust whom England bore, shaped, made aware,
Gave once her flowers to love, her ways to roam;
A body of England's, breathing English air,
Washed by the rivers, blest by suns of home.
And think, this heart, all evil shed away,
A pulse in the eternal mind, no less
Gives somewhere back the thoughts by England given;
Her sights and sounds; dreams happy as her day;
And laughter, learnt of friends; and gentleness,
In hearts at peace, under an English heaven.

---

[1] "The Soldier" is probably the most famous of Brooke's *War Sonnets*. Its idealistic tone is very different than Siegfried Sassoon's sardonic, dark war poetry.

Marianne Moore

(1887–1972)

Marianne Moore was a distinguished American Modernist poet who won a Pulitzer Prize in poetry. She was raised by her mother in Kirkwood, Missouri and graduated from Bryn Mawr in 1905 where she was a classmate of H.D. and the two became lifelong friends. Moore had written poetry from childhood and she started publishing poetry after moving with her mother in 1914 to Greenwich Village in New York City. Moore was published in many journals, including *Poetry*, under the editor Harriet Monroe. T. S. Eliot was an admirer of her work and he wrote an introduction to her *Selected Poems* (1935). She received many honors during her lifetime including a Pulitzer Prize, a National Book Award, election to the National Institute of Arts and Letters, the Bollingen Prize, and the Gold Medal for Poetry from the National Institute. She died when she was eighty-four years old.

Poetry[1]

I, too, dislike it: there are things that are important
  beyond all this fiddle.[2]
    Reading it, however, with a perfect contempt for it,
      one discovers in
    it after all, a place for the genuine.
      Hands that can grasp, eyes
        that can dilate, hair that can rise
          if it must, these things are important not
            because a

high-sounding interpretation can be put upon them but
  because they are
  useful. When they become so derivative as to
become unintelligible,
    the same thing may be said for all of us, that we
      do not admire what
      we cannot understand: the bat
        holding on upside down or in quest of
          something to

eat, elephants pushing, a wild horse taking a roll,[3] a
  tireless wolf under
  a tree, the immovable critic twitching his skin like a
    horse that feels a flea, the base-
  ball fan, the statistician—
    nor is it valid
      to discriminate against 'business documents and

---

[1] Later Moore pared her poem down to three lines: "I, too, dislike it./Reading it, however, with a perfect contempt for it, one discovers in/ it, after all, a place for the genuine."
[2] Fussy trifling.
[3] "Taking a roll" means rolling in the dust, as to get rid of lice, etc.

school-books';[4] all these phenomena are important.
    One must make a distinction
however: when dragged into prominence by half poets,
    the
        result is not poetry,
        nor till the poets among us can be
        'literalists of
        the imagination'[5]—above
            insolence and triviality and can present

for inspection, 'imaginary gardens with real toads in
    them',[6] shall we have
    it. In the meantime, if you demand on the one hand,
    the raw material of poetry in
        all its rawness and
        that which is on the other hand
            genuine, you are interested in poetry.

---

[4] Moore is referring to Leo Tolstoy's *Childhood, Boyhood, and Youth*
    in which he notes "Where the boundary between prose and
    poetry lies, I shall never be able to understand. The question is
    raised in manuals of style, yet the answer to it lies beyond me.
    Poetry is verse: prose is not verse. Or else poetry is everything
    with the exception of business documents and school books."
[5] A quote from William Butler Yeats's "Ideas of Good and Evil."
[6] The source of this quote isn't confirmed but it could be that
    Moore was referring to "the garden front of Toad Hall" in Ken-
    neth Grahame's *The Wind in the Willows.*

EDITH SITWELL

(1887–1964)

EDITH SITWELL was a highly influential British poet and critic of the first half of the 20th century although her reputation has since diminished. Born in Scarborough, Yorkshire, she was the eldest daughter of an eccentric baronet, Sir George Sitwell. Her two younger brothers, Osbert and Sacheverell, were also distinguished literary figures. Sitwell had a tempestuous relationship with her parents and wrote in her autobiography that they remained strangers to her. When Sitwell was twenty-five she moved into a small apartment with her governess, Helen Rootham. Later the two moved to Paris together. When Sitwell's mother died in 1937, she did not attend the funeral. During World War II, Edith left France and returned to her childhood home where she lived with her brother Osbert and his lover. Sitwell toured the United States with her brothers in 1948 where she gave poetry readings and recorded some of her poems. In 1955 she converted to Roman Catholicism. She wrote two books about Queen Elizabeth I that were very successful, as well as *English Eccentrics* in 1933 and *Victoria of England* in 1963. She also wrote a novel based on the life of Jonathan Swift, *I Live Under a Black Sun*. In 1962 Edith Sitwell gave her last poetry reading and died two years later of a cerebral hemorrhage.

Sitwell published her first poem in 1913 in the *Daily Mirror*. She edited an annual poetry anthology from 1916 to 1921 with the collaboration of her brothers and they became known as "the Sitwells," a literary clique.

Sitwell wrote many poems during the war, including "Still Falls the Rain" about the London blitz. This poem remains her most famous and was set to music by Benjamin Britten. Her early work was inspired by the French Symbolists[1] and later she championed new poets such as Dylan Thomas and Wilfred Owen. During her lifetime she was a controversial figure and had many public disputes over her strong opinions, including one with the playwright Noel Coward.

----

[1] A late 19th century movement practiced by such poets as Stephane Mallarmé and Paul Verlaine that favored imagination and dreams over naturalism and realism. It had its roots in Charles Baudelaire's *Les Fleurs du mal* or *The Flowers of Evil.*

Aubade[2]

Jane, Jane,
Tall as a crane,
The morning light creaks down again;
Comb your cockscomb-ragged hair,
Jane, Jane, come down the stair.
Each dull blunt wooden stalactite
Of rain creaks, hardened by the light,
Sounding like an overtone
From some lonely world unknown.
But the creaking empty light
Will never harden into sight,
Will never penetrate your brain
With overtones like the blunt rain.
The light would show (if it could harden)
Eternities of kitchen garden,
Cockscomb flowers that none will pluck,
And wooden flowers that 'gin to cluck.
In the kitchen you must light
Flames as staring, red and white,
As carrots or as turnips shining
Where the cold dawn light lies whining.
Cockscomb hair on the cold wind
Hangs limp, turns the milk's weak mind...
Jane, Jane,
Tall as a crane,
The morning light creaks down again!

---

[2] An aubade is a morning love poem.

T. S. Eliot

(1888–1965)

T. S. Eliot (Thomas Sterns Eliot) is a towering figure in poetry, and can be said to be the most influential poet of the 20th century and the progenitor of Modernism. He made his mark both as a poet and a critic of poetry and literature. "The Love Song of J. Alfred Prufrock," published in 1915 inaugurated Eliot's career. It is one of the most anthologized English language poems. "The Love Song of J. Alfred Prufrock" is written as a dramatic form and uses the "stream of consciousness" technique. For many 20th century readers, *Prufrock* embodies the feelings of isolation, powerlessness, and despair that went along with the zeitgeist of the time.

Born in St. Louis, Missouri, he studied at Harvard University, receiving a B.A. and M.A. in philosophy. He taught there briefly and then studied at the Sorbonne in Paris, in Munich, and at Merton College, Oxford, but never received his Ph.D. In 1915 he married Vivienne Haigh-Wood and he separated from her in 1932. She died in a mental institution in 1947. In 1957 Eliot married his private secretary, Valerie Fletcher, who became his literary executor after he died.

Eliot's first books of poetry were *Prufrock, and Other Observations* (1917), *Poems* (1919), *Ara Vos Prec* (1920), *The Waste Land* (1922), and *Poems* (1909–1925). Eliot was inspired by French Symbolist poetry early on in his career as a poet and he drew heavily on the friendship and advice of Ezra Pound, who edited "The Waste Land."

In London, Eliot earned his living as a literary journalist, as a teacher, and as a clerk at Lloyds Bank (1917–1925). From 1917 to 1919 he acted as assistant editor of *The Egoist*; and he founded and edited *The Criterion* from 1922 to 1939. In this way Eliot helped many younger writers, including W. H. Auden and Stephen Spender.

Around 1927 Eliot permanently converted to the Anglican Christian faith. His poetry from this time on reflected his religious beliefs: *Journey of the Magi* (1927), *Animula* (1929), *Ash Wednesday* (1930), *Marina* (1930), and the *Four Quartets* (1935–1942), by many considered the greatest long poem of the 20th century. Eliot also proved himself an important literary critic, starting with the publication of *The Sacred Wood* in 1920 to one of his last, *On Poetry and Poets*, in 1957. He received many awards in his lifetime, including the Nobel Prize for Literature. Eliot's masterpiece "The Waste Land" is probably the most famous English poem of the 20th century, a landmark meditation on human anxiety with the modern world.

THE LOVE SONG OF J. ALFRED PRUFROCK

S'io credesse che mia risposta fosse
A persona che mai tornasse al mondo,
Questa fiamma staria senza piu scosse.
Ma perciocche giammai di questo fondo
Non torno vivo alcun, s'i'odo il vero,
Senza tema d'infamia ti rispondo.[1]

Let us go then, you and I,
When the evening is spread out against the sky
Like a patient etherized[2] upon a table;
Let us go, through certain half-deserted streets,
The muttering retreats
Of restless nights in one-night cheap hotels
And sawdust restaurants with oyster-shells:
Streets that follow like a tedious argument
Of insidious intent
To lead you to an overwhelming question . . .
Oh, do not ask, "What is it?"
Let us go and make our visit.

---

[1] Eliot took the poem's epigraph from Dante's *Divine Comedy*. In the *Inferno* Count Guido da Montefeltro, who is being punished for giving false advice by being consumed eternally in flame, answers Dante's question about his identity with these words: "If I believed that my answer would be to someone who would ever return to earth, this flame would move no more, but because no one has ever returned alive from this gulf, if what I hear is true, I can reply with no fear of infamy."

[2] Anesthetized.

In the room the women come and go
Talking of Michelangelo.[3]

The yellow fog that rubs its back upon the window-
    panes,
The yellow smoke that rubs its muzzle on the window-
    panes,
Licked its tongue into the corners of the evening,
Lingered upon the pools that stand in drains,
Let fall upon its back the soot that falls from chimneys,
Slipped by the terrace, made a sudden leap,
And seeing that it was a soft October night,
Curled once about the house, and fell asleep.

And indeed there will be time
For the yellow smoke that slides along the street,
Rubbing its back upon the window-panes;
There will be time, there will be time
To prepare a face to meet the faces that you meet;
There will be time to murder and create,
And time for all the works and days[4] of hands
That lift and drop a question on your plate;
Time for you and time for me,
And time yet for a hundred indecisions,
And for a hundred visions and revisions,
Before the taking of a toast and tea.

In the room the women come and go
Talking of Michelangelo.

---

[3] Michelangelo was the famous Renaissance painter and sculptur
   who lived from 1475 to 1564.
[4] Refers to Hesiod's *Works and Days*, an 8th-century (B.C.)
   description of rural life.

And indeed there will be time
To wonder, "Do I dare?" and, "Do I dare?"
Time to turn back and descend the stair,
With a bald spot in the middle of my hair—
(They will say: "How his hair is growing thin!")
My morning coat, my collar mounting firmly to the
    chin,
My necktie rich and modest, but asserted by a simple
    pin—
(They will say: "But how his arms and legs are thin!")
Do I dare
Disturb the universe?
In a minute there is time
For decisions and revisions which a minute will reverse.

For I have known them all already, known them all:
Have known the evenings, mornings, afternoons,
I have measured out my life with coffee spoons;
I know the voices dying with a dying fall
Beneath the music from a farther room.
  So how should I presume?
And I have known the eyes already, known them all—
The eyes that fix you in a formulated phrase,
And when I am formulated, sprawling on a pin,
When I am pinned and wriggling on the wall,
Then how should I begin
To spit out all the butt-ends of my days and ways?
  And how should I presume?

And I have known the arms already, known them all—
Arms that are braceleted and white and bare

(But in the lamplight, downed with light brown hair!)
Is it perfume from a dress
That makes me so digress?
Arms that lie along a table, or wrap about a shawl.
And should I then presume?
And how should I begin?

      *   *   *   *

Shall I say, I have gone at dusk through narrow streets
And watched the smoke that rises from the pipes
Of lonely men in shirt-sleeves, leaning out of windows?

      *   *   *   *

I should have been a pair of ragged claws
Scuttling across the floors of silent seas.

      *   *   *   *

And the afternoon, the evening, sleeps so peacefully!
Smoothed by long fingers,
Asleep . . . tired . . . or it malingers,
Stretched on the floor, here beside you and me.
Should I, after tea and cakes and ices,
Have the strength to force the moment to its crisis?
But though I have wept and fasted, wept and prayed,
Though I have seen my head (grown slightly bald)
   brought in upon a platter,
I am no prophet—and here's no great matter;
I have seen the moment of my greatness flicker,
And I have seen the eternal Footman hold my coat, and
   snicker,
And in short, I was afraid.

And would it have been worth it, after all,

After the cups, the marmalade, the tea,
Among the porcelain, among some talk of you and me,
Would it have been worth while,
To have bitten off the matter with a smile,
To have squeezed the universe into a ball
To roll it toward some overwhelming question,
To say: "I am Lazarus, come from the dead,
Come back to tell you all, I shall tell you all"—
If one, settling a pillow by her head,
  Should say: "That is not what I meant at all;
  That is not it, at all."

And would it have been worth it, after all,
Would it have been worth while,
After the sunsets and the dooryards and the sprinkled
    streets,
After the novels, after the teacups, after the skirts that
    trail along the
    floor—
And this, and so much more?—
It is impossible to say just what I mean!
But as if a magic lantern threw the nerves in patterns
on a screen:
Would it have been worth while
If one, settling a pillow or throwing off a shawl,
And turning toward the window, should say:
  "That is not it at all,
  That is not what I meant, at all."

*   *   *   *

No! I am not Prince Hamlet, nor was meant to be;
Am an attendant lord, one that will do
To swell a progress, start a scene or two,
Advise the prince; no doubt, an easy tool,
Deferential, glad to be of use,
Politic, cautious, and meticulous;
Full of high sentence, but a bit obtuse;
At times, indeed, almost ridiculous—
Almost, at times, the Fool.

I grow old . . . I grow old . . .
I shall wear the bottoms of my trousers rolled.

Shall I part my hair behind? Do I dare to eat a peach?
I shall wear white flannel trousers, and walk upon the
    beach.
I have heard the mermaids singing, each to each.

I do not think that they will sing to me.

I have seen them riding seaward on the waves
Combing the white hair of the waves blown back
When the wind blows the water white and black.
We have lingered in the chambers of the sea
By sea-girls wreathed with seaweed red and brown
Till human voices wake us, and we drown.

INDEX OF FIRST LINES

635

Index of Poets and Poems

Poets are typeset in boldface